P9-CAN-190

PATHWAYS TO THE PRESENT

PATHWAYS

TO THE PRESENT

U.S. DEVELOPMENT AND ITS
CONSEQUENCES IN THE PACIFIC

Mansel G. Blackford

University of Hawai'i Press
Honolulu

Library of Congress Cataloging-in-Publication Data
Blackford, Mansel G.
Pathways to the present : U.S. development and its consequences in the Pacific /
Mansel G. Blackford.
p. cm.
Includes bibliographical references and index.
ISBN 978-0-8248-3073-1 (hardcover : alk. paper)
1. Pacific States—Economic conditions. 2. Pacific States—History. 3. Islands of the
Pacific—Economic conditions. 4. Islands of the Pacific—History. 5. Aleutian Islands
(Alaska)—History. 6. United States—Territories and possessions—History. 7. United
States—Insular possessions—History. 8. Islands of the Pacific—Relations—United
States. 9. United States—Relations—Islands of the Pacific. I. Title.
HC107.A18B63 2007
338.995—dc22

2006035362

University of Hawai'i Press books are printed on acid-free
paper and meet the guidelines for permanence and durability
of the Council on Library Resources.

Designed by University of Hawai'i Press production staff
Printed by The Maple-Vail Book Manufacturing Group

For my wife, Victoria.

Thank you for coming on the journey with me.

Contents

Preface

I have long been fascinated by the Pacific. As a child, I grew up in Seattle during the 1940s and 1950s, decades noted for the dominance of the Boeing Company in the Pacific Northwest. During those years, my father captained a fishing vessel that pioneered in the opening of Alaska's king crab industry, and I had the opportunity to visit the north on several occasions. I attended college and graduate school on the Pacific Coast, mainly in northern California, during the 1960s and early 1970s, a time when Silicon Valley was booming, beefed up by Cold War defense contracts. My interest in Japan dates back to the 1950s. Trawling in the North Pacific, my father came into close contact with Japanese fishermen, trading American cigarettes for Japanese curios. Later, in the 1980s, I spent two years living with my family in southern Japan, where I taught in Fukuoka and Hiroshima as a Fulbright Lecturer and learned about Japanese society. Traveling to and from Japan, I stopped over in the Hawaiian Islands, and during the 1990s I had the opportunity on several occasions to teach on Maui for the University of Hawai'i—experiences that brought me into close contact with a broad range of Pacific Islanders, including Chamorros transplanted from Guam and American Samoans.

My professional work, including this volume, has allowed me to combine interests in business, environmental, and urban history with an abiding concern for the history of the American West and the Pacific. Many of my books have explored intersections of these fields. There have been, we shall see, commonalities in the development of the United States' Pacific possessions. Those commonalities have been perhaps nowhere more striking than in interactions in economic and environmental decision making. However, there have also been marked regional patterns of development within this vast area; after all, the Pacific covers one-third of the globe and has always been complex. Yet, especially with several forms of economic and geopolitical integration that have taken place since World War II, it is possible to begin thinking of the Pacific, including American possessions there, as one region.

It would be easy to romanticize developments in the Pacific. I remember many wonderful moments spent living there: sailing part of the Inside Passage to Alaska in a small open boat as a teenager, a voyage cut short, however, by a summer gale; eating Dungeness crabs from the shell in northern California; and swimming in ocean swells off white-sand beaches near Fukuoka. There is another side to the Pacific. Until very recently, and even now in much of the region, the economy evolved as a boom-and-bust affair based on extractive industries, just as that of the American West did in the 1800s. I am one of those who can recall, during a recession in the early 1970s, a billboard on Interstate Highway 90 on the eastern outskirts of Seattle that read, "Will the Last Person Leaving Please Turn Out the Lights?"

It is on the interactions between economic developments, environmental issues, and political decision making that this volume focuses. My study casts a wide net. Ranging from the sun-kissed beaches of the Hawaiian archipelago to the snow-swept shores of the Aleutian Islands and from congested Silicon Valley to rural Guam, it looks at contests over the exploitation of natural resources, land-use issues, and urban planning, among other matters. Beyond individual regional topics lie general debates and decisions over quality-of-life concerns. By looking at this array of issues, my book captures both the commonalities and the complexities of the changes that have occurred throughout the Pacific possessions of the United States.

⤸

Few scholarly studies are truly individual efforts, for most build on the works of others, especially in the field of history. I would like to take this opportunity to thank the many people who helped bring this work to fruition. David Lincove, the history librarian at The Ohio State University, aided me in tracking down many elusive sources, as did librarians at the Hamilton Library at the University of Hawai'i, Mānoa and librarians at the Suzzallo Library at the University of Washington. Dirk Ballendorf, James Bartholomew, William Childs, Stewart Firth, Hal Friedman, James Kraft, William McCloskey, Lucy Murphy, Daniel Nelson, Darrin Pratt, Dorothy Pyle, Robert Rogers, Mark Rose, Randy Roth, David Stebenne, Tetsuo Taka, William Tsutsui, Richard Tucker, and Judy Wu read and commented on earlier drafts of all or parts of this study. More generally, I would like to thank my colleagues at Ohio State for providing a stimulating and collegial environment in which to work. I am indebted to the College of Humanities of The Ohio State University for released time from teaching, which allowed me to conduct research on this project and for a publication subvention for this resulting book. Finally, I would like to thank Masako Ikeda, Acquiring Editor for the University of Hawai'i Press, and the two anonymous readers for the press, for their valuable comments and help in bringing my manuscript to publication.

I presented earlier versions of parts of Chapters 2 and 5 as papers at meetings of the American Society for Environmental History in 2003 and 2004 and part of Chapter 6 as a paper at the annual meeting of the Business History Conference in 2005, and my work benefited from suggestions made at those gatherings. An earlier version of Chapter 2 was published as "Environmental Justice, Native Rights, Tourism, and Opposition to Military Control: The Case of Kaho'olawe," in the *Journal of American History* 91 (September 2004): 544–571; and part of Chapter 6 was published electronically as "Tourism, the Environment, and the Military: The Case of Guam, 1962–2002," in the 2005 Proceedings of the Business History Conference at <http://www.thebhc.org/publications/BEHonline/beh.html>.

Finally, I must say a few words about languages. I have followed standard practices in including diacritic marks in words wherever they are called for, but I have not added them when they did not appear in the original, as in quotations or book titles. I have chosen to write Japanese names with the given name first and the surname second, adhering to English-language practice, which is the reverse of that in Japanese.

Introduction

Writing in his diary on May 29, 1943, Dr. Paul Nobuo Tatsuguchi of the Japanese Imperial Army observed, "All the patients in the hospital were made to commit suicide. I am only 33 years old and am to die. Have no regrets. Banzai to the Emperor. I am grateful that I have kept the peace of my soul which Enkist [Jesus Christ] bestowed on me at 8 o'clock." The medical officer stationed with the Japanese occupation force on Attu, one of Alaska's far-western Aleutian Islands, Tatsuguchi correctly foresaw his future. He tried to surrender to American soldiers who were retaking the island on May 30, shouting to them in English, "Don't shoot! Don't shoot! I am a Christian!" His actions were misunderstood. The Bible he waved in one hand was mistaken for a weapon, and Tatsuguchi was killed.[1]

By the time of World War II, Tatsuguchi and his family had moved back and forth across the Pacific Ocean on numerous occasions. Native to Hiroshima, Tatsuguchi's father had emigrated to California in 1895. There the elder Tatsuguchi converted to Christianity and attended Heraldsburg College, specializing in dentistry. In 1907, he returned to Hiroshima as a medical missionary for the Seventh Day Adventist (SDA) Church, where he married. Paul was one of six children. He attended college in California, graduating from Pacific Union College in 1932. When his parents died a year later, Paul returned to Japan to settle family affairs. In 1933, however, he went back to California to enroll in the College of Medical Evangelists at Loma Linda College, graduating four years later. In 1938, he returned to Japan with a bride who was the daughter of a SDA pastor in Honolulu. In Tokyo, Tatsuguchi concentrated on medical work in a tuberculosis sanitarium and, with his wife, on SDA church activities. Drafted in 1941, he found himself on Attu with Japan's invading forces a year later.[2]

The Tatsuguchi family story, nonetheless, was not one of unmitigated tragedy. At the close of World War II, Tatsuguchi's wife found employment with American forces occupying Japan. In 1954, she moved with her two daughters to Honolulu to work as a translator, with the three of them becoming naturalized American citizens. Still later, the three moved to California. One of the daughters followed in her father's footsteps, graduating with a degree in nursing from Loma Linda College and then returning to Japan as the wife of an SDA church member who served as the temperance secretary for the Japan Union Conference in Tokyo. The other daughter, also a registered nurse from Loma Linda College, married a California businessman and settled in the Golden State.[3] Although unusual in the frequency of their movements across the Pacific, members of the Tatsuguchi family typified the growing mobility of Pacific peoples. In their travels between California, Hawai'i, Japan, and Alaska, the Tatsuguchis illustrated the increasing military, economic, and social integration of the Pacific.

Dealing with the Pacific as a distinct region, not simply looking at the Pacific Rim or the Pacific "donut" empty in the middle, my study analyzes relationships among business developments, cultural changes, and environmental alterations in United States' possessions across the Pacific created by that integration.[4] World War II militarized most of the Pacific, and after that conflict the affected areas had to chart new developmental courses, which often differed substantially from both prewar and wartime situations. The result was several trajectories. Still, there were commonalities.

My thesis about those developments is simple, at least in outline. World War II, building on alterations often already under way, accelerated and intensified major changes in the Pacific, among the most important of which was increased geopolitical and economic integration.[5] That integration—especially the trade ties and, in some areas, the rise of tourism—brought faster economic development. The growing presence of the American military, as American policy makers came to view the Pacific as an American lake, also brought some forms of economic growth to the region and, of course, eliminated domination of areas such as Micronesia by the Japanese military. While American military spending became an important source of economic expansion and rising standard of living for many people, not all benefited from it equally. Many of the profits went to handfuls of developers, often outsiders. Moreover, growth impinged on traditional lifestyles, especially for indigenous peoples. Not surprisingly, there arose considerable resistance to some forms of American military and economic developments, especially, as time progressed, on environmental grounds. That opposition set the stage for conflicts, from which compromises usually emerged, and with agreements came the creation of important parts of today's Pacific.

My book explores how and why people worked in the ways they did to influence their economic, social, and physical environments, and what the consequences of those labors have been. The question was never whether America's Pacific possessions were going to be developed. Rather, questions included: In what ways would they be developed? Within what limits? For whose benefit? And, of course, it is important to bear in mind that considerable development had occurred in earlier times. Individuals, the many organizations they formed, including businesses, and governmental agents emerge as key actors in answering these questions. In examining the actions of individuals and groups throughout the Pacific, I hope my work will contribute to our knowledge of environmental history, business and economic history, Pacific history, and the history of the American West.[6]

Environmental historians have created a field of study over the past generation. Environmentalism has assumed various forms, and developments in the Pacific illustrate well the movement's complexity. Historians have increasingly related the development of modern environmentalism to alterations in society, politics, and culture. For example, Adam Rome has found the wellsprings of American environmentalism in the 1960s in "the revitalization of liberalism, the growing discontent of middle-class women, and the explosion of student radicalism and countercultural protest."[7] Similarly, in her 2003 presidential address to the American Society for Environmental History, Carolyn Merchant observed links among environmentalism, social and cultural changes, and the writing of environmental history. As she has pointed out, a growing number of scholars have become involved in documenting America's environmental justice movement, a campaign begun in the 1970s and 1980s to address the placing of garbage dumps, hazardous-waste sites, power plants, and other nuisances in neighborhoods populated mainly by poor people of color.[8]

Developments in the Pacific resonate with environmental efforts elsewhere. As my study shows, much of what took place in the Pacific connects especially with America's environmental justice movement. Not all wanted to rid the Pacific of Americans. Exactly how Pacific peoples viewed trade-offs between economic development and environmental protection matters varied from place to place and from time to time, but one common denominator was their dislike of outside influences and, as many viewed matters, colonial oppression. In the post-1945 era, that determination meant for many trying to lessen or end American dominance in the region, especially as memories of World War II waned. Issues of sovereignty were involved.

Some scholars looking at the development of environmentalism have recently stressed its origins in colonial possessions. In his pathbreaking work, Richard H. Grove has cogently argued that much of modern environmentalism has its sources not in the United States or western Europe, but rather in experiences in the colonies. "As colonial expansion proceeded," he has stated, "the environmental experiences of Europeans and indigenous peoples living at the colonial periphery played a steadily more dominant and dynamic part in the construction of new European evaluations of nature and in the growing awareness of the destructive impact of European economic activity on the peoples and environments of the newly 'discovered' and colonized lands." He concludes, "Any attempt to understand the foundations of western environmental concerns actually involves writing a history of the human responses to nature that have developed at the periphery of an expanding European system." Similarly, Peder Anker has traced concerns about ecology to experiences in the British Empire in the late nineteenth and early twentieth centuries, observing that "broad ecology owes its success to its patrons in the economic administration of the environmental and social order in the British Empire."[9] Like these studies, my work looks beyond the "center" to the "periphery" to find some of the origins of modern environmental actions in the work of indigenous peoples as well as in that of colonizers.[10]

My study seeks to contribute to business history as well as environmental history. Business historians have been slower than many scholars to examine environmental issues. Focusing especially on the business firm and its management, they have not probed deeply into the externalities that helped frame business actions. As historians Christine Rosen and Christopher Sellers have observed, "Business history has never paid much attention to the environment" and in fact has given "little attention to the effects of resource extraction and use on plants, animals, land, air, or water, much less entire ecosystems and climate." That situation has begun to change, as business historians increasingly look at connections among business firms, their societies, and their cultures. Such an approach is a fruitful way to understand many Pacific developments, including relationships among tourism, environmental changes, and cultural alterations.[11]

While some of the findings of my study connect with those of the works of business and environmental historians, they also illuminate efforts by scholars to deal with the Pacific as one large region of the globe, thus increasing our understanding of Pacific history. Although it is difficult to speak just yet of a trans-Pacific community in quite the same senses that Fernand Braudel has written of the Mediterranean Sea or as Bernard Bailyn and many other scholars have written about a transatlantic community, there have long been extensive linkages throughout the Pacific, and those connections have increased since World War II. My study contributes to work done by historians, geographers, anthropologists, and others in rethinking Pacific history over the past generation.[12] There is tremendous diversity in the approaches and conclusions of these scholars, but several major themes stand out: a need to view Pacific history through non-western eyes; a need to see the Pacific as a major unified region of the world; and a need to examine interactions among Pacific peoples, their natural environments, and their economies. Some connections have been mainly economic in nature—trade and tourism, for example. Others have been more social and cultural in orientation— such as the movement of peoples, often called a "Pacific diaspora." Standing behind many of the linkages has been the military presence of the United States in the Pacific, which has motivated transnational protests by Pacific peoples.[13]

The United States' Pacific possessions shared major elements of history in common with other parts of the Pacific. Because they were American-owned or American-controlled, however, their histories also diverged in some ways from those of other sections of the Pacific. Historians have long looked at parts of the Pacific as an American frontier, sharing developments with those of the evolution of the trans-Mississippi West. As Americans moved across the North American continent and then traveled farther west into the Pacific as explorers, whalers, traders, and fishermen, they took with them familiar patterns of thinking and acting.[14] Capitalistic development based on the rapid exploitation of natural resources was the norm in Alaska, Hawai'i, and Guam. Extractive industries, which tended to create boom-and-bust economies with little thought for the future, dominated developments in the American West and in the American Pacific.[15] In the twentieth century, especially after about 1970, tourism seemed to offer a chance for economic diversification and stabilization at little cost to the environment in the West and in the Pacific. Tourism became the leading industry in Guam and Hawai'i and was important in the other regions as well. Leaders in Hiroshima considered leaving the ruins of their city intact as a form of nuclear tourism. Yet, tourism brought neither economic stability nor unadulterated environmental progress to either the West or the Pacific. Still other themes connect western American history to the history of America's Pacific: the importance of federal government and military spending in both regions (and, conversely, local attitudes that were often hostile to that government); and the fact that economic growth was very uneven, usually benefiting indigenous peoples—Native Americans, Alaskan Natives, native Hawaiians, and the Chamorros of Guam—less than other groups. After enduring repression or neglect for decades, members of indigenous groups became important actors in the decision-making process on economic and environmental issues.[16]

⌔

Six chapters compose my study. To set the stage for the rest of the volume, Chapter 1 offers a brief survey of the history of the Pacific. The chapter shows that a considerable degree of integration existed before the coming of Euro-Americans to the region but looks in most detail at connections forged after World War II. It focuses especially on postwar changes caused by America's growing Pacific presence. Taking the Hawaiian Islands as the center of American activities in the Pacific, Chapter 2 looks at interactions among native Hawaiian, developmental, military, and environmental issues in the archipelago after World War II.[17] The chapter examines land-use matters concerning Kahoʻolawe, one of the eight major Hawaiian Islands. Environmentally degraded by western ranching, the island was further damaged by the U.S. Navy, which used it as a shelling and bombing range until 1990. Most recently, Kahoʻolawe has been partially restored by native Hawaiian groups. Viewing their efforts as having broad implications, some native Hawaiian leaders took what they saw as their anticolonial campaign to other parts of the Pacific. The chapter closes by comparing developments on Kahoʻolawe to conflicts about naval live-fire ranges elsewhere in the Pacific and Caribbean, for the Kahoʻolawe controversy had trans-Pacific and transnational ramifications.

Moving to the United States' Pacific Coast, Chapter 3 examines explosive growth in the Seattle region and the San Francisco Bay area, especially Silicon Valley. High-technology developments have often been seen as "green," having minimal environmental downsides. However, events on America's Pacific Coast, my study shows, belie this easy assumption. As in the Hawaiian Islands, specific land-use and water-use matters intersected with more nebulous quality-of-life concerns to generate policy controversies in northern California and the Puget Sound region. Environmental-justice matters surfaced, as immigrant workers, often Hispanic and Asian women, suffered. Then, too, Native Americans were hurt by high-technology developments, particularly in the Seattle region. Chapter 3 also compares efforts to create high-technology districts in the San Francisco Bay area and Seattle to attempts to construct them in South Korea and the Hawaiian Islands.

Chapter 4 looks at economic development and environmentalism in

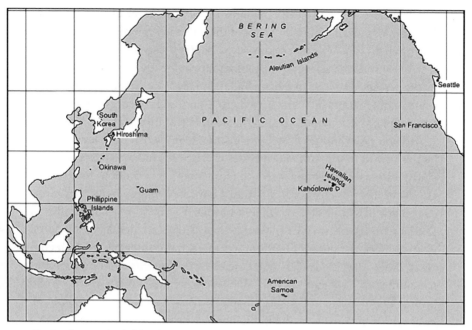

The Pacific, one-third of the globe.

Alaska through the lens of changes occurring along the Aleutian Islands. Because their state remained particularly dependent on extractive resources, Alaskans faced controversies that revolved mainly around how those resources should be exploited and who should benefit from that exploitation. In the Aleutians, heated conflicts pitted groups of fishermen against each other, and fishermen against oil prospectors. Still, even in Alaska general quality-of-life matters were of significance, as revealed in efforts to create the Beringia Heritage International Park. Until recently, Alaskan Natives found themselves pushed aside in efforts to develop Alaska's resources, including parks used for tourism, much as happened to native Hawaiians in the rush to develop their islands.

From Alaska, my study moves southwest. Chapter 5 examines developments in Hiroshima after its destruction by the atomic bomb in 1945, looking at why residents chose a new type of future for their city and how they implemented their wishes. Americans were very influential in Japan for about a decade after World War II, and their ideas helped to reshape Hiroshima. Hiroshima's residents tried to combine urban-planning concepts, including environmental protection measures, with economic development. How they resolved conflicting goals resonates with urban developments in the

San Francisco Bay and Seattle regions. In the resolution of their conflicts, Hiroshima's citizens generally ignored the wishes of minority groups, again raising environmental justice concerns. Chapter 5 also investigates efforts to recreate Hiroshima as a high-technology city in the 1990s, attempts inspired by the perceived success of Silicon Valley. Finally, the chapter describes postwar planning efforts on Okinawa, where American influences were particularly strong, and compares them to those in Hiroshima.

Chapter 6 examines developments in Guam, particularly issues raised by the growth of tourism and the use of Guam for military purposes. Specific questions arose about where to place a new ammunition dock for the U.S. Navy, how to construct a national park to commemorate the Pacific campaigns of World War II, where to locate a national seashore, and how to deal with the brown tree snake, an alien species accidentally introduced by the American military. Questions on these matters intersected with concerns about what kinds of lives the residents of Guam, including Chamorros, wanted to have and the roles the American government might play in turning those desires into reality. Chapter 6 also compares what occurred on Guam to developments in the Philippines to the west and American Samoa to the south.

Common themes permeate my work. The study's chapters focus on twentieth-century developments, especially on economic and environmental choices made since 1945. As historian John McNeill has shown in his remarkable global environmental history, the pace of change greatly accelerated in the twentieth century, making that time period "something new under the sun."[18] Change was certainly the case for the Pacific possessions of the United States. The chapters of my study look at varied areas of the Pacific in an attempt to see whether there has been something unique to economic and environmental developments in this region. All examine American territories or American-dominated regions in the Pacific. Even Japan was such an area between 1945 and 1952, and Okinawa for an additional two decades. The chapters probe relationships among American military desires, economic development, environmental issues, and peoples' rights, the last especially as defined by indigenous groups. The areas dealt with in this volume were chosen to represent the many aspects of America's postwar presence in the Pacific: in urban and rural regions, parts of the eastern and western Pacific, near-tropical to near-arctic areas, and mainland and island regions. Still, this work does not examine all of the many places in America's Pacific in detail, probably omitting as much as it includes. The book is not meant to be fully inclusive. Indeed, it is my hope that this work will stimulate future research about the United States' developmental and environmental impacts on Pacific areas. More generally, I also hope that my study will encourage research into the interactions between economic development and environmental protection issues globally, for many of the changes occurring in the Pacific have, of course, been taking place elsewhere in the world. Throughout, my work differentiates among local, regional (that is, pan-Pacific), and global developments.

To foreshadow my arguments a bit, let me close this introduction with a listing of my study's major findings. First, the Pacific, at least American territories in the Pacific, may be considered as composing one major region, especially in modern times. Second, within this region World War II and the Cold War acted as major catalysts for changes, but those alterations occurred within the long scope of earlier regional developments. Third, many of the changes resulted from the reactions of local residents, including indigenous peoples, against western political and economic colonialism and, more specifically, against America's massive postwar military presence in the Pacific. Fourth, the state was often the arena within which actions were worked out. Politics and governmental policies mattered.

We begin our voyage by examining in Chapter 1 the development of the Pacific from pre-contact times to the present. Several themes stand out in this investigation: first, that large parts of the Pacific have long contained elements of integration; but, second, that since World War II the degree of integration has increased; and, third, that even now that integration is incomplete. It is essential to look at the degrees and types of integration in various time periods, because it was these connections that formed the platforms on which people made decisions about economic development and environmental protection.

CHAPTER 1

Pacific Developments

In 1976, native Hawaiians and others sailed the *Hōkūleʻa*, a replica of a Polynesian twin-hulled voyaging canoe, using only traditional navigational techniques, to and from Tahiti, two thousand miles in each direction. In doing so, they demonstrated the feasibility of earlier large-scale migrations by canoe throughout the Pacific. Equally important, their actions helped unite many indigenous Pacific peoples in a consciousness of their common heritage. Some fifteen thousand celebrants met the *Hōkūleʻa* when she entered Tahiti's Papeʻete harbor the first time. "Now you have returned," observed one orator addressing the canoe's crew members in a reference to the ancient Polynesian origins of Hawaiians. "The people of Polynesia have been overjoyed to hear of your voyage," he concluded, "you are brothers." On her return voyage to the Hawaiian Islands the *Hōkūleʻa* carried representatives from New Zealand, Samoa, Tahiti, Tonga, and the Marquesas. After another roundtrip between Hawaiʻi and Tahiti in 1980, those in charge of the *Hōkūleʻa* undertook a still longer trip, which they labeled a "voyage of rediscovery." In the mid-1980s, the *Hōkūleʻa* traversed twelve thousand miles of the Pacific, bridging seven archipelagos from the Hawaiian Islands to Tahiti, Tonga, and New Zealand. The *Hōkūleʻa* set sail from the fishing village of Miloliʻi on the southwestern coast of the island of Hawaiʻi on January 10, 1985, and returned to Kualoa, a sandy point on Oʻahu, over two years later on May 23, 1987.[1]

Hawaiians were not alone in their movements through the Pacific. In 1988, far to the north, Russian and American officials permitted Alaskan Natives to pay ceremonial visits to their counterparts across the Bering Sea in the Chukotka region, where they were, according to reporters, "welcomed enthusiastically by hundreds of Soviet adults and school children." Their trip was part of a movement toward visa-free visits by Russian and Alaskan Natives across national boundaries.[2] Since World War II, there has been an

The voyages of the *Hōkūleʻa* helped reunite parts of the Pacific. Here the *Hōkūleʻa* sails off Honolulu in 1995. (Courtesy of the Polynesian Voyaging Society)

increasing integration—perhaps "reintegration" is a more accurate term—of the Pacific, in part through the migration of people.[3]

Integration has taken other important forms as well: economic integration, especially through trade; social and cultural integration, encouraged among other means by the expansion of tourism; and growth in unity among Pacific peoples as they threw off what they viewed as the repressive yoke of western colonialism. Overarching much of the integration was the new and immense military and economic power of the United States in the Pacific. That strength was both a legacy of the increased presence of the United States in the Pacific during World War II and a result of recognition on the part of American officials of the importance of the Pacific for the Cold War. America's growing Pacific presence must, in fact, be seen as part of the development of a cold war with the Soviet Union (which, like the United States, greatly increased its Pacific military forces after World War II) and the People's Republic of China, with the vast region of the Pacific caught between the Great Powers.

While focusing on the post–World War II development of the Pacific as an "American lake," this chapter begins by examining earlier developments. Before contact with westerners, many Pacific peoples lived in oceanic associations and empires. To some extent, they inhabited in an integrated Pacific. Colonization of the Pacific by western nations, including the United States, disrupted native associations by dividing the Pacific into European territorial possessions. Only later, with changes wrought by World War II, the Cold War, and other developments, did reintegration occur. The long history of the Pacific played important roles in influencing how people regarded economic development matters and environmental protection issues and how they fought and cooperated with each other to make their visions realities.

Early Indigenous Integration and Later Colonial Disintegration

The Pacific Ocean is the largest geographical feature on Earth, covering one-third of the globe, host to more than twenty thousand islands, 80 percent of the world's total. It is a "water continent." With each square mile of land come 130 square miles of ocean.[4] Scholars have emphasized the importance of the Pacific Ocean and its peoples to world history for at least a generation now. They have stressed how long-term trends have affected recent developments and have highlighted that those developments need to be seen through non-western eyes. Geographer Gerard Ward expressed the views of many scholars when he observed in 1989 that, while the Pacific seemed empty to most Europeans, it was anything but vacant for the people living there at the time of contact, "They were skilled navigators for whom the Pacific was neither trackless nor empty."[5] Writing in 1994, anthropologist Ben Finney, who had spearheaded work on the *Hōkūle'a,* called on scholars to focus on more than just the rim of the Pacific by looking at interactions among peoples of the islands and relationships between island peoples and those living beyond the islands.[6]

Scholars examining the Pacific have been keenly aware of difficulties in considering the Pacific as one region. After observing in 1989 that the Pacific is "a hard place to identify with—so much ocean, too many islands," Greg Dening stated that he would have "fewer qualms about the term 'Pacific history' if by it we meant history *in* the Pacific rather than history *of* the Pacific, and if by history *in* the Pacific we were much more tolerant of all the varieties of histories there are."[7] Similarly, Arif Dirlik has stressed the diversity of cultures in the Pacific. After rejecting such conceptions as the Pacific Rim and the Pacific Basin because they leave out the Pacific Ocean and most of its islands, he has claimed that the "Pacific region is an idea," with political and economic structures coming from both Asia and America.[8] Jocelyn Linnekin has also observed that "Clearly there can be no single, seamless history of the many peoples who inhabit the Pacific Islands."[9]

Increasingly, however, scholars have seen the Pacific Ocean as a comprehensive region, in much the same ways that they have viewed the Mediterranean Sea, the Indian Ocean, and the Atlantic Ocean. As early as 1979, Kerry R. Howe, the editor of *Pacific Studies,* urged scholars to look at "the Pacific islands within the much wider geographic, economic, and political framework of the Pacific Ocean involving, as it must, its adjacent shores—the Americas, Russia, Japan, Korea, China, Southeast Asia, and Australasia." Such would be, he observed, "an Oceanic as opposed to insular orientation."[10] In 2000, Dennis O. Flynn and Arturo Giraldez, the editors of a book series on the *Pacific World,* stated that their premise was "that the Pacific represents as coherent a unit of analysis as the Atlantic Ocean, the Indian Ocean, and the many seas throughout the world."[11] Typical of the scholars taking broad approaches to the Pacific have been historians Paul D'Arcy and John McNeill. Their recent works have contributed greatly to reconceptualizations of the Pacific.

D'Arcy has been a leader in showing that the Pacific was "no empty quarter" before the entrance of the first Europeans. People probably moved, he has noted, into "the western margins of Oceania . . . around 50,000 years ago," when ocean levels were low because water was locked up in glaciers and ice sheets in this cool time. People may have also crossed into North America via a land bridge across the Bering Strait called Beringia. Warm temperatures brought oceans to near their current levels about ten thousand years ago, by which time "human settlement had spread to Australia, New Guinea, and some of New Guinea's more accessible offshore neighboring islands in Island Melanesia." The rest of Oceania, D'Arcy has observed, "seems to have been colonized in a 2,000-year period beginning around 3,500 years ago by what appears to have been a relatively coherent culture that is associated with the distribution of the Austronesian family of languages, a highly developed maritime culture based on outrigger sailing canoes, and a distinct style of pottery known as lapita ware."[12]

D'Arcy has cogently argued that the "seas of Oceania were bridges rather than barriers" and that "mobility was integral to the yearly cycle for most Oceanic communities." The Tongan scholar Epeli Hau'ofa made much the same point when he observed in 1994 that "Oceania denotes a sea of islands with their inhabitants." Further, he noted, "The world of our ancestors was a large sea full of places to explore, to make their homes in, to breed generations of seafarers like themselves." Associations, even empires, held together by long-distance canoe voyaging, partially integrated large sections of Oceania before contact with Europeans. "The Pacific world was not one of isolated island worlds that were suddenly opened up by the arrival of European and American explorers and traders," D'Arcy has concluded.[13]

While voyaging never completely died out in Oceania, it decreased with the acquisition of much of the region by European powers, especially in the nineteenth century. It may have been in some decline even earlier, as local societies matured and less in the way of voyaging was needed between them. Colonial prohibitions on long-distance travel and European control of the islands further broke up much of the earlier native integration of Oceania. Only much later, from the 1960s on, was long-distance canoe voyaging partially reestablished. With that reestablishment came some sense of unity among indigenous peoples of the Pacific. A peak was reached in 1992, when a Pacific Festival of the Arts was held in Rarotonga, with sailing canoes converging on the island from throughout Oceania to celebrate canoe voyaging.[14]

Like D'Arcy, McNeill has looked at relationships among people, flora and fauna, and environmental changes. In a seminal article published in 1994, McNeill observed, "The pattern of environmental history of the Pacific Islands exhibits eras of calm interrupted by spurts of torrential change," with the pace of change "governed primarily by spurts and lulls in human transport and communication throughout the ocean." For McNeill, the important stages in settlement and development were "the ages of the outrigger, the sailing ship, and the steamship." He has emphasized the instability of island environments and the "transforming power of intrusive species, including *Homo sapiens.*" He has stressed that "Isolation over millions of years caused Pacific ecosystems to become labile, that is, prone to sudden change." People moving into Oceania, perhaps especially Polynesians, "significantly changed the fauna of the islands they settled" by hunting birds and animals to extinction and by introducing new species. Similarly, their cultivation, which included the use of fire to clear lands, greatly altered the flora of the islands, as did the importation of chickens, pigs, dogs, and rats. "Some people," McNeill has noted, "fondly maintain that islanders lived in harmony with their environments," but he has concluded that "the weight of the evidence suggests that this is romantic exaggeration." In fact, he has further observed, "Pacific islanders, wherever they were numerous, strongly shaped their environments and frequently degraded them," for "they were people not ecological angels."[15]

The coming of westerners to the Pacific further altered environments, especially after Captain James Cook entered the region for a decade of exploration in 1769. The Spanish were the first westerners to reach the Pacific, hailing land at Guam in 1521, but they had relatively little impact initially. Spanish galleons traveled back and forth between Acapulco on the west coast of New Spain and Manila in the Philippines from 1571 to 1815 without stopping elsewhere except at Guam. Captain Cook and those Europeans who followed him caused more extensive alterations.[16] "The 1760s were to the Pacific what the 1490s were to Atlantic America," McNeill has written. "Europeans brought to the Pacific a new portmanteau biota, and new economic principles and possibilities, all of which eventually combined to disrupt biotic communities, not the least human ones." Following exploration, Europeans and Americans moved into the Pacific to exploit its natural resources, which they treated in an extractive, nonrenewable manner: sandalwood, sea slugs, fur-bearing animals such as sea otters and seals, and whales. Meanwhile, diseases unintentionally carried by westerners decimated indigenous populations of Pacific islands. The initial death rate was often 80–90 percent.[17]

European colonization followed hard on the heels of exploration. Historian Steven Fischer has aptly summarized the situation: "Britain assumed control of most of the southwestern Pacific, France dominated most of Eastern Polynesia, while Germany extended its authority over most of the equatorial and northern regions of the Western Pacific." Australia came to exercise control over New Guinea and Nauru, and during World War I New Zealand took over control of German Samoa, which became Western Samoa. Many motives enticed Europeans into colonization. Trade in some items led to the acquisition of land for plantations to produce cotton, sugarcane, and coconuts for coconut oil. Worldwide imperial rivalries played important roles, especially after Germany emerged as a united nation in 1871. Then, too, Pacific islands were sought as coaling stations for naval ships and as stations for communications cables.[18]

The division of the Pacific into European empires shattered, or at least greatly eroded, earlier ties among indigenous peoples. Only Tonga and the Kingdom of Hawai'i remained independent in the late nineteenth century, and Hawai'i's days were numbered. Hau'ofa has been most eloquent on this point, observing, "Nineteenth-century imperialism erected boundaries that led to the contraction of Oceania, transforming a once boundless world into the Pacific Island states and territories we know today." As a result, "People were confined to their tiny spaces, isolated from each other.... No longer could they travel freely to do what they had done for centuries." Instead,

"They were cut off from their relatives abroad, from their far-flung sources of wealth and cultural enrichment."[19]

Nor were these changes limited to Oceania, as the arrival of Euro-Americans led to major alterations throughout the Pacific. Inspired by notions of Manifest Destiny and economic gain, Americans crossed the North American continent, displacing Mexicans in California. The Gold Rush brought hundreds of thousands of newcomers to California. In 1848, California's population, exclusive of Native Americans, was about 15,000. By 1852, that population had exploded to roughly 223,000, and by 1860 it stood at 380,000. The world rushed into California, as historian J. S. Holliday has written; and California became a state of the Union in 1850. Disease, small wars of extermination, and other factors decimated the Native-American population. There were about 100,000 Native Americans in California in 1846, but a scant 30,000 remained in 1870, and just 16,000 in 1900. Early San Francisco became an American town and soon a city. It already had close to 300,000 inhabitants by 1890 and 417,000 by 1910.[20]

Much the same story was played out farther north. Americans pushed aside the British in the Pacific Northwest. Retired British and American fur trappers had jointly occupied the Oregon country for decades, but the movement of American farmers overland to Oregon tipped the balance in favor of the United States, and the nation acquired the Oregon Territory in 1846. Founded in 1844, Portland had 46,000 residents by 1890 and 207,000 in 1910. Seattle was founded in 1851 and boasted 102,000 inhabitants by 1890; twenty years later it had 320,000.[21] Still farther north, Russians moving eastward across their nation's frontier of Siberia in the 1600s and 1700s crossed the Bering Sea into the Aleutian Islands and southwest Alaska. (They also moved southward into Japan's northern islands.) Their hold on Alaska was, however, always tenuous, and the United States acquired the region in 1867. With the discovery of gold in parts of Alaska in the mid-1890s, the non-native population of the territory rose from 430 in 1880 to about 36,000 in 1900. Conversely, the number of Alaskan Natives dropped from 33,000 in 1880 to 25,000 in 1910.[22]

Americans also moved beyond the North American continent into the Pacific, taking their cultural baggage and economic ideas with them. As a consequence of its victory in the Spanish-American War, the United States acquired Guam and control over the Philippines in 1898. The Hawaiian Islands became American in the same year and were organized as a territory in 1900. Even earlier, Americans had forced open trade with Japan. In the mid-1850s, ships of the U.S. Navy steamed into Tokyo Bay to end Japan's isolation from most western nations. As Japan successfully modernized in succeeding decades, it became as imperialistic as the United States and the nations of western Europe, taking much of Micronesia from Germany during and after World War I and integrating those islands into its growing empire in the 1920s and 1930s. With its defeat in World War II, however, Japan forfeited those islands to the United States, whose officials were active in their postwar reconstruction. Americans also took part in significant ways in the rebuilding of Japan's home islands.[23]

Americans thus played important roles in Pacific developments well before World War II, to the extent that some historians have considered the Pacific to have been a maritime frontier for Americans. American ships carried New England trade goods to the Pacific Northwest and Russian Alaska, where they were exchanged for furs, especially sea otter pelts. From Alaska, those ships sailed to the Hawaiian Islands to pick up sandalwood, which they then took, along with the furs, to China. The traders in turn carried Chinese tea, porcelain products, and other goods back to Philadelphia, Boston, and New York. By the early 1800s, about 10 percent of the furnishings of Philadelphian houses came from China. Slightly later, American whalers hunted in Alaskan waters, periodically putting into the Hawaiian Islands to refit. In the 1840s and 1850s, hundreds of the whaling ships wintered in Hawaiian ports. This trade lasted into the 1870s, when petroleum products replaced whale oil in many uses, especially lighting.[24]

American Reintegration after 1945

Although Americans had long been involved in the Pacific, their engagement with the region increased during and after World War II. The American presence provided much of the impetus for regional economic growth and reintegration. Throughout much of the Pacific, trade and economic development came to revolve around American actions. Increased economic activity brought higher standards of living to many people in the Pacific. However, just as globalization has had many critics, so has development sponsored by the United States in the Pacific. America's military activities at times also seemed overwhelming. Most Pacific peoples were glad to be rid of Japanese militarism and thanked Americans for that. However, by the 1960s memories of World War II had begun to fade, and opinions about the American military's impacts on the Pacific to change. Despite positive contributions made by the military to economic development in some areas, a growing number of local residents came to resent the American presence. Groups arose to oppose, for example, nuclear and thermonuclear testing in Micronesia and the Aleutian Islands, leading to the formation of transnational antinuclear movements, themselves integrating forces in the Pacific.[25]

In summarizing the impact of World War II on Pacific Islanders, historian Stewart Firth observed, "The outside world—above all the American military machine—came to the Pacific in prodigious proportions, dwarfing anything that had ever come before." In its impact on the Pacific, World War II resembled the importance of the Gold Rush to California. Echoing Firth and other scholars, Fischer concluded of Oceania, "Nothing in the region would ever be the same again."[26] Much the same can be said for the other areas: Japan, certainly, but also the Hawaiian Islands, the Philippines, Guam, Alaska, and America's Pacific Coast. World War II was a major watershed in the history of the Pacific. Changes were occurring well before the conflict, but the war altered economic and social systems in ways that changed how people thought about and sought to deal with issues of economic development and environmental protection. For instance, the perceived abundance brought to Oceania by Americans stimulated a desire for more material goods on the part of Pacific Islanders, many of whom had worked as laborers for the American armed forces or served in the armed forces. This demand in turn affected how Pacific Islanders viewed plans for economic development in their homelands.

One important change in the Pacific was the breakup of European colonies, just as also occurred in Asia and Africa. In 1962, Western Samoa became the first Pacific Island nation to reestablish its independence, and within a generation most of the territories held by Great Britain, New Zealand, and Australia had followed suit. Pacific areas under American trusteeship, mainly in Micronesia, gradually achieved more self-rule and, in some cases, independence. The Hawaiian Islands and Alaska became states in 1959, though heavy economic dependence on the mainland continued long after that time. Military connections increased with the Cold War. American rule of Japan ended in 1952, when that nation regained full independence, but collective security agreements and economic ties between the United States, Japan, and South Korea tightened. The situation was different in the areas controlled by France. Generally viewing their Pacific Islands as part of greater France, not as areas slated for independence, French politicians increased central control over them, yielding ground to local advocates of self-determination only very grudgingly.[27]

While the end of World War II heralded the beginning, or in some cases the resumption, of independence movements in the Pacific, it also vastly increased the presence of the United States in the region. Cold War concerns boosted American interest. The victory of communists in China in 1949 especially shocked many Americans, and the Korean War of the early 1950s drove home the point that the Pacific was of tremendous strategic value. As part of their containment policy enunciated in the late 1940s, American politicians looked anew at military and diplomatic issues in the Pacific. President Dwight D. Eisenhower told his advisers in mid-1954 that one of their main goals should be "to keep the Pacific as an American lake."[28] Accordingly, the United States built new military facilities or greatly expanded existing bases in Japan, South Korea, Alaska, Hawai'i, the Philippines, and Guam. Clashes soon arose between local residents, especially indigenous peoples, and federal authorities over political, economic, and environmental matters.

The United States used parts of the Pacific as test sites for nuclear and thermonuclear bombs. The nation conducted above-ground tests in Micronesia between 1946 and 1958, most notably at the Bikini and Enewetok atolls. American atmospheric testing also took place on the Johnston Atoll, about eight hundred miles southwest of O'ahu, and on Christmas Island, about the same distance to the southeast of O'ahu, in 1962. Beginning in 1963, American testing went underground as the result of a treaty banning atmospheric tests signed with Great Britain and the Soviet Union, and shifted to Amchitka Island in the Aleutian Islands, where three below-ground tests were conducted between 1965 and 1971. Nor was the United States alone. Between 1946 and 1996, the United States, Great Britain, and France exploded more than 250 nuclear devices in the Pacific. This extensive testing, often carried out against the wishes of local residents, who in some cases were not warned beforehand of the tests, has led Firth to label the Pacific a "nuclear playground" for western powers. Antinuclear sentiments often blended with more general antiwestern thoughts, as locals sought to oust the American military from their areas.[29]

America's economic reach equaled its military extension into the Pacific. As historian Jean Heffer has observed, commercial exchanges between the United States and the Pacific region rose rapidly after World War II. Measured in current dollars, American imports from the Pacific soared from $1.5 billion to $200 billion between 1948 and 1990, and American exports to the Pacific increased from $2.3 billion to $130 billion during the same years. Texan ports and West Coast cities such as Los Angeles, San Francisco, and Seattle increased their share of America's foreign trade from 25 percent to 38 percent during the 1970s. "This accelerating trade in goods and services,"

Heffer has written, "transformed the Pacific into an economic zone no less vital to United States interests than the Atlantic." In fact, by the mid-1980s the value of America's trade with the Pacific exceeded that of its trade with Europe. In the early 1990s, the Pacific received 30 percent of America's exports and accounted for an even higher 40 percent of its imports.[30] The openness of the American market to goods from Pacific nations spurred economic development in them, allowing those nations to pursue growth strategies based on developmental ideas other than ineffective import-substitution policies.

Not all regions of the Pacific shared equally in the economic growth fueled by American actions, however. Growth was uneven. Most of the increase in trade occurred in the North Pacific—commerce between the United States, Japan, Southeast Asia, and the "four little dragons" of South Korea, Taiwan, Hong Kong, and Singapore. In 1990–1991, those regions accounted for 80 percent of the Pacific's exports to and 83 percent of the imports from the United States. Trade with Oceania was much lighter. The same was true of direct foreign investment by American firms in the Pacific: the lion's share went to Central America, Japan, and Australia, with much less going to Oceania.[31]

In part because of their legacy of colonialism and in part because of their failure to participate fully in trade with America, many of the smaller Pacific islands developed what have been described as MIRAB economies. These were (are) economies based on the *MI*gration of people away from the islands to New Zealand, Australia, and the United States, *R*emittances that those migrants sent home, and foreign *A*id which sustained the growth of government *B*ureaucracies. In other words, many of the islands failed to develop truly self-sustaining economies and were kept afloat only by wages earned elsewhere and foreign aid.[32] Their small sizes, lack of resources, and great distances from major markets hindered economic growth.[33] Guam, American Samoa, and even the Hawaiian Islands long showed signs of having MIRAB economies. Many native Hawaiians, Chamorros, and American Samoans migrated to mainland America, and governments in all three areas, buoyed by federal spending, were important parts of the economies.

For parts of the Pacific, tourism seemed to offer pleasing prospects for economic growth at little environmental cost, as American and Japanese tourists flocked into the region seeking relaxation and imagined exotic sojourns away from reality. Writing in 1997, two economists observed, "It has now become a cliché to describe the Pacific as the world's fastest growing region for international tourism." Between 1980 and 1996, international tourist arrivals at Pacific Rim destinations rose from 76 million to 191 million, far outpacing the overall growth in international world tourism arrivals, which increased from 286 million to 592 million, or the increase in tourism in any other single part of the globe. Tourism had become important for national economies in Melanesia, Micronesia, and Polynesia, accounting for 5 percent, 54 percent, and 9 percent respectively of the gross national products (GNPs) of nations in those regions.[34] By the 1970s and 1980s, tourism was quickly replacing military spending as the mainstay of the economies of Guam and the Hawaiian Islands, a circumstance that led residents in both regions to reassess the value of the military for their lives.

Residents of the Pacific were soon wrestling with issues stemming from tourism similar to those with which people in the American West had grappled for several decades: how to create or preserve various sorts of socioeconomic systems; how to provide infrastructures for those systems; and how to ensure a desirable quality of life. Far from being cost-free and "green," tourism, they found, imposed significant burdens on host nations and regions. Land-use issues, water matters, and stress to an area's infrastructure accompanied touristic developments in the Pacific. Tourism also raised questions about ethnic and national identities. As occurred worldwide, tourism often led to some homogenization of culture and identity throughout the Pacific, a trend that caused backlash against tourism and tourists in parts of the region, including Guam and Hawai'i, by local residents.[35] United Nations (UN) officials recognized that tourism did not offer easy answers to the economic challenges facing Pacific Island nations, especially small ones. A 2005 UN report observed correctly that, "Unregulated tourism practices could have adverse consequences for the environment and, in turn, the tourism industry itself." The report also noted that, "if not well planned and managed, tourism can increase gender disparities and cultural erosion" and that "much of the wealth from the tourism sector does not trickle down to the community level."[36]

As they dealt with common economic issues, Pacific residents, like people throughout the world, worked through organizations, and these bodies contributed to the reintegration of the Pacific. Tangential to the parts of the Pacific dealt with in this study, but still significant, was the Association of Southeast Asian Nations (ASEAN) formed by Indonesia, Malaysia, Thailand, the Philippines, and Singapore in 1967. Set up originally as an anticommunist organization, this body pursued an "ASEAN way" of consensual decision making, and membership broadened in the 1980s and 1990s. More important in the early 2000s, however, was the Asia-Pacific Economic Cooperation forum (APEC), which embraced most of the Pacific in what has been described as "an amorphous, unstructured grouping stretching over four continents." Committed to trade liberalization, leaders of APEC encouraged commerce throughout the Pacific. By 2003, APEC officials were also beginning to address joint security concerns, such as the development of nuclear weapons by North Korea.[37]

Organizations also dealt with economic issues of special concern for Oceania. Longest-lived was the South Pacific Commission, later renamed the Secretariat of the Pacific Community. Started in 1947 by Great Britain, France, the United States, the Netherlands, Australia, and New Zealand, the secretariat eventually included twenty-two Pacific states and territories committed to social and economic development. The South Pacific Forum was, however, more representative of the newly independent nations of Oceania. Founded by sixteen nations in 1971, it was based in Suva, Fiji, and was dedicated to opposition to colonialism and neocolonialism in economic and political affairs. Its work was instrumental in the creation of the South Pacific Nuclear Free Zone Treaty signed by representatives of ten nations in 1985. Still other organizations sought to deal with common environmental challenges, the South Pacific Action Committee for Human Environment and Ecology and the South Pacific Regional Environmental Programme, for example.[38]

Migration has also bound together parts of the Pacific. As the editors of the definitive study have observed, "People of the islands—of Hawai'i and Guam, Aotearoa [New Zealand] and Fiji, Kiribati and Papua New Guinea, and two dozen other island groups—have been moving from village to city, from island to island, and back and forth to the industrialized nations of the Pacific periphery, throughout the second half of the twentieth century." While they have noted that this movement "is not an entirely new phenomenon" because "Islanders have been moving around the Pacific for as long as memory recalls, for many hundreds of years," they have concluded that "the velocity and impact of such movements have increased dramatically in recent decades."[39] This migration was part of an increase in the global movement of people after World War II following stagnation in such movements in the 1930s. As many nations, led by the United States in 1965, eased barriers to some forms of immigration, people around the world, but especially from Asia and the Pacific, moved to the United States, Canada, and Australia in large numbers.[40]

Although the movement of temporary workers, refugees, and permanent settlers rose globally after 1945, it was probably most pronounced in parts of the Pacific. By the mid-1980s, about one-tenth of Pacific Islanders lived outside of their home countries, searching for economic and social opportunities. Especially relevant for my study is the fact that by 1990 about 154,000 people identifying themselves as Pacific Islanders lived in mainland America. American Samoans, Chamorros, and native Hawaiians moved in large numbers to the mainland. There were more Chamorros living on the mainland than on Guam, and about one-third of all native Hawaiians resided on the mainland, especially in California and Nevada.[41]

Whether or not this movement of people would eventually create a new pan-Pacific identity remained uncertain in the early 2000s, but migrations had clearly led to cultural sharing.[42] Two brief examples illustrate that trend. After the Second World War, native Hawaiians in the American armed forces introduced American-style football, with Hawaiian twists, as "barefoot football" to Guam. On Guam, some Chamorros eagerly adopted the game and added their own variations. Football thus served as both an assimilative force and as means by which locals maintained their own identities.[43] Another example also involved interchanges between native Hawaiians and Chamorros. Native Hawaiians used the Native American Graves Protection and Repatriation Act (1990) to preserve elements of their culture, blocking resort developments where they might disrupt ancient burial sites. Inspired by native Hawaiian successes, some Chamorros employed the congressional legislation in a similar way.[44]

Flora and fauna, as well as people, have moved throughout the Pacific for thousands of years. People entering Micronesia, Melanesia, and Polynesia took plants and animals with them from Southeast Asia. Others brought in the sweet potato from South America. Polynesians, in turn, carried pigs, dogs, chickens, rats, and some thirty-two plant species to the Hawaiian Islands in their voyaging canoes. The pace of biotic change accelerated with the entrance of westerners. As early as 1840, for example, westerners had introduced 111 plant species to the Hawaiian Islands. Introduced species dramatically altered environments, especially in the Hawaiian Islands, Guam, and Alaska, and those changes had ideological overtones for indigenous peoples, as they equated losses of their plants with erosions in their cultures.[45]

Despite all the changes that have taken place since World War II, it would be wrong to overemphasize the integration of the Pacific. Caveats are in order. Oceania, for example, remains an identifiable subregion of the Pacific, with much of its own distinct history and present-day concerns. In the North Pacific differences based on nationalities linger. Anger over Japanese militarists' actions in World War II, for instance, have hindered the development of a regional trading bloc there, as divisions and disagreements between

China and Japan have remained pronounced. Historian Roger Buckley has correctly observed that "it remains highly problematic to envisage an Asia-Pacific region of genuine cooperation and mutual respect for all members, whether large or small." He has concluded that "The creation of a common future would require decades of diplomacy among rival states that to date have found it immensely difficult to work together."[46]

Conclusions

Historian John McNeill accurately pointed out in 2001 that "As yet there is no field of Pacific environmental history" though there is "a sizable scholarly literature devoted to environmental histories of various parts of the Pacific basin." McNeill then went further than other scholars in discerning commonalities in environmental developments throughout the Pacific and in suggesting avenues for future research. He highlighted "threads that bind most if not all of the Pacific together," ranging from natural ones, such as geological instability and the El Niño influence, to cultural connections and economic ties. He stressed the fragility of much of the Pacific and "the thread of biological change" as having "bound the shores of the Pacific together."[47] Other scholars have identified environmental issues of particular importance for Pacific peoples. They have often cited global warming as a special concern for several reasons: that rising ocean waters threaten low-lying islands with inundation; that salt water may infiltrate freshwater lenses under the islands, ruining the water supplies needed for human consumption and agriculture; and that weather patterns may be growing unstable.[48] Researchers for the UN have recently also recognized the great vulnerability of much of the Pacific to environmental changes.[49]

Informed by these analyses, my study looks at how people in America's Pacific possessions have tried to balance economic development issues with environmental concerns, how residents and nonresidents have sought to shape their lives in an ever-changing region of the world, and what the results have been. In doing so, my work differentiates Pacific from global issues. Of course, global and Pacific matters have often overlapped. Rising sea levels threaten islands in the Indian Ocean and the Caribbean Sea as well as in the Pacific. The rights of indigenous peoples, especially their right to preserve traditional relationships to their environments, extend far beyond the Pacific. Economic integration is a global as well as a Pacific issue. Still, many matters have had distinct Pacific meanings. The American military and economic integration of the Pacific, in particular, has formed bedrock upon which economic development and environmental protection conflicts have been resolved.

Let us begin our voyage with the Hawaiian Islands at the center of the Pacific. The next chapter examines developments on the island of Kahoʻolawe, one of the eight major islands in the Hawaiian archipelago. Here many of the issues running through deliberations about developmental matters were dramatically worked out in the 1970s, 1980s, and 1990s. Environmentally degraded by western ranching before World War II, Kahoʻolawe was further damaged by its use by the U.S. Navy as a shelling and bombing range during and after the conflict. As native Hawaiians and others came to oppose the continued use of Kahoʻolawe as a live-fire range, they raised issues that reverberated across the Pacific.

CHAPTER 2

The Hawaiian Islands

The "Healing" of Kahoʻolawe

In the late 1960s and early 1970s, American fighter-bombers training for the Vietnam War repeatedly swept down on targets placed on Kahoʻolawe, the smallest of the eight major islands of the Hawaiian archipelago and the only one then being used as a live-fire range. Between 1968 and 1970, the warplanes dropped 2,500 tons of bombs on Kahoʻolawe, and in the latter year alone they bombarded the island for 315 days, solidifying its reputation as "the most bombed island in the Pacific." The American military had used Kahoʻolawe as a target range since the 1930s, and even earlier, goats, sheep, cattle, and horses introduced by westerners had overgrazed the island, degrading its environment. The ground was severely eroded, and with much of its original vegetation gone Kahoʻolawe became home to alien plant species. Unexploded bombs made traveling on the island dangerous and fishing in nearby waters unsafe. Sediment from runoffs killed nearshore reefs.[1]

Beginning in the 1960s, ranchers, environmentalists, native Hawaiians, and politicians throughout the Hawaiian Islands sought to return Kahoʻolawe to environmental circumstances before western contact. For native Hawaiians, restoration involved cultural renewal. George Helm, a major native Hawaiian leader, claimed that it was his "moral responsibility to attempt an ending to this desecration of our sacred aina [land] ... for each bomb dropped adds further injury to an already wounded soul." "What is national defense," he wondered, "when what is being destroyed is the very thing the military is entrusted to defend, the sacred land of (Hawaii) America?" Similarly, Dr. Noa Emmet Aluli, another important native Hawaiian leader, observed: "The work to heal the island will heal the soul of our people. Each time we pick up a stone to restore a cultural site on the island, we pick up ourselves, as Hawaiians." As native Hawaiians rediscovered their culture, the restoration of Kahoʻolawe along Hawaiian lines became a burning topic for them, a major catalyst for a native Hawaiian renaissance.[2]

This chapter looks at how disparate issues fused in the movement to halt the environmental degradation of Kahoʻolawe. It begins by discussing the environmental changes that ranching and military usage brought to Kahoʻolawe and then investigates how and why some Hawaiian residents began to oppose those alterations. Not particularly concerned initially with native Hawaiian rights, ranchers, environmentalists, and local politicians mounted the first challenges for reasons ranging from their dislike of federal government authority, to their desire to use Kahoʻolawe as a park, to their hope that the island could be preserved as a pristine counterpart to touristic development taking place on the nearby island of Maui. In the mid-1970s, native Hawaiians became the most important group advocating change in the status of Kahoʻolawe. For native Hawaiians, restoring the island physically and using it as a site for cultural renewal went hand in hand. Ultimately, they secured the removal of Kahoʻolawe from American military control and its restoration to the State of Hawaiʻi, with the state pledged to give the island to them when they established their own sovereign nation. How they succeeded in convincing other Hawaiian residents to support their goals is an informative story of intergroup dynamics. The chapter closes by comparing developments with regard to the Hawaiian Islands to those surrounding the navy's live-fire operations in Micronesia and the Caribbean.

In their movement to recover Kahoʻolawe, native Hawaiians created a distinctive postcolonial variant of the United States' environmental justice campaign. Viewing the United States as a colonizing power, they hoped to rid the island of its influence, especially that of the U.S. Navy. The attempt to restore Kahoʻolawe resembled in some ways the work of residents of urban areas in the United States, often poor people of color, to keep their neighborhoods from being used as sites for landfills, sewage stations, electric power plants, and the like. However, far from being an urban area, Kahoʻolawe was an unpopulated rural island, and efforts to end its use for bombing and begin its restoration show the working out of cleavages, as well as cooperation, within the ranks of environmentalists, native groups, politicians, and the general public.

At its heart, the success of native Hawaiians rested on a blend of culture, politics, and public policy—a combination of rediscovered native symbols, direct action, and astute use of courts. Native Hawaiians could succeed because federal law devolved some aspects of environmental management to locals, with lawsuits a major mode of management. While local in their origins, environmental actions to restore Kahoʻolawe were nonetheless transnational in their implications. Many native Hawaiians came to see their labors as part of a wide movement to remove colonial controls over the lives of Pacific Islanders, and some native Hawaiians played active roles in antimilitary movements throughout the Pacific. They engaged in pan-Pacific organizing, contributing to the region's reintegration.

Traditional Hawaiian Life and Western Ranching

The smallest and southernmost of the four islands of Maui County, Kahoʻolawe lies seven miles off Mākena on southwest Maui and sixteen miles from Lānāʻi. About eleven miles long and seven miles wide, Kahoʻolawe covers 28,600 acres. Puʻu Moaʻulanui, the island's highest point, rises to 1,477 feet, with smaller hills dotting the island. Kahoʻolawe's southern and eastern shores rise dramatically from the ocean, forming steep cliffs. The northern and western shores slope more gradually and contain small sand beaches. Surrounded by the ocean channels, Kahoʻolawe is often difficult to approach from the sea due to winds and strong currents that frequently produce rough water. Northeastern trade winds blow for part of the year, exacerbating wind erosion on the eastern side and crest of Kahoʻolawe. Erosion caused by overgrazing and bombing had removed six feet of topsoil from Kahoʻolawe by the 1990s. Lying in Maui's rain shadow, Kahoʻolawe is arid, with rainfall generally limited to showers occurring during periods of southerly winds. Rainfall varies from about ten inches annually on the west coast to twenty-five inches at the summit. All of the streams on the island are intermittent. A 1988–1989 study estimated that 50–100 thousand gallons of water could be collected from rainfall annually, if catchment basins and storage systems were built. The study also concluded that groundwater impounded in a thirteen-square-mile aquifer might be tapped to supply an additional 500 thousand gallons per year.[3]

In pre-contact times, before Captain James Cook "discovered" the Hawaiian Islands in 1778, Kahoʻolawe supported a semipermanent population. "Traditional habitation sites" developed on Kahoʻolawe, according to a definitive report, "wherever potable water and/or food sources were available." The earliest archaeological sites date to A.D. 900–1000, and as many as 300 people lived on Kahoʻolawe as late as 1750. In the late 1700s and early 1800s, wars to unify the Hawaiian Islands by Kamehameha I combined with diseases unintentionally introduced by westerners to decimate the population of Kahoʻolawe, which fell to about 160 by 1805.[4] Traditional life on Kahoʻolawe revolved around fishing and, to a lesser extent, farming. Both offshore and near-shore fishing grounds were rich, with Hawaiians practicing long-line and net fishing in the former and net and pole fishing in the latter environments. Hawaiians gathered squid and limpets at the rocky shorelines. They also grew various vegetables, including sweet potatoes. However, the lack of reliable, year-round water sources precluded cultivating taro, the food staple throughout most of the Hawaiian Islands. Instead, residents of Kahoʻolawe traveled to Maui to exchange their fish for poi made from taro. Those on Kahoʻolawe usually suspended work during the rainy winter months to visit friends and relatives on other islands. Although arid compared to the other major islands of the Hawaiian archipelago, Kahoʻolawe supported fairly varied agriculture and vegetation. There may have been more rainfall on the island than in later times, for a "sky bridge" of moisture-bearing clouds often connected Maui's high volcanic peak Haleakalā to the summit of Kahoʻolawe well into the nineteenth century.[5]

Kahoʻolawe was important as a spiritual center and as a navigation marker. The island, scholars and native Hawaiian activists have noted, "was originally named Kohemālamalama O Kanaloa and just simply Kanaloa, after the Hawaiian and Polynesian god of the ocean currents and navigation. Kahoʻolawe is the sacred *kino lau*, body form of the god Kanaloa." The island was, they observe, viewed as "one of the residences of Kamohoaliʻi, the shark god brother of the volcano goddess Pele." Thus, Kahoʻolawe was considered to be a *wahi pana* (sacred place) by ancient Hawaiians and is so considered by many native Hawaiians today. Creation myths reinforce the island's significance as a *wahi pana,* for they tell of the island as being born of the union of Papa, earth mother, and Wakea, sky father. Hawaiians also thought of Kahoʻolawe as a *puʻuhonua* (place of refuge). The only Pacific island named after a major Polynesian god, Kanaloa, the island was seen in a special light by Hawaiians. The name Kohemālamalama O Kanaloa, scholars and activists have maintained, "can also be interpreted as meaning the sacred refuge or *puʻuhonua* of Kanaloa." Moreover, Kahoʻolawe, they have pointed out, "figured significantly in the long voyages between Hawaiʻi and Tahiti." The island's southern tip was a launching place and ceremonial area for such voyages. A strong southerly current runs through the Kealaikahiki Channel toward Tahiti and is still known locally as the "Tahiti Express." The high central part of the island was the location of a traditional training school for navigators. Offering sweeping views of the Hawaiian Islands, the crest of

Kahoʻolawe housed a platform used as a navigational school and a dwelling for the *kahuna* (priests) who taught the students in navigation.[6]

A letter from a visitor in 1858, at the close of the period of traditional life on Kahoʻolawe, captured well what circumstances were like and suggested changes about to occur. William F. Allen, the Kingdom of Hawaiʻi's minister of foreign affairs and a person soon to be deeply involved in ranching on Kahoʻolawe, noted the existence of "good soil" on various parts of the island and observed that "the natives have some Sugar Cane growing; melons, pota-toes, and pumpkins grow well here." He found the men "engaged in fishing, which is very good there most of the year," and thought the Hawaiians lived in three villages. Foretelling a different future for the island, he concluded that it could support twenty thousand sheep and reported that "the natives are anxious to remain here, and some of them are willing to be employed as shepherds."[7]

By this time, Kahoʻolawe's physical environment had already begun to change.[8] Significant ecological alterations were under way on the Hawaiian Islands in the late 1700s and early 1800s. Before the coming of the first people, there were about 2,700 species of plants, 4,000 species of insects, and seven species of land birds on the Hawaiian Islands. There was also one land mam-mal, the Hawaiian bat, but no reptiles or amphibians. In their colonization of the Hawaiian Islands, Polynesians introduced thirty-two plant species, in-cluding taro, sugarcane, bananas, breadfruit, and sweet potatoes, along with chickens, dogs, pigs, and rats. As they established plots for taro and other crops, and as their plants and animals competed with native species, Polyne-sian settlers changed the biota of the Hawaiian Islands. The clearing of low-land forests and more selective cutting in the uplands started to transform the composition of trees and plants on the islands. Some species of birds were driven into extinction, mainly large flightless ones, just as occurred with the coming of the Maori to New Zealand. In addition, new uses brought ecological alterations to Kahoʻolawe. During the 1830s and 1840s, the King-dom of Hawaiʻi, which was created through the efforts of Kamehameha I and his successors, used the island as a penal colony. Expected to be as self-suffi-cient as possible, the prisoners planted gardens and altered the landscape in other ways. At the height of its use as a penal colony Kahoʻolawe possessed about eighty residents, but with the end of its use for that purpose only about seventeen remained. As Helm and other late-twentieth-century native Hawaiians believed, their ancestors lived close to the land on Kahoʻolawe, but in a very dynamic, not static, relationship.[9]

The pace of ecological change accelerated with the coming of westerners. Captain Cook's men brought melons, onions, and pumpkins in 1778, and Captain George Vancouver's crew added oranges, lemons, almonds, and grapes fourteen years later. Westerners introduced 111 plant species, including 65 fruits and vegetables, to the Hawaiian Islands by 1840. Altogether, westerners brought in about 5,000 species and varieties of plants by the 1980s. Westerners also introduced animals very destructive of native plants, even before ranching began. Vancouver introduced the first goats to Kaho'olawe in 1793. As western sea captains did on many of the seemingly "unpopulated" Pacific islands, Vancouver dropped off the goats on Kaho'olawe so that their progeny might be available as food sources for shipwrecked sailors. Or, according to some accounts, he gave the goats to a Maui chief, who sent some of them to Kaho'olawe. By whatever means they arrived, the goats multiplied and began causing trouble. As early as 1850, they were damaging trees by chewing on their trunks. Sheep, cattle, and horses came a bit later, with attempts to establish ranching on Kaho'olawe.[10]

Eager to raise funds for its operations, increasingly influenced by westerners, and not at the time overly concerned about the island's cultural or spiritual importance, the Hawaiian government leased all of Kaho'olawe to Robert Wyllie and Elisha Allen, the chief justice of the supreme court of the kingdom, in 1858. By 1887, about nine hundred head of cattle, twelve thousand sheep, and an unknown, but large, number of goats roamed the island. The destruction of vegetation through overgrazing and concomitant soil erosion were recognized as substantial problems by the late nineteenth century.[11]

A concerned territorial governor, Walter Frear, publicized the destruction. Close to United States Secretary of the Interior James Garfield and Director of the United States Reclamation Service F. H. Newell, Frear was imbued with Progressive-era notions of conservation. In talking to a women's group in 1908, Frear observed that "in Hawaii the relation between forest, streams and lands are [sic] closer than in most other countries." Turning specifically to developments on Kaho'olawe, he noted that "I saw more clearly than I had ever seen before the results of continued neglect and wastefulness in the use of forests." The island, he continued, was "formerly covered with forest," but now "for miles and miles the vegetation has been killed off and the soil simply blown away."[12] Governor Frear signed a proclamation designating Kaho'olawe a forest reserve in August 1910.

For the next eight years, Kaho'olawe was one of a number of forest reserves in the Hawaiian Islands. Ranching was phased out, and about five thousand goats and a number of sheep were removed or eradicated. Perhaps five hundred to a thousand goats and sheep remained on Kahoʻolawe as the island's forest-reserve period came to a close. Archaeological work began, under the auspices of the Bishop Museum. Reforestation efforts accelerated in an attempt to stabilize the soil and halt erosion. There was also some hope that forests would bring back rains that had, by tradition, fallen from clouds connecting Maui to Kahoʻolawe (traditional chants called these *naʻulu rains*). *Kiawe,* spineless cactus, ironwood trees, and candle and grape trees—all alien species—were used in this effort. Australian salt bushes were also introduced and spread widely. The use of alien species was a common response to forestry problems in the Hawaiian Islands and elsewhere at this time. For example, when a natural die-off killed 8,500 acres of forest in east Maui in the early 1900s, governmental officials and business leaders reforested the land with eucalyptus trees from Australia.[13] In typical Progressive-era fashion, the goal was not to preserve a pristine native forest, but to put the land to productive use to avoid waste.[14]

The experiment of creating a forest reserve on Kahoʻolawe ended in 1918. Strapped for funds—the federal government failed to deliver the expected sums—the territorial government decided to lease the island once again for private ranching. An investigation near the end of the forest-reserve era concluded that ranching and conservation could coexist, that "under a carefully prepared lease of the island with due restrictions and limitations good use could be made of these [Kahoʻolawe's grasslands] and at the same time goats could be required to be exterminated."[15] Conservation work would, it was hoped, continue in private hands. There was little doubt that such work was needed. Writing in 1916, C. S. Judd, the superintendent of forestry in Hawaiʻi, observed, in words reminiscent of Governor Frear's statement eight years earlier, "innumerable sheep and goats cropped the grass and other herbage so closely, that the sod cover was broken." He continued, "the unprotected and exposed soil could not stand the force of the strong trade wind but was lifted little by little and carried southwest across the island and out to sea in a great red cloud." As a result, Judd concluded, "the top of the island which was once covered with four to eight feet of good soil has been largely reduced to hardpan."[16]

The territorial government leased Kahoʻolawe to Angus MacPhee in 1918. A former Wyoming cowboy, MacPhee had been the champion rodeo roper of the world between 1902 and 1907 and a top bronc buster in Buffalo Bill Cody's Wild West Show. He had learned of possibilities on Kahoʻolawe in several ways. As the manager of a ranch on Maui, he could clearly see

Kahoʻolawe across the ocean channel separating the two islands. What he saw disturbed him, his daughter later recalled, "By noon each day, the Moaʻe Wind was sending a red-dust plume from the island to the western horizon." As she remembered, her father told her, "much of the western land where I was born came to look like badlands too. Kahoʻolawe has life! Given the opportunity I could make the land blossom." There was more to MacPhee's decision to try ranching there than simply a desire to restore the island, however. He was a friend of the person who had leased Kahoʻolawe right before the island became a forest reserve and was well aware of the possibility of making a profit.[17] Under the terms of his lease, MacPhee was to remove all of the goats and sheep before restocking the island with cattle. The lease's provisions also limited the number of cattle that could be grazed on the island at any one time.[18]

Brash and full of optimism, MacPhee sailed for Kahoʻolawe on his newly acquired boat, the *Kahoʻolawe Maru,* with lumber needed to build redwood water tanks, so necessary for cattle raising in the arid land. MacPhee put in ten 10,000-gallon and several 5,000-gallon tanks. Other improvements came quickly, a ranch house and outbuildings. Perhaps most important initially, MacPhee constructed a seven-mile-long fence across the middle of the island to control goats and sheep. During his first two years there, MacPhee captured and sold or exterminated some twelve thousand goats and sheep— moves that greatly reduced but did not completely eliminate the animals from Kahoʻolawe. Twelve Hawaiian cowboys led by Jack Aina conducted these operations. For a time, remembered MacPhee's daughter, "the land smelled horribly of death."[19] As required by his lease, MacPhee also worked to restore the land by planting trees and bushes. Some were alien species: eucalyptus trees, Australian salt bushes, and *kiawe* trees, for example. Others were indigenous, such as sandalwood and Hawaiian tobacco.[20]

Pleased by the results of MacPhee's labors, territorial officers renewed his lease in 1920. In the new lease, MacPhee was joined by Harry Baldwin, a member of a well-known missionary and landowning family. The two men formed the Kahoolawe Ranch Company. By this time, MacPhee had invested $38,000 in his ranching operations and was strapped for additional funds needed to continue making improvements. Baldwin initially paid in only $1 to the joint venture but was expected to soon invest much more. His interest in Kahoʻolawe was as a potential site for the raising of purebred cattle and thoroughbred horses. In 1929, severe storms hammered Kahoʻolawe, damaging or destroying many of MacPhee's improvements, including a large cistern for water. Baldwin pumped tens of thousands of dollars into the ranch over the next twelve years, until the total investment in the ranch had climbed to $190,000 by 1941.[21] In 1939, there were a reported 500 cattle, 200 sheep, 25 goats, 17 horses, 3 mules, and 500 turkeys on Kahoʻolawe.[22]

Military Use of Kahoʻolawe and Early Opposition to Live-Fire Operations

Another stage in western use of Kahoʻolawe began as military training replaced ranching. As early as the 1930s, army pilots hanging out of the cockpits of their biplanes dropped hand-held bombs on targets on part of the island. Seven months before the Japanese attack on Pearl Harbor, Baldwin and MacPhee subleased the southern tip of Kahoʻolawe to the United States for use as a bombing range by the Army Air Corps in an arrangement to be renewed annually and not to run beyond 1954. With the Japanese attack on Pearl Harbor, the U.S. military took over the entire island as a bombing and shelling range, and ranching ended.

Military use of Kahoʻolawe generated criticism. As the Second World War continued, the Pacific front moved farther west, well away from the Hawaiian Islands, prompting the first questions about the military's use of Kahoʻolawe; and those questions mounted once the war ended. MacPhee and Baldwin wanted compensation for the loss of tens of thousands of dollars' worth of improvements that they had made on Kahoʻolawe. Moreover, they hoped to return to ranching on the island, a desire thwarted by the navy. The navy raised the rent it paid to them but did not allow them back on the island until 1945, and then only for a short visit. All they found of the ranch during that visit, wrote Inez Ashdown, were "heaps of rubble."[23] Harry Baldwin died in 1945, but a year later MacPhee sued the United States government for eighty thousand dollars in compensation. When MacPhee passed away in 1948, his daughter kept up the pressure, but in the end received nothing.

The navy cancelled its lease of the island from the Kahoolawe Ranch Company in the fall of 1952. Some territorial officials joined MacPhee and Baldwin in questioning the navy's actions. As early as 1942, a few officials discussed how best to rehabilitate the island. Visitors noted that sheep and goats, which had been kept under control by the Kahoolawe Ranch Company, were increasing in number and again denuding the island. After the war ended, the navy nixed a proposal for joint usage of Kahoʻolawe. The territorial government wanted to rid Kahoʻolawe of goats and sheep and restock it with game birds for hunters. Noting that there were many unexploded shells and bombs on the island, navy officials rejected that plan as unsafe. The same logic led them to oppose returning the island to ranching. Then, too, Cold War concerns combined with a very hot war in Korea seemed to justify continuing use of Kahoʻolawe as a target range for bombing and shelling.[24]

Navy officials believed that military requirements necessitated the reservation of Kahoʻolawe as a live-fire range, and President Dwight D. Eisenhower transferred the island to the jurisdiction of the navy by executive order in 1953. Although it kept Kahoʻolawe for the navy, Eisenhower's order also contained provisions for environmental restoration, at the insistence of territorial authorities. The agreement specified that the navy would eradicate feral goats, or at least limit their number to no more than two hundred. Then, too, territorial officials were to be allowed "at reasonable intervals to enter and inspect the island to ascertain the extent of forest cover, erosion, and animal life thereon, and to sow or plant suitable grasses and plants under a program of soil conservation." Very important in light of later events, when the navy no longer required the use of Kahoʻolawe, it was to return the island to the territory of Hawaiʻi in a condition "reasonably safe for human habitation, without cost to the Territory."[25]

The navy maintained an important presence in the Hawaiian Islands, but its significance lessened over time. America's Pacific command (Commander in Chief Pacific or CINCPAC) was headquartered at Pearl Harbor. CINCPAC's scope of operations extended throughout the Pacific and into the Far East, South and Southeast Asia, and the Indian Ocean. CINCPAC decisions greatly influenced environmental developments on Guam, for example. A unified command of the nation's military services, CINCPAC was nonetheless mainly a naval show. In the late 1980s, the navy had 116 facilities and the marines another 98 in the Hawaiian Islands. Even so, the relative importance of the military to the Hawaiian economy declined over time. The number of military personnel in the islands came to between 50,000 and 60,000 annually from the early 1950s into the mid-1980s. Military personnel, including dependents along with civilian employees of the military and their dependents, composed about 35 percent of the population of the Hawaiian Islands in 1955. However, as the population of the islands increased and economic diversification occurred, they came to make up only about 20 percent of it by 1988. Military expenditures accounted for nearly one-third of the personal income of Hawaiian residents in 1949, but only 7.5 percent in 1988. By way of contrast, tourism accounted for just 2.4 percent of the personal income of Hawaiian residents in 1949, but nearly one-third by 1988. As the importance of the military to their economy declined and memories of

World War II faded, many Hawaiian residents rethought their relationships to the U.S. Navy. That reassessment had important consequences for how they viewed the continued use of Kahoʻolawe as a live-fire range.[26]

As a 1972 report issued by navy officials explained, throughout the 1950s and 1960s the navy used Kahoʻolawe "for training in air-to-ground weapons delivery and shore bombardment." The navy set up seventeen air-to-surface targets and twenty-one surface-to-surface targets on Kahoʻolawe, mainly at its center. Exceptional tests punctuated routine training. In 1965, for example, the navy simulated small atomic bomb explosions to explore the effects of blasts on ships anchored near the island. One detonation of 500 tons of TNT left a large ocean-filled crater that remains to the present day. Kahoʻolawe was especially utilized, however, by navy and marine pilots and gunners preparing for service in Vietnam.[27]

Increased bombing, combined with a growing environmental awareness in the Hawaiian Islands, brought the first major opposition to the use of Kahoʻolawe as a military range. The passage of clean air, clean water, wilderness protection, and endangered species acts by Congress in the 1960s and 1970s and the establishment of the Environmental Protection Agency (EPA) in 1970 signaled that environmentalism had reached a new stage of maturity in the United States. Many Americans came to see having a clean environment almost as a birthright, with the natural environment as something to be consumed in leisure-time activities. In the Hawaiian Islands, the explosive growth of tourism unified many local groups and people in early environmental efforts. In 1959, the coming of statehood and the arrival of jet airplanes boosted tourism. Between 1958 and 1973, the number of tourists visiting the Hawaiian Islands rose an average 20 percent each year, increasing from 171,000 to 2,631,000. This very rapid growth of tourism placed enormous stresses on the physical environment of the Hawaiian Islands and on established social and cultural practices. Land-use issues, water matters, community development topics, and quality-of-life concerns soon dominated politics and policy making in the islands.[28]

Nowhere were these concerns more pressing than in Maui County, and particularly on the island of Maui, which experienced exuberant growth during the 1970s and 1980s. In 1956, just 29,000 tourists visited Maui, which possessed 247 hotel rooms. By 1964, 131,000 people were coming to Maui each year, housed in 885 hotel rooms. A scant thirteen years later 1.1 million visitors enjoyed Maui; and by 1980 the number had risen to 1.4 million. A peak came in 1990 with 2.5 million tourists visiting Maui, staying in 18,000 hotel and condominium rooms.[29] Appalled by the rapid growth of tourism on their island, many Mauians saw the navy's use of Kaho'olawe, which was separated from their island by only an eight-mile-wide channel, as part of the more general problem of environmental protection.

Even as she kept up her ultimately unsuccessful effort to secure compensation from the navy for ranch improvements lost on Kaho'olawe, Inez Ashdown increasingly criticized the navy for its environmental insensitivity. Replying to navy officials who repeatedly declared that Kaho'olawe was an essential training target, she observed in an interview published in the *Los Angeles Times* in the fall of 1968, "Hogwash! Kahoolawe could be a paradise. It has gorgeous beaches, spectacular valleys, cliffs and ravines." She continued, "If the U.S. Navy has its way, Kahoolawe will be bombed off the map. . . . The Navy is destroying Kahoolawe."[30]

Political leaders soon joined Ashdown in her opposition to the navy. Elmer Cravalho, a leading politician in the Hawaiian Islands, led the charge against the navy. As Maui County's very forceful mayor, Cravalho came to view the bombing with a jaundiced eye. Bombs, he thought, were bad for business, especially tourism. A staunch believer in home rule, he also greatly disliked any actions of the federal and state governments that impinged on his local political power. In early 1969, Cravalho complained to Rear Admiral Fred Bakutis, commandant of the Fourteenth Naval District, that bombing might have an adverse "impact on development here." As Cravalho explained, "We're talking about the investment of millions of dollars on this coast in the next 20 to 25 years." All bombardment should cease, Cravalho thought. Bakutis agreed to give Maui's residents prior notice of any bombing activities and said the navy would look into relocating targets to the side of Kaho'olawe farthest away from Maui, but he insisted that the bombing continue.[31]

Ironically, this effort to end the bombing focused, not on the value of preserving Kaho'olawe as a pristine place, but on opening Maui to more tourism. How those opposing the bombing viewed tourism was complex. The initial objective of many opponents of the bombing was to make Maui more attractive to tourism. Yet attitudes changed. By the 1980s and 1990s, many pushing for the preservation of Kaho'olawe, particularly most native Hawaiians, came to see preservation as an antidote to what they viewed as all-too-successful resort development of Maui, a real shift in values from those of a few decades earlier.[32]

Cravalho soon deepened his criticism to include environmental concerns. In September 1969, he called the navy to task for not eradicating the goats on Kaho'olawe, as specified by the 1953 executive order. Then came a blockbuster discovery. An unexploded 500-pound bomb, accidentally dropped on Maui by a navy plane, was found on land in which Cravalho had a commercial interest. Navy technicians exploded it harmlessly, but the damage had been done. Cravalho attacked the navy for having "wantonly ravaged and destroyed" Kahoʻolawe. In a mixed appeal to preservation and use, Cravalho called for "productive use of the island" at a time "when the rallying cry of our citizens is focusing attention on the protection of our environment." By mid-1970, he was suggesting the use of Kahoʻolawe as a park, saying "It's an ideal place for just lying around, swimming or fishing; it's a beautiful place."[33]

Led by Cravalho, other politicians came to oppose the navy's bombing of Kahoʻolawe. In 1969, members of the Maui County Council (given the absence of city councils, the governing body in local politics) called for the termination of all bombing in 1969, a stance reaffirmed in later years. Three representatives of the state's congressional delegation—Representative Patsy Mink, Representative Spark Matsunaga, and Senator Hiram Fong—like Cravalho greatly disturbed by the discovery of the bomb on Maui, urged Secretary of Defense Melvin Laird to halt all bombing on Kahoʻolawe to avoid, in Matsunaga's words, "a major disaster." In 1971, Senator Daniel Inouye joined his Hawaiian colleagues in Congress in urging that Kahoʻolawe be returned to the state of Hawaiʻi. Inouye was an influential figure in Washington, and his opposition counted. Inouye was a veteran of the famed 442nd Regimental Combat Team, composed of Americans of Japanese ancestry, and his break with the navy on the bombing of Kahoʻolawe was telling. In opposing the navy, politicians such as Inouye were concerned about more than the environment. Like the political leaders of many western American states, they wanted to wrest control of their land from the hands of federal officials. Like Cravalho, they resented having others tell them what to do.[34]

Grassroots environmental groups added their support. Most important was Life of the Land, an organization formed in 1968 to clean up beaches on Oʻahu. Led by the charismatic Tony Hodges, members of this group made halting the bombing one of their goals. In 1971, Hodges filed suit against the navy in federal court, charging that the use of Kahoʻolawe as a target range violated the National Environmental Protection Act of 1969, which required that federal agencies prepare and file for public comment environmental impact statements for any actions that might harm the environment. The navy, as Hodges noted, had failed to do so. Hodges employed sarcasm and irony in his public statements. "I hope the navy pilots have learned to recognize their targets a little better," he told a newspaper reporter in a reference to the bomb discovered on Cravalho's land. "Both I, and, I am sure, Alexander and Baldwin, would hate to see bomber pilots mistake the Wailea resort area for Kahoolawe." Wailea was a multimillion-dollar resort being constructed on South Maui directly across an ocean channel from Kahoʻolawe. It was being built by Alexander and Baldwin, one of Hawaiʻi's "Big Five" agricultural firms then making a transition to tourism. Hodges concluded, "Perhaps A&B should include some sort of anti-aircraft batteries in its master plan." Asked to join the suit against the navy, Cravalho was delighted to do so, observing that the navy's attitude was "arrogant" and that it had "completely ignored the County."[35]

Navy officials prepared an environmental impact statement in early 1972 in response to the lawsuit. The statement admitted that shelling and bombing hurt Kahoʻolawe, stating that "the adverse effects are cratering, comouflets, sprays of shell and bomb fragments, ground disruptions, water pollution, destruction of vegetation and animal life, and other related effects." Even so, the statement highlighted perceived "beneficial environmental effects of military use," ranging from pulverizing the island's soil, thus making it amenable to the growth of vegetation, to the accumulation of rain runoff in bomb craters. Then too, navy representatives argued that "the mineral content per acre of the target sites, from [shell and bomb] fragmentations, might someday prove economically worthwhile from the standpoint of salvage and retrieval of some of the metallic alloy material involved." "Unexploded dud ordnance" did constitute "a major problem," but it was one "without noticeably adverse effect on the human population spread within the Hawaiian archipelago." In short, according to navy officials, "thirty years of use of the island as a target site" had "slightly improved the balance of the island's ecosystems."[36]

Nor, according to navy officials, were alternative uses worthwhile. The navy's report claimed that Kahoʻolawe "contains no areas of particular aesthetic value." Unlike Cravalho, navy officials thought it unsuitable for picnicking, hiking, or hunting. The navy did increase its efforts to reduce the goat population and boosted its restoration work, planting fifteen thousand trees and shrubs, mainly alien species—eucalyptus and tamarisk trees—but also some native species, *wiliwili* and *Acacia koai*. However, many of these trees and bushes died when the navy failed to water them. Nonetheless, navy officials adamantly refused to yield on the main bone of contention: their right to bomb and shell Kahoʻolawe. After surveying other possible sites in the Pacific and even debating the possibility of constructing an artificial island, navy officers concluded that no other option fit their needs. Cost considerations, ownership issues, distances from military bases, and the inability

Overgrazing and bombing left Kahoʻolawe badly eroded. (Courtesy of the Kahoʻolawe Island Reserve Commission)

to use other sites year-round ruled out the possibilities. Only Kahoʻolawe would do. Such would remain their stance into the 1990s. The federal court, satisfied that the navy had completed a meaningful environmental impact statement, dismissed the case in late 1972.[37]

Native Hawaiians and Direct Action

In the mid-1970s, native Hawaiians became the leading opponents of military use of Kahoʻolawe, turning what had been a local conflict into a major statewide issue that attracted national and international attention. Their actions took place as part of the native Hawaiian renaissance, a movement that sought the return of lost lands, the revival of Hawaiian culture, and political sovereignty. Beginning in response to the removal of native Hawaiian farmers from lands on Oʻahu in the late 1960s, the movement later broadened. According to Haunani-Kay Trask, a faculty member at the University of Hawaiʻi and a leading native Hawaiian activist, efforts expanded from "an ongoing series of land struggles throughout the decade of the seventies" to "a larger struggle for native Hawaiian autonomy" in the 1980s. The movement, she noted, also "branched out politically to link up with American Indian activists on the mainland, anti-nuclear independence struggles throughout the South Pacific, and international networks in Asia and at the United Nations." The many sailings of the *Hōkūle'a* helped to spread ideas and stimulate a shared consciousness.[38]

By this time, native Hawaiians had lost most of their lands—the Hawaiian Islands contained 4.1 million acres—over a century and a half of western economic development. Western traders extracted sandalwood from Hawaiian forests to trade in China as early as the 1790s, leading Hawaiian chiefs to force commoners to harvest the wood but keeping most of the profits themselves. Further commercialization of the economy of the Hawaiian Islands followed in the 1830s and 1840s, as the islands became important supply points for whaling fleets plying the Pacific. Later in the nineteenth century, sugarcane replaced the supply trade as the major commercial enterprise in the islands. More than any other factor, the desire of planters to maintain their exports of sugar to mainland America led to the overthrow of the Kingdom of Hawai'i in 1893 and the annexation of Hawai'i by the United States five years later. Sugar dominated the Territory of Hawai'i, with pineapple developing as a secondary crop. With the spread of sugar and pineapple plantations, land ownership became concentrated, until by the early 1940s about one-half of the land in the Hawaiian Islands was owned by just eighty estates, corporations, or individuals. Most of the rest lay in the hands of the territorial government, which leased desirable tracts to planters at low rates. Native Hawaiians lost out as land was reapportioned. Congress passed legislation in 1921 to return about 200 thousand acres to native Hawaiians, but this measure proved ineffective. It was toward regaining their land base, and with it economic and political power, that native Hawaiians directed their rights movement.[39]

Land loss and other factors, according to a detailed report prepared for Congress by native Hawaiians in 1983, had had important "psychological, social, and cultural consequences for Native Hawaiians." They had the lowest life expectancy, the highest infant mortality rate, and the highest suicide rate of any ethnic group in the Hawaiian Islands. Only 4.6 percent of native Hawaiians completed college (compared to a statewide average of 11.3 percent), and 30 percent of native Hawaiian families lived in poverty. The report concluded, "by all major indices—health, education, income—Native Hawaiians display distinct disparities with their fellow citizens." Many native Hawaiians left Hawai'i. By 1990, about one-third of all native Hawaiians were living on the mainland, where they sought better social and economic opportunities, just as many Pacific Islanders in the South Pacific lived in New

Zealand and Australia. In Australia the number of Pacific Islanders more than doubled between 1976 and 1981, and the number of Pacific Islanders in New Zealand almost doubled between 1971 and 1981.[40]

More native Hawaiians stayed, however; and an increasing proportion became involved in the native Hawaiian renaissance, and then in pan-Pacific movements. As Trask observed, native Hawaiian leaders—like some other indigenous Pacific peoples, such as some of the Maori of New Zealand—became proponents of a nuclear-free Pacific and took their antimilitary campaign from Kahoʻolawe to other Pacific islands. The Maori also sought to reassert their control over lands lost to the British in the 1840s and later. Native American efforts, especially after the Second World War, aimed at regaining land, water, and fishing rights lost in broken treaties, objectives similar to those of many native Hawaiians. Ties between Native American and native Hawaiian groups were usually tenuous, however; for native Hawaiians identified much more closely with Pacific peoples and did not consider themselves to be a Native American tribe. Still, there were examples of cooperation, especially by the 1990s. Both groups made effective use of the Native American Graves Protection and Repatriation Act, passed by Congress in 1990, to protect sacred burial sites from development, and in the early 2000s some native Hawaiians favored the passage of congressional legislation giving them many of the rights possessed by Native American tribes recognized by the federal government. In a meaningful division, however, some native Hawaiians opposed the proposed legislation, arguing that if they accepted it, they would be giving up their rights to political independence and sovereignty.[41]

Over time, a pan-Pacific, transnational identity began to form, largely based on indigenous peoples' opposition to the American, and in some areas the French and British, military in the Pacific. Native Hawaiians involved in opposition to the U.S. military in Hawaiʻi soon became engaged in anticolonial activities throughout the Pacific. This transnational Pacific identity was, in turn, part of growing global indigenous people's movements.[42]

Some of the native Hawaiian opposition to the bombing of Kahoʻolawe began with Charles Kaulewehi Maxwell. A resident of Maui, Maxwell organized a group of native Hawaiians as the Aboriginal Lands of Hawaiian Ancestry (ALOHA) in the early 1970s. As he informed the Maui County Council in late 1973, the ALOHA's "primary objective is to seek land or money reparations from the United States Congress" in compensation for lands the body's members thought had been taken illegally in the late 1800s. The "Island of Kahoolawe will be among the lands we are seeking," Maxwell observed. He lobbied Congress to allocate reparation funds for native Hawaiians to no avail. Upon returning to the Hawaiian Islands from Washington, DC, Maxwell focused his energies on Kahoʻolawe, largely as a result of an epiphany he experienced in the summer of 1975. Despite a navy prohibition of the activity, he was hunting with several friends on Kahoʻolawe when they were surprised by a navy helicopter flying overhead. As his friends hid under *kiawe* trees, Maxwell stood his ground. The thought came to him, Maxwell explained: "I am a native Hawaiian. I have prior rights. . . . I should not hide, this was my land, my aina." He took off his shirt and waved it at the helicopter, which, however, ignored him. While looking out over the ocean from a cliff on Kahoʻolawe that evening, he "felt that the presence of my ancestors was very close to me." Maxwell returned to Maui and, in his words, "started this movement of Kahoolawe."[43]

Maxwell was not alone. In 1975, native Hawaiians on the nearby island of Molokaʻi formed Hui Alaloa (the Group of Long Trails), an organization that soon became important in the fight to change how the navy treated Kahoʻolawe. Hui Alaloa sought to regain public access to the trails, roads, and beaches, which was being cut off by large landowners involved in economic development activities. Hui Alaloa was aided by Cravalho, who as the mayor of Maui County sought public beach access. The organization's founders noted that they had "recovered part of the dying Hawaiʻi culture." Hui Alaloa soon turned its attention to Kahoʻolawe, which was quickly becoming the preeminent symbol, in the eyes of many native Hawaiians, of their oppression. Writing to presidential candidate Jimmy Carter in 1976, Walter Ritte, Jr., the head of Hui Alaloa, explained why the bombing seemed to them so heinous: "The Hawaiian people recognizes Kahoʻolawe as a place where their culture is being desecrated as bombs blow up their sacred heiaus, or places of worship, destroy many koas or fishing shrines along the shore, wipe out the historical village site of old, kill the reef surrounding the island which was teeming with food, and especially killing the entire Hawaiian island." Ritte voiced the thoughts of a rapidly growing number of native Hawaiians. "The renaissance, which is going on in Hawaii today, has picked Kahoʻolawe as the place of revival of a living Hawaiian culture."[44]

Following the initial work done by ALOHA and Hui Alaloa, landings on Kahoʻolawe led to the formation of additional organizations and challenges to the navy. Influenced by the seizure of Alcatraz Island in San Francisco Bay by Native American militants in 1969, native Hawaiian groups sponsored unauthorized—the navy called them "illegal"—landings on Kahoʻolawe to protest the bombing of the island and to dramatize their demand for the island's return to native Hawaiians. In 1976 and 1977, as Ritte and Walter Sawyer explained, there were "five symbolic landings on Kahoʻolawe . . . chosen to represent the five fingers of limahana (the working hand)."[45]

The first landing was timed to coincide with the bicentennial of American independence. Before dawn on January 4, 1976, as Maxwell later recalled, the protestors set out in several boats from Maui for Kahoʻolawe. Many of those sailing for Kahoʻolawe were members of Hui Alaloa and wanted to secure native Hawaiian access to the island. Others were fishermen irked by the closure of the island's waters most of the time. Near Kahoʻolawe they were turned back by the coast guard. Only nine people, who became known as the "Kahoʻolawe Nine," returned later on the same day to "occupy" the island, including a Muckelshoot Indian from the Pacific Northwest who was visiting the Hawaiian Islands for a Native Claims Association meeting. Seven of the nine protesters were quickly captured, but Aluli and Ritte remained at large for two days.[46]

Within two days of their forced departure from Kahoʻolawe, Aluli, Ritte, and George Helm spearheaded the formation of a new group, soon named the Protect Kahoʻolawe ʻOhana (PKO; ʻohana means family), which became the leading body in the fight against the navy. The PKO sponsored two more landings in the winter of 1976. Even as the landings occurred, navy officials displayed continuing insensitivity to native Hawaiians. In March 1976, they denied a request from five Molokaʻi kūpuna (elders) to visit Kahoʻolawe, saying that unexploded ordnance made a visit too dangerous. In the same month, a particularly heavy bombing run rattled homes on Maui, alarming that island's residents. A South Maui resident was reported as exclaiming, "We ran out of our house, we thought it was an earthquake." The mayor's office, police stations, and the coast guard were deluged with calls asking whether a natural disaster had occurred. A bit later, the marines came out with a T-shirt bearing the slogan "Bomb the Kahoolawe Ohana."[47]

Public opinion throughout the Hawaiian Islands began to turn against the navy. The state's leading newspaper editorialized in early 1976: "It's not a question of whether Kahoolawe will be returned. The question is when." After holding discussions throughout the Hawaiian Islands, members of an investigatory committee of the state legislature concluded that most residents favored the goals of the PKO, reporting that "the majority of the people meeting with the Committee expressed their strong support for the ʻOhana on seeking the return of the Island and a stop to the bombing." Support for the PKO was not unconditional, however. Many people, including many native Hawaiians, disliked the group's tactics. "Many disagreed," the committee observed, "with the methods of the 'Ohana including trespass and any other law breaking." Some older native Hawaiians, in particular, said that they thought that the actions of PKO members "destroyed the dignity and grace for which Hawaiians had long been known."[48]

The work of the PKO, especially its dramatic landings, helped change attitudes, but so did altered economic matters. Simply put, the navy was becoming less important to Hawaiian life, and memories of World War II were growing distant (or completely nonexistent for young people). In 1976, the Hawaiian Chamber of Commerce, the state's leading business organization, came out publicly against the navy's bombing. The chamber had earlier been a staunch supporter of the navy, mainly on economic grounds, but now the chamber changed its stance. The growing significance of tourism may well have influenced the decisions of chamber members, as, like Cravalho, they came to see the bombing as bad for tourism. The investigation by the committee of the state legislature reached findings backing up the altered position of the chamber. The committee concluded that claims by the navy of large economic losses to the state should the navy be forced to abandon its activities on Kaho'olawe were "unsubstantiated" and should be ignored.[49]

The campaign to end the bombing broadened as more groups found common cause, but such was not always the case with regard to environmental issues in the Hawaiian Islands. Native Hawaiians, environmentalists, and developers often found themselves at odds. They differed, for example, on the proposed construction of a large geothermal electric power plant on the island of Hawai'i. Many environmentalists favored building the facility as a way to free the Hawaiian Islands from dependence on oil-fired plants, but many native Hawaiians opposed the proposition because it would have to be built in an area they considered to be sacred to their volcano goddess, Pele. No plant was built. Environmentalists, resort developers, and native Hawaiians also disagreed about how a part of South Maui right across the strait from Kaho'olawe should be treated. Developers wanted to put in a new hotel; native Hawaiians hoped to preserve their shoreline trail; and environmentalists wanted to create a state park, even if doing so meant relocating the trail. Eventually, a compromise was worked out, with Cravalho acting as mediator. Nonetheless, as late as 1988 Aluli viewed the agreement with dismay, stating that it was "just another compromise for us. It says our culture is for sale, our water's for sale. Our concerns have been sold out."[50]

Thus, cleavages often divided native Hawaiians, environmentalists, and other Hawaiian residents—but not over ending the use of Kaho'olawe as a live-fire range. The island's geography and lack of reliable water supply made resort development unlikely, and by their actions native Hawaiians were able to convince environmentalists and others that the island was special for them. Many questions remained. How and when might a transfer occur? How would the island be used in the future? What would cleaning up the island cost? A new environmental impact statement in late 1977 suggested that it would cost about $5,000 per acre to clean up the island, for a total of $78 to $131 million, depending on how much land was cleaned—figures navy officials stood by two years later.[51] More immediately, there was the question of how to convince federal government authorities to relinquish Kahoʻolawe and return the island to the state, for navy officials remained adamantly opposed to any such action.

George Helm increasingly led the opposition to the navy, especially for native Hawaiians. Born in 1950, he was raised on rural Molokaʻi, the son of a part-native Hawaiian father and a native Hawaiian mother. Music was an important part of his life. His father gave Helm a ukulele and, as one commentator observed, "passed on to George, Jr., his love of Hawaiian music." At the age of fifteen, Helm moved to Honolulu to attend high school. He continued to find time for music, studying as a vocalist with a well-known teacher of Hawaiian chants. Within a few years of graduating from high school, Helm pursued a career in music, playing in leading clubs and restaurants in Honolulu. Performing songs important to native Hawaiians was part of his act. That move into performing music full-time was a major turning point in his life. From then on, as his mother later observed, Helm "spent any spare time he had reading and researching his Hawaii culture," traveling to "other islands to meet with the kupunas and Hawaii people to learn first hand all that was true Hawaii." It was a short step for Helm to become an activist. His brother Adolph introduced him to others who were starting Hui Alaloa and the PKO. Helm was a bundle of energy, researching native Hawaiian land claims, speaking at community gatherings, and helping his compatriots when the navy took them to court for trespassing. He was, by all accounts, charismatic, with a lilting, melodic voice that projected well. Beyond Helm's specific words lay an intensity and impatience to get things done, leavened by a sense of humor. His message, if often fuzzy, was powerful. When asked in early 1977 about long-range plans for Kahoʻolawe, he replied that it would be a "spiritual place," where native Hawaiians could "discover themselves," and "experience the ocean, the aina," a place where he and others might "spread our thoughts out, see and experience ourselves as Hawaiian."[52]

Two meetings at which Helm presided stand out. At an early 1977 gathering with Hawaiian elders on Maui, Helm overcame initial resistance through music. At first dismissed as "hippies" and "radicals," Helm and his friends won acceptance by singing old Hawaiian songs. The elders responded positively: "You boys are not radicals, you are *hui o hoʻoponopono,* those who will set things right." Later that year, Helm addressed the Hawaiian state legislature—the first time a nonmember had been allowed to do so—calling for the ending of bombing and the return of Kahoʻolawe to the state. "Helm moved his audience, some of them to tears," one Hawaiian resident recalled. That same day the legislature approved a resolution urging the navy to halt the bombing and return Kahoʻolawe to Hawaiʻi.[53]

Nonetheless, navy officers remained intransigent, and federal officials dragged their feet, leading to additional landings on Kahoʻolawe. The fourth landing was destined to be the longest and most tragic. On January 30, 1977, Helm, Ritte, Sawyer, and two others landed on the island. Within a few days, all but Ritte and Sawyer had given themselves up to authorities. Ritte and Sawyer remained until March 5, when they surrendered by flagging down a navy helicopter. Meanwhile, unaware that they had left the island, Helm returned to Kahoʻolawe to aid them. Helm recruited James "Kimo" Mitchell of East Maui. A graduate of Fresno State University, Mitchell was a twenty-five-year-old ranger in the National Park Service. Helm and Kimo Mitchell in turn linked up with Billy Mitchell (no relation to Kimo) and Polo Simeona, a Honolulu fireman who provided a boat. Around 2:30 a.m. on March 6, the group set out for Kahoʻolawe. Upon nearing the island, Helm and the Mitchells went over the side of the boat onto two surfboards.[54]

On reaching the shore of Kahoʻolawe, Helm and the Mitchells searched for Ritte and Sawyer. When a pickup boat failed to arrive, the three men attempted to paddle back to Maui on their surfboards in the early morning of March 7. Exactly what transpired at this point is unclear. Billy Mitchell, the only survivor, later said that he last saw Kimo Mitchell and Helm struggling in the surf near Molokini, an islet in the channel separating Kahoʻolawe from Maui. Unable to help them, he returned to Kahoʻolawe. After hiking across the island, he convinced a group of marines to aid him. By that time, however, almost two days had passed. The navy mounted a search, but no trace of Kimo Mitchell or George Helm was ever found. The weather was stormy, and Helm and the Mitchells were already tired when they attempted to paddle back to Maui. Most likely, they were lost at sea.[55]

The deaths of the two activists thrust the PKO into the limelight. Although in momentary disarray after the disappearance of Helm and Mitchell, PKO members soon rallied. A 1978 report by the state government offers an incisive contemporary look at the PKO. "The ʻOhana," the report observed, "is not the kind of group that is run on the basis of by-laws or headed by an elected group of officers." It was, instead, "a rather nebulous group held together by the belief in a common goal—the cessation of the bombing of Kahoʻolawe and its return to the State of Hawaiʻi." As the report explained, concepts of ʻohana (family and cooperation), aloha ʻaina (love of the land), pule (prayers), naʻau (gut feelings or emotions), and hoʻoponopono (a desire to make things right) permeated the work of the organization. A loose organization, the PKO had a membership that fluctuated greatly over time, probably with several hundred members as its core constituency and several thousand others as strong supporters.[56]

The PKO encompassed disparate groups. Many native Hawaiian leaders were young, urban, and college-educated—similar to the leadership of some Native American groups such as the American Indian Movement (AIM). However, far from all PKO members fit that mold. Coming from distinctly rural areas such as Molokaʻi, many had to overcome what one observer in 1977 called "a traditional Hawaiian ʻcrab mentality' and a ʻmake no waves' ethic." It was at a series of meetings that members of the PKO resolved their differences. There, older native Hawaiians, or kūpuna, played significant roles, as many of the younger activists looked to them for instruction in Hawaiian culture. At an important meeting on Molokaʻi in April 1977, those present were divided on how to proceed after the deaths of Helm and Mitchell. Ritte appealed to Aunty Clara Ku, the oldest kupuna in the room, "Aunty, give us your naʻao." According to a reporter at the meeting: "Out comes a voice like a lioness: Have you forgotten yourself? . . . We are here to save that aina. That aina is being bombed and you all here hukihuki [are quarreling] . . . we have to listen to our hearts." After Ku sat down, the members of the PKO voted unanimously to stand firm on their demand for a six-month cessation of all bombing, long enough for a joint committee of Hawaiian residents and congressmen to study the situation.[57]

At many such PKO meetings young and old worked together to alter how Kahoʻolawe would be used. Both "heart" and a savvy understanding of federal legislation guided their next steps. As the PKO matured, the body broadened its leadership. Working to advance what was fast becoming their cause, native Hawaiians followed new leaders. Dr. Noa Emmett Aluli and Harry Mitchell typified the diversity of those leaders.

Aluli combined in his life urban and rural approaches to activism. Born in 1944, he grew up on Oʻahu. He graduated with a Bachelor of Science from Marquette University in 1966 but, drawn to medicine, returned to his homeland to graduate in the first class of the John A. Burns School of Medicine

Dr. Noa Emmett Aluli was very
active in ending the U.S. Navy's use
of Kahoʻolawe as a live-fire range.
(Courtesy of the Kahoʻolawe Island
Reserve Commission)

at the University of Hawaiʻi in 1975. After completing his residency there a
year later in an integrated surgery/family medicine program, Aluli moved
to Molokaʻi to join the Family Practice Clinic. As Aluli later explained, he
hoped "to deliver health care to rural areas." Some of the professors with
whom he had studied were, Aluli remembered, "interested in developing an
alternative approach, one that was more Hawaiian," which included "*laʻau
lapaʻau,* or the use of herbs." Aluli was early drawn to Hawaiian rights issues
and became deeply involved in them on Molokaʻi. Working with Helm and
others, he was one of the founding members of the PKO and a participant
in the first landing on Kahoʻolawe. He became one of the foremost leaders of
the PKO in the 1980s and 1990s, eventually heading the commission overseeing the regeneration of Kahoʻolawe.[58]

The *kupuna* Harry Mitchell, the father of Kimo Mitchell, shared many
of Aluli's concerns. Born in 1919 in Keʻanae, a traditional area in East Maui,
he worked as a taro grower, cowboy, fisherman, and hunter. Mitchell also became a renowned native healer, skilled in the use of plants and herbs. Active
in Hui Alaloa's efforts to gain beach access, he helped start the PKO, becoming especially convinced of Kahoʻolawe's significance as a spiritual place

for native Hawaiians. Mitchell opposed military exercises on Kahoʻolawe, even making a solo surfboard trip to the island at night to protest shelling and bombing in 1982. Mitchell instructed the younger generation of native Hawaiians in their cultural, linguistic, and healing practices. From Mitchell, Aluli learned some of his geographic knowledge of Kahoʻolawe, including ancient meanings of place-names there. Mitchell also connected with Aluli as a native healer. Throughout his work, Mitchell stressed that people needed to "give back to the aina." He is perhaps best remembered as the author of "Mele o Kahoʻolawe," a chant/song, which became the unofficial anthem of the PKO.[59]

Like many others in the PKO, Aluli and Mitchell took the message of native Hawaiian activists abroad. Together they served as ambassadors from the PKO to nuclear-free-Pacific conferences on the island nations of Fiji and Vanuatu. At one meeting a smiling Mitchell held up a banner reading "No More Hiroshimas." Mitchell also testified on behalf of Greenpeace activists in Japan. Aluli, Mitchell, and other native Hawaiians came to consider their work in the Hawaiian Islands as part of a broader movement to remove western military powers from the Pacific. As people of color, they saw the federal government's efforts to maintain its control over Kahoʻolawe as a form of cultural repression. Ending the bombing and winning control of the island became part of a Pacific-wide, anticolonial movement. At a large rally in Honolulu on May 26, 1984, "Nuclear Free Pacific" banners intermingled with "Malama K" ["Care for Kahoʻolawe"] and "Aloha Aina" banners in the crowd. Marchers in that demonstration chanted, "Make the Pacific Nuclear-Free."[60] The Native Hawaiian campaign had taken on transnational meanings.

Changing Navy Policies and Native Hawaiian Use of Kahoʻolawe

While the actions of the PKO raised public consciousness about the bombing of Kahoʻolawe, environmental results nonetheless depended upon legal decisions and sympathetic judges. In 1976, the PKO filed suits in federal court against the secretary of the navy and the secretary of defense for violating clean air, clean water, historic site, and freedom of religion laws. The suits claimed that the navy's 1972 environmental impact statement was inadequate and that the navy was not complying with a court order calling for the protection of archaeological sites on the island. In 1977, the judge hearing this case told the navy to follow the order and to identify sites on Kahoʻolawe that might be nominated to the National Register of Historic Places. In fact, he ordered the navy to obtain the secretary of the interior's opinion for the possible inclusion of the entire island in the National Register. The navy was also instructed to draft a more complete environmental impact statement detailing the results of its activities on Kahoʻolawe.[61]

In late 1977, navy lawyers responded with a supplement to the 1972 environmental impact statement in which they grudgingly gave ground. "It is concluded," noted the report, that the "U.S. Navy, in conjunction with other users, has no suitable alternative to the use of Kahoolawe as a target site." Pointing out that they had planted additional trees and had eradicated sixteen thousand feral sheep and goats in the 1970s, navy officials praised their environmental restoration efforts. They also claimed that they had followed the order directing them to sponsor archaeological work on the island.[62] Public hearings on the supplemental environmental impact statement in 1978 showed, however, just how dissatisfied many Hawaiian residents were with the navy.

Members of the PKO led the opposition in the hearings. Walter Ritte offered a detailed critique of the navy's findings, concluding that "inside I'm pissed off" and that "the credibility of the United States Navy stinks!" Like Ritte, Aluli denounced the navy for violating federal laws and orders. At the close of his testimony Aluli stated: "Listen. Stop the bombing, cross the cultural gap. You're big enough and powerful enough. We are a rising nation, and we are going to be recognized." Isaac Hall, who was just beginning a distinguished career as an environmental lawyer on Maui, testified on behalf of the PKO, noting that "basically, we have pitted the national military needs of the navy against the cultural needs of the people of Hawaii."[63]

Members of other native Hawaiian groups and representatives of environmental bodies echoed the sentiments of those in the PKO. After asking for "a few seconds of silence for Brother George Helm and Brother Kimo Mitchell," a member of Hui Alaloa observed, "it is my firm belief that we Hawaiians today have every right to walk and hunt our mountains, to fish and surf and camp on our beaches." Similar testimony came from members of the Hawaii Coalition of Native Claims and the Mama Loa Foundation. Representatives of Life of the Land condemned the navy for what they viewed as its callous treatment of animal and plant life. A representative of the Sierra Club called the bombing a "sad display of natural and archaeological destruction" and drew an analogy that an increasing number of Hawaiian residents accepted. "Kahoolawe," he said, "is in a very real sense the Plymouth Rock of the Polynesian pilgrims who came to Hawaii."[64]

Faced with hostile testimony, in 1979 the navy accepted a consent decree setting new rules for the use of Kahoʻolawe. Endorsed by the PKO, the federal court decree began a period of joint use of Kahoʻolawe by the navy and native Hawaiians in 1980. The decree stipulated that the navy clear about one-third of the island's surface of all ordnance. The PKO was to select the areas to be cleaned up according to their significance for "restoring the religious, cultural, historic and environmental values of Kahoʻolawe." Moreover, the navy was to give the PKO access to Kahoʻolawe for at least four days each month for ten months of the year for religious, cultural, scientific, and educational purposes. Furthermore, the navy was to submit to the secretary of the interior an application for the inclusion of all of Kahoʻolawe in the National Register, and a few months after the navy signed the consent decree the island was indeed so listed. The navy was ordered to eradicate all goats still on the island, implement a soil conservation program, begin revegetation, and draw up an ocean management plan for surrounding waters. Finally, the navy was told to recognize members of the PKO as stewards of Kahoʻolawe.[65]

A jubilant PKO won a major victory with the consent decree. In 1982, native Hawaiians reinstituted Makahiki celebrations, end-of-the-year festivities of peace, relaxation, and religion. By 1992, some four thousand people had visited Kahoʻolawe, mainly for spiritual and educational purposes. That fall, cultural ceremonies rededicated Kahoʻolawe as a center for the spiritual well-being of the Hawaiian people. Still, there was nothing in the consent decree to prevent the navy from using some of Kahoʻolawe as a gunnery and bombing range, and it reserved about one-third of the island as a live-fire range.[66]

Rim of the Pacific (RimPac) exercises, which involved the bombardment of Kahoʻolawe by the U.S. Navy and the navies of America's allies in the Pacific every two years, particularly irked those trying to put an end to military use of the island. The 1982 exercises led to a protest landing on Kahoʻolawe by PKO and Greenpeace members in kayaks, causing political leaders of Australia and New Zealand to halt their navies' ships from firing on the island. In the wake of the 1982 exercise, the PKO broadened its protests by seeking international help. In 1983, PKO members met with members of the South Pacific Peoples Foundation, who at the time were deeply involved in efforts to stop nuclear testing in the Pacific. Aluli denounced RimPac exercises in 1984 for failing to protect Hawaiian sites on Kahoʻolawe, leading Japanese leaders to bar their ships from firing on the island.[67] However, it was the 1988 RimPac exercises that attracted the most protests. Together with PKO members, Hannibal Tavares, the mayor of Maui County, landed on Kahoʻolawe during a lull in the military maneuvers, planted a county flag on the island,

and called upon the navy to return the island to the people of Hawai'i. Accompanied by Harry Mitchell, Tavares then toured parts of the island, attentive to Mitchell's admonition, "from the land alone can come life, not out of cement," a derogatory reference to resort development taking place on Maui.[68]

The 1988 protests strengthened ties between the PKO and other Pacific groups. As Aluli explained at the time, the PKO's work was "all part of a network of groups involved in issues such as the rights of indigenous people, peace, and the environment." Specifically, Aluli named three Japanese groups with which he was in contact: Jinshukoza, Jensuikin, and Jensuiky. The first body was involved in supporting the rights of indigenous peoples; the other two took part in antiwar protests. As a Honolulu newspaper observed, "While the Navy prepares for biennial Rimpac exercise in May, the Protect Kahoolawe Ohana can turn to a network of international contacts to protest in their countries the bombing of the target island in Hawaii."[69]

Political action followed the protests. Pushed by Senator Daniel Akaka of Hawai'i and supported by Senator Inouye, the chair of the Senate Defense Appropriation Committee, the Senate passed and the House concurred in a 1990 measure creating the Kaho'olawe Island Conveyance Commission (KICC) to set terms for the return of Kaho'olawe to the state of Hawai'i. At the same time, President George H. W. Bush instructed his secretary of defense to end use of Kaho'olawe as a firing range. This temporary halt was later made permanent, and after 1990 no bombs fell on Kaho'olawe. With Tavares as its chair and Aluli its vice-chair, the KICC held public hearings throughout the Hawaiian Islands in 1991 to encourage further discussion of the island's future. Those who had once been in opposition now ran the show, and their leadership created a new mood at the hearings. Tavares urged those testifying to "speak from the mind and the heart" in "any language you want, Hawaiian, Portuguese, Japanese, Filipino, whatever." He called upon native Hawaiian elders to begin the meetings with prayers and chants.[70]

Testimony strongly favored ending military use. A representative of the PKO articulated what was in the minds of many native Hawaiians, stating that "the aina is alive with mana [power], and we all know that it is wounded, and we need to heal it." Dana Naone Hall, a native Hawaiian activist on Maui and wife of the environmental lawyer Isaac Hall, called for "a complete cessation of military use" and the immediate return of the island to the state of Hawai'i "prior to its ultimate conveyance to a sovereign Native Hawaiian entity." Charles Maxwell voiced similar sentiments. Politicians of every stripe, representatives of the Sierra Club, members of the International

Longshoremen and Warehousemen's Union, and officers of Maui Historical Society supported the testimony of native Hawaiians. Most poignant was the testimony of Inez Ashdown, the last living descendant of those who had once been ranchers on Kahoʻolawe. Ill and unable to attend the hearings, the ninety-two-year-old Ashdown had a priest present her testimony. The priest began by noting that Ashdown was one of the few people alive who had known the Kingdom of Hawaiʻi's last queen, Liliʻuokalani. "Though her body is very weak and old," the priest said, Ashdown "speaks vehemently against those who have hurt it [Kahoʻolawe], those who have destroyed it."[71]

In the testimony given at the hearings and the results of a 1992 state-wide public opinion poll, the KICC found overwhelming support for an end to military use of Kahoʻolawe. Some 77 percent of the 252 people testifying at the public hearings, as well as 71 percent of 1,200 Hawaiian residents chosen at random for polling by the governor of Hawaiʻi's Office of State Planning, wanted to halt all military activity immediately. Of those testifying, 79 percent thought Kahoʻolawe should be given into the stewardship of the PKO and held by the state of Hawaiʻi until some form of sovereignty for native Hawaiians was recognized. Of those polled, 77 percent believed that Kahoʻolawe should be relinquished by the federal government to their state government, but only 45 percent wanted the PKO to manage the island (40 percent wanted the state government to do so). A poll of 2,000 Hawaiian residents in the February 1992 edition of *Honolulu Magazine* revealed similar findings. It revealed that there was "nearly universal agreement" that the "best thing about Kahoʻolawe" was "the efforts to save the island/stop the bombing."[72]

The polling and the hearings revealed a remarkable degree of support for the PKO and native Hawaiians, backing that had been much less widespread just ten or fifteen years earlier. Much had changed to explain the growing support. First and foremost was the work of native Hawaiians themselves. Their landings, along with the deaths of George Helm and Kimo Mitchell, had dramatized and simplified issues for many residents of the Hawaiian Islands, as Helm and Mitchell became almost unquestioned icons for those in the movement. Moreover, the maturing of the native Hawaiian renaissance, especially the PKO's increasing reliance on lawsuits, made native Hawaiian demands seem less radical.

The PKO's changing approach also won acceptance from other Hawaiian residents. Even though they benefited from the spending of the federal government in their islands, such as its support of military establishments, Hawaiian residents resented what they saw as their colonial, second-rank status. Such a reaction should not be surprising. Many western American residents harbored deep dislikes and suspicions of the federal government, even though their region had benefited inordinately from federal spending. The Sagebrush Rebellion of the 1970s and 1980s is perhaps the best-known manifestation of this feeling. Rebels in western states like Nevada called upon the federal government to give vast tracts of the public domain to the states, presumably so that the land might then be sold to private purchasers. Permeating the opposition of Hawaiian politicians to the navy's bombing of Kahoʻolawe was a desire to take control of affairs away from the federal government. Much the same thinking, we shall see, affected developments in many of the other regions dealt with in this study, most notably in Alaska and Guam.[73] Then, too, Hawaiian residents found that they could back the PKO for their own reasons. Environmentalists, whose numbers greatly increased during the 1980s and 1990s, saw the movement to end the bombing as a major issue. While they might not agree with native Hawaiians about every detail of Kahoʻolawe's future, they could easily agree that bombing should stop.

Finally, navy officials were, at times, their own worst enemy. Throughout the 1970s and 1980s, they fought all efforts to limit their usage of Kahoʻolawe, giving ground only when forced to do so; they failed to move with the times. Consistently arguing that no other spot in the Pacific had the advantages offered by Kahoʻolawe for live-fire exercises, navy officials persisted in their stance even as the world around them changed. As America's role in the conflict in Vietnam ended in the 1970s, and as the Soviet Union disintegrated and the Cold War wound down in the 1980s and 1990s, the unwavering stance of the navy came to seem anachronistic to many Hawaiian residents: the navy simply became less relevant to their lives. Fewer and fewer Hawaiian residents were willing to accept the argument that bombing Kahoʻolawe was essential to America's national security. In addition, the relative importance of military spending to the economy of the Hawaiian Islands decreased, making it easier for Hawaiian residents to forsake the navy. To some, the bombing even seemed to threaten desired touristic developments on nearby Maui.

As the "major finding" of its final report to the federal government, the KICC declared that Kahoʻolawe was "a special place with unique and important cultural, archaeological, historical, and environmental resources" and recommended that all "commercial activity and exploitation of resources" be prohibited. It concluded, moreover, "that all military use of Kahoʻolawe must cease, and that the State of Hawaiʻi must guarantee in perpetuity that the island and its surrounding water be used exclusively for the practice of traditional and contemporary Hawaiian culture, including religion—and for educational and scientific purposes." The KICC asked that Kahoʻolawe be returned to the state "without conditions" and that the federal government "be responsible for the removal of unexploded ordnance . . . and that the island be restored to a condition reasonably safe for human habitation and human use." The recommendations hearkened back to President Eisenhower's 1953 order, which had stated that Kahoʻolawe would someday be returned to Hawaiʻi in an appropriate condition for civilian use.[74]

The Return of Kahoʻolawe

At sunrise on May 8, 1994, native Hawaiians and their supporters on Kahoʻolawe walked down to the beach at Hakioawa—a major settlement in precontact days, and in the 1990s the base camp for the PKO—to celebrate the island's return to the state of Hawaiʻi. In the early morning, the celebrants cleansed themselves by bathing in the ocean, changed into traditional dress, and gathered in front of a stone platform where a ceremony giving thanks for the return of Kahoʻolawe took place. "Linked in prayer" and with "feet rooted in the ʻaina," the celebrants chanted and sang in the sunrise. As the sky turned blue, an ʻawa ceremony began, honoring those who had helped bring about the transfer. Offerings were made by PKO leaders to Kanaloa, god of the ocean, and to Lono, god of agriculture. Later in the day, the celebrants visited a rock where plaques honoring George Helm and Kimo Mitchell had been placed. Here Aluli spoke: "George Helm dreamed of the re-greening of the island. Now the island is home. It's up to us to come back, to learn from the ʻaina and make it grow." Finally, those on Kahoʻolawe formed a circle, joined hands around the Hawaiian flag, and exclaimed, "I ku wai! [stand together]."[75]

The official documents transferring Kahoʻolawe from the federal government to the state of Hawaiʻi had been signed the day before at a meeting on Maui. By their terms, the federal government gave up all claims of ownership to Kahoʻolawe to the state of Hawaiʻi and agreed to clear unexploded ordnance from the island and complete its restoration within ten years. While the cleanup was under way, the navy would control access to the island, doing so, however, in close consultation with state officials. A congressional appropriation of $400 million was to pay for the cleanup. After a decade, the navy would transfer all control to the state. State actions reinforced those of the federal government. Hawai'i established the Kaho'olawe Island Reserve, consisting of the island and its surrounding ocean waters, for the preservation of native Hawaiian cultural, spiritual, and subsistence practices. No commercial uses were allowed. State legislation also set up the Kaho'olawe Island Reserve Commission (KIRC) to lead the cleanup in cooperation with the navy. Aluli, the former PKO activist, became the chair of the KIRC and was joined on the body by other PKO members. The KIRC recognized the PKO as "the landowner of the island, holding it in trust for the sovereign native Hawaiian entity when it is re-established and recognized by the state and federal governments."[76]

Meanwhile, the KIRC set policies in a use plan promulgated in late 1995. The commission was empowered to decide how thoroughly the many sections of the island were to be cleaned up. Under various agreements between the federal and state governments, about one-quarter of the surface of Kaho'olawe was to be cleared of ordnance to the extent that it would be completely suitable for human use. Roughly three-quarters of the island were to be made reasonably safe. Working closely with the PKO, the KIRC listed thirteen areas for complete cleanup. As the land was cleared of ordnance, it was to be restored through the control of erosion, revegetation with native plant species, and the recharging of water tables. The KIRC's plan also designated areas for the establishment of educational centers/work camps, overnight campsites, cultural/historical preserves, and botanical/wildlife preserves.[77]

Both the navy and the KIRC felt increasingly pressed for time to meet the cleanup deadline of 2003, resulting in a change in priorities. While the KIRC initially insisted that the surface of the entire island be cleaned, it later agreed to the cleaning of 70 percent. The KIRC also agreed to less subsurface cleaning, selecting only those places that would be in high use. Federal efforts ended in November 2003, with about 60 percent of the surface and 7 percent of the subsurface of Kaho'olawe cleaned up. The management of access to the island was at that time turned over to the state of Hawai'i. Kaho'olawe was well on its way to becoming a religious, cultural, and educational center for Hawaiians.[78]

Naval Live-Fire Operations Elsewhere in the Pacific and Caribbean

Despite the resolution of matters on Kaho'olawe, the navy remained embroiled in controversies elsewhere in the Pacific. In 2002, a federal court ordered the navy to cease using the tiny island of Farallon de Medinilla in

Native Hawaiians restored Kahoʻolawe in the 1990s, with federal government funding. (Courtesy of the Kahoʻolawe Island Reserve Commission)

the U.S. Commonwealth of the Northern Mariana Islands, about fifty miles from Saipan, as a live-fire range. With Kahoʻolawe closed to shelling and bombing, this islet, which was about 0.3 miles wide, 1.7 miles long, and 260 acres in area, was one of the few live-fire ranges the navy had in the Pacific. Although uninhabited by humans, it was the home of extensive birdlife, including masked, brown, and red-footed boobies and great frigates. The international environmental group Earthjustice Legal Defense for the Center for Biological Diversity argued that the navy's bombing was destroying the birds and their habitat. Navy officials opposed closing the island to live-fire exercises. Showing just how complex matters could be, the congressional delegate from Guam and Saipan's business leaders, who were often at odds with the federal government on other issues, supported the navy on this occasion. They feared that any move by the navy to lessen its operations in the Northern Marianas would harm the region's economy. On appeal, navy lawyers succeeded in having the stay on its bombing lifted.[79]

Naval officers were less successful in getting their way in the Caribbean, as demonstrated by events involving the small American island of Vieques, located a few miles east of Puerto Rico. In 1999, 2000, and 2001, protestors decried the navy's use of large parts of Vieques as a bombing and gunnery range in terms and with methods very similar to those employed by native Hawaiians a generation earlier. A local referendum of the island's residents revealed that two-thirds of them wanted the navy to stop all military use of their island. In statements reminiscent of the early opposition to the bombing of Kahoʻolawe, residents said that they feared that the bombs might go awry (an errant bomb killed a civilian in 1999) and that they thought that the bombing was bad for tourism and fishing. When the navy refused to stop the bombing, activists led by the vice president of Puerto Rico's Independence Party moved onto the bombing range to dramatize their protests, and fishermen piloted their boats into forbidden waters around the island. Supported by the governor of Puerto Rico, the activists forced navy officials to the bargaining table in 2001, and a year later a compromise had been worked out. The navy greatly limited its military use of the island and restored parts of the bombing range to civilian use.[80]

The navy clearly needed ranges for live-fire bombing and shelling as the twenty-first century opened. The world remained an unsafe place, and America's armed forces required places to practice their operations. But where would they be? The growing opposition to live-fire operations in both the Pacific and the Caribbean from the 1970s onward left the navy with fewer options than had been the case in earlier times. Moreover, that opposition became more than a NIMBY (not in my backyard) affair. As opposition increasingly equated environmental with cultural matters, the navy found itself beset in ways that had not occurred in previous decades.

Conclusions

The campaign to end military use of Kahoʻolawe is revealing for what it illuminates about the development of environmentalism, particularly within the United States. As distinct from conservation movements, environmentalism developed as part of consumerism in the United States, particularly during the 1960s and 1970s. Americans came to regard a clean environment as almost an entitlement, similar to their right to possess advanced consumer goods, such as color televisions. As historian Samuel P. Hays has observed, "Environmentalism was a part of the history of consumption that stressed new aspects of the American standard of living."[81] As might be expected, local environmental groups composed mainly of middle-class Caucasians, joined by local politicians, mounted the first major opposition to the navy's bombing of Kahoʻolawe. The degradation of the island did not fit in with the advanced consumer society they thought they should have. It was not that they wanted to build shopping malls on the island but that many of them, such as Cravalho, hoped that the island could be used (consumed) as a park or a place for leisure-time activities such as fishing or hunting. They also saw a halt to bombing as a boon to the development of tourism on Maui. For them, nature had become something of a commodity.

Many native Hawaiians viewed matters differently, and their entrance onto the environmental stage during the mid-1970s changed the nature of the campaign against the navy. Many thought of the island as a spiritual and cultural home and only secondarily, if at all, as a place for leisure-time hunting, fishing, and picnicking. They sought cultural renewal as well as environmental restoration. No hotels, resorts, or appurtenances of consumerism, they insisted, should be allowed. For example, there would be no organized bicycle riding down Kahoʻolawe's hills, nothing like the very popular ecotourism bicycling on Maui. A KIRC commissioner spoke for many native Hawaiians when she contrasted the restoration of Kahoʻolawe as an undeveloped, spiritual place to what she viewed with dismay as the touristic development of Maui. Kahoʻolawe, she observed, "has a basis of culture that does not require condominiums, does not require cement walkways."[82] The landings of native Hawaiians in the 1970s, along with their work through the courts in later decades, convinced other Hawaiian residents to accept the idea that Kahoʻolawe had special meaning for them and that they should become stewards for the island.

The environmental activism of native Hawaiians resembled the drifting of some Americans into an environmental justice movement in the 1970s and later. Garbage dumps, electric power plants, sewer facilities, and hazardous waste sites seemed to be located near Indian reservations and in lower-income, often black and Hispanic, urban areas. For instance, in his recent examination of Chicago, historian David Pellow has examined "conflicts over solid wastes and pollution in urban areas, particularly in communities of color" and "workplaces where immigrants and low-income populations live and labor." By 1988, about 4,700 local groups had been formed across the United States to oppose toxic-site placements. The environmental justice movement was interested as well in changing workplace conditions. In doing so, the movement, scholar Robert Gottlieb has written, began "to shift the definition of environmentalism away from the exclusive focus on consumption to the sphere of work and production."[83] Native Hawaiians faced some of the same challenges as other minorities in the United States in environmental justice matters, and for native Hawaiians the continuing destruction of what they viewed as their land, the island of Kahoʻolawe, by an outside force, the U.S. Navy, came to symbolize all that was wrong with how they had been treated by Americans for over a century.

With its emphasis on the spiritual and cultural value of the land, however, the native Hawaiian version of environmentalism also differed from the ideas espoused in the environmental justice movement. The efforts of native Hawaiians to reassert control over Kahoʻolawe resembled closely the work of other indigenous peoples—ranging from Native Americans to the Maori of New Zealand to the Chamorros on Guam—to regain lands lost to western powers. Many native Hawaiians came to see their work as part of a larger transnational, anticolonial movement, part of a reintegration of the Pacific, and continue to do so to the present day. The native Hawaiian effort to "heal" Kahoʻolawe came to stress a perceived sacredness of the earth and was incompatible with any efforts to put the island to economically productive use, even environmentally friendly use. As Helm had written in introspective notes not intended for publication: "My veins are carrying the blood of a people who understand the sacredness of the land and water. This is my culture & no matter how remote the past is, it does not make my culture extinct." He concluded, "We are Hawaiians first, activists second." While partially romanticizing the lives and thoughts of the Hawaiians who had once lived on Kahoʻolawe (for Hawaiian actions, especially their agricultural plantings, had begun altering the island well before the first westerners arrived), Helm voiced sentiments shared by some other leaders of Pacific peoples. Like Helm, they partially mythologized the pasts of their groups as a way of understanding and achieving goals in the present.[84]

Kahoʻolawe's story is mainly a rural one, though many of the native Hawaiian and environmental leaders involved in it were urbanites. The next chapter turns to two major urban areas of the Pacific: Silicon Valley in the San Francisco Bay area and Seattle in Puget Sound. In these regions seemingly different economic development and environmental issues were played out; but beneath the surface, and not very far underneath it at that, many of the same Pacific and global issues raised in restoring Kahoʻolawe surfaced again.

CHAPTER 3

The Pacific Coast

Seattle and Silicon Valley

Writing in 1967 about the Seattle area, Philip Herrara, a journalist for *Fortune Magazine,* observed that the region was "a lovely land blessed with a mild, moist climate" and "tall, rugged mountains." The area was, however, "in the grip of a tremendous boom" about which the "two million presumed beneficiaries seem to have decidedly ambivalent feelings." The reason for doubt was not far to seek, Herrara thought. Economic growth was creating "a monster city actually known by the monstrous name Pugetopolis." That awkward-sounding name came from Puget Sound, the inlet of the Pacific Ocean on which Seattle fronted. "With roads, housing subdivisions, and strip developments encroaching on the landscape," Herrara concluded, "the region's residents are naturally beginning to see further development as a threat to the unique charm that has made their way of life so attractive."[1] By 2004, the Seattle region covered an area a hundred miles long and sixty miles wide and was home to more than 3 million residents.[2]

Much the same transition from rural to urban and suburban occurred around other Pacific Coast cities.[3] Benefiting from military spending for World War II and the Cold War, the cities boomed. Here, as in other Pacific possessions of the United States, the federal government was of great importance. Nowhere was population growth and expansive development more apparent than in parts of the San Francisco Bay region, especially the southern section known as Silicon Valley. For decades, fruit growing and processing had, in the words of a publication of the California state government in 1928, led many to think of the region as " 'The Valley of Heart's Delight' because of its scenic attractions, mild climate, and diversified agriculture."[4] The situation dramatically changed during the 1950s and 1960s and later, as high-technology firms, supporting businesses, new highways, and housing blanketed the area. The white blossoms of plum and apple trees became rare as orchards were uprooted. Writing in 2001, journalist Cathy Newman aptly described Silicon Valley as "an extended suburb of flat monotony . . . a terrain made visible by the grace of fluorescent and halogen light, connected by concrete tentacles of freeway."[5]

This chapter examines the development of Silicon Valley and the Seattle region as high-technology and industrial districts after World War II and looks at what those developments meant for people living in the areas. High-technology firms created tens of thousands of jobs, as those companies kept Americans on the cutting edge of technological advances in their industries worldwide. However, exuberant growth created problems. The rearrangement of the physical landscape was a major part of the story, and reactions against those alterations led to the birth of grassroots environmentalism. Economic development was uneven, as some sections of Pugetopolis and Silicon Valley benefited more from growth than others. Moreover, the burden of health hazards in making computer chips fell on production-line workers, many of whom were immigrant Asian women—part of the Pacific-wide migration—who were paid low wages. Then, too, Native Americans were displaced. Environmental justice was at stake, in some ways similar to what was taking place on Kaho'olawe.

The Development of Silicon Valley

The name "Silicon Valley" originated with a reporter for *Electronic News* who wrote a journalistic history of the San Francisco Bay area's semiconductor industry in 1971.[6] The name stuck, because the region was home to building computer hardware, which used silicon in great quantities. The geographic area came to include about 1,500 square miles running from the outskirts of San Francisco south along the San Francisco Peninsula through Santa Clara County, with the city of San Jose at its center.[7] Silicon was (and is) a primary raw material used in making semiconductors and integrated circuits. Silicon transmits electricity well, and is thus a semiconductor, and so could be used in making transistors, which are in effect very small switches to control the flow of electricity. In 1947, William Shockley and others at Bell Laboratories in New York invented the transistor. Seven years later, Shockley moved to Silicon Valley, where he started Shockley Transistor Laboratories. Soon, leaders of firms in Silicon Valley and Texas combined transistors with other devices on silicon wafers to make integrated circuits. Integrated circuits were (and are) capable of sending complex electrical signals from miniaturized components. Transistors and integrated circuits quickly replaced bulky and less reliable vacuum tubes in such tasks. By the early 1970s, Silicon Valley firms were assembling not just integrated circuits but also microprocessors, the hearts of personal computers.[8] Resulting environmental problems—heavy metal pollution of water supplies and the emission of poisonous fumes—were not addressed for nearly a generation.

Small and medium-size firms were the lifeblood of California's Silicon Valley. Nimble, ever-changing, and amorphous, they made the region the foremost high-technology center in the world after World War II. As scholar Annalee Saxenian has explained, these companies formed "a regional network-based industrial system that promotes collective learning and flexible adjustment among specialist producers of a complex of related technologies."[9] There was, however, more to the development of Silicon Valley than a collection of small firms. A wide variety of developments came together in what might be called a "hot mix" to create the high-technology region. The work of people at nearby universities, the labors of business entrepreneurs, and the availability of federal government spending for military purposes were all central in the initial development of the Valley.[10]

Silicon Valley did not spring up overnight. Although sometimes overlooked, high-technology developments in the San Francisco Bay area predated the emergence of Silicon Valley. In the early 1900s, engineers, businessmen from Sacramento, and the president of Stanford University formed the Federal Telegraph Company (FTC) in Palo Alto. FTC employees developed new ways to send radio messages for the U.S. Navy. World War I brought in orders from the navy and army, but orders declined after the conflict. Patent disputes with the very aggressive Radio Corporation of America (RCA) also pummeled the FTC, leading the firm to move in new directions and to spin off new ventures: Magnavox in 1910, Fischer Research Laboratories in 1936, and Litton Industries in 1932. Such spin-offs would become a hallmark of the Valley in later years. The FTC itself moved from the San Francisco Bay area to New Jersey in 1931. The FTC had been purchased by another company, which decided to consolidate its research work in Newark. Many other engineers and high-technology companies were active in the San Francisco Bay area, demonstrating the first all-electronic transmission of a television image in 1927 and developing the gammatron tube a bit later.[11]

Particular individuals were important. "If anyone deserved to be called the 'father of Silicon Valley,'" historians Stuart Leslie and Robert Kargon have written, "it was Frederick Terman." As a faculty member in engineering, later as the dean of engineering, and finally as the provost of Stanford University, Terman pioneered in the establishment of connections between academia and industry, trained students in high-technology fields, and helped those students get started in business. Two of his best-known graduate students, William Hewlett and David Packard, formed Hewlett-Packard in 1937, using a loan of $538 from Terman to begin the business. Other start-ups, often formed by Terman's students, were also important. Charles Litton established Litton Industries in 1932, and Sigurd and Russell Varian started Varian Associates a few years later.[12]

Prodded by Terman, Stanford University established the Stanford Industrial Park in the early 1950s. Renamed the Stanford Research Park (SRP) in 1961, this land became the nation's first high-technology park. Its development, historian Margaret Pugh O'Mara has explained, benefited from being on the "right side" of important demographic and economic trends in the United States. First was the growing importance of research universities in higher education. Located in Palo Alto, a close-in suburb of San Francisco, Stanford evolved as a regional educational facility before World War II, but federal spending transformed it into a national powerhouse in electronics and engineering during the Cold War. Second, Stanford was suburban at a time when more and more Americans, including engineers and scientists, wanted to live in suburbs. Its suburban location also meant that Stanford had the land upon which a research park could be built. Third, Stanford's location fit in with the decentralization and dispersal tactics begun by the Department of Defense during World War II, an effort to move plants out of the Northeast where, it was feared, they might be vulnerable to enemy attack.[13]

The SRP soon bustled with activity. In a bucolic, campus-like setting, where buildings seemed to blend into the rolling hills of the countryside, the SRP accepted Varian Associates as its first tenant, a move that successfully brought together academic researchers and businesspeople. By 1963, the SRP housed forty-two companies employing 12,000 workers. Six years later, the SRP boasted sixty firms with almost 18,000 employees.[14] As some of the high-technology firms in the SRP and nearby areas developed, they "hived off" many new, smaller companies. A case in point was Fairchild Semiconductor, founded in 1957 by Robert Noyce and other scientists who broke away from Shockley Transistor Laboratories. During the 1960s, employees who left Fairchild to capitalize on their specialized knowledge founded over two dozen semiconductor-related companies. Called "Fairchildren," these small firms added greatly to the vibrancy of Silicon Valley. Noyce himself left Fairchild to help start the firm that became Intel in 1968.[15]

Military spending linked different eras in the development of the SRP and, more generally, of Silicon Valley. As historian Stuart W. Leslie has pointed out, "it may not be too much of an exaggeration to say that the Department of Defense was the original 'angel' of Silicon Valley—a relationship that . . . goes back to before World War I." From the early radio days, the military was a significant purchaser of electronics products, but it was World War II that gave the "infant West Coast industry a chance to show what it could do."[16] Hewlett-Packard, which had been founded near San Jose a few years earlier, saw the number of its employees jump from nine in 1940 to one hundred in 1943 and its annual sales mushroom from $37,000 to $1 million in the same years. The Cold War and the very hot Korean War further benefited California's high-technology companies. Between 1951 and 1953, California firms received $13 billion in prime defense contracts, allowing the state to displace New York as the nation's leading recipient of defense contracts. Aerospace ventures in Southern California received much of the funding, but those in Silicon Valley, Leslie has noted, "won their share." By the late 1950s, the Valley trailed only Los Angeles (and surpassed San Diego) as a recipient of defense funding in the Golden State. Sensing opportunities, eastern high-technology firms moved west. Lockheed Missiles and Aerospace opened a major manufacturing facility in Sunnyvale, near Stanford University, in 1956. Soon employing 28,000 workers there and at a research facility in Palo Alto, Lockheed served as "a crucial catalyst for further high-technology growth."[17]

By the early 1970s, what had been a small cluster of companies had expanded into a full-fledged high-technology district. At first, executives located their operations near Stanford University, but they soon spread them southward down the San Francisco peninsula. Confined by natural boundaries of mountains and ocean, the companies formed a very dense network of enterprises. As Silicon Valley matured, individual entrepreneurs and small firms remained at its core, and their work helps explain the Valley's success as a high-technology district.[18] Most of the makers of computer hardware and software, producers of communications equipment, and manufacturers of defense products were smaller firms that consciously avoided vertical integration. (Vertically integrated companies embrace all or most of the stages of production and sales within one corporate entity.) Instead of trying to internalize all facets of their companies' work in single firms, Silicon Valley entrepreneurs got ahead by forming a large, informal, flexible network of linked but independent companies. Located in one region, this agglomeration of many small businesses allowed producers to benefit from economies of scale without forming big businesses. Proximity encouraged communications among the firms and stimulated growth. Bars and restaurants, along with institutions such as professional and business associations, where scientists and entrepreneurs could meet informally, encouraged the spread of information among the firms. Then, too, workers moving from job to job—for job-hopping was very common—spread information across firm boundaries. By the late 1970s, Silicon Valley possessed nearly three thousand electronics firms, 70 percent of which had fewer than ten employees and 85 percent of which had fewer than 100.[19]

Not all Silicon Valley firms were small, however. As early as 1959, Lockheed Missiles and Aerospace employed 19,000 workers at its Sunnyvale establishments and soon gave jobs to thousands more. Hewlett-Packard employed tens of thousands of workers in the 1970s and 1980s. Some of the larger firms were branches of foreign companies, which wanted to have "eyes and ears" in the Valley. Korean and Japanese companies established sizeable operations during the 1980s. Many of the big businesses tended, at least in the 1960s and 1970s, to act in ways typical of smaller ventures. Hewlett-Packard was long known, for example, for its informal management style and paternalistic work practices, popularized as the "HP Way."[20]

Companies of all sizes benefited from continued federal government spending for defense. In 1989, San Jose, the capital of Silicon Valley, was the leading community in the United States in terms of the value of prime defense contracts per employed worker—at $4,590, more than four times the average for workers in American cities. Washington, DC, was a distant second at $3,863, and Los Angeles–Long Beach trailed in ninth place at $2,234. Seattle-Everett was eleventh at 2,127.[21] The relative significance of military spending to the economic development of Silicon Valley declined in the 1990s, as defense spending plummeted early in that decade.[22] A sign of the changing times was that Lockheed employed only about six thousand workers in Silicon Valley by 2000.[23] Nonetheless, defense contracts remain important to the Valley to the present day.

Specialized service firms aided the maturation of the Valley as a high-technology region. Adopting the informal style of their high-technology clients, law firms proliferated with the Valley's development. The number of Palo Alto law firms rose from thirty-five in the mid-1970s to sixty-nine in 1988. Moreover, they increased in size. In the mid-1970s, the largest Palo Alto firms had only 12 lawyers apiece, but by 1988 they boasted as many as 150 attorneys each. The firms specialized in patent, copyright, and intellectual property law, but their members did much more than simply handle legal cases for their clients; they acted as business counselors and deal makers of all sorts.[24] Similarly, venture-capital firms performed many functions for the high-technology enterprises. Their members provided much of the financing for the expansion of high-technology companies. Between 1968 and 1975, thirty venture-capital firms located in Silicon Valley, many of them on Sand Hill Road in Palo Alto. Their members assumed a "hands-on" relationship with their clients, just as did members of the law firms. Taking substantial equity positions in their client firms, they sat on their boards of directors, offered business advice of all types, and often helped spread information from firm to firm.[25]

The flexibility of the many small firms, and of Silicon Valley as a whole, spelled success for decades. The suburban nature of the Valley and the small, decentralized character of the thousands of companies reinforced each other to create a high-technology juggernaut. Between 1959 and 1976, forty-five semiconductor firms began business in the United States, and forty of these were in the Santa Clara Valley, at the south end of the Silicon Valley. During the same period, about 210,000 new jobs were added to the region.[26] Many of these were high-technology jobs. (Not all were, for some were in companies servicing the high-technology firms.) Silicon Valley firms employed about 115,000 high-technology workers in 1975. By 1990, that number had jumped to 265,000.[27]

Even so, Silicon Valley companies faced a major crisis in the mid-1980s and early 1990s, when they lost the market for semiconductors to fierce competition from Japanese companies. In 1980, American companies were making about 57 percent of the world's semiconductors, but by 1989 their share had dropped to only 36 percent. Semiconductors had shifted from being a custom to a commodity product, in which low-cost production had become the watchword. Between 1985 and 1986, about 20 percent of the semiconductor employees in the Valley lost their jobs.[28]

Silicon Valley partially recovered in the 1990s. It boomed with the advent of commercial applications for the Internet for most of the 1990s, only to partially collapse in a "dot-com" bust as the decade closed. As late as 1999, the market for high-technology stocks remained hot.[29] Soon, however, the respected British business magazine *The Economist* expressed growing doubts about there being "a new era" in business in which "the economy would grow by 5.5 percent a year forever" and in which "inflation and the business cycle were dead." It was all, the journal feared, "a bubble."[30] Stock prices plummeted in the spring of 2000. By May, reporters for the *Wall Street Journal* wrote about "a pileup of corpses in the land of dot-coms," and in July journalists for the *Economist* discussed high-technology firms as going "from dot.com to dot.bomb."[31] The *Wall Street Journal* reported in mid-2001 that losses incurred by high-technology firms in the previous year had wiped out all the profits they had earned since 1995. Looking at the earnings of the 4,200 companies that listed their stocks on the Nasdaq, the paper concluded that recent losses were so great that it was as if the boom of the mid- and late 1990s had never occurred.[32]

Still other problems assailed Silicon Valley. Even as some firms generated new jobs there, others outsourced jobs abroad, especially by setting up silicon-chip-fabrication and computer-assembly operations in Southeast Asia. Fairchild put up a plant in Hong Kong as early as 1963, and in the 1990s many other firms followed suit. Many production firms relied on "temporary" workers who received few benefits. Those companies followed additional strategies to cut their costs, as was happening in a broad range of companies across America.[33]

Silicon Valley's overall success in job generation led to efforts to replicate the high-technology district elsewhere. As early as the 1950s and 1960s, Terman was involved in these actions. In New Jersey he worked with Bell Labs, high-technology firms, and university leaders to try to establish a "Silicon Valley East." The venture failed when the companies and the educational facilities proved unable to cooperate. New Jersey's high-technology firms developed, as a consequence, more as individual companies than as part of an industrial district. In the Dallas–Fort Worth area, Terman's work with high-technology companies and Southern Methodist University was cut short by a recession that dried up funding.[34]

Leaders in other regions sought with mixed results to emulate the development of Silicon Valley. Despite efforts by the president of Rensselaer Polytechnic Institute and leaders of nearby businesses, it proved impossible to develop a full-fledged high-technology district around Troy, New York, in the 1980s. The lack of a strong regional industrial base thwarted such efforts.[35] Similarly, attempts to build a high-technology district around the Georgia Institute of Technology, in conscious emulation of Terman's work in the San Francisco Bay area, only partially succeeded. State legislators proved fickle in financing Georgia Tech. Similarly, lacking massive federal spending and an adequate land base, the University of Pennsylvania experienced only partial success in trying to create a high-technology district in the 1960s and 1970s.[36] There were some successes. Working with university leaders, North Carolina Governor Luther Hodges used the research and development capabilities of the University of North Carolina and two other state universities to attract high-technology companies. In the mid-1960s, he succeeded in creating the Research Triangle Park, which became the chief southern challenger to Silicon Valley. Another high-technology district emerged in Austin, Texas, with the University of Texas at its center.[37] In the Boston area, large high-technology firms clustered along Route 128. Lacking the flexibility of Silicon Valley, however, the Boston region declined, in relative terms, as a high-technology district after the 1960s.[38]

A pattern of mixed successes and failures characterized attempts to bolster economies in the United States' Pacific possessions. Among the many regions to embrace high-technology business as its economic savior were the Hawaiian Islands, especially the island of Maui. Hard-hit by declines in the plantation-agriculture crops of sugarcane and pineapple, Maui's residents turned to other avenues of economic advance. Some sought economic growth through the development of tourism, but that industry experienced ups and downs with fluctuations in the global economy. And, of course, not all Hawaiian residents, certainly not all native Hawaiians, favored touristic developments. Well into the 1990s, high-technology businesses seemed to offer solutions to Maui's economic difficulties without harming the island's environment. However, problems arose in trying to turn high-technology dreams into realities.

Well aware of their island's economic difficulties, Maui's political and business leaders formed the Maui Economic Development Board (MEDB) in 1982 to diversify their island's economy, especially by nurturing high-technology ventures through the creation of the Maui Research and Technology Park (MRTP). Those forming the MEDB, and its child the MRTP, believed that high-technology businesses could become a "third leg" of Maui's economy, along with agriculture and tourism.[39] The MEDB entered into agreements with the state of Hawai'i, the University of Hawai'i, Maui County, and the federal government to try to make the MRTP a reality.[40]

State and federal funding helped. State Senator Mamoru Yamasaki persuaded the state government to finance the first major building to serve as an incubator for newly formed high-technology companies. The state's agreement to participate in the MRTP broke an impasse. Private firms constructed a second building, a state-of-the-art commercial office complex. Next came the Maui High Performance Computing Center, complete with a very powerful supercomputer, made possible by funding from the federal government secured by Senator Daniel Inouye. Other installations followed in the 1990s. Still, it proved difficult to attract tenants. A major challenge lay in a dearth of scientists and technicians on Maui. MEDB members hoped to upgrade scientific education in the island's public schools and labored to improve higher education as well. They wanted especially to turn Maui Community College into a major four-year research institution. They failed in this unrealistic goal, for state funding to do so was not available. The lack of a four-year university on Maui hurt badly.[41]

Only in the late 1990s did the MRTP begin to fulfill its promise. By the winter of 1998, about twenty companies, mainly small businesses, and organizations there employed about 350 people. High-technology companies had not, however, yet become a third leg of Maui's economy.[42] Nor, despite considerable government support, had that occurred elsewhere in the Hawaiian Islands, which lacked many of the factors needed to attract high-technology businesses—elements ranging from the possession of a first-class scientific research university to the existence of government policies favorable toward businesses. High tax rates hurt business development in Hawai'i, for example. In 1999, *Forbes Magazine* ranked Honolulu 160th out of 162 regions—third from the bottom of the list—in the United States as a desirable place in which to conduct high-technology businesses.[43]

There was more success in another Pacific region influenced by the United States, South Korea. Here Terman was important. Korean leaders had long stressed technical education and research as important parts of its development strategy, and Chung Hee Park continued this policy after he took power in 1961. The United States government was also very important, its cooperation part of its efforts to build up allies in the Pacific. In 1965, Park secured $150 million in development loans from the United States, including some for the Korean Institute of Science and Technology (KIST). American officials selected Terman to head a committee to assess the feasibility of KIST's proposals and projects, and Terman, along with two of his protégés, who were also on that committee, toured Korea in 1970, meeting with government officials and business executives.[44]

From those meetings, and earlier conferences, came the idea for the Korean Advanced Institute of Science and Technology (KAIST), situated in the Korean government's Ministry of Science and Technology. KAIST was originally envisioned as a graduate-only institution, to have 200 masters-level and 200 doctoral-level students in such fields as electronics, polymers, and pharmaceuticals. The institute would have close ties with industry, just like those binding Stanford to the many firms in Silicon Valley. Backed partly by American funding, the KAIST succeeded. By the mid-1980s, it had 1,200 students, two-thirds of whom were at the masters level. Its graduates contributed in important ways to South Korea's advances in high-technology fields, for example in the making of D-RAM chips. In 1987, KAIST moved from

Seoul to the Taedok Science Town, about sixty miles to the south, and South Korean planners transformed that city into a technopolis. A combination of American aid and advice and South Korean know-how had worked over a decade and a half of consistent effort.[45]

As developments across the United States and its Pacific territories demonstrated, it was not a simple matter to replicate Silicon Valley. Many factors had to come together for high-technology districts to succeed. Having flexible, entrepreneurial firms seemed necessary, but they were not by themselves a guarantee of success. Governmental spending, such as the defense spending so important for Silicon Valley firms, helped. So did the presence of a nearby research university, such as Stanford, especially if researchers from that institution interacted with high-technology entrepreneurs and service businesses such as specialized venture-capital firms and law firms. Even though success was difficult, many areas hoped to become new Silicon Valleys in the early twenty-first century. In their aspirations, people in these regions tended to overlook the many downsides of Silicon Valley's development.[46]

Environmental Problems in Silicon Valley

The problems in Silicon Valley constituted a dark side to the region's growth. In their recent wide-ranging historical account, David Pellow and Lisa Park have observed, " 'The Valley of the Heart's Delight' is often referred to as the 'Valley of the Toxic Fright' by environmentalists and occupational health advocates." They have noted that the "Valley holds many dubious distinctions, including hosting the highest density of federally designated toxic Superfund sites anywhere in the nation."[47] Looking at the status of women workers in the Valley, Glenna Matthews has written that the development of Silicon Valley was achieved only at considerable human cost. The "biggest cost," she has concluded, "has been paid by the assembly workers: exposed to toxic chemicals, poorly compensated."[48] In his account of Mexican Americans, the largest minority group in Silicon Valley, the historian Stephen Pitti has also decried the costs to workers of the district's development. While stressing that they were not simply victims, Pitti has pointed out that "few ethnic Mexicans enjoyed runaway economic success in the Gold-Rush atmosphere of the late-twentieth-century information age."[49] Many lived in poverty.

Far from being clean and offering opportunities to all, Silicon Valley's high-technology industries created a host of environmental problems, which raised serious quality-of-life questions. Crowding, congestion, and air and water pollution affected nearly everyone in the region by the 1970s and 1980s. Health issues, however, most affected production-line workers. As late as 1999, making an eight-inch silicon wafer required 3,023 gallons of deionized water (in addition to gallons of regular water), 4,267 cubic feet of bulk gasses, 29 cubic feet of hazardous gasses, and 27 pounds of chemicals. Production processes created 3,787 gallons of waste water and 9 pounds of hazardous waste.[50]

Unless handled carefully, these substances harmed the health of workers. Too often, few safeguards were in place, especially in the early days. Chemical fumes, corrosive acids, and other toxic substances assailed production-line workers, who were usually not warned of the dangerous circumstances under which they labored as they fabricated wafers and assembled electronics products. According to a 1980 report by the state of California, workers in semiconductor plants suffered from illnesses at a rate three times greater than that of workers in general manufacturing. A year later, another state report, this one about forty-two California semiconductor firms, revealed that nearly half of elevated illness rates their workers incurred came from systemic poisoning or toxic exposure.[51]

A pioneering investigation in 1984 summarized many of the dangers. Prepared by the director of the Labor Occupational Health Program at the University of California, Berkeley, and the safety coordinator in the Santa Clara County Office of Education, the report was damning. It found that "electronics is not a sterile, clean industry," but rather one using "hundreds of potentially dangerous substances." Organic solvents used in cleaning operations caused "a range of health problems, including dermatitis; central nervous system effects, such as nausea, dizziness, and headaches; liver and kidney damage; and even cancer." Corrosive acids caused "serious burns" and "lung damage." Moreover, "other toxic substances, including gasses such as arsine and phosphine, metals such as lead and other solders, and epoxies, pose[d] additional risks." Finally, "reproductive hazards" included "radiation and various chemicals."[52]

These dangers fell heavily on a largely immigrant workforce. Liberalization of America's immigration laws in 1965, combined with the lure of jobs in California, pulled new workers into the San Francisco Bay area. Many ended up in Silicon Valley. Hispanics and Asians, especially, took part in the new immigration into the United States. The movement of Asians into the San Francisco Bay area was an important element in the Pacific Diaspora. In the two decades after 1965, for example, 622,000 Filipinos came to the United States, with nearly 70 percent settling in western America. Filipino women were a very important component of Silicon Valley's workforce.[53]

Relatively few of the immigrants to the San Francisco area found managerial positions. In 1970, Latinos held a scant 7 percent and Asians only 17 percent of Santa Clara Valley's high-technology managerial white-collar jobs. Another 17 percent of the craft jobs were held by Latino employees, 14 percent by Asian workers. By way of contrast, Latinos filled 57 percent of the jobs classified as belonging to "operatives" or "laborers," and Asians held an additional 36 percent of them.[54] In the early 1980s, about 75 percent of the electronics workers were women, and at least 40 percent of them were minorities, mainly Hispanic and Asian. By way of contrast, white males comprised 90 percent of the managers. Fifteen years later, the situation remained about the same. In 1997, Hispanics held only 7 percent of the white-collar jobs in Silicon Valley's high-technology industries, but 23 percent of the blue-collar ones in original manufacturing firms and 14 percent of those in contract companies. Asians had 31 percent of all white-collar positions, but 59 percent of the blue-collar jobs in original manufacturers and 77 percent of those in contract firms.[55]

Environmental challenges caused by high-technology manufacturing extended beyond the workplace. Nowhere were problems worse than in the pollution of groundwater supplies. Silicon Valley drew mainly on groundwater in aquifers for its industrial and drinking water. By the early 1980s, it was becoming apparent that toxic-waste water from high-technology manufacturing was contaminating the aquifers. The discovery of toxic chemicals, which were used to clean microchips and computer boards, in the soil and water near a Fairchild plant and an IBM plant in the early 1980s turned out to be just the tip of the iceberg. Testing by governmental authorities soon revealed that 65 of 79 companies examined had released toxic chemicals into the ground beneath them. Some 104 wells providing drinking water had been contaminated, and 66 plots of land were too toxic for humans to walk on. Making the problem worse than it might have otherwise been was the fact that some 10,000 old wells, uncased and uncapped, once used to provide water for the irrigation of orchards allowed chemicals easy access to Silicon Valley's groundwater. By the late 1990s, the Environmental Protection Agency had designated twenty-nine Superfund sites in the Valley, more than in any other county in America. Twenty-four of the sites resulted from pollution by electronics firms.[56]

Among those districts hit hardest by the water pollution was east San Jose, home to the barrio in which many Chicanos lived. Long neglected by San Jose's city officials, east San Jose had historically lacked services found throughout the rest of the city. As late as the 1950s, children played in gulches containing raw sewage. Many streets remained unpaved and without sidewalks or public lighting. After 1960, San Jose's "Latino community boomed in size" until it came to "comprise more than 25 percent of the city by 1990, but its recent history only highlighted the Valley's greatest constant, the power of race for structuring local political and cultural developments," Pitti has observed.[57] Not surprisingly, perhaps, it was the water supply for the Los Paseos neighborhood that was among those found to be most contaminated—by seepage from tanks on Fairchild's property. An investigation revealed "an apparent clustering of birth defects, miscarriages, stillbirths" over a three-year period.[58]

Complaints from women in the area, together with the efforts of activist lawyers, led to the formation of a grassroots environmental movement. Traditional national environmental groups held back, perhaps because many of their members were managers in high-technology firms. Two local organizations were of most importance. Having held community workshops about chemical solvents even before the discovery of the first release, the one at the Fairchild plant, the Santa Clara Center for Occupational Safety and Health (SCCOSH) greatly expanded its operations after it. Formed in response to the Fairchild spill, the Silicon Valley Toxics Coalition (SVTC) also soon increased the scope of its work. That work soon brought results. Fairchild closed its plant in south San Jose in 1983 and spent $40 million on remediation work. In contrast, many other companies persisted in denying any responsibility for damages to the environment or to the health of their workers. In fact, many executives initially blamed their workers for the health problems, accusing women employees who complained about illnesses as suffering from "hysteria."[59]

They changed their stances in the 1990s as a result of continuing pressure from local environmental groups and the federal government. In her discussion of workers' health issues in Silicon Valley, Matthews observed that by the opening years of the twenty-first century there had been "real and important progress," but she has also noted that "the problem is still serious."[60] Similarly, Pellow and Park conclude their account of quests for labor and environmental justice in the Valley with the observation that "labor and environmental justice organizations have made their mark on Silicon Valley's political and economic terrain." Still, they question "whether they can continue to reform an industry that is growing more rapidly around the globe than any other."[61]

Although environmental concerns involving toxic substances were of the most immediate concern to production-line workers in Silicon Valley, planning matters, especially urban planning issues, were not far behind. Just as the development of high-technology businesses brought many more benefits to white-collar than blue-collar workers, it also brought greater benefits to some sections of the San Francisco Bay area than to others. The development of Silicon Valley exacerbated earlier uneven patterns of growth in the region, as did high-technology developments in the Seattle region slightly later. Private market forces, not government planning, with the important exception of military spending, dictated the early economic development of Silicon Valley. Land-use planning and planning for water resources were minimal, setting the stage for later problems such as traffic congestion and groundwater pollution.

Unplanned growth in California replicated a general lack of planning elsewhere in the nation. This situation might be expected, for the San Francisco Bay area had long developed in a chaotic way. Efforts to rebuild San Francisco after its horrific 1906 fire and earthquake in a designed manner proved largely abortive, despite the fact that a city plan had been drafted in 1905. Then, too, regional planning efforts for the development of transportation, though much discussed, won scant approval and were not implemented in the years before World War II. None of these facts should be surprising; America's Pacific Coast cities developed in mainly unplanned ways in these decades. They simply contained too many different groups of people with many diverse ideas and were growing too quickly, at least into the 1920s, to embrace urban planning.[62]

Increased planning efforts, especially regional planning, accompanied World War II and continued after that conflict. In 1943, federal officials established a Metropolitan Defense Council (MDC) composed of local businessmen and politicians to try to improve the San Francisco Bay area's infrastructure for the war effort. The MDC in turn led to the creation of the Bay Area Council a year later. Led by prominent businessmen, the council was dedicated, in its officers' words, "to the proposition that the San Francisco Bay Area is an integrated economic unit." Over time, council members became pro-suburban in their mind-sets and tried to attract new industries whose employees would be won over by "a good climate, beautiful landscape, and cultural amenities." What had begun as regional planning became decentralized boosterism.[63]

A major result of decentrist thinking was to widen differences among localities in the San Francisco Bay area. Not all communities, and certainly not all people, benefited equally from the high-technology boom. Richmond and Oakland, which had gained in job creation from World War II, were largely bypassed as Silicon Valley expanded to the south. San Francisco initially found few benefits. Not until the 1990s and later did the city profit much from high-technology developments. Most of the growth and the bulk of the new jobs were concentrated on the west and south sides of San Francisco Bay.

One of the first signs that uneven development might cause environmental problems occurred in the "Battle of the Hills" in Palo Alto during the early 1960s. Seeking to expand the SRP, Stanford University officials faced opposition from some of the local residents. Locals wanted to keep the foothills into which an expanded SRP would intrude free of commercialization. Moreover, the expansion proposal acted as a lightning rod for those who had come over the previous decade to dislike noise and fumes from some of the businesses in the supposedly "green" SRP. In the end, Stanford officials carried the day and expanded the SRP, but only in a scaled-back fashion, as grassroots environmentalism had an impact on development.[64]

A more dramatic event highlighting inequalities was the seizure in late 1969 of federally owned Alcatraz Island by seventy-eight Native Americans calling themselves "Indians of All Tribes." At issue was the matter of sovereignty, just as it would later be on Kahoʻolawe. Responding to demands that they leave the island, Native Americans exclaimed that it "is the hope of Indian People to advance themselves culturally and spiritually. . . . We will no longer be museum pieces, tourist attractions, and politicians' playthings." Those seizing Alcatraz declared it to be Indian land and vowed to build a cultural and educational center there. However, they were soon divided by leadership struggles and harmed by a lack of adequate food, water, housing, and electricity on Alcatraz. Those few Indians still remaining on Alcatraz were removed by federal officials in June 1971.[65]

The development of Silicon Valley's high-technology industries led to rapid population growth, which gobbled up land for urban use and led to further environmental problems. San Jose's population mushroomed from 95,000 in 1950 to 920,000 in 2000. This population explosion outpaced that for the state of California as a whole, which increased from 10.5 million to 33.9 million in the same decades, and that of the San Francisco Bay area, which rose from 2.6 million to 6.5 million. Uneven development continued. As one urban historian has explained with understatement, San Jose's expansion "consumed considerable adjacent farmland, including some of California's finest vineyards and numerous orchards." California being the most urbanized state in America in 2000, some 93 percent of Californians lived in metropolitan areas. Quality-of-life issues caused by urban sprawl, the disappearance of green space, and a lack of affordable housing were epidemic.[66] They were nowhere more pressing than in Silicon Valley.

Pushed by a progrowth city government, San Jose expanded rapidly through the 1960s. Using control over their city's sewer treatment facilities as a club, San Jose's political leaders convinced people in many contiguous areas to agree to annexation, until by 1970 the city covered 132 square miles.[67] San Jose's rampant growth, which sparked fears about increased costs for city services and, at the same time, generated concerns that bucolic lifestyles were in danger, led to the formation of an antigrowth coalition. Women were in the forefront of this campaign. As early as 1962, the conservative Virginia Shaffer had won election to the city council on the strength of promises to reduce city taxes. By 1969, she and others had succeeded in removing San Jose's progrowth city manager from office. Still more women won election to the city council in the 1970s. In 1974, San Jose voters chose Janet Gray Hayes, one of the councilwomen, as their city's mayor, making her the nation's first woman to be mayor of a city of five hundred thousand or more people. Hayes campaigned on the promise to "make San Jose better before we make it bigger" and was an advocate of parks and green areas.[68]

State legislation framed local actions, but local measures often had greater impacts. Already in the 1950s, farmers and slow-growth advocates secured state legislation limiting the power of municipalities to annex farmland and guaranteeing that farmland would be assessed for taxation on the basis of its value as agricultural land, not on the basis of its market value as real estate. This legislation, however, had little effect in Silicon Valley, where many farm owners were small landowners eager to sell at hefty profits to developers. Closer to home, San Jose's voters approved Measure B in 1973, an ordinance limiting new zoning for homes wherever schools were overcrowded.[69] Measures like that one did reduce the pace of growth within San Jose's city limits, but urbanization continued outside of them. San Jose, after all, was far from the entirety of Silicon Valley. Then, too, ways to continue annexation were found, leading to an overall tenfold increase in the size of San Jose between 1950 and 2000.

Affordable housing became rare in the Valley, in part because of the movement of so many new people into the area and in part because of limitations on building such as Measure B. In 2001, only 16 percent of the region's residents could afford the $540,000 median house price. The problem was that house prices had more than doubled since 1990, while per capita income had risen by a much smaller 36 percent (and for the bottom quartile of wage earners' real incomes had actually fallen). Even renting an apartment was difficult, with a median apartment rental price of $1,600 per month. All-too-typical was the family of John Singh. Singh worked on a contract basis for Hewlett Packard, and his wife had employment as a registered nurse. Together, they earned $105,000 annually. However, with three children they could not afford to buy a house and lived, instead, in the Boccardo Reception Center, a shelter for the homeless in San Jose. They were not alone; 40 percent of the shelter's residents had jobs.[70] High-technology workers were not the only ones hit hard by high housing prices. Service workers such as teachers, firemen, and policemen found it increasingly difficult to live in the Valley.[71]

Even for those who could afford Valley homes, life was far from easy. A study of some forty communities across the United States in the late 1990s revealed that, "although Silicon Valley ranked high in interracial trust and diversity of friendships, it landed near the bottom in civic engagement, charitable giving, volunteering, and civic leadership—and in sense of community as well."[72] In a region where vacations had come to be derided as "downtime," even some successful high-technology entrepreneurs questioned what they were doing with their lives as the twenty-first century opened. In such an environment, growing traffic congestion was, not surprisingly, particularly resented as a waste of time.[73]

Thus, Silicon Valley, and more generally the San Francisco Bay area, experienced exuberant growth in the twentieth century, especially after World War II. Buoyed by entrepreneurial ambitions and defense spending, the region boomed as a high-technology region, well known and imitated around the globe. Areas throughout the Pacific, from would-be high-technology districts in the Hawaiian Islands and Japan to a more successful one in South Korea, sought to become new Silicon Valleys. In trying to emulate the Valley's apparent success, residents in other regions overlooked the negative aspects of such expansion. For instance, many of the same issues emanating from industrial and high-technology growth arose in an expansive Seattle after World War II.

Economic Growth and Environmental Problems
in Seattle and Pugetopolis

Traffic tie-ups were even worse in the Seattle area than in Silicon Valley. As a scholar of urban planning observed in 2002, "traffic congestion in Greater Seattle is arguably the worst in the nation." Every nook and cranny from

Everett in the north to Tacoma in the south was being filled with urban and suburban developments, and Pugetopolis was quickly coming to resemble the linked cities of Boston, New York City, and Washington, DC. From an overgrown town of 368,000 people in 1940, Seattle became a major metropolis of 2.6 million residents fifty years later.[74]

The Seattle region suffered from some of the same growth problems as Silicon Valley, but there were differences as well. Beyond transportation congestion loomed runaway housing prices, land-use questions, and water-quality problems. Seattle boomed in the 1980s and later, in part, from the expansion of high-technology firms such as Microsoft. However, because these companies engaged more in software production than in the fabrication of computer chips and hardware, there was less contamination of the region's water supply by toxic chemicals. True, Seattleites and people in nearby suburbs polluted Lake Washington with their sewage, but in a rare show of regional cooperation they succeeded in cleaning up that body of water.[75]

Seattle's first period of rapid development started with the acquisition of rail connections to the Midwest and East in the 1880s and 1890s. Seattle's business leaders were well situated to take advantage of new economic developments. With much of the Great Lakes cut over, the United States came to depend more heavily than before on the Pacific Northwest for its timber. Seattle-area mills helped supply that demand. Even more explosive, though short-lived, was the impact of the Klondike Gold Rush to Alaska in the mid- and late 1890s. Possessing a fine natural harbor and ambitious merchants, Seattle benefited greatly as the leading outfitting point for the north. Slightly later, Seattle fishermen and corporations came to control most of Alaska's salmon industry. Local railroads also opened up areas near Seattle to coal mining and farming. Seattle thus developed as a commercial city more than as a manufacturing center. Still, as the city grew in size and population, it became a large enough market to spur the development of local industries such as shipbuilding and ironworking. Between 1890 and 1920, the city's population rose more than fivefold, from 43,000 to nearly 240,000, growth that made Seattle a large regional center on America's Pacific Coast.[76]

Faced with the rapid expansion of their city, some Seattleites turned to planning to channel the forces of change. In some matters, largely engineering ones aimed at the commercial expansion of their city, they succeeded. Seattle's chief engineer, R. H. Thomson, oversaw a major regrading effort that lowered the heights of Seattle's hills by using hydraulic monitors (apparatus similar to large fire hoses) to wash them away. He then utilized the resulting dirt and gravel to fill in parts of Seattle's waterfront. This action both removed a significant barrier to Seattle's commercial and residential expansion and created new sites for industrial development. Seattle's officials also seized new water supplies for their growing metropolis, especially by securing a watershed area off-limits to most types of development around the Cedar River. At about the same time, the federal government built a major set of locks on a waterway connecting Lake Washington to Puget Sound, a project that further enhanced the city's commercial potential.[77]

There were environmental downsides to these actions, however—problems only dimly perceived and rarely acknowledged by Seattleites in their scramble for wealth. Entire ecosystems were greatly altered. The building of the locks, for example, sent Lake Washington's water out to sea by a new route. Doing so lowered the lake's level considerably and completely eliminated the Black River, which had earlier been its outlet. Environmental justice issues were involved, as public works especially hurt Native Americans. Once again, benefits from growth were unevenly distributed. For instance, the industrial development of newly created areas on Seattle's waterfront and the banks of nearby rivers, especially the Duwamish, impinged on the livelihood of Native Americans in the area. They found it impossible to maintain a subsistence lifestyle based on hunting, fishing, and gathering, and had to move away. Only in the 1990s and later did small groups return.[78]

Seattleites proved less successful in redesigning the spatial layout of their city. Like the residents of other Pacific Coast cities, they considered a comprehensive city plan for their metropolis. Called the Bogue Plan after Virgil Bogue, the engineer who drew it up, the scheme envisioned the coordinated construction of new harbor facilities, streets, parks and boulevards, and a civic center. Presented to voters by the city council in 1912, the plan embraced an area of 150 square miles and sought to prepare Seattle for a population of one million people, roughly four times its population then. The Bogue Plan failed to win approval. Like the Progressive-era city plan for San Francisco, it initially attracted a lot of favorable comment, as many business and professional groups came out for it. Yet, those organizations soon split on particular aspects of the scheme. Many Seattleites also feared that approval of the plan would raise their taxes. Feeling themselves already heavily burdened to pay for engineering works such as the regrading of their hills, they opposed any measure that might hike their taxes still more. While some parts of the Bogue Plan were put in place over the following decades, the idea of comprehensive city planning was relegated to the back burner for many years to come.[79] A major reason for this turn of events was a slowdown in the rate of Seattle's growth. Like most Pacific Coast cities, with the notable exception of

Los Angeles, Seattle grew more slowly in the 1920s and 1930s. Consequently, the urgency for comprehensive planning dissipated.[80]

Seattle's population resumed its upward trajectory during and after World War II, as its shipbuilding firms, and especially the Boeing Company, boomed.[81] Into the 1970s, Seattle's fate was tied directly to that of Boeing. While Boeing's expansion brought economic growth to the Seattle region in the form of tens of thousands of jobs, challenges also trailed in the wake of the rapid development of the firm. People lived ever farther from Seattle's downtown, as suburbs proliferated. Downtown businessmen tried to arrest this trend, with only partial success. A climax to their actions came in the late 1960s, when they sought through regional planning to address district-wide infrastructural issues, nearly all of which impinged upon the physical environment of the Seattle area.

Describing Seattle after World War II, urban historian Carl Abbott has accurately observed, "The engine that was obviously driving the new Seattle was Boeing."[82] It was during and right after the conflict that Boeing became central to Seattle's economy, and it was really only then that Seattleites from many walks of life—business leaders, many labor leaders, and politicians—united, for a time, in pushing for Boeing's agenda at the national level. In the importance of Boeing to the Seattle region can be glimpsed, once again, the significance of the American military, World War II, and the Cold War in the Pacific. While many of Boeing's sales were commercial, many others were military, especially in the 1940s and 1950s.[83]

Founded shortly before World War I, the Boeing Company expanded during the conflict, only to contract after it. Established on the banks of the Duwamish River close to Seattle's waterfront, the company was one of the manufacturing ventures that displaced Native Americans there. Boeing had become Seattle's largest industrial venture by 1928, with 900 employees. Hurt by the Great Depression, Boeing boomed from the 1940s into the late 1960s, as the firm developed military aircraft and, after World War II, civilian airplanes as well. It delivered its 707, the first American commercial jetliner, to airlines beginning in 1958. Boeing's employment in the Seattle region jumped from about 4,000 in 1940 to roughly 50,000 four years later. Employment slumped to 9,000 in 1946, but climbed to 58,000 in 1958 and reached about 100,000 by 1967. By the mid-1960s, about 20 percent of all of the jobs in King County were with the Boeing Company.[84] The company's expansion also spurred population growth in the Seattle area. In 1950, about 468,000 residents made Seattle their home, up from 368,000 a decade before. In 1970, some 530,000 people lived in the city of Seattle, with many more in its suburbs. By that time, 1.4 million people were living in Seattle's standard metropolitan area.[85]

Although Seattle's leaders backed Boeing's efforts to win Defense Department contracts, some came to harbor doubts about the impacts the firm was having on their region's economy and development. By the early 1960s, they voiced two major critiques: they thought that Boeing's dominance was precluding the development of a diversified economy (some even came to see Seattle as being simply a "colony" of Boeing); and they believed that too much of the economic growth and spatial development was occurring outside of Seattle in its suburbs, thus endangering downtown businesses. There was considerable truth to these perceptions, especially the second one. Needing space for runways, large assembly plants, and research facilities, Boeing located most of its facilities beyond Seattle's city limits, eroding the city's tax base. Then, too, as Boeing attracted workers to the region, an increasing proportion lived outside of Seattle. In the decade of the 1950s, the outlying parts of Seattle increased in population by 46 percent, but within the city limits the rise was less than 1 percent. The first regional shopping center, Northgate, opened in 1950, just north of Seattle's city limits. The trend toward suburbanization, aided by the construction of interstate highways, continued in the 1960s, until by 1970 about 63 percent of Seattle-area residents lived in suburbs.[86] These decades were, one disgruntled Seattleite observed, "the era of the bulldozer, the ranch-style house, the shopping center, and long runs of commerce on arterials."[87]

Seattle's business and political leaders responded in several ways. Like San Jose's leaders, they embraced annexation, sometimes using their control over water and sewers to persuade outlying regions to agree to become part of the city of Seattle. The sixty-block area in which Northgate was located was annexed in 1955, bringing revenues from taxes on the shopping center into the city's coffers. In 1962, they also mounted a world's fair in a section of Seattle not far from the city's downtown. Seattle's leaders hoped that the exposition would both attract new businesses to their region and showcase the downtown as the center of the Seattle area. The exposition drew nearly 10 million people. However, it proved to be too isolated from the downtown to help the downtown area much. Its emphasis on aerospace and science, as in the construction of the landmark Space Needle, did more to boost Boeing than other firms in the public's imagination.[88]

Nonetheless, Seattle's downtown did not stagnate. At the hands of political and business leaders, it developed as an international center for finance and trade, complete with a host of shimmering skyscrapers soaring above its hills. During the 1950s and 1960s, choices made by Seattle's elite moved their city ahead of other regional rivals such as Portland to become a globally "networked" city. Historian Abbott credits civic initiatives undertaken in these decades—the world's fair, the building of a downtown sports complex, including a domed stadium (the Kingdome, since torn down to make way for a newer stadium), harbor improvements designed to handle containerships, and the construction of a new park system—with helping Seattle to attain international standing.[89]

Still, Seattle's downtown never regained the dominance it had once exerted over its surrounding area. Despite some success at annexation, new areas continued to spring up beyond the city limits, as suburbs marched ever deeper into the countryside. Increasingly, those suburbs sought independence from Seattle; more and more people in the new suburbs refused annexation, as they came to realize that it did not automatically bring sidewalks, streetlights, and other amenities. As a result, Seattle's city boundaries were basically fixed by about 1960.

In terms of suburban expansion, the greatest growth, and the most worrisome for Seattle's downtown leaders, occurred to the east of Seattle. As environmental historian Matthew Klingle has observed, "the most dramatic gains were in the smaller towns that ringed Lake Washington, especially in the Eastside region across the lake." About thirty miles long and one to three miles wide, Lake Washington runs north–south along Seattle's eastern boundary. Two bridges, one opened in 1940 the other in 1963, connect Seattle to the metropolis' Eastside. Only four incorporated towns, including Seattle, touched Lake Washington in 1942, but twenty years later nine new towns bordered the lake on the Eastside alone. The Eastside's population more than doubled in the 1950s.[90]

Of the rapidly growing Eastside communities, Bellevue attracted the most attention. Incorporated in 1953, Bellevue's expansion was chaotic. "There was nothing orderly about it," noted George Bell, the Eastside's prime housing developer. In the mid-1960s, Bellevue was, as one Seattle magazine exclaimed, "the fastest-growing chunk of Washington" and "one of the fastest-growing areas in all of America." Rapidly becoming an independent city, Bellevue nonetheless was home to many residents who had moved there hoping to enjoy a country existence. It was a place that "proudly proclaims its own unique, non-metropolitan identity," the Seattle journal noted. However, its character was changing. "Already the Bellevue landscape is a kaleidoscope of contrasting scenes," the journal mused, with "the most obvious contrast" being "between the remaining belts of rusticity and the highly developed

Just east of Seattle, Bellevue sported its own downtown skyscrapers. (Courtesy of Elizabeth Lawrence)

sections of town." By 1972, 62,300 people were living in Bellevue, up from just 7,700 in 1954.[91]

As in the San Francisco Bay area, economic growth was very uneven in Pugetopolis. Generally speaking, Seattle and the Eastside suburbs benefited at the expense of southern Puget Sound and Indian reservations throughout King and Pierce Counties. For instance, the Duwamish–Green River corridor became poorer and more polluted, while Lake Washington and the Seattle suburbs grew wealthier and cleaner.[92]

Political contests over two groups of economic development and environmental protection issues laid bare divisions between Seattle and its suburbs and demonstrated the limits of power wielded by the metropole. In the late 1950s, Seattleites and their suburban neighbors cleaned up Lake Washington, which had become polluted by sewage from surrounding towns. Such cooperation proved difficult to achieve and had partially hidden environmental costs, however. About a decade later, voters in the Seattle region considered a package of issues designed to improve both their economic and physical environments, but approved only some of them.

Pollution problems in Lake Washington worsened dramatically after World War II.[93] Seattle's sewers dumped into Puget Sound for the most part, but the sewers of Eastside communities had their outlets in the lake. By 1955, ten new sewer systems discharged treated and untreated sewage into Lake

Washington, and leaking septic tanks added to the problem. Even Seattle's sewage, which coursed through the same pipes as rain runoff, spilled into Lake Washington in times of heavy rainfall. Combined sewage overflows lay at the heart of the problem. In a wake-up call to Seattleites, a University of Washington professor of zoology proclaimed the lake "dead" in 1956. For months over the next three summers, large sections of the lake were closed to swimming and recreational activities, further alarming Seattleites.

Worried that the deteriorating condition of Lake Washington might hurt the growth and image of their city, Seattle's leaders, beginning to dream of a world's fair, joined forces with younger professionals and educators to change matters. Doing so would be difficult, they realized; for, like many regions, Seattle was characterized by fragmented government. There were about 180 separate local governments in King County, including 21 sewer districts representing 40 communities around Lake Washington. Nonetheless, led by James Ellis, a young Seattle attorney active in civic affairs, they sought to build consensus for change. They initially failed. In March 1958, voters turned down a plan for a comprehensive sewer system. Two factors led to the defeat. First, it was presented to voters as part of a package that also included a regional mass transit system and plans for regional zoning. Even many who wanted to clean up Lake Washington hesitated to vote for that expansive package. Then too, Seattleites and the residents of Bellevue approved the plan, but it lost heavily in South King County, whose residents in many suburbs viewed it as a power grab by Seattleites.[94]

Sewer advocates quickly reworked their proposition. They stripped it of any connections to mass transit and regional zoning and limited the vote to residents of communities directly bordering on the lake. Approved by a wide majority in September 1958, the measure provided for the construction of huge interceptor sewers around Lake Washington, soon making the lake a "textbook example on how 'bioremediation' can pull aquatic ecosystems back from the brink of collapse."[95]

There was a dark side to even such a dramatic environmental victory, however. The new sewers dumped into Puget Sound, increasing pollution there, and into the Duwamish River, where what little remained of aquatic life was almost snuffed out. These actions occurred just as Native Americans in the state of Washington were beginning to reassert their historic fishing rights. Only in later decades were some remediation efforts taken to improve the quality of water in the Duwamish River, allowing a few Native Americans to fish there again. More broadly, the rehabilitation of Lake Washington helped draw more people to the Seattle region, thus ironically increasing some forms of pollution and congestion. With only slight hyperbole, historian Klingle has observed that a "rising tide of concrete and asphalt began to flow up the Sammamish River [which drains into Lake Washington] and onto the Issaquah Plateau, engulfing more and more acreage with every year."[96]

As growth continued, Seattle-area residents sought to control sprawl through "Forward Thrust" proposals. Extensive bond issues to fund the proposals were voted on separately, not as single entities; proponents had learned from the defeat of the initial Lake Washington sewer measure. With Ellis again playing a leading role, some proposals won relatively easy acceptance in 1968: area-wide parks and recreation centers, the Kingdome, additional sewers, flood-control measures, and various neighborhood improvements.[97]

Transportation measures, on the other hand, mainly failed at the polls. Voters were asked to approve the building of new arterial streets (streets just short of being freeways) through Seattle. These propositions drew immediate fire. One street, named R. H. Thomson after Seattle's early-twentieth-century engineer, would have sliced through Seattle's world-famous arboretum, an oasis of nature in the city. Another would have destroyed much of Seattle's black community. Yet another would have crossed Lake Washington on a third bridge. There was more to Forward Thrust's transportation plans, however. A mass transit scheme was also part of Forward Thrust: four coordinated rapid-rail lines serving major travel corridors into Seattle from the suburbs. The results at the polls were mixed. Some of the proposed arterials were built, but not all. Even those that were constructed were greatly modified in light of public concerns. No arterial bisected the arboretum (instead, half-built on-ramps today provide diving platforms for swimmers enjoying Lake Washington), and a third Lake Washington bridge was not built. The street extending through part of the black neighborhood was greatly modified to do much less damage than the one originally proposed.[98]

The opposition to freeways in Seattle was part of a nationwide antifreeway movement that had begun in San Francisco in 1959 and spread throughout much of the United States in the 1960s and 1970s. Urban historian Raymond Mohl has identified a number of commonalities in successful freeway revolts: "persistent neighborhood activism" and "interracial alliances," strong journalistic and political support, a tradition of planning in the affected localities, and ways for proponents to take their concerns into court systems. In Seattle, many of these characteristics were present. Very strong local neighborhood organizations coalesced into a large citywide umbrella organization, Citizens Against Freeways, well able to flex its political muscles. Its leaders were well-positioned professionals similar to those in Forward Thrust, and they could not easily be brushed aside. The journal *Seattle Magazine* and Seattle's major newspapers initially provided support for many of Forward Thrust's plans, but in time questioned its freeway ideas, as did local and statewide politicians. While never as important as in some other areas, court cases sometimes were used to slow construction plans. Most important in Seattle, however, were the votes on bond measures.[99]

No mass transit system was approved. The mass transit plan included in Forward Thrust, and backed as well by many members of Citizens Against Freeways, won a bare majority of the vote, 51 percent, but not the needed 60 percent. The major reason the issue failed was that the proposed routes aimed simply at moving people into and out of the downtown area, not between the rapidly developing suburban communities, what some observers of urban developments were beginning to call "edge cities." Even the editor of the progressive *Seattle Magazine* had doubts about this plan.[100] The failure of the mass transit proposals and the inability to construct some of the arterials set the stage for the clogging of Seattle-area roads, which has resulted in a high degree of congestion to the present day.[101] Saving the arboretum and Seattle's black area from highways and protecting Lake Washington from a third bridge entailed environmental costs. Choices on economic development and environmental protection matters, the example of Seattle's Forward Thrust shows, are rarely easy.

At about the same time that Seattleites addressed problems of urban growth and congestion, residents throughout Pugetopolis began changing their attitudes toward the region's defense industries. By the late 1960s, and especially in the 1970s and 1980s, inhabitants of the Puget Sound region began to oppose defense developments on environmental and antiwar grounds. Historian Brian Casserly has cogently written, "Puget Sound communities traditionally welcomed the local military presence for the economic benefits that it brought but . . . this changed in the 1960s and 1970s . . . as groups of citizens challenged the traditional cozy relationship between local civic and business leaders and the military." That alteration, he has concluded, resulted from "the development of environmental concerns about the impact of military related growth, such as the destruction of natural areas like Hood Canal, increased urban sprawl, etc." "In addition," Casserly observed, "new, more critical approaches to the military were also influenced by the growth of peace activism in the 1970s."[102]

A case in point lay in efforts to stop the building of a Trident nuclear submarine base at the Bangor Ammunition Depot near Bremerton on Hood Canal just across Puget Sound from Seattle. In the 1970s, a loose coalition of local property owners worried about the costs of infrastructure improvements and higher taxes, environmentalists who were concerned about changes that an increase in population might bring to the landscape and quality of life in their region, and peace activists sought to shut down the project. Like those challenging the navy's use of Kahoʻolawe at about the same time, they relied on demonstrations to dramatize their opposition. One group invaded the base illegally to plant a garden "to symbolize the conflict between issues of world hunger and 'the tremendous amount of money being spent on a nuclear first strike offense.'" Again like the navy's opponents in Hawaiʻi, they went to court to challenge the navy's environmental impact statements to try to halt the construction of the base. They lost, and the Trident base opened in 1982. However, the widespread opposition heralded, Casserly has explained, "the emergence of a new phase in western relations with the military, especially regarding facilities associated with nuclear weapons."[103]

A second instance of local opposition to the military, this time successful, occurred with regard to Fort Lawton right in Seattle. Seattle's civic and business leaders had lobbied hard for the creation of Fort Lawton during the early 1900s, but once established, the base never generated the anticipated economic growth. When military officials proposed using part of its grounds as an Anti-Ballistic Missile facility in 1968, local leaders mounted spirited opposition, arguing that the base's grounds could better be used as a park to enhance the quality of life for Seattleites.[104] They were joined by Native American leaders. Inspired by the 1969 Indian occupation of Alcatraz Island, Seattle-area Indians took over some of Fort Lawton's grounds in early March, 1970. Jane Fonda joined them in their protests several weeks later. In the end, the base's lands were transferred to Seattle for use as a park, which included an Indian cultural center.[105]

High-Technology Developments in Seattle

The only-partial success at regional planning by Forward Thrust advocates combined with an economic downturn in the early 1970s to usher in a new period in Seattle's history. Boeing was hit hard by the national recession and laid off 60,000 workers between 1969 and 1971.[106] As unemployment in Seattle climbed to 14 percent, a billboard on Interstate Highway 90 asked, "Will the Last Person Leaving Please Turn Out the Lights?" Boeing eventually recovered from this downturn, but never again dominated Seattle's economy the way it had in the 1950s and 1960s. The city developed a more diversified economy, based in part on high-technology industries.[107] This change did not, however, halt environmental alterations, as suburbanization continued apace. In fact, the choices made by Seattle-area residents in rejecting many of the plans proposed by Forward Thrust continued to affect them as the twenty-first century began.

While less important to Seattle's economy than before, Boeing remained significant. Consequently, Seattleites continued to benefit and suffer as the company endured cyclical ups and downs in its production and sales. Buoyed by both commercial and military orders, the firm's employment in the Seattle region recovered to 93,000 by 1989. Another recession and cutbacks in military spending led to layoffs in the mid-1990s, but employment rose again later in the decade. Surprises came in the opening years of the twenty-first century. In 2001, Boeing moved its headquarters, although no factories, to Chicago, and a few years later ethics scandals rocked Boeing, costing the firm several large federal government orders.[108]

However, Boeing was no longer the only game in town. Lumber and fishing remained significant industries; ocean-borne trade through new harbor facilities was important; and a research-oriented University of Washington and new research institutions, such as a major branch of the Columbus-headquartered Battelle Memorial Institute, added a fillip to the region's development. Tourism boomed. Recognizing these alterations and the development of a significant high-technology component to the Seattle-area economy, *Fortune Magazine* named Seattle America's number-one city for business in 1992.[109]

Seattle's high-technology segment differed from that in Silicon Valley. It was not an agglomeration of many independent, tightly linked firms. Instead, Seattle's high-technology development took more of a "hub-and-spoke" design. Boeing acted as a hub for aerospace developments. It both subcontracted work to other companies in the region and spun off start-up aerospace firms, although not to the extent that high-technology firms such as Fairchild did in Silicon Valley. In 1989, there were eighty-six companies making aircraft and aircraft parts and another five producing guided missiles and space vehicles in the Seattle area. Microsoft formed part of a hub for software companies. Some six hundred software firms made the state of Washington their home by 1992, with the great majority of them located in the Seattle region. Often less well recognized was Boeing's role in the development of software enterprises. Founded in 1970, Boeing Computer Services

(BCS) employed 6,000 people by 1989. Established to serve Boeing's internal needs, BCS ventured into commercial markets and spun off independent companies. There were already over a hundred software companies in the Seattle region by the time Microsoft was incorporated in 1981. Finally, the University of Washington and its Fred Hutchinson Cancer Research Center served as the hub for a fledgling group of biotechnology firms. By the mid-1990s, some sixty such enterprises employed 5,000 workers. The various types of high-technology businesses provided about 10 percent of the jobs, and a higher percentage of the payroll, in the Seattle region by 1989.[110]

Renewed economic growth led to further expansion in Seattle's suburbs, until by 1990 the Seattle region contained 2.6 million residents. The Eastside especially boomed. Bellevue soon boasted its own downtown, complete with skyscrapers rivaling those in Seattle. Bellevue had become a classic edge city, largely independent of Seattle. By 2002, Bellevue boasted 117,000 residents.

Rapid population growth and spatial expansion resulted in renewed calls for planning and controls. As in California, some localities in Pugetopolis sought to limit development though the adoption of "no-growth" or "slow-growth" ordinances. When these generally proved only partially effective, Washingtonians turned to their state legislature for help.[111] In 1990, the Washington State Legislature passed the Growth Management Act (GMA). This legislation required that local governments make plans channeling growth in specific areas by designating areas as either growth or nongrowth corridors. The GMA also required that infrastructure improvements— schools, water and sewer facilities, roads, and the like—be put in place before residential or commercial development could occur. Moreover, the state's twelve most populous counties had to submit comprehensive land-use plans.[112] The GMA proved less effective in controlling growth than many of its advocates had hoped. One scholar of urban development observed, the "result has been even more rivalry among entities," as little cooperation to curb growth occurred. Continuing, he noted, "Although expansion of built-up areas into exurban areas has been reduced, each community has vigorously tried to increase its share of the employment and population pie." Indeed, he has concluded, "within the growth boundaries, traditional zoning regulations have been relaxed in favor of higher densities."[113]

The Seattle region was too popular for its own good. A writer for *Newsweek* observed in 1996, "Sooner or later, it seems, everyone moves to Seattle, or thinks about it, or at least their kids do." Seattle, he concluded, had come to "consist entirely of people who were born somewhere else. Rootless youths seeking alienation beneath Seattle's brooding skies, but with plenty of girls to keep them company. Middle-aged strivers betting that Microsoft can create one more millionaire." Seattle's motto had become, he suggested, "Seattle: if you can make it there, so what?"[114] Growth extended far into the countryside. A reporter for the *Seattle Post-Intelligencer* observed the trend accelerating in 2004, as many Seattleites lived ever farther from the city's center. Writing about Issaquah, he described how "3,330 homes are planned to the northeast in Issaquah Highlands ... where a new Microsoft campus is planned." "As a result," he noted with dismay, "the broad greenswards that helped attract settlers to Issaquah Creek's flood plain more than a century ago have been covered with blacktop and storefronts."[115]

Conclusions

Military spending for World War II and the Cold War helped America's Pacific Coast cities, just as such spending boosted other Pacific regions. The cities experienced rapid economic growth and attained national, even international, stature. Seattle and Silicon Valley created measurably high economic standards of living for their residents. In 1970, and even more so twenty years later, residents in Seattle enjoyed a per capita income quite a bit higher than that of the average Washingtonian. Similarly, Silicon Valley residents had incomes on average considerably higher than those of other Californians.[116] In Silicon Valley and, increasingly, in the Seattle region the rising incomes came from high-technology companies.

However, major environmental costs accompanied economic growth. Some costs were obvious, others hidden. Congestion and high home prices were in plain view. So was water pollution by sewage. In both Silicon Valley and Seattle, urban and suburban development altered physical landscapes in ways similar to those described by environmental historian Adam Rome for communities across America.[117] As in the rest of postwar America, suburban growth spawned environmental efforts to control sprawl, with, at least in the cases of Seattle and Silicon Valley, only partial success.[118] Groundwater contamination, especially by toxic chemicals, was much less obvious. Even further from public view were questions of environmental injustice, as high-technology development fostered uneven economic growth. The health problems of immigrant women workers in Silicon Valley's wafer fabrication plants and the loss of fishing grounds on the Duwamish River by Native Americans were two deleterious results.

Environmental justice concerns were, of course, central to policy making for Kahoʻolawe. Trade-offs between economic development and environmental justice matters also occurred in Alaska, the subject of the next chapter. Those issues became apparent in efforts to create a new international park in cooperation with the Russians. That effort seemed to infringe on the rights of Alaskan Natives and was initially opposed by some of them. Trade-offs between business development and environmental protection in Alaska revolved, however, mainly around the exploitation of fishery and oil resources.

CHAPTER 4

Alaska

The Aleutian Islands

Returning to her home port of Cordova, Alaska, on April 28, 1976, the king crab boat *Master Carl* developed mechanical problems in the face of a fierce storm, a blow featuring waves more than thirty feet high. Water entered the vessel's hull as she passed near Montague Island just outside of Prince William Sound, and at midnight the ship's flooded engine died. Tossed by waves, the *Master Carl* rolled onto her side and her captain and crew members had to abandon her. After donning survival suits, they clambered into a life raft and, with great difficulty, cast off. Caught in three-storey-high waves, the raft overturned on several occasions, spilling the men out into the rampaging sea. Against the odds, they climbed back in, and eventually two of the crewmen made it to shore. The captain and another crew member died in the attempt. Once on shore, the two surviving men, exhausted and suffering from hypothermia, huddled together through a cold night. They were harassed by a grizzly bear, which they fended off by throwing rocks. Only after a horrific night were they rescued the next day by a coast guard helicopter.[1]

The loss of the *Master Carl* was typical of accidents afflicting king crab vessels in Alaskan waters. In early 1983, the *Americus* and her sister ship, the *Altair,* went down in 80-knot winds, sinkings that cost the lives of thirteen men. Even earlier, in the winter of 1962–1963, thirteen king crab boats were lost, most with all hands, in storms whose winds exceeded 140 miles per hour.[2] Men and women were willing to endure extreme hardships in Alaska's fisheries for the same reason that they did so in exploiting the state's other natural resources: they wanted to get rich quick.[3] Whether hunting sea otters, mining gold, fishing for salmon and king crabs, drilling for oil, cutting down forests, or boosting a burgeoning tourism industry, Alaskans—like Ameri-

A large king crab. (Author's
collection)

cans on frontiers before them—sought personal enrichment and adventure.[4]
A national park service planner who had spent five years in Arctic Alaska
observed in the mid-1970s that the state's coat of arms should be a shield divided into quarters with each bearing one of four mottos: "Dig it up; chop it
down; fish it out; shoot it." Even those who failed to strike it rich in Alaskan
ventures—and there were many—aspired to riches.[5]

Relatively little thought was given at first to the conservation of natural
resources or to more general environmental matters. However, as development continued and resources seemed to be in danger of depletion, conservation matters, and sometimes environmental issues, were taken more seriously by Alaskan residents.[6] By the late-nineteenth and the early-twentieth
centuries there were stirrings of concern about the conservation of natural resources, especially wildlife. After World War II, that concern broadened and deepened to include land-use and water-management matters and
quality-of-life issues.

This chapter examines conservation and environmental issues in Alaska
since the Second World War; World War II in Alaska, as throughout so much
of the Pacific, was a watershed in history. After surveying Alaska's development through the 1960s, the chapter first analyzes efforts, only partly successful, to preserve fishing stocks in Alaskan waters, particularly those along

the Aleutian Islands and in the Bering Sea. The chapter looks next at controversies surrounding drilling for oil on the state's continental shelf, especially its outer continental shelf. This development brought oil prospectors into conflict with fishermen, and how those disputes were resolved is a revealing story of resource management. The chapter closes by investigating joint efforts on the part of the American and Russian governments to create a Beringia Heritage International Park on both sides of the Bering Strait and what those attempts have meant for people already living in that region.

The developments dealt with in this chapter took place in what might be called "Island Alaska" and shared similarities with occurrences elsewhere in America's Pacific possessions. Several major themes permeate this story. Once again, politics emerge as very important in determinants of resource allocation. In the political arena, businesspeople, environmentalists, politicians, and others worked out compromises on how to use and preserve Alaska's lumber, fish, and minerals. Then, too, the rights of indigenous people, Alaskan Natives and Eskimos (Inuit), played important roles similar in some ways to those played by native Hawaiians and, as we shall see in a later chapter, by Chamorros on Guam. Finally, economic and social developments in Alaska passed through different stages of integration, disconnection, and reintegration with other parts of the Pacific.

Alaska's Development

From the beginning, Euro-American explorers rightly described Alaska as immense. Russians called it "Bolshaya Zemlya," the "Great Land." Today's state of Alaska embraces 591,000 square miles (378 million acres), an area one-fifth the size of the lower forty-eight states sweeping across four time zones. A map of Alaska superimposed on one of the lower forty-eight states shows it touching the Atlantic and Pacific Oceans and the Canadian and Mexican borders. Alaska is as diverse as its geography is large, with six regions having distinct topographies and climates. The state possesses 34,000 miles of seacoast, 50 percent more than the total of the lower forty-eight states combined. Two oceans and three seas wash Alaska's shores.[7]

Russian fur traders and merchants moving east from Siberia and Kamchatka were the first non-natives to enter Alaska. Private individuals, they sought profits by trading the pelts of sea otters found in Alaskan waters for goods in China. The Russian adventurers established an extensive fur-trading empire dependent on the Aleuts as hunters. Stretching by the early 1800s from the Aleutians through Alaska's panhandle and south to an outpost in northern California, that empire was beset by problems. Its great distance from Russia meant that needed supplies were often scarce; there were conflicts with native groups in southeastern Alaska; and there was growing competition with traders from the United States and European nations. Always lightly held—there were never more than about seven hundred Russians in Alaska—Alaska was sold to the United States in 1867.[8]

Russian work in Alaska set trends that Americans continued. Despite attempts to rein in the slaughter, the Russians and other westerners hunted sea otters to near extinction. Coming a bit later, most Americans also looked upon Alaska's natural resources as treasures inviting plunder. As historian Stephen Haycox has noted, Alaskans have generally been "insensitive to their impact on nature and landscape, regarding the land as infinitely renewable and its resources as inexhaustible, and theirs to appropriate for their own uses." Some of that same insensitivity long governed relations with native peoples. Torn from their homes and overworked, Aleut Indians fell prey to diseases unintentionally introduced by Russians to which the Aleuts had no natural immunities. Aleut numbers dropped from 15,000–25,000 in precontact times to a scant 900 in 1848. As with Hawaiians and Chamorros, disease was the big killer of the Aleuts, just as it was for Native Americans across North America.[9]

Alaska long remained colonial in its economy. Most of the capital necessary to develop Alaska came from outside of the region, most recently in the case of the oil and lumber industries, earlier in mining and fishing.[10] To the extent that people succeeded in developing Alaska's economy in the early days, they did so through their engagement in the Pacific economy. Sea otter pelts were traded in China, with food to support the Russian venture arriving from such diverse sources as Russia, the Hawaiian Islands, the Pacific Northwest, and California. For a while in the late nineteenth and early twentieth centuries, Alaskans turned their backs a bit on greater Pacific connections, focusing on just the Pacific Coast of North America. However, after World War II salmon fishermen and king crabbers, along with most miners, lumbermen, and oilmen, returned to a full involvement in the Pacific economy. In these varied Pacific relationships, Alaskans remained dependent on outside regions for development funds, markets, and their general economic well-being, just as were residents in the Hawaiian Islands, Guam, and (for many years) the Seattle area. Alaskans' work was part and parcel of the economic integration of the Pacific stimulated by Americans.

Even the nature of later federal–state governmental relations during

American times was foreshadowed in the Russian period, for in both time periods the relationship between the metropole and the periphery was a love-hate one. Alaskans recognized that they needed the support of the federal government, but were most reluctant about acknowledging that necessity. Like Hawaiians and Guamanians, they resented what they regarded as outside federal interference in their affairs.[11] Americans were active in Alaskan developments even in Russian times, including Russian Alaska in their Pacific maritime frontier from about the 1820s. American ships carried New England goods to the Pacific Northwest and Alaska, where they were exchanged for furs, especially sea otter pelts. Later, American whalers hunted in Alaskan waters, periodically putting into the Hawaiian Islands to resupply. By the 1840s and 1850s, hundreds of American whalers wintered in Honolulu on Oʻahu and Lahaina on Maui.[12]

Like many regions dependent on just a few resources, Alaska developed a boom-and-bust economy. Mining was the first major industry to go through that cycle. Hard-rock gold mining in southeastern Alaska flourished from the 1880s, with the mines and smelters paid for by outside capital and with most of the profits leaving Alaska. Copper mines operated in south-central Alaska by the Kennecott interests two decades later also depended heavily on outside capital and organization. However, it was the discovery of gold in Canada's Klondike in 1896 that boomed Alaska. In 1897–1898, 60,000–100,000 gold rushers left Seattle and San Francisco for the Klondike. By 1907, fifty new gold-mining camps had been established in Alaska. Alaska's non-native population rose from about 430 people in 1880 to roughly 30,000 in 1900. Conversely, the region's native population fell from 33,000 to 30,000 over the same decades.[13] The mining boom quickly became something of a bust. Gold production peaked in 1906, and copper production began falling in the early 1920s. By 1930, only 4,800 Alaskans were working in mines. By 1920, Alaska's non-native population had fallen to 28,000, a figure only slightly higher than the 27,000 natives living in the region.[14]

The territory's fisheries proved more long-lived, but showed the same boom-and-bust characteristics. Moving their operations north from California and the Pacific Northwest, salmon companies set up their first canneries in Alaska during the 1870s and 1880s. In 1889, thirty-seven canneries packed 714,000 cases of salmon (a case was 48 net pounds). Capitalized at $4 million, they employed about 6,000 people. Most of the workers were brought in from outside Alaska for the summer and fall canning season, and few local residents found employment in the canneries. Nor, initially, did residents benefit much by catching fish for the canneries. Instead, the canneries relied mainly on their own fish traps and nets set at the mouths of rivers up which the salmon swam to spawn. By 1910, the Alaskan salmon pack came to 2.5 million cases. About 6.7 million cases were packed in 1918, as the U.S. Army bought canned salmon for its troops. Output fell to fewer than 3 million cases in 1921, but recovered to more than 8 million cases in 1936, an all-time high.[15]

Efforts to regulate Alaska's salmon industry were sporadic political footballs pitting the salmon canneries against local Alaskan fishermen and federal officials against territorial ones. As early as 1889, an inspector for the U.S. Fish Commission, worried that the fish traps were depleting Alaska's salmon runs, recommended conservation measures. The packers disagreed on what to do and accomplished little. Instead, the federal government and the packers turned to artificial propagation in fish hatcheries, which, however, did little to help. Alarmed by failures at conservation, Secretary of Commerce Herbert Hoover convinced President Warren Harding to establish a salmon-fishing reservation in southwestern Alaska in 1922. Local fishermen opposed this action as unfairly limiting their activities. Legislation following Harding's executive order, the White Act of 1924, named after Representative Wallace H. White of Maine, who introduced it in the House, was ineffective. Its two most controversial sections—one prohibiting the use of fish traps, as desired by Alaskan residents, the other establishing more fishing reservations, as desired by the packers—were deleted before passage. The White Act did give the secretary of commerce the power to limit fishing in parts of Alaskan waters and allowed him to set the types of fishing gear that could be deployed, although not the amount, a crucial omission. The legislation also decreed that half of the salmon be allowed to swim upstream to spawn. Even this last requirement was only rarely enforced at the time, however.

Little more was accomplished over the next two decades. Significant in its own right—the industry employed more workers than any other industry in the territory during the 1920s and 1930s—the Alaskan salmon industry was important for precedents it set. The conflict between local and outside interests was replicated in many later industries, including the king crab industry. In addition, Congress' actions in trying to conserve salmon greatly angered many Alaskans, contributing to their dislike of the federal government.[16]

At the time of World War II, Alaskans still lived a colonial existence, with their economy based on the extraction of minerals, fish, and furs. Nearly all of the capital came from outside. In the case of infrastructure improvements, such as the building of the Alaska Railroad, completed from Seward to Fairbanks in 1923, the source was the federal government. In the case of private businesses, funds came from across the United States. In the instance of the salmon industry, the sources lay in Pacific Coast companies. Not surprisingly, most of the business profits left Alaska, repatriated to corporate offices elsewhere. The economy of Alaska had become less of a Pacific economy by about 1910. Alaskans still had ties with America's Pacific Coast, but they temporarily turned away from Asia and Hawai'i. Only later were those connections fully reestablished.[17]

Developments during World War II and the Cold War partially changed Alaska, but earlier precedents remained significant. Billions of federal government dollars flowed into Alaska, linking the region closely to the rest of the United States. The achievement of statehood further boosted Alaska in the eyes of many. Even so, sustained economic growth was, as before, elusive. As one prominent Alaskan historian explained in 1967, the state's progress depended on "minerals, oil, coal, timber, and furs," supplemented by "high-grade fish." More than elsewhere in western states, Alaskans acted out the paradox of the centrality of the state and the conviction of personal responsibility and autonomy.[18]

In Alaska, World War II revolved around Japan's attack on the Aleutian Islands in 1942, including the taking of the islands of Attu and Kiska, and the United States' successful counterattack to recapture the islands a year later. American bombers also flew 1,500 sorties from bases in the Aleutians against Japanese positions in the Kurile Islands, and nearly half of the lend-lease materials reaching Russia was carried in ships traveling the northern circle route, which went through the Aleutians. As elsewhere in the Pacific, the war greatly increased the American presence in Alaska. At its peak in 1943, the American military stationed 152,000 troops there (as late as 1939 only 524 military personnel had been in the territory). The war brought infrastructure improvements, many of which were later put to commercial use. These included building the first all-weather highway connecting Alaska to the lower forty-eight states, the Alaska/Canadian (ALCAN) highway, making improvements to harbors, and constructing numerous air bases.[19]

Not all benefited from wartime developments. As elsewhere in the Pacific, economic growth was uneven. Aleut Indians, in particular, were hurt, as they were evacuated by the American military from their settlements on the Pribilof and the Aleutian Islands. Some of their villages were razed to prevent Japanese use of their buildings. Many Aleuts spent the war in unsanitary relocation camps in southwestern Alaska. Still others were taken prisoner by the Japanese on Attu. Placed in an internment camp on Hokkaido,

40 percent died. The survivors found that they could not return to Attu at the close of the conflict, for the island was littered with war debris. They joined other Aleuts in a resettlement colony on Atka Island. Like Chamorros on Guam, Aleuts were innocent victims of the Pacific conflict. Only in the 1980s and later did Aleuts receive some compensation for their wartime losses.[20]

The Cold War extended changes that had begun in World War II. After briefly slumping at the close of World War II, military construction in Alaska averaged about $250 million per year between 1949 and 1954. Although military expenditures declined in real terms after the mid-1950s, they remained important, amounting to $932 million in 1980. Similarly, the number of military personnel, after falling to 19,000 in 1949, rose to 50,000 in 1952, before dropping to 30,000 in 1970. Alaska's population rose from 73,000 in 1940 to 129,000 in 1950 and then soared to 226,000 in 1960. The nature of that population changed. As late as 1940, natives comprised 44 percent of Alaska's population, but by 1960 they made up only 19 percent of it.[21]

The Cold War threatened to alter Alaska through the uses of nuclear and thermonuclear energy. In 1957, the Atomic Energy Commission (AEC) approved Operation Plowshare as part of an effort to find nonmilitary uses for nuclear explosives. A year later, the AEC devised Project Chariot as part of Operation Plowshare. Project Chariot was to use hydrogen bombs to blast out a harbor near Point Hope on Alaska's northwest coast at the northern reaches of the Bering Strait. A considerably scaled-down plan using nuclear bombs was presented to Alaskans in early 1959, and a still more modest scheme was laid out in 1960. Even the smaller 1960 plan would have used bombs having an explosive power over twenty times that of the blast that had destroyed Hiroshima. To be exploded underground, the bombs would allow the AEC to experiment with nuclear weapons as a possible tool for building canals and harbors. With military spending in Alaska winding down a bit, all of Alaska's chambers of commerce and most of the territory's political leaders initially supported Project Chariot.[22]

Little thought was given to the Eskimos eking out a subsistence existence in the area, but by their actions the Eskimos changed that situation. Very worried by reports of harm to Pacific Islanders caused by nuclear tests, they publicized possible negative outcomes of the blasts. They also were alarmed by the fact that the federal government would reserve a considerable amount of land for Project Chariot, making it difficult for them to acquire lands to which they were entitled. In late 1959, the Point Hope village council voted unanimously against Project Chariot and turned to other Alaskan Natives for support. At a meeting at Point Barrow in 1961, Eskimos and Alaskan Natives united in opposition to Project Chariot. In 1964, they held their first state-wide conference, resulting in the establishment of the Alaskan Federation of Natives two years later. This organization was an important factor in later environmental and Alaskan Native issues. In their opposition, Alaskan Natives were joined by a pioneering Alaskan environmental organization, the Alaska Conservation Society, and by national groups such as the Wilderness Society and the Sierra Club. When environmental studies revealed that proposed blasts might harm birds and caribou upon which the Eskimos relied for food, and that the explosions might also release unacceptable amounts of radio-activity into the atmosphere, the AEC backed off from Project Chariot and, despite continued support for the project from many of Alaska's business and political leaders, abandoned it.[23]

Opponents were less successful in halting nuclear and thermonuclear weapons tests on the Aleutian Island of Amchitka. The AEC and the Department of Defense chose the uninhabited island as the site for a series of above-ground and below-ground tests, but the adherence of the United States to an international treaty prohibiting atmospheric tests in 1963 meant that explosions would be underground. Global developments thus intruded into the Pacific. Opposition to the first test in 1965 was muted, as Cold War concerns ruled the day. Plans for additional tests generated more controversy. Scientists and environmentalists pointed out that Amchitka lay near a geologic fault line and that nuclear testing might set off earthquakes and tidal waves. For those reasons, too, the governments of Japan and Canada opposed the tests. Environmental groups, including the Sierra Club and Friends of the Earth, joined Alaskan Native bodies to try unsuccessfully to block the tests through court appeals, as did the Aleut League in a suit of its own. The tests went ahead in 1969 and 1971. Fortunately, although Amchitka and its wildlife were damaged, no seismic activity occurred. One result later to have significance throughout the Pacific and the world was the formation of the environmental group Greenpeace. Set up initially to halt the explosions, the group adopted its name in 1972.[24]

With World War II and the Cold War drawing more people into their territory, Alaskans voiced successful calls for statehood. In 1959, President Dwight D. Eisenhower signed the proclamation admitting Alaska as the forty-ninth state in the Union. Statehood brought important changes to the management of natural resources. The new state's constitution urged governmental officials to "encourage the settlement of its land and development of its resources by making them available for maximum use consistent with the public interest." Federal officials agreed to give the state 103 million acres from the public domain, 28 percent of Alaska's area, with state officials to select the land over twenty-five years. The state also gained control over Alaska's continental shelf and the waters above it for a distance of three miles out to sea. To administer hunting and fishing, the state government created an Alaskan Board of Fish and Game. One of the board's first jobs was to enforce a ban on fish traps, hated by independent Alaskan salmon fishermen as a symbol of outside interests. The traps had been provisionally outlawed by a 1956 ordinance and were permanently banned three years later.[25]

However, even after statehood the federal government remained very important in Alaska. Of the 110,600 working Alaskans in 1971, some 17,300 were employees of the federal government. All of the public domain not selected by the state and all of the waters above the continental shelf more than three miles from shore remained under federal control. The federal government extended its authority over fishing activities beyond the three-mile zone up to six miles out to sea in 1958, and much farther out in the 1960s and 1970s.

Statehood did not automatically bring boom times to Alaskans. The search for stable economic growth continued. The salmon industry continued a decline begun in the 1940s. Not even the imposition of limited-entry fishing, which used a system of permits to regulate the amount of fishing gear in use, helped much. Beset by problems of its own making and by the overfishing of salmon stocks on the high seas, the Alaskan salmon industry became less important to the Alaskan economy than it had been in prewar times. After peaking at more than 8 million cases in 1936, the Alaskan salmon pack plummeted to fewer than 2 million cases by 1960 and rebounded to only 3 million cases a decade later. Not even a later recovery in salmon fishing fully revived the fortunes of fishermen, as prices dropped. Military spending in Alaska peaked in the mid-1950s and then fell in real terms. Nor did mining, fur trapping, or farming offer much hope for economic growth.[26]

There were some bright spots. One was the lumber industry. Alaska's first large pulp mill opened in Ketchikan in 1954, and five years later a second mill, owned by a Japanese firm, began operations in Sitka. Both were supplied with logs from the nearby Tongass National Forest. By 1967, Alaska produced $78 million worth of wood products. Then, too, the development of new fisheries such as king crabs partially offset the decline in the salmon industry. By 1965, the wholesale value of Alaska's fish catch came to $167 million. Tourism, which became one of Alaska's key industries in later years, was in its infancy. So was the state's oil industry. By 1965, five oil and gas fields had been developed in Alaska, and the state had taken in $122 million in payments from oil companies.[27]

Despite the promise of expansion in fisheries, lumber, tourism, and oil, Alaskan economist George W. Rogers was correct when he stated in 1967 that there was an "urgency for understanding" economic development matters that was "greater in Alaska than in the nation as a whole." In fact, he continued, "Every Alaskan is aware of the need for economic development if our state is to survive and prosper as a viable political entity." He was heartened that "The political leaders and candidates of both parties campaign under the banner of economic development."[28] Yet matters were more complex than Rogers suggested. While most Alaskans continued to favor putting their state's natural resources to use with little thought for the future, some were beginning to question this approach—as the defeat of Project Chariot suggested. Developments in king crab fisheries along the Aleutian Islands and in the Bering Sea raised important questions about resource usage and conservation over the next four decades.

Conservation in Alaska's King Crab Industry

As fishery expert Terry Johnson explained in 2003, "Commercial fishing in Alaska is a diverse, colorful, tough, dangerous, thriving and—with skill and luck—lucrative enterprise." Alaska's varied fisheries accounted for about half of the United States' seafood harvest, with a dockside value of about $1.4 billion. "Not only does the Alaska seafood harvest outrank in quantity and the value of the harvest of the rest of the United States' combined," Johnson observed, "this bounty outranks the individual harvests of Norway, Denmark, Iceland, and Canada." Alaska's fisheries products industry employed about 70,000 workers. Crabs composed about a quarter of the value of Alaska's fishery products, with most of the crabs taken along the Aleutian Islands and in the Bering Sea.[29]

The Aleutian Islands and the Bering Sea comprise western and southwestern Alaska. Extending almost 1,500 miles west from the Alaskan Peninsula toward Russia and Japan, the Aleutian Islands are mainly volcanic in origin. They have vegetation described by scientists as consisting of "alpine heath meadows and lichen communities, with moist tundra at some lower elevation sites." There are few trees. The islands and the Bering Sea just to their north endure weather that is foggy, rainy, and stormy. However, weather on the whole is less severe than that of the interior of Alaska. Temperatures fall below 0°F only occasionally in the winter and rarely rise above 55°F in the summer. Covering an area as large as the United States west of the Mississippi, the Bering Sea benefits from climactic conditions, currents, and geographical features that make it one of the most productive fishing grounds in the world. Much of the sea is shallow. Its continental shelf to a depth of 300 feet covers 400,000 square miles, and a section of the shelf the size of California lies fewer than fifty feet under the surface.[30]

It was in the coastal waters of Alaska, especially those around the Aleutian Islands and in the Bering Sea, that king crabs were found.[31] Largely unexploited by Americans before World War II, king crabs were heavily fished after the war. No one was more active in fishing these waters for king crabs than Lowell Wakefield. As overfishing developed by the 1960s, Wakefield and others involved in the industry strove to ensure their future through conservation measures. The resolution of conflicts over the utilization of the Alaskan king crab fishery—disputes between Alaskan fishermen and fishing companies headquartered outside of the state and contests pitting American, Japanese, and Soviet fishermen against each other—illustrated how complex conservation issues had become.

Lowell Wakefield pioneered the development of the Alaskan king crab industry through the formation of Wakefield Seafood. Wakefield came from a family with an extensive background in Alaska's salmon and herring fisheries.

Lowell Wakefield (*left*) with two other founders of Wakefield Seafood in the Aleutian Islands in the 1950s. (Author's collection)

He became acquainted with king crabs through exploratory efforts made by the federal government in the 1940s. Searching for new sources of protein for the American public and the armed forces during World War II, the government sponsored fishing expeditions along the Alaskan coast. These ventures suggested that king crabs could become a significant fishery. Surveys were conducted in front of a Wakefield cannery and revealed a large number of crabs in the water. Wakefield's knowledge of the surveys and his realization that Alaska's herring and salmon industries were in decline led him to abandon his family's business and set up his own company.[32]

Wakefield spearheaded the formation of his new enterprise under the laws of the state of Washington in 1945. Breaking with past experience, he assigned a single ship to catch, process, and freeze king crabs and bottom fish. Previous operations had employed small ships to catch crabs and fish, which they then transferred to shore plants or large mother ships for processing and canning. Processing on board the catching vessel, a specially built ship named the *Deep Sea,* was favored by Wakefield as highly efficient. He expected to reduce costs greatly by decreasing spoilage and by integrating previously separated stages of fish processing into one continuous-flow operation. Freezing, which came into common use for food processing in America in the 1930s and 1940s, appealed to him as an ultramodern method and as a way to differentiate his crab from the canned crab of competitors. After processing, the crab and fish would be stored on board the ship in refrigerated holds until they could be packaged and sent to market.[33]

Getting started proved difficult. Unable to secure financing for his speculative venture from commercial banks, Wakefield turned to the federal government. The Reconstruction Finance Corporation (RFC), a federal agency set up to help businesses during the Great Depression, agreed in 1946 to grant a substantial loan to Wakefield Seafood. Family and business ties brought in additional needed funds. The founders and investors were young men in their twenties and thirties on the make. World War II had disrupted their lives, and they found themselves at loose ends at the conclusion of the conflict. All were extremely optimistic, expecting that their new company would be returning hefty profits within two or three years of starting operations. Motivated by more than money, they were looking for adventure in setting up their new business.[34] The expected quick profits did not materialize, for the company encountered difficulties in every stage of its operations. The problems nearly brought Wakefield Seafood to its knees. Only a timely loan from Wakefield's father and a charter of the *Deep Sea* for work for the federal government saved the firm from bankruptcy in 1948.[35]

King crabs on board the *Deep Sea* preparatory to butchering, cooking, and freezing. (Author's collection)

Wakefield Seafood emerged as a profitable enterprise in the mid-1950s. Several related elements accounted for that success. The company's officers eagerly embraced technological advances, many of them spin-offs from World War II. Their ship was the first to use radar, sonar, and loran (a navigational aid) in fishing. The captain of a minesweeper in the Aleutian Islands for several years during World War II, the skipper of the *Deep Sea* was well versed in advanced nautical technologies. Then, too, those starting the company were willing to endure hard times. When unable to attract fishing and processing crews, the owner-managers manned the nets and processing lines themselves. Moreover, the personal ties that had been important in starting Wakefield Seafood helped account for the firm's survival. Friendships between the founders of the company and the heads of the Seattle branch of the RFC, Seattle's commercial banks, and the suppliers of fishing gear secured extensions on loans. Though internal factors help to explain the success of Wakefield Seafood, so do external elements. As on many western American frontiers and throughout America's Pacific possessions, the federal government was significant in many ways in the development of Alaska's king crab frontier, from financing the initial fishing surveys to the provision of the RFC loan.[36]

In developing its operations, Wakefield Seafood was one of a handful of fishing ventures to employ Aleut Indians at that time. Most of the *Deep Sea's* processing crew was composed of Aleut natives from Akutan Village just northeast of Dutch Harbor. Both humanitarian and practical considerations led Lowell Wakefield to hire them. Wakefield's background was important. He had done graduate work at Columbia University in anthropology, studying with the famed Franz Boas. After finishing there, he worked for the International Labor Defense. He became involved in the Harlan County, Kentucky, coal disputes—"Bloody Harlan"—and in the Labor Defense's southern organizing drive before returning to Alaska. He hoped the king crab industry would provide jobs for Aleuts, who had few employment prospects. Then, too, he imagined that employing locals might burnish his firm's luster with Alaskans at a time when some were beginning to see the company as a predatory outside interest. All was not sweet harmony, however. After serving on board the *Deep Sea* for a month or more, non-native deck crew members cast aside inhibitions when they received shore leaves. They drank to excess and caroused. They brought liquor into native villages and cohabited with native women, acts about which Aleut village chiefs bitterly complained.[37]

No sooner had Wakefield Seafood escaped from near-bankruptcy than it expanded its operations dramatically. Relying increasingly on independent fishermen to catch crabs, the firm built shore plants in the Aleutians to process and freeze the crabs. Wakefield Seafood's success attracted competition. In 1950, the company put up 70 percent of the American king crab pack, but by 1966 it accounted for only 18 percent. Nor was competition confined to American firms, as Japanese and Soviet ventures reentered Alaskan waters. In 1959, American companies accounted for two-thirds of the king crabs caught in the Bering Sea and from waters above Alaska's continental shelf, but in 1962 the share of American firms had dropped to just over half. With more ships placing more fishing gear in the water, Alaska's king crab catch soared from 23,000 pounds in 1946, to 1.5 million pounds in 1950, to 29 million pounds in 1960, and to 160 million pounds in 1966, a high point. The catch crashed to just 60 million pounds in 1969 and to only 50 million pounds in 1974.[38]

To deal with their problems, especially the decline in the crab catch, fishermen turned to state and federal governments, and conservation measures often became tools for economic competition, just as had occurred earlier in the salmon industry. Of most immediate concern in the 1950s were regulations governing the catching of crabs within Alaska's three-mile limit. Most of the initial fishing regulations sought to mediate fishing-gear conflicts. Wakefield Seafood's ships were mainly trawlers, which dragged nets across the ocean bottom scooping up everything in their paths. By way of contrast, most of the smaller boats manned by independent Alaskan fishermen employed crab pots. Like very large lobster pots, they were lowered to the ocean floor. Once crabs crawled into the baited pots, they could not get out. Raised to the surface, the pots were emptied on board the boats, which then delivered crabs alive to the nearest processing plant. As early as the mid-1950s, clashes occurred in Cook Inlet, especially Kachemak Bay, with local fishermen claiming that the trawls operated by the ships of Wakefield Seafood were destroying prime fishing grounds and their pots. Federal and territorial authorities were able to work out compromises regulating when and where different types of gear could be employed.[39]

When Alaska gained statehood, control over near-shore fishing was transferred to state agencies. Pushed by Kodiak fishermen, the state took a number of actions that hurt the larger non-Alaskan firms. The state banned trawling operations completely in 1961 and severely limited the movement of ships from one fishing area to another. As local crab shortages began to show up in some fishing areas, state agencies sought to limit the number of crab pots a boat could carry. This effort proved ineffective as a conservation measure, for it placed no restrictions on the number of boats entering the fisheries. The state then moved in the direction of limited-entry fishing, as desired by Lowell Wakefield and executives of other large companies. Limited-entry fishing restricted the number of boats that could fish for crabs, usually by granting licenses only to boats already engaged in the fishery.[40]

However, little was achieved until after the crash in the crab catch in the late 1960s, for the smaller, local companies viewed limited-entry fishing as an infringement on their economic rights. In the 1970s, the state established a quota system by dividing Alaska's king crab grounds into six areas, setting a maximum allowable catch (MAC) for each and closing the grounds to fishing each season once the MACs were reached. This system seemed to work. By 1976, the crab catch was back up to 106 million pounds, and in the late 1970s it averaged 180 million pounds per year.[41]

The state scheme was helped by changes in national and international fishing regulations. Even as they fought each other over the regulation of near-shore fishing, Alaska's king crabbers united in opposition to Soviet and Japanese fishermen. Clashes first occurred over the types of gear to be used. The Japanese employed stationary tangle nets across large reaches of the ocean, much to the annoyance of American fishermen trying to move through the same fishing grounds with trawls. Then, too, American fishermen wanted their Japanese counterparts to agree not to fish for crabs east of 175 degrees west longitude, a line that would exclude them from much of the Bering Sea. The Japanese had agreed to such a restriction with regard to salmon and halibut. Led by Lowell Wakefield, American crabbers took their concerns to the International North Pacific Fisheries Commission (INPFC). Set up in 1952 with the United States, Japan, and Canada as signatories, the INPFC was charged with studying and regulating fisheries resources in the North Pacific. Arguing that the king crab fishery was not fully developed, the Japanese refused to accept limitations on their high-seas crab fishing in the 1950s. International conflict flared up anew in the early 1960s, when large Soviet crab fleets, some with as many as two hundred vessels, entered Alaska's offshore waters. Gear conflicts multiplied, and local shortages of crabs became common.[42]

Actions by the United Nations helped resolve matters, with consequences that extended far beyond the North Pacific. In 1958 and 1960, the UN sponsored Law of the Sea Conferences. Of greatest importance for American king crabbers, the conferences adopted a convention giving coastal nations almost exclusive control over the exploitation of their continental shelves—specifically over oil, minerals, and some fish (sedentary creatures on the bottom) found on or under them to a depth of 200 meters.[43] Backed by many third-world nations but initially opposed by the United States, whose leaders were concerned about global access for its fishermen and about navigation rights for its commercial and military vessels, this convention had a major impact on king crabbing. King crabs were deemed to be sedentary, for they crawl but do not swim. Thus, the crabs were judged to be attached to the continental shelf. Consequently, this convention would place crabs in the mostly shallow waters of the Bering Sea and the Aleutian Islands in American hands. By 1963, enough countries—including the United States, which had reversed its earlier position, and the Soviet Union, but not Japan—had ratified the convention to put it into effect.[44] In 1964, Congress gave the convention bite by passing legislation confirming the United States' ownership of creatures on the nation's continental shelf, over vehement protests from Japan. Further talks with Japanese and Soviet representatives in 1964 and 1965 led to their reluctant acceptance of the continental shelf convention and restrictions in their fishing for king crabs.[45]

Additional international agreements helped the American king crab industry. Here global matters merged with Pacific ones. What fisheries expert Terry Johnson has recently called "the most profound change in the world's commercial ocean fisheries" occurred with the adoption of 200-mile exclusive economic zones (EEZs) by a growing number of nations in the 1970s. After first opposing the concept, the United States proclaimed such a zone in 1976 with the passage by Congress of the Federal Fishery Conservation and Management Act (reenacted, with some changes, in 1996). This legislation extended the federal government's control over fishing 200 miles out to sea from American shores, regardless of ocean depths. Eight regional management councils set Total Allowable Catches (TACs) for different types of fish in their areas. Foreign vessels could fish within the 200-mile zone only if American ships did not take all of the TACs. Lowell Wakefield acted as an industry representative at UN Law of the Sea Conferences in 1974–1976, at which many of the concepts embodied in the 200-mile EEZs were discussed.[46]

Another UN Law of the Sea Conference in 1982 resulted in global recognition of 200-mile EEZs.[47] Objecting to some of the details set by the conference governing the management of the EEZs, the United States did not sign this convention, but did insist on its 200-mile economic exclusionary zone. The 1982 convention was implemented without American adherence in 1994. By then some 60 nations had signed it, 145 nations by 2003. Many Pacific Island nations declared 200-mile EEZs, and by the 1990s some were beginning to reap substantial benefits from them, as they leased fishing and mineral rights to people from other countries.[48]

Not all actions represented progress toward conservation, however. A UN Law of the Sea Conference in 1993 failed to regulate fishing on the high seas beyond the 200-mile limit. This meeting was called the UN Conference on Straddling Stocks and Highly Migratory Fish Stocks. A follow-up meeting in 1995 gave rights to manage such fish to regional fishery organizations, but it gave those organizations no right to exclude anyone from fishing and gave the bodies no enforcement powers. The 1993–1995 conferences were toothless in their outcomes.[49]

None of these agreements ensured that global or regional fishery resources would be used in a sustainable manner, and many world fisheries, including some in the Pacific, were overfished. Too often nations controlling the 200-mile EEZs permitted more fishing than fish stocks could sustain, and beyond the 200-mile limits just about anything went. New England's cod fishery, which in the mid-1970s accounted for 23 percent of the entire global fish catch, crashed a few years later and has not recovered.[50] One careful investigator observed in 1998, "After a steady rise from twenty million tons per year just after World War II, the production capacity of the ocean peaked at 90 million tons in 1988 and then flattened out. The catch has grown no further despite the fact that the world's fishing nations are pumping $230 billion a year into fleets to produce seafood worth about $175 billion."[51]

By the 1990s, the world's fisheries were in a state of crisis. As early as 1992, *U.S. News & World Report* carried a lengthy article on "the rape of the oceans," exposing to the general public what was already well known by fishing-industry members. Three years later, the *Economist* reported that navies around the globe were gearing up to defend fishing rights. An article in the same journal in 2002 observed, "The world's fish catch may be much smaller than previously thought." In 2003, the *Economist* wondered if it was "the ocean's eleventh hour" for fishing. There were valid reasons for concern. According to the American Academy for the Advancement of Science, the global fish catch of 2000 was only half that of fifty years before, despite a tripling of the world's fishing effort. In June 2005, a thousand scientists signed a letter asking the UN to declare a moratorium on industrial fishing techniques, which they suspected were sweeping the high seas clean of fish. The letter was submitted to the UN Law of the Sea Conference in Costa Rica.[52]

Alaskan fisheries experienced roller-coaster rides in the 1980s and 1990s. There was tremendous optimism that the proclamation of a 200-mile EEZ there would aid the fisheries. *Fortune Magazine* exuded faith in 1979 that "opportunities in the northern Pacific region appear almost boundless."[53] And, indeed, the Alaskan king crab catch did reach new heights in the late 1970s. But then it crashed in the early 1980s, falling by 90 percent in 1981 alone. The catch recovered somewhat later in the 1980s, only to collapse again in the mid-1990s.[54] No one fully understood the dynamics of the king crab population as the twenty-first century opened, but research showed that developments in different fisheries were interrelated and suggested that a seemingly small change in climate might have "cascaded" in its effects to produce large changes in them.

A possible scenario went as follows. There was a rise in the temperature of Alaskan waters amounting to 2°C in 1977. The warmer water caused plankton to disappear. Tiny copepod and krill, which feed on plankton, soon also disappeared. Shrimp and crab, deprived of their food, nearly vanished—hence the king crab crash in the early 1980s. Nor were they the only species affected. Lacking food, Steller sea lions declined in numbers. There were about 300,000 sea lions in Alaskan waters in the 1960s, but only 60,000 by the 1990s; and in 1997 the Steller sea lion was declared an endangered species. Killer whales, which had fed mainly on sea lions, turned instead to sea otters. In the 1980s, there were about 100,000 sea otters living along the Aleutian chain, but by 2000 just 6,000 remained.[55]

As a result of their continuing problems, many in the king crab industry had in the early 2000s come to favor the establishment of Individual Transferable Quotas (ITQ), also called Individual Fishery Quotas (IFQ), for fishermen going after crabs. Successful as a conservation measure in fisheries in Iceland, New Zealand, and some other nations, ITQs gave fishermen property interests in their fishery resources, a nearly assured percentage of the TACs. The ITQs thus placed fisheries on sustainable bases.[56] Successful in the Alaska halibut fishery, ITQs were extended to the state's snow and king crab fisheries as well, even to the extent of giving some ITQs to processors who received delivery of catches.[57]

Not all species suffered. Salmon, which adjusted better to the warmer water than did king crabs, exploded in numbers. Recovering from their low points in the 1950s and 1960s, salmon catches rose in later decades, again for reasons not completely understood. American fishermen, protected from foreign competition by the 200-mile EEZ, swarmed into Bristol Bay in the Bering Sea and other Alaskan waters. They often entered into joint-venture agreements with Soviet, Japanese, and Korean companies. Americans caught the salmon (and halibut and pollack), which they then sold to factory ships owned by foreigners for processing. By the mid-1990s, the catch was too large. The number of salmon landed in Alaska rose from 22 million in the mid-1970s to 217 million two decades later. In 1996, the *Wall Street Journal* reported that "Alaska is awash in salmon." Record Alaskan catches, along with the development of fish farming for salmon in some nations, glutted world markets. Prices plummeted, leading Alaskan officials to conclude, once again, that their state's salmon industry was on the ropes.[58] Their very success also brought fishermen into conflict with Alaska's oil prospectors, setting the stage for additional conservation controversies.

Fish and Oil

Although drillers had discovered oil and gas in Alaska earlier, it was Atlantic Richfield's announcement in 1968 that its roughnecks had hit paying quantities of oil at Prudhoe Bay on Alaska's North Slope that set off the state's oil boom. The discovery turned out to be mammoth, the largest ever found in

North America and the twelfth largest in the world, ten billion barrels of re-coverable oil. (By way of comparison, an earlier gigantic field, the East Texas Field, had contained about two billion barrels of petroleum.)[59] There were considerable technical challenges in developing the Prudhoe Bay field: how to drill in the frozen arctic and how to transport the crude oil to market. Equally daunting were political challenges, especially how to deal with land claims by Alaskan Natives. Once these matters were addressed, the success of the oil companies on the North Slope led the firms to look intensively for petroleum throughout Alaska, including the state's continental shelf. This quest brought oilmen into conflict with fishermen.

The state of Alaska sold oil-drilling leases on 179 tracts of North Slope land to several consortia of oil companies in the fall of 1969 for a whopping $900 million. All of the previous twenty-two oil leases had brought in less than $100 million to the state's coffers. Alaskans immediately had visions of what the oil bonanza could finance: schools, hospitals, community centers, roads, and scholarships—the list seemed endless. Technical problems, while formidable, could, most believed, be overcome. A long-distance pipeline, the Trans-Alaska Pipeline System (TAPS), would carry the oil south to a terminal at Valdez, a warm-water port not far from Anchorage. However, long-standing land claims put forward by Alaskan Natives for some of the land that the pipeline had to cross halted construction of TAPS. Claims also called into question the matter of future leases for oil exploration and production. Until the claims were settled, no development could occur.[60]

What followed was a scramble to craft congressional legislation to deal with and extinguish native claims. Many parties needed to be satisfied: Alaskan Natives, federal and state government officials, oil-company executives, Alaskan businessmen and workers, and environmentalists. Historian Peter Coates, who prepared a comprehensive account of North Slope oil development, observed, "The pipeline proposal spawned a debate commensurate to the size of the project . . . the most passionately fought conservation battle in American history since the controversy (1908–1913) over the city of San Francisco's proposal to dam Hetch Hetchy Valley in Yosemite National Park to provide itself with a water supply from the Sierra Nevada."[61] For three years, proposals were bandied about Congress, until the passage of the Alaska Native Claims Settlement Act (ANCSA) in 1971. ANCSA gave Alaskan Natives title to 40 million acres of their state's public domain, provided them with $963 million in compensation for the settlement of all land claims, and established twelve regional corporations owned by Alaskan Natives to administer this settlement.[62] ANCSA also called for an additional 80 million acres of Alaska's public domain to be set aside for public purposes. This last provision led to renewed debate among environmentalists, business leaders, and others inside and outside of Alaska for nearly a decade, until issues were resolved with a second major piece of congressional legislation, the Alaska National Interest Lands Conservation Act (ANILCA) of 1980. ANILCA set aside 104 million acres of Alaska's public domain for national parks, wild-life refuges, national monuments, conservation areas, and wild and scenic rivers.[63]

With native land claims addressed and with land issues in general settled, pipeline construction could begin. Authorized by Congress in 1974, TAPS was quickly built, and oil began flowing in 1977.[64] By 1980, oil revenues ac-counted for 90 percent of the state of Alaska's income, and a decade later still comprised around 80 percent of state revenues. The success of drilling on the North Slope led to a surge in interest in oil exploration elsewhere, including possible underwater reserves in the state's continental shelf. Much of that interest focused on drilling in the continental shelf north of Prudhoe Bay, but many other regions or, as they were called in the oil industry, "basins," attracted notice.

The same principles that regulated Alaskan fisheries governed oil explo-ration and production on Alaska's continental shelf, but specific laws regu-lated the actual granting of oil and gas leases. State governments regulated leasing and drilling on the continental shelf three miles out to sea, with the federal government doing the same at distances beyond the three-mile limit. Congressional legislation governed leasing and drilling by companies be-yond the three-mile limit, and those terms were often followed by state gov-ernments setting terms for near-shore leases. Under the terms of the Outer Continental Shelf Lands Act of 1953, the Department of the Interior sold leases on the basis of a cash-bonus bid plus an annual royalty on produc-tion fixed at one-sixth of the value of that production. Twenty percent of the bonus bid had to accompany the bid, with the remaining 80 percent paid, along with the first year's royalty, when the lease was assigned. Oil companies were given five years to begin developing leases, or forfeit the leases. If oil was found, leases were generally extended for as long as oil (and/or gas) was produced.[65]

Leasing laws changed in 1978, when Congress passed the Outer Conti-nental Shelf Lands Act to amend the bonus-bid system required in the 1953 legislation. The 1978 law allowed the Department of Interior more flexibility in structuring leases. Pushed by environmentalists in the wake of a major oil spill in California's Santa Barbara Channel and passed over the protests of most oil companies, this law stressed the need for "orderly" and "balanced" oil development, with more protection for marine and coastal environments. At the same time, the Alaska Legislature enacted a similar law designed to give state officials more leeway in arranging near-shore leases and increasing its revenues from those leases, an action again taken over the protests of oil companies. The state and federal laws specified eight possible bidding systems and tightened government regulatory controls over the oil companies.[66]

Under this mélange of laws, development of oil and gas on America's continental shelf proceeded. The earliest offshore production occurred just off the coast of California in 1896. A major oil field was developed in the Gulf of Mexico in 1938 and another one there in 1947. By 1976, some 12,605 wells in federal waters had produced 3.6 billion barrels of oil and 24 trillion cubic feet of gas.[67] In Alaska, the continental shelf beyond the huge North Slope strikes attracted the most attention from both oil company executives and governmental officials during the 1970s and 1980s.[68] It was under the waters of the Chukchi and Beaufort Seas that the greatest quantities of offshore oil and natural gas were expected to be found.[69] Even so, considerable notice went to continental shelf regions in south-central Alaska, the Aleutian Islands, and parts of the Bering Sea. Cook Inlet, the Kodiak Basin, and the North Aleutian Shelf, along with a number of basins in the Bering Sea seemed promising.[70] In fact, a few were already being developed by oil companies, and these actions brought them into conflict with well-established fisheries businesses.

Offshore oil leasing and drilling began early in Cook Inlet. Between 1959 and 1974, the state leased 1.9 million acres there, and the Cook Inlet Basin had yielded 700 million barrels of oil and 743 billion cubic feet of natural gas by 1976. Already in the 1960s, offshore wells and wells on the adjacent Kenai Peninsula were pumping $50,000 per day in taxes and royalties into the state's coffers. Small oil spills occurred as a result of this activity. In the decade after 1965, some 223 "incidents" dispersed 10,011 barrels of oil onto the inlet's water. Although some environmentalists had their doubts, most Alaskans accepted the spillage as a small price to pay for what they viewed as economic progress.[71]

Despite the development of offshore oil production there, Cook Inlet remained a very productive fishing area. Cook Inlet, and especially its Kachemak Bay, it will be recalled, had been the scene of many fishing-gear conflicts in the 1950s. By the mid-1970s, Cook Inlet was producing annual salmon catches totaling 4,600 metric tons worth $6.9 million to fishermen, king crab catches of about 2,000 metric tons valued at $1.8 million, catches of shrimp coming to 2,500 metric tons worth $1.2 million, along with catches of halibut, herring, and some other types of crab and fish. The bulk of these catches came from Kachemak Bay and nearby Kamishak Bay.[72] Those catches, many feared, might be damaged by oil spills likely to accompany increased oil exploration, drilling, and production. A spill resulting from a tanker discharging ballast crude oil into the ocean near Kodiak Island in 1970 sullied 1,000 miles of beaches in the northern Gulf of Alaska, killed 10,000 sea birds, and oiled fishing gear. This incident turned many fishermen against oil developments at sea.[73]

In the 1970s, additional government plans for offshore oil activities caused heated disputes in Cook Inlet. Controversies first revolved around the state of Alaska's offer to sell oil and gas leases to 93,000 acres in Lower Cook Inlet, including 5,000 acres in Kachemak Bay, in late 1973. This offer created what historian Daniel Nelson has rightly called "a firestorm."[74] Fishermen complained bitterly that state officials ignored their protests and failed to keep them informed of plans for the region. They pointed out that the state refused to hold public hearings on proposed oil and gas leases, even when biologists for the Alaska Department of Fish and Game (ADFG) and the National Marine Fisheries Service (NMFS) requested a delay to examine the impact of oil and gas activities on fishing. An ADFG scientist observed, "We believe, and have evidence to support our belief, that Kachemak Bay . . . is one of the most highly productive marine environments in the world," and a NMFS scientist added that one of the proposed drilling locations was "located in a spot that is a very critical habitat" for shrimp. Beyond objecting that oil exploration and production might pollute fishing waters, fishermen added that increased boat traffic would lead to the accidental destruction of fishing gear, especially crab pots.[75] Nonetheless, the leases won approval in December 1973.

That was far from the end of the matter. Local fishermen, some state legislative leaders, themselves fishermen, and scientists raised an increasing number of questions about the compatibility of oil and fish.[76] A 1975 analysis by Alaska's leading economist supported the fishermen, noting that oil and gas "operations and transportation will inevitably cause varying degrees of destruction to fisheries, chiefly through contamination of water by chronic discharges and accidents." The report suggested that the state might earn greater revenues in the short term from oil and gas leasing than from taxes on fishing, but pointed out that the oil resources would be exhausted in ten to twenty years, whereas fish were a renewable resource and thus a better long-term bet for Alaska's economy.[77]

What to do with Cook Inlet became a hotly contested issue. Eager for revenues, the state went ahead with its leasing plans for the inlet in the mid-1970s. This was several years before the huge royalties started rolling in from the North Slope leases, and Alaska's government needed income. Fishermen initially failed in their effort to halt the drilling when an Alaska district court refused to hear their case against the leasing. Still, their protests continued and found a political solution, which altered how the development of Cook Inlet was carried out. With a new governor elected, in part through a promise to be more environmentally sensitive than earlier governors, the state legislature designated Kachemak Bay as a marine sanctuary in 1976. Oil and gas leasing was prohibited. Over the next few years, the state used its powers of eminent domain to buy back leases.[78]

The federal government thus inherited a legacy of protest when it began leasing oil tracts beyond the three-mile limit in Cook Inlet. First made in 1977, federal leases covered 495,000 acres and brought in nearly $400 million to the nation's treasury. A second and even larger sale of leases was set for 1981. However, protests and lawsuits from fishermen and environmentalists proved effective in imposing fairly strict restrictions on the development of the tracts covered by the 1977 leases and in delaying indefinitely leasing the tracts proposed in 1981.[79] In its environmental impact statement for the proposed 1981 leases, the federal government recognized that there was "a large potential for resource-conflict between the oil and gas industry and commercial and sports fisheries." The 1978 Outer Continental Shelf Lands Act established a Fishermen's Contingency Fund of $1 million to reimburse commercial fishermen for any damage to their vessels or gear due to oil and gas activities.[80]

Much of the conflict between fishermen and oilmen shifted to the Bering Sea in the 1980s and 1990s. As early as 1981, a journalist observed, "Like a new species colonizing a remote bay, the oil folks were starting to hit Dutch Harbor." Five of the seven basins there—the Navarin Basin, the North Aleutian Basin, the St. George Basin, the Norton Basin, and the St. Matthew-Hall Basin—were believed to contain commercially recoverable amounts of oil. The Minerals Management Service (MMS) of the Department of Interior estimated that the basins contained 2 billion barrels of oil and 45 billion cubic feet of gas. Many of the basins were also prime fishing grounds for king crabs, salmon, halibut, herring, and other fish species. An investigation by the Department of the Interior reported in 1979 that the St. George Basin "supports a large and growing king crab fishery," that the Northern Aleutian Shelf (western Bristol Bay) "is the immigration route for the majority of the sockeye salmon that support the largest salmon fishery in the world," and that the Navarin Basin had "an expanding king crab fishery." All of these fisheries would be affected by oil and gas development activities, as would subsistence fishing by Alaskan Natives. Nonetheless, the federal government sold leases for 2 million acres in the mid-1980s.[81]

The sales led to conflict with fishermen. Graffiti in the men's room at the bar of the King-Ko Inn in King Salmon on Bristol Bay read, "Stick your oil money up your ass, Bristol Bay will sail again." When wells in most of the basins produced insignificant amounts of oil and gas, exploration in those regions lessened. Abetting the decisions of oil companies to stop drilling was an action taken by environmentalists. In 1985, actor Robert Redford's Institute for Resource Management, a nongovernmental organization (NGO), interceded to work out a compromise among oilmen, fishermen, environmental groups, and Alaskan Natives on how to develop much of the continental shelf underlying the Bering Sea. Some 240 million acres in the Navarin Basin, the St. George Basin, and Norton Sound, especially sensitive near-shore areas, were placed off-limits to oil and gas development. In return, environmental groups and fishermen agreed not to oppose the leasing of 48 million offshore acres in other areas.[82]

Exploration then came to focus on the North Aleutian Basin on the edge of western Bristol Bay, one of the most productive fishing grounds and a region that was not subject to the agreement negotiated by Redford's organization. In 1988, oil companies bought twenty-three leases there. However, continuing protests from fishermen operating in those waters, a $1-billion-per-year fishery, led Congress to approve a one-year moratorium on oil and gas exploration there in 1989.[83]

There was, in fact, growing sensitivity on the part of MMS officials to the harm oil could do to fisheries. In 1989, it sponsored a symposium on that issue. MMS officials observed that "The coastal and offshore waters of the United States are a source of abundant natural resources." "This abundance," they further noted, "does not preclude conflict among those who use these waters." One of the papers presented at the conference specifically singled out the North Aleutian Basin as a region where "some impact assessments prepared by the U.S. Minerals Management Service have incorrectly predicted the adverse affects of oil spills by greatly underestimating the area covered by potential spills." The moratorium passed by Congress in 1989 was implemented by the MMS a year later. It was later extended one year at a time and currently remains in effect until 2012. The oil companies relinquished their leases in 1995. This was not quite the end of matters. The MMS began a five-year leasing program for part of Norton Sound in 2003, and the state of Alaska leased some near-shore areas for exploratory drilling.[84]

The Beringia Heritage International Park

The movement to create a Beringia Heritage International Park was another flash point in the northern Bering Sea and nearby regions during the 1990s. Proposed as a joint Soviet-American venture, the park, sponsors hoped, would celebrate the end of the Cold War and encourage the scientific study of the vast region of Beringia. "A Beringian park," observed a National Park Service (NPS) historian in 1988, "could be a showcase where the warmth of international cooperation offsets the arctic chill."[85] After promising beginnings, however, legislation to establish the park stalled in Congress, and no such park existed as the twenty-first century began. Instead, park advocates regrouped, started a series of joint Russian and American activities called the Shared Beringia Heritage Program, and renewed their efforts to set up an international park.

The proposed park was huge, encompassing the waters over and adjacent lands of an ancient land bridge that had once linked Alaska and Siberia. During extended cold periods in the past, tremendous volumes of water had been locked in ice and snow, causing the levels of seas and oceans to fall. The Bering Sea dropped by about 300 feet twelve to fifteen thousand years ago, opening a land bridge a thousand miles wide between Asia and the Americas. By the 1990s, Beringia was seen in scientific circles as having composed a coherent region extending from the Kolyma River in the Russian Far East to the Mackenzie River in the Northwest Territories in Canada. It was across this land bridge, nearly all scientists believe, that people first traveled to the Americas, and it was a large segment of this region that advocates wished to include in a Beringia Heritage International Park.[86]

Park ideas took several decades to attract meaningful support. Walter Orr Roberts, who had been a special consultant to President Harry S. Truman and who was the founding director of the National Center for Atmospheric Research in Boulder, Colorado, proposed the idea of a joint park in the 1960s. In an international climate colored by the Cold War little was immediately accomplished. Still, some steps were taken. In 1972, the United States and the Soviet Union signed an "Agreement on Cooperation in the Field of Environmental Protection" and set up a working group to investigate the "conservation and management of natural and cultural heritage[s]." That group developed "themes" to investigate further, and in 1987 one theme specified the "research, conservation, and management of the Beringian heritage" as a goal to be pursued. Meanwhile, the two nations agreed to treaties governing the management of migratory birds, whales, polar bears, fur seals, and fish in their northern waters. In 1987, an American woman was allowed to swim across the Bering Strait, and the next year Alaskan Natives were permitted to visit the Chukotka region in the Soviet Union across the strait from Alaska. In 1989, American and Soviet planning teams presented the concept of an international park during joint visits to native villages on both sides of the Bering Strait. Published as the *Beringian Heritage Reconnaissance Study* in 1990, the results of the work of the planning teams set the stage for an international agreement to create the park.[87]

President George H. W. Bush and Premier Mikhail Gorbachev signed a joint statement endorsing the establishment of an international park bridging the Bering Strait on June 1, 1990. Bush asserted that such a park would "preserve the unique natural, environmental, and cultural heritage of the Bering Sea region" and added, moreover, that it would serve as "a bridge of hope" between America and Russia. Gorbachev echoed Bush's sentiments, arguing that the park would help the two nations in "moving toward a healthier international environment." Legislation to establish the park was submitted to Congress in the fall of 1991. The measure authorized the president to designate an already existing 2.8-million-acre Bering Land Bridge National Preserve as the American portion of the park (with additional lands to be added later) as soon as a similar protected area was created by the Russians on the Chukotka Peninsula. Endorsed by the native population on the Chukotka Peninsula, park planning went ahead in Russia, with the Leningrad State Institute of Urban Planning as the agency designated to prepare actual park plans.[88] By way of contrast, park planning languished on the American side of the Bering Strait.

Congress did not act on the enabling legislation when several important groups opposed the establishment of the park. Only partly reconciled to the national legislation settling land issues in Alaska, oil and mining companies fought "locking up" any more Alaskan acreage in parklands. At the time American mining executives were pursuing the possibility of joint ventures with Russian counterparts and spoke against creating the park. The head of the Alaska Miners Association added, "We have no respect for the National Park Service," because he thought the NPS had broken promises to miners in the establishment of other national parks in Alaska. Then too, Alaskan Natives, unlike their Russian counterparts, were generally against the establishment of the park. As a member of the Inuit Circumpolar Conference explained, "Parks haven't always been good for us." Continuing, he observed that "park officials won't let us use snow machines to get to our fishing streams in the Bering Land Bridge National Preserve."[89] Representatives of the NPS belatedly realized that they had not done enough to urge interested parties to support park legislation. As they observed, the legislation failed to win approval in Congress in 1991, and "subsequent attempts to redraft the legislation with the cooperation of native groups in Northwest Alaska and conservation organizations were not successful."[90]

The evolving situation in Alaska with regard to the Beringia Heritage International Park provides a valuable contrast to the much more inhumane treatment meted out to Native Americans in the earlier creation of many national parks on the American mainland. In the establishment of the Yellowstone, Yosemite, Grand Canyon, and Glacier national parks in the late nineteenth and early twentieth centuries, Native Americans living on parklands were simply thrown out.[91] Nor did native groups always fare well in the establishment of national parks in Alaska.[92] However, times change, and, at least in the case of the Beringia Heritage International Park, the NPS came to recognize, as one of its spokespersons explained, "that it was necessary to encourage more local support and involvement in the activities that an international park designation would promote, before efforts to introduce legislation that would be supported by a wide range of interests would be successful." Organized Alaskan Natives, now full participants at the political table, could not be ignored.[93]

From the mid-1990s, the NPS made sustained efforts to involve Alaskan Natives in decisions about the proposed park. In 1996, it set up a five-member Beringia Panel to make recommendations on priorities for the funding of Beringia projects. Even though no park existed, the NPS received annual appropriations for a Shared Beringian Heritage Program. Two panel members represented the NPS, but the others were representatives of three of the twelve regional native corporations set up by ANCSA, corporations owned by Alaskan Natives in north and northwestern Alaska. The Shared Beringian Heritage Program stressed goals important to Alaskan Natives: "to provide for the continued opportunity for customary and traditional subsistence uses of resources within Central Beringia, and recognition of unique and traditional activities by indigenous people"; "the reestablishment of cultural traditions"; "to meaningfully involve indigenous people and local communities of the Beringia region in the administration and management of programs"; and "to encourage and assist in the return, retention, storage, display, and interpretation of native artifacts from the Beringian region in or near the communities from which they originated."[94]

By the early twenty-first century, Russian and American leaders had made renewed progress toward the creation of an international park, a sign of the modern reintegration of the Pacific. The NPS reported that several projects had been "developed and initiated at the local level," ranging in scope "from cultural celebrations to educational opportunities for village youths." An official of the NPS had also instituted a Beringia Days celebration every October in Anchorage to provide visibility for this work. After the collapse of the Soviet Union, the Russian Federation reaffirmed support for the park, and the regional Chukotka Administration established a Nature-Ethnic Park Beringia. The Chukotka Administration also commissioned a feasibility study for the creation of the Russian component of the Beringia Heritage International Park, which might encompass the Nature-Ethnic Park Beringia. The results of that study are due soon.[95]

Conclusions

The controversies surrounding fishing rights, oil exploration, and the creation of parks in Alaska illustrate how complex economic development and environmental issues have grown in the Pacific and in the world since World War II. State, national, and international governmental bodies were involved in working out arrangements among the various interest groups, and the number and variety of those groups had exploded from earlier times. Alaskan fishermen battled out-of-state companies, just as they had in territorial days, but more than in the past they also had to contend with Japanese and Russian competitors. Nor was that all. By the 1970s and 1980s, other industries, most notably the oil industry, found the Aleutians and the Bering Sea enticing, forcing fishing firms to seek agreements with companies from those industries. Much of this type of conflict had taken place between different interests seeking to use the public domain in earlier periods in American history. As historian Samuel P. Hayes has shown in his classic study of conservation during the Progressive Era, ranchers, farmers, timbermen, and others battled for rights over the public domain.[96]

More was involved in Alaska after World War II, however. Alaskan Natives gained seats at the political bargaining tables, as the recent fight over the Beringia Heritage International Park has amply demonstrated. Then, too, environmental groups and NGOs played expanding roles in the north. Interested in a broad spectrum of topics, these groups increasingly championed quality-of-life issues, such as the right of natives to continue using snow machines in their travels, as well as the conservation of natural resources.

Changing attitudes lay behind altered practices in Alaska with, again, events occurring along the Aleutians and in the Bering Sea serving as valuable barometers of those alterations. In their attitudes toward king crabs, those who established Wakefield Seafood closely resembled Americans surging west across the North American continent and into the Pacific in how they viewed the natural resources: they hoped to put them to immediate profitable use, with little thought for the future. Whalers, oilmen, timber operators, and others in Alaska shared that point of view as they developed their industries, and some continue to adhere to that outlook to the present day. Old attitudes died hard. In 2005, Alaskans expanded their hunting of wolves from airplanes, a form of hunting renewed in 2003 after years of being outlawed.[97] New ways of thinking, on the other hand, resulted in a changed appreciation of Alaska's environment, including the state's natural resources. Some Alaskans, often prodded by out-of-state individuals and groups, adopted a longer-term approach to resource management. Lowell Wakefield came to recognize that new methods were needed. Writing in 1965, he observed in a thoughtful essay, "Commercial fishing has not progressed very far beyond buffalo hunting on the Western Plains." However, he continued, "just as homestead rights and grazing leases have stabilized and greatly increased production from the plains, some such approach will one day come for the oceans. . . . The sort of thing that I can picture will be fishermen's cooperatives."[98] What he was searching for, of course, was a way to break free from the "tragedy of the commons," a path, unfortunately, never fully followed, with today's world fisheries crisis as a result.

As Alaskans sought a balance between economic development and environmental preservation, they rejoined the Pacific economy and, more generally, the Pacific world. Alaskans had never completely left that world, but between about 1910 and 1940 they had been tied more closely to Washington, Oregon, and California than to other parts of the Pacific. World War II reaffirmed Alaska's full Pacific presence, and after the conflict ties between Alaska and other Pacific regions were tightened. For example, much of the pulp from the Tongass National Forest went to Japan. No doubt North Slope oil would have done so as well, had it not been for national legislation forbidding that trade. Salmon roe from the native fisheries in the Yukon was consumed in Asian-Pacific regions. The movement of people across national boundaries in the North Pacific may be just beginning. Alaskan Natives have paid ceremonial visits to Chukotka. Less heralded has been the movement of Russians back into Alaska. In the 1960s, a small group of *Staroveri* (Old Believers), whose ancestors had left Russia in the 1800s, established several villages on the southern Kenai Peninsula and near Kodiak. Some became "major participants" in the Bristol Bay salmon fishery. Moreover, with the breakup of the Soviet Union, "many people" emigrated from Russia to Alaska, where they took up jobs, including some in the salmon industry.[99]

CHAPTER 5

Southern Japan during
American Occupation

Hiroshima and Okinawa

At 8:15 a.m. on August 6, 1945, an atomic bomb destroyed Hiroshima. Michihiko Hachiya, the director of the Hiroshima Communications Hospital, described what he saw in his diary: "The morning was still, warm, and beautiful . . . shimmering leaves, reflecting sunlight from a cloudless sky, made a pleasant contrast with shadows in my garden." Then came the bombing: "Suddenly, a strong flash of light startled me . . . garden shadows disappeared. The view where a moment before all had been so bright and sunny was now dark and hazy." Hachiya quickly realized that his clothes had been blown away and that he had been injured by the bomb's blast. "To my surprise I discovered that I was completely naked," he recorded, "all over the right side of my body I was cut and bleeding." [1] Though injured, Hachiya was more fortunate than the tens of thousands of people immediately killed. The bomb leveled much of Hiroshima, and fires burned most of those parts of the city not immediately destroyed by the blast. Hiroshima's major business district, government and military centers, and some industrial and residential areas were obliterated. Only the port, because of its distance from the bomb's hypocenter, the point at which it exploded, survived unscathed. [2]

This chapter examines the rebuilding of Hiroshima, a process requiring decades to complete. It begins by looking at Hiroshima's development before 1945 and then explores the human and physical damage resulting from the atomic bomb as a prelude to examining the difficult choices made in rebuilding. Those choices involved environmental and economic trade-offs that have affected the city to the present day. Shinzō Hamai, Hiroshima's mayor, stands out as an influential political actor in the crucial late 1940s. National legislation passed by the Japanese Diet in 1949 with American support, for which Hamai strenuously lobbied, was essential in laying the groundwork for rebuilding. After assessing the impact of postwar planning on Hiroshima, the chapter describes recent efforts to turn part of Hiroshima into a high-technology city, a less successful venture in planning. While modeled to some degree on Silicon Valley, the attempt to create a technopolis helped Hiroshima's development very little, in marked contrast to the more successful high-technology efforts in South Korea. The chapter closes by comparing reconstruction in Hiroshima to that which occurred in Okinawa, where Americans played even larger roles.

This chapter investigates Hiroshima in the context of urban planning in Japan and American involvement in that planning. Until recently, scholarship on Japanese city planning, especially that available in English, has been limited. Andre Sorensen, a Canadian political scientist, however, has done a great deal to correct this situation. His *The Making of Urban Japan* presents a valuable overview of city growth and urban planning in Japan, emphasizing continuities, especially the centralized nature of such planning.[3] Japanese historians have made many of the same points. Yorifusa Ishida, for instance, has observed that city planning in Japan "had long been centralized under the national government" by the time of the Second World War and remained so after the conflict.[4] Other scholars have joined Sorensen and Ishida in explaining Japan's urban experience, especially postwar rebuilding. Still, much remains to be accomplished.

Looking specifically at Hiroshima, historian Cherie Wendelken has observed, "Surprisingly little has been written on the planning and rebuilding of Hiroshima."[5] The Japanese scholar who has studied Hiroshima's rebuilding most fully has observed, "Hiroshima shares some characteristics with other war-damaged cities, but, at the same time, together with Nagasaki, has its unique characteristics as an atomic bombed city."[6] One difference lay in the degree of American involvement in reconstruction, which was greater in Hiroshima than in most Japanese cities, although not as great as in Naha City on Okinawa. Another difference was the considerable amount of local initiative in reconstructing Hiroshima, especially in the early postwar years. While it is certainly true that national planners were important, so were people at the local level.

Hiroshima's Prewar Development

Before the mid-sixteenth century, few people were living at the future site of Hiroshima. A handful of fishermen inhabited hamlets loosely linked as an entity called "Gokason" (Five Villages) on islands in the delta of the Ota River where it poured into the Inland Sea. At that time, Niho, Eba, and Ujina (later Motoujina) were islands in a shallow bay. Connecting these islands and filling in the river delta created the space on which much of Hiroshima was later constructed. *Hiro* means wide and *shima* means island in Japanese, so Hiroshima may be translated as "broad island." [7]

Improvements began with the creation of Hiroshima as a castle town in 1589. That year, Terumoto Mori left Koriyama Castle in nearby Yoshida to build a new castle near the mouth of the Ota River. In 1590, he had the grounds for the castle, its moat, and the beginnings of a castle town laid out at Hiroshima. At the time, his family was seeking to extend its influence from its home base and hoped to control traffic on the Inland Sea from the new castle at Hiroshima. As the castle went up, a town developed around it. The castle lay at the center of the growing town, and planning by the Mori clan defined the use of urban spaces, as roads, bridges, and canals were constructed outward from the castle. Markets for fruits and vegetables and for handicrafts such as tatami mats and baskets operated in designated places, and neighborhoods developed that remained important until they were destroyed in 1945. However, in 1600 the Mori clan found itself on the losing side in a civil war that raged throughout Japan and was forced by the victorious Tokugawa clan to give up its control of Hiroshima and its castle. The end of the civil war ushered in a period of peace and political unity called the Tokugawa period in Japanese history, roughly the years 1600–1867. [8]

Dominated from 1619 by the Asano clan, allies of the Tokugawa, Hiroshima continued to develop as a castle town. The Asano family added land by filling in shallows in the Ota River delta and by leveling nearby hills. Hijiyama, Nihonshima, and Eba, all originally islands, became part of Hiroshima. Hiroshima developed a rich samurai or military culture as a castle town but, as was typical of castle towns in Japan, also possessed a commercial culture. In Hiroshima and the nearby area, trade and early industry focused on salt making, fishing, shipbuilding, and iron making. In the last industry, artisans exploited iron sands along streams in the mountains. Quarrying iron often resulted in the heavy flow of silt in the rivers, which became clogged and flooded, destroying the rice paddies of farmers downstream. This environmental issue was solved by refraining from mining during planting times. Eventually, mining upstream from Hiroshima was forbidden by the Asano leadership. All of these economic activities, together with nearby farming, brought growth to the town. Hiroshima had about seventy thousand inhabitants by the mid-1800s. [9]

During Tokugawa times, Japan had about two hundred castle towns like Hiroshima, of which some thirty to forty supported populations of at least ten thousand, as merchants and artisans moved in to serve them. The castle towns functioned as military and administrative centers, but they were also foci for economic development, at least into the 1800s, when smaller villages became relatively more important. The growth of many of the castle towns, including Hiroshima, represents a case in development from above. The local lords, called daimyo, following directions from the shogun, Japan's supreme military ruler, determined where the towns would be sited, how they would be laid out, and how they would function. The desires of the daimyo were, especially initially, more important than the free flow of social and economic forces.[10]

While some urban centers in Japan grew up in a haphazard manner, there was also a tradition of planning. In 645 A.D., the emperor constructed the port city of Naniwa, where present-day Osaka stands, with a gridiron street system modeled on the Chinese city of Chang-an. In 694, the succeeding emperor moved the capital to Fujiwara and again ordered a city constructed with a gridiron street pattern. Fujiwara soon became too small, and in 710 the capital was moved to Nara. Measuring about two and one-half by three miles in size, Nara was divided by a major north–south boulevard and subdivided into eighty districts of sixteen sections each. Finally, in 794 the emperor relocated the capital to Kyoto, where it remained until 1868. Kyoto, influenced by urban designs in China, was also laid out in a gridiron fashion, with a north–south boulevard separating the city into halves corresponding to the division of the government between the Ministry of the Left and the Ministry of the Right.[11]

Centralized urban planning was a major legacy of the Tokugawa period that would influence the rebuilding of Hiroshima. In castle towns like Hiroshima, daimyo were important to the selection of sites and in the determination of spatial layouts. In Japan's capitals, the emperor performed much the same functions. However, not all choices were made in a fully centralized manner. Merchants and artisans had some options and influenced some developments. Even daimyo had to consider their desires if they wanted to attract them to their castle towns and thus encourage economic development in their regions. So, although centralized decision making was typical of the Tokugawa era, the leaders making those decisions had to recognize the wishes of other groups in society.

In the 1850s and 1860s, when Japan was forcibly opened to expanded trade with the West, the Tokugawa regime lost control of the nation and modernization intensified. The Emperor Meiji officially returned to power and moved his capital from Kyoto to Tokyo in what was known as the Meiji Restoration of 1868. In fact, most of the political power in Japan was shared by a group of oligarchs and, a bit later in the nineteenth century, by a two-house legislature called the Diet, modeled on the British Parliament. As Japan modernized, the new regime launched successful wars against China in 1894–1895 and Russia in 1904–1905.[12]

Japan's expansive overseas policy brought prosperity to Hiroshima, which continued to develop as a military and economic center. Crucial was the construction of a major harbor at Ujina. Ignoring the opposition of fishermen who rightly feared the loss of traditional fishing grounds, the prefectural governor of Hiroshima, successor to the local daimyo, had the harbor built between 1884 and 1889. In the process, dredging operations formed some two million square meters of new land near what had been Ujina Island. Railroads linked the harbor and the city of Hiroshima to other parts of Japan. Its harbor and railroads made Hiroshima a major embarkation point for troops bound overseas in Japan's conflicts with China and Russia. In the Sino-Japanese War, the emperor moved to Hiroshima, where he set up imperial headquarters and planned military strategy. The Diet held meetings in a building on the west drill ground of the Hiroshima castle. Transportation links also made Hiroshima significant as a center of commerce and home to stock exchanges, banks, and mercantile establishments. Heavy industry came to Hiroshima. Large factories for Toyo Industries, a maker of cars and trucks, Mitsubishi Shipyards, Mitsubishi Machinery, Nippon Steel, and two rayon-making plants operated in Hiroshima's suburbs or at its harbor. As it matured, the city also hosted the Hiroshima Teachers' College in 1902 and the Hiroshima College of Science and Literature, later Hiroshima University, in 1929.[13]

With Hiroshima's growth came efforts at planning. About 141,000 people lived in the city in 1909 and 344,000 in 1940. Covering twenty-seven square kilometers in 1889, Hiroshima had expanded to sixty-nine square kilometers forty years later. As part of the formation of the new national government in the Meiji Restoration, old political designations were abolished and Japan was divided into large districts called prefectures and smaller districts—cities, towns, and villages—in the 1870s. The prefecture of Hiroshima was established, administered by a governor, with the town of Hiroshima consisting of four smaller subdivisions, each administered by a municipal officer. Hiroshima was officially recognized as a municipality by Japan's national government in 1889, along with thirty-eight other urban centers, and a physician was appointed as mayor. In that year, too, Hiroshima opened its first city hall.[14]

These changes occurred, as they did throughout Japan, in a top-down manner. Prefectural governors, mayors of cities, and other city officials were generally appointed, not elected by local residents. The Home Ministry of the national government tightly controlled regional and local governmental developments, with prefectural governors usually appointed from that ministry's roster of bureaucrats. Decisions made in Tokyo and prefectural offices were most important in shaping Japan's expanding urban areas. Those decisions emphasized efforts to "reduce the risk of fire, build broad, straight, paved streets, and improve the water supply," as Japan sought in urban affairs, as in other matters, to catch up with the West.[15]

The primacy of Japan's central government in urban planning was most apparent in the Diet's passage of City Planning and Urban Building Laws for the entire nation in 1919. Administered by the Home Ministry, the laws allowed little room for local variance. Growing out of earlier efforts to remake Tokyo and influenced by western ideas, these laws were a first attempt at a "comprehensive planning system that applied to whole urban areas and all major cities, that could structure activity on the urban fringe, and provide controls on individual buildings." With only minor changes, the measures remained in effect into the late 1960s.[16]

The 1919 laws had five major provisions. First, they divided urban lands into four zones: residential, commercial, industrial, and unrestricted. This effort came about a decade after a number of major American cities, led by New York and Los Angeles, had embraced zoning. However, the system in Japan differed from zoning in the United States in two major ways. In Japan, zoning was imposed from above—in the United States each city worked out its own zoning scheme—and was much less exclusive than American zoning schemes. That is, there was much greater intermixture of land uses in Japan than in the United States; for example, workers' housing continued to be built right next to factories. Second, the legislation set building codes for construction in the different zones—such as allowable building materials, building heights, and building lot coverage. Third, the laws established building lines by designating the edges of roads as building lines and stipulating that construction could occur only on lots fronting those lines. Fourth, the measures provided for the designation and construction of public facilities ranging from parks to sewer systems. Finally, the laws, expanding on earlier practices and stiffened by additional legislation passed in 1923, included land readjustment schemes, especially for the development of land on the outskirts of cities. The government could require landowners to donate up to 10 percent of their holdings for public purposes—such as the construction of roads—without compensation, the assumption being that they too would benefit from the improvements.[17]

The measures accomplished less than had been hoped in remaking cities. The destruction of much of Tokyo by an earthquake and fire in 1923 made it imperative that Japan's government focus planning efforts and funding on the capital for the rest of the decade, which left little in the way of national planning expertise and money for other cities. Moreover, the opposition of local landowners to land readjustment schemes stymied some planning efforts. Finally, despite the growth in population and size of their cities, many Japanese simply did not think that their areas yet needed much in the way of planning and found ways to delay its onset. Zoning was adopted only slowly, with just twenty-seven of the largest ninety-seven urban areas having established zoning plans by 1930.[18]

Hiroshima was one of the cities to adopt zoning. The City Planning and Urban Building Laws of 1919 were applied there in 1924 with the establishment of a city planning area, and zoning into residential, commercial, industrial, and unrestricted districts began. In 1928, city planning roads were designated, though not actually built, in the form of a grid pattern of east–west streets across branches of the Ota River intersecting with north–south streets running down each of Hiroshima's main islands. In 1933, areas were targeted for land readjustment, and in the late 1930s and early 1940s locations for public facilities, including parks and green areas, were added to Hiroshima's basic city plan. However, as was true in most of Japan's hinterland cities, planning in Hiroshima remained in the form of wishes, not reality—lines on maps, not actual roads, parks, or other facilities—before the Second World War. One major accomplishment, however, was begun as a wartime measure, the construction of a hundred-meter-wide boulevard traversing Hiroshima east to west as a firebreak.[19]

On the eve of Japan's entrance into World War II, Hiroshima was a major military, commercial, and industrial center and was becoming more spatially differentiated. Military headquarters were in the castle and buildings near Hiroshima's center, with barracks close by. A retail area blossomed not far from the castle, expanding from the Nakajima district that had existed in Tokugawa times. Industrial establishments grew up in several areas. The city's five largest manufacturing firms employed nearly half of Hiroshima's workforce and were located mainly on the outskirts of town. There were also hundreds of small manufacturing companies near the city center. Residential areas were interspersed with retail and industrial ones, but many were located a kilometer or two out from the city center, with developing suburbs such as Koi farther away. As Hiroshima's population mushroomed, governmental officials struggled to put in place an adequate infrastructure of roads and water and sewer lines, but they fell behind burgeoning demands. As in most Japanese cities, for example, human waste was collected by nightly "honey" wagons, for few sewer lines existed until well after the Second World War. As abortive efforts at providing parks suggested—many were planned, but none were built for lack of funding—there was also a growing concern about the quality of life for Hiroshima's residents. Shrubs and plants along or sometimes down the center of streets, and along river banks, government officials began to realize, were not adequate.[20]

Destruction and Recovery

Hiroshima continued to develop as a military center during the Second World War. Navy headquarters were established in the port of Ujina in 1942, with military units stationed up and down the coast near the city. As Japan suffered defeats in the Pacific, the home islands were divided into two parts for defense purposes. The Second General Headquarters, established to defend southern Japan from invasion, was set up in Hiroshima's castle just north of the city's center. There were 343,000–353,000 people in Hiroshima when the atomic bomb was dropped on the city. These consisted of a resident population of 280,000–290,000 and some 10,000 additional Japanese workers from nearby areas, including junior high school students brought to Hiroshima as laborers. On August 6, many were tearing down houses to prepare fire lanes. Hiroshima residents lived in one of only a handful of major Japanese cities not yet heavily bombed and were trying to prepare for expected fire bombing. There were also about 43,000 Second Army troops in Hiroshima.[21]

Exploded in the air 575 meters above the center of Hiroshima, the atomic bomb released energy equivalent to 12,500 tons of TNT. Heat, shock, and radiation waves shot out from the hypocenter, which formed a fireball. Intense heat from the bomb ignited many fires, and still others began when braziers, upon which many Hiroshima residents were preparing breakfast, overturned. The bomb's shock wave traveled outward at a speed of two miles per second for a short distance before slowing to the speed of sound, knocking down buildings in its path. Gamma rays carried radiation from the bomb outward for several kilometers. Later in the day, a "black rain," composed of water and minute particles of carbon from the fires, fell to the north and northwest of Hiroshima, carrying radiation well beyond the initial range of the gamma rays.[22]

The atomic bomb left much of Hiroshima as what observers at the time called an "atomic desert."[23] About five square miles of the city were laid waste. Hiroshima had been chosen as the number one target for the atomic bomb in part because of its topography. Aside from a few small hills, the city proper was flat. Moreover, it was surrounded on three sides by high hills that were expected to contain the blast and perhaps amplify it. Only a small area of Hiroshima near the hypocenter, the Danbara section that was partially shielded from the blast by the hill Hijiyama, survived without extensive damage. Elsewhere nearly all of the wooden buildings in Hiroshima were destroyed or extensively damaged, and most concrete buildings were damaged. Only 8 percent of the city's buildings remained usable after the blast and fire. Some 60,000 homes were destroyed or damaged. The destruction included the prefectural office, the city hall, most fire stations, the railroad stations, the post offices, the telegram and telephone offices, and the broadcasting station. Streetcars, electricity, gas, water, and sewage systems were put out of operation. Some six hundred of the city's smaller industrial facilities were destroyed near the city center. Larger factories on the outskirts of town were damaged but not destroyed. Eighteen emergency hospitals and thirty-two first-aid clinics were destroyed.[24]

The death toll was huge. The heat and shock waves killed outright many residents within one or two kilometers of the bomb's hypocenter. Thousands more died of radiation poisoning from the initial blast, and still others contracted deadly radiation poisoning when they entered Hiroshima from nearby areas to aid the bomb's victims or to look for lost family members. Some 90 percent of the doctors and 93 percent of the nurses in Hiroshima died in the blast, limiting the immediate availability of medical aid needed by survivors. The exact number of deaths caused by the atomic bomb in Hiroshima is a matter of debate. The most reliable estimate puts the number at about 130,000 dead by the beginning of November 1945. Radiation sickness continued to kill people after that date, and by 1950 perhaps 200,000 residents of the city had died as a result of the bomb. A significant number of the dead were non-Japanese: 30,000 Koreans forcibly brought to the city as conscript laborers, several hundred Chinese workers, an unknown number of the 3,200 Japanese Americans living in Hiroshima, ten American POWs, and a handful of Europeans.[25]

The death toll in Hiroshima was unprecedented, not in absolute numbers but as a proportion of a city's population. Heavy bombing of Tokyo in March 1945 resulted in about 100,000 deaths among the city's estimated population of 1 million, a death rate of 10 percent; the rate was as high as 20 percent in Tokyo's Fukagawa ward. However, in Hiroshima the death rate was even higher, 38 percent for men and 30 percent for women within the city's boundaries. About 80 percent of those within one kilometer of the bomb's hypocenter died. Deaths caused by the atomic bomb, combined with the movement of survivors out of Hiroshima after the bombing, depopulated much of the city. Between February 1944 and November 1945, Hiroshima lost 58 percent of its people.[26]

Less affected than the people in Hiroshima or the city's physical plant were Hiroshima's flora and fauna. Temperate in climate, and washed annually by summer monsoon rains, the city boasted a wide range of plants. Rice paddies dotted nearby fields, and orange groves blanketed hillsides on islands in the Inland Sea close to the city. The impact of the atomic bomb in this respect was relatively mild. Mosquitoes, birds, and carp in shallow ponds near the hypocenter were killed. So were many trees, plants, and shrubs. Rice plantings as far as four to five kilometers from the hypocenter were damaged, as was bamboo to a distance of five to six kilometers. However, little lasting damage occurred. Indeed, Hiroshima residents soon found that they could grow bountiful truck crops of tomatoes, eggplant, and soybeans in their city's ashes.[27]

Rebuilding the lives of the survivors and reconstructing the city of Hiroshima occurred in two stages. For several years the emphasis lay in providing for the immediate physical needs of the people remaining. Only from about 1949 onward did more long-term reconstruction take place.

Right after the bombing, survivors had to rely on their own resources and those of nearby communities. "Despite the desolation of the cities and the sufferings of the A-bomb victims, the response from the Japanese government was exceedingly passive," Japanese scholars have noted.[28] The magnitude of the war damage across their nation slowed relief efforts by the national government. American bombing and naval shelling had damaged 215 Japanese cities, not including those in the Ryūkyū Islands. In 1946, the Japanese government decided that 115 of those cities, including Hiroshima, were so heavily damaged that they needed to be rebuilt with central-government planning. The destruction in those cities covered about 160,000 acres and included 2.3 million houses. Some 331,000 citizens living in those areas had been killed, with another 427,000 injured. About 9.7 million Japanese were homeless. With the Japanese economy in tatters—in 1945 the nation's industrial output was only one-tenth of what it had been in 1930—funds simply were not forthcoming from the national government to help localities.[29]

There was also an initial reluctance to make special provisions for just one or two cities, Hiroshima and Nagasaki. In the face of tremendous overall national needs, the central government found itself stretched precariously thin. In Japan's capital of Tokyo alone, some 50,000 acres and 750,000 houses had been destroyed. Nor did Americans immediately step into the breach. As one scholar has correctly observed, "On the American side, there was a tendency to avoid placing any stress upon atomic bomb aftereffects, and when the problem was attacked, an emphasis was more on research than treatment." More generally, American authorities viewed the bombing of Japanese cities as just compensation for Japan's attack on Pearl Harbor and the high rate of casualties inflicted by Japanese forces in battles at Okinawa and Iwo Jima.[30]

The most urgent need was medical aid. Those few surviving doctors and hospitals in Hiroshima were overwhelmed. Typical was the situation at the damaged Red Cross Hospital, Hiroshima's most modern and largest, with six hundred beds. On the day of the bombing, about ten thousand people sought aid there. Only six of the hospital's doctors were able to function, as were just ten of the more than two hundred nurses. One of the few unwounded doctors soon found himself working as "an automaton, mechanically wiping, daubing, winding [bandages], wiping, daubing, winding."[31] He labored for three days with only brief snatches of sleep. Two days later, doctors at the Red Cross Hospital were joined by a fresh doctor and ten nurses from the nearby town of Yamaguchi, who brought with them sorely needed antiseptics and bandages. Several days later, another physician and a dozen more nurses came in from the town of Matsue. Even five weeks after the bombing, an American doctor visiting the hospital observed, "Rooms and equipment have been unbelievably damaged and there are many patients, again attended by the families, amid shattered surroundings."[32]

In the first weeks after the bombing, medical aid arrived in Hiroshima piecemeal. Military units from Ujina, the nearby islands of Ninoshima and Etajima, and the close-by naval base at Kure sent doctors and first-aid workers. Civilian first-aid teams from towns throughout the Hiroshima and Okayama prefectures followed. Fifty-three first-aid stations were established in school buildings one or two kilometers from the bomb's hypocenter. About a month after the bombing, Red Cross supplies, including fifteen tons of medical supplies, reached the city, and more followed later. Finally, help came from the American occupying forces that entered Hiroshima in numbers in early October, though a few teams of American doctors had arrived earlier.[33]

After medical care, water, food, and shelter were the most pressing needs. By the early afternoon on the day of the bombing, a filtration plant about two miles from the bomb's hypocenter was supplying parts of the city with some water. Nonetheless, this plant proved inadequate, since many of the city's underground pipes had been destroyed, making distribution difficult. Thirst remained a real problem in Hiroshima for months, and drinking polluted water from the Ota River threatened to spread disease. Food was another problem. Some produce came into Hiroshima from the surrounding countryside, but not enough. Nor was the amount of food supplied by aid organizations sufficient. Children went to newly reopened schools with empty stomachs.[34] Shacks in which to live went up helter-skelter. Aided by government-provided seeds, many survivors planted small truck gardens around them. An American army doctor working in the city recorded in a diary entry for mid-October, "bamboo scaffolding was beginning to appear on some of the larger buildings." Reconstruction had begun.[35]

Some essential city services were soon restored. Within two days of the bombing, electricity generated in an undamaged station in Danbara reached Ujina and that part of Hiroshima near its main railroad station. Railroad lines connecting the city to the outside world were back in operation within two weeks. Some streetcar and bus lines were reopened within three days of the bombing, and many of the telephone exchanges were back in operation at new locations within a week and a half. Radio broadcasting resumed the day after the bombing from a studio in the suburbs.[36]

The speedy restoration of these services was a remarkable achievement, and Hiroshima residents long employed the analogy of a phoenix rising from ashes when describing the rebirth of their city. There is considerable truth to this interpretation. Hiroshima did recover from its disaster fairly rapidly in certain respects. Part of the explanation lies in the fact that some of its infrastructure escaped destruction. Some transportation facilities, water plants, and so forth either survived or could be quickly repaired. Then, too, the prefectural and city governments were soon reestablished, developments crucial for a society accustomed to centralized decision making.

Setting up a new government began even while Hiroshima's ashes were still hot. On the evening of August 6, thirty surviving political, military, and business leaders, together with a representative of the prefectural police, formed a temporary prefectural government, which asked for help from the national government, aid from nearby prefectural governments, and assistance from military bases.[37] Together with what little remained of the military command in Hiroshima—most military bases and offices had been destroyed by the bomb, notably the Second Army Command at the castle—the prefectural government sought to coordinate relief activities. The marine transport commander from Ujina was especially important as well, as he became the acting police chief for Hiroshima. Military and prefectural authorities supervised the disposal of corpses and the provision of food and water from surrounding areas. Most military aid ended, however, with Japan's surrender on August 15.[38]

It was more difficult to reestablish a workable city government. Located just 1.2 kilometers from the atomic bomb's hypocenter, Hiroshima's city hall was gutted, leaving only the outer reinforced concrete structure standing. Most civil servants, some 280 in all, along with Hiroshima's mayor, died in the blast. By mid-August, about 80 city officials had joined their counterparts in the prefectural government in overseeing relief activities. In October, a reconstituted city assembly chose a new mayor, a politician who had long represented Hiroshima in the Diet. Described by some as "a sickly old man," the new mayor, Shichiro Kihara, was much less important than the person chosen as vice-mayor, who by his actions pushed Kihara aside.[39]

That man was Shinzō Hamai. Formerly a municipal section head born in Hiroshima, but educated at the elite Tokyo University, Hamai got things done. A young man in his thirties, he was a bundle of energy and an inspiration to those around him. At his home three thousand meters from the hypocenter at the time of the bombing, Hamai entered the city's center almost immediately after the bombing, only to find city hall in flames. As soon as the fire died down, he set up an office in one of the few rooms still intact and began working with prefectural and military authorities on relief measures. He worked, ate, and slept there for weeks, venturing forth only to oversee the provision of food and medical aid. Learning that Hiroshima's mayor was dead, he took over the reins of the city government without hesitation. "They say I shouted at and directed the deputy mayor and other officials who were my superiors," he later remembered, "I did not know I was doing this, as I was working like a man in a dream." Hamai was lucky; in Hiroshima's harbor he discovered a tanker filled with vegetable oil; in town he located a warehouse full of food; elsewhere he discovered military uniforms, which could be used as clothing. He distributed all of these supplies to aid those suffering in Hiroshima. Hamai was popularly elected mayor of Hiroshima in April 1947 and was a leader in the city's government for the next two decades.[40]

As they labored for Hiroshima's recovery, prefectural and city authorities did so in a new political framework. Laws passed by the Diet, at American insistence, reshaped relationships among the national, prefectural, and city governments, at least on paper. In an effort to encourage democracy, American authorities had the Diet pass a Local Autonomy Law in 1947, which for the first time provided for direct elections for prefectural governors and mayors of cities. It was under the terms of this law that Hamai won election. The law also expanded the powers of prefectural and city assemblies, especially by giving them some authority to levy taxes. The Home Ministry was abolished in the same year. Even so, the national government retained much of its power over urban planning. Prefectural governors often thought of themselves as serving the national government more than the local citizens who had elected them. A new Ministry of Construction took over the planning responsibilities of the old Home Ministry, with little change in personnel or ideas. Local governments could not issue bonds to fund improvement projects without approval from the Ministry of Construction. In short, little in the way of power really devolved to local citizens.[41]

Even with the reestablishment of a workable government, relief and rebuilding were more difficult than a celebratory view of Hiroshima's recovery suggests. Although many basic city services were available fairly soon, it required several years for Hiroshima to renew its population base. By 1946, people who had fled to the outskirts of the city and nearby towns were returning to the edges of Hiroshima's burnt-out sections. Most settled on the fringes. Far fewer moved into the area near the atomic bomb's hypocenter. As late as mid-1948, the large section of Hiroshima within two kilometers of the hypocenter contained only about 55 percent of its prebombed population. The suburbs were crowded. Sections of Hiroshima three or more kilometers out contained twice as many people as before the bombing. By the late summer of 1948, Hiroshima as a whole had regained the population it had possessed three summers before.[42]

Still other population changes occurred, which raised environmental justice issues, at least in hindsight. Hiroshima's *burakumin* or *eta*, a group of "untouchables" shunned by most Japanese as unclean because they slaughtered animals and worked with leather against the teaching of Buddhism, had lived in their own enclaves on the outskirts of town. With the bombing, other Hiroshima people moved into these areas and mingled with the *burakumin*. Similarly, the *burakumin* found opportunities to leave their ghettos. In like fashion, Koreans and Chinese in Hiroshima were reclassified as members of liberated nations with Japan's defeat, against whom the Japanese police were not entitled to act. They soon formed gangs that fought pitched battles with Japanese gangs around Hiroshima's main railroad station for control of a black market in food and other necessities. These alterations proved only temporary, however, as most of the Koreans and Chinese were soon repatriated and most of the *burakumin* retreated to ghettos.[43]

At the same time that Hiroshima was experiencing internal population shifts, the city was upset by the arrival of outsiders eager to take advantage of its destruction. Survivors of the atomic bomb, who came to be known as *hibakusha,* found themselves challenged by newcomers.[44] There was "a surge of 'outsiders'" who "quickly repopulated the city." These included "Hiroshima natives stationed elsewhere during the war, people deprived of their homes in overseas possessions now taken from Japan, others from the nearby Kansai area and especially from business districts around Osaka." Osaka had long been the mercantile center of Japan—the city was often characterized by Japanese as the mouth or, sometimes, the stomach of Japan—a metropolis known for the shrewd dealing of its inhabitants. Physically stronger than most of the *hibakusha,* who often suffered from radiation sickness, and coming from a part of Japan with an aggressive subculture, the newcomers from Osaka elbowed their way into Hiroshima.[45]

Life in Hiroshima during 1945 and 1946 was remarkably fluid. New groups jostled for power; recovery existed side by side with continuing problems over water and food; and lawlessness seemed to rule the day in parts of the city. Still, with aid beginning to come in from the outside, and through their own efforts, survivors managed to eke out an existence. In this day-to-day scramble to live, little care was taken for Hiroshima's natural environment. Nor did quality-of-life matters concern people. Only when their immediate problems of daily living were brought under control were residents able to return to a consideration of broader issues that had begun cropping up in the 1920s and 1930s, such as zoning and other forms of planning. When they did so, however, they accomplished more than did residents in most of Japan's other war-damaged cities.

The Hiroshima Peace Memorial City Construction Law

Even as officials in Hiroshima's city and prefectural governments were struggling with immediate relief, some began to think about long-term rebuilding. At first, suggestions about planning did not achieve much, for neither city, prefectural, nor national governments possessed the necessary resources. Only in 1949 did the Diet pass, with substantial American approval and support, a national law providing funding and authority for the rebuilding of Hiroshima and Nagasaki along new lines. Only later in the 1950s and 1960s, as economic prosperity returned to Japan, was that reconstruction accomplished.

As they approached reconstruction, those in Hiroshima faced new national measures that framed their actions. In December 1945, the Diet approved a Basic Policy for War-Damaged Areas Reconstruction Law, which set ambitious targets for urban rebuilding. This measure established guidelines for reconstruction, including strengthened land-use and building-standards controls. The measure urged that 10 percent of all urban areas be reserved as parks and that cities be surrounded by extensive greenbelts. In addition, it called for the creation of broad boulevards as firebreaks and streets capable of handling increased automobile traffic. In September 1946, the Diet passed the Special City Planning Act, which created a War Damage Reconstruction Board to examine rebuilding projects nationally and which altered the land readjustment provisions of earlier legislation. Under the 1946 legislation as much as 15 percent of a landowner's property could be taken without compensation by the state, 5 percent more than previously allowed. This part of the law, however, was altered at American insistence in 1949 to provide compensation to landowners for any lost properties. In 1954, two years after Japan had become fully independent, new legislation reversed the situation, once again setting the proportion of land that could be taken without compensation at 15 percent. Though amending details of the 1919 laws, the legislation of 1945–1946 did not fundamentally change them.[46]

New planning laws might have gone much further, as Japanese architects, planners, and others discussed sweeping changes. However, a lack of funding, ministerial disagreements in the national government, disputes over property ownership, and American opposition doomed more extensive planning. American occupation authorities, in particular, thought that flamboyant planning simply was not appropriate for their former enemy and concluded that retrenchment and austerity should be the order of the day for the Japan.[47] In the end, only about 70,000 of the 163,000 acres designated for reconstruction in Japanese cities were rebuilt in a planned way. Only a few wide boulevards were constructed, and only a handful of new parks and greenbelts were created. The zoning plan of just four designations, inherited from the 1919 legislation, remained in force.[48]

Hiroshima proved to be an exception to the rule that relatively little was accomplished in postwar Japanese cities—even more than in Nagasaki, which had weaker local political leaders. Because of its destruction by an atomic bomb, more notice, especially American attention, focused on Hiroshima than on most damaged Japanese cities. Then, too, Mayor Hamai, urged on by local citizens, argued forcefully for national aid. Even so, while more in the way of planned rebuilding was accomplished in Hiroshima than in most other Japanese metropolises, reconstruction was a tortuous path.

Soon after the bombing, surviving Diet members from the Hiroshima region set up a War Disaster Restoration Committee, which in turn established a War Disaster Restoration Group composed of business and political leaders in Hiroshima. The group, according to a city publication, "stimulated public discussion on the restoration work and generally strengthened the commitment to vigorously pursue the reconstruction goals."[49] But what would those goals be?

In late 1945 and early 1946, well before the Diet passed the Special City Planning Act, both the city and prefectural governments began grappling with the issue of what type of city Hiroshima would become. Less damaged than the city government, the prefectural government made preliminary reconstruction plans in very late 1945, led by Satoshi Nagoshima, who had been involved in urban planning at Nagoya. City officials soon followed this lead. In January 1946, a Hiroshima Restoration Bureau (sometimes called the Reconstruction Office) was set up as a new section within the city government, headed by a civil engineer with experience in city planning. Within a month, this section of the city government was making recommendations to the mayor. Cooperation between prefectural and city officials followed. In February 1946, the prefectural governor invited a number of the city's leaders to a Hiroshima Restoration Symposium to discuss plans for Hiroshima's future.[50]

At that symposium, Hiroshima residents expressed a wide variety of views. A writer testified that he hoped that the banks of Hiroshima's rivers would "become green areas and parks" and that trees would be replanted throughout the city. Housing should be built, he observed, on the outskirts of Hiroshima for "the A-bomb victims who are now compelled to live in shacks." A painter echoed his thoughts about greenbelts and added that he wanted Hiroshima to become "a modern city displaying the highest quality of original Japanese culture." The head of broadcasting for NHK in Hiroshima hoped that culture would not be lost sight of in the rebuilding and called for the construction of libraries, movie theaters, and playhouses. A Buddhist priest urged that major roads be immediately rebuilt and that Buddhist temples be constructed in the various sections of town, where they could be used as community centers.[51]

Not everyone favored reconstructing Hiroshima along new lines, or
even rebuilding the city at all. The deputy mayor of nearby Kure City stated
that he wanted "to keep the vast expanse of the burned-out area intact as
a memorial graveyard for the sake of everlasting world peace" and added
that he had "reservations about building a city on the place where countless
numbers of people ha[d] died." In fact, he thought it would be a good idea to
"search for a new place in the suburbs and construct a new Hiroshima there."
The president of Asahi Industries urged the preservation of an area within
a two-mile radius of the bomb's hypocenter as ruins, with a new city built
outside of those limits. A scholar of religion added that he was "opposed to
the idea of rebuilding Hiroshima as a large city."[52]

Debates continued at meetings of the city government at which a broad
spectrum of ideas was floated. Some thought that Hiroshima's future lay with
tourism to its nuclear wasteland. Others argued that the city should become
mainly a governmental center. Still others believed that Hiroshima should
be made into an Asian Venice, with canals connecting the branches of the
Ota River upon which imported gondoliers might ply their craft. A few suggested that Hiroshima be rebuilt as a Japanese Monte Carlo, with casinos for
the wealthy. One person urged that Pablo Picasso be invited to Hiroshima to
preside over the establishment of an artist colony.[53]

Foreigners also offered advice. Major S. A. Jarvis, an Australian adviser
greatly influenced by American city-beautiful ideas, played a significant role.
Building on plans put forward at the various conferences, he urged Hiroshima residents to think big in reconstructing their city. Tam Deling, an
American park planner, was among the first to suggest the preservation of
bombed-out buildings near the hypocenter as a memorial. Miles Born, the
vice president of the United Press, was among the first to urge the construction of a Peace Park in the Nakajima district.[54]

For a while, all things seemed possible. Nonetheless, little was immediately accomplished, for funding was not available. Revenue from taxes fell by
85 percent in Hiroshima in the years right after the bombing, and rents and
public fees dropped 75 percent. The city government had to depend even
more than in the past on funds from Japan's national government for its
operations. City officials estimated that they needed at least $6 million to
initiate planned reconstruction, but they had only $200,000.[55] When city
officials appealed to the national government for a special subsidy in the
summer of 1946, they were rebuffed. Strapped for funds, the Diet had no
money to spare.[56]

Even so, planning ideas survived. Late in 1946, the national government's

War Disaster Restoration Institute called upon the architect Kenzō Tange, then just thirty-three years of age, to develop a plan for Hiroshima. Born in 1913, Tange graduated from the University of Tokyo in 1938. After working for four years in the office of an important disciple of the Swiss modernist Le Corbusier, he returned to the University of Tokyo to study city planning. A believer in discipline in planning, Tange thought that cities should be designed to expand along straight lines and not be allowed to grow in a hodgepodge fashion. Influenced greatly by Le Corbusier, he thought that form should follow function. Also like Le Corbusier, he believed in the value of large "brutalist" buildings to impress the public. In 1945 Tange was an associate professor at Tokyo University serving part-time as a land-use planner for the national government. After working on a plan for Hiroshima, he would go on to other noteworthy projects: a Tokyo Plan for an assembly hall, park, and two towers in 1960; Tokyo's Olympic stadium in 1964; the Osaka Expo 70 in 1970; a new Tokyo city government complex in 1991; and the Fuji Television Building in 1996. Outside of Japan, Tange was well known for work in Singapore, the United States, China, and Western Europe. In 1987, he became the first Japanese to win the coveted Pritzker Architecture Prize. Upon his death in 2005, his obituary in the *New York Times* observed that "Tange may best be remembered for his transformation of Hiroshima."[57]

For Hiroshima, Tange urged the construction of a major east–west boulevard one hundred meters wide stretching across the city from Hijiyama to the suburb of Koi. The boulevard would facilitate the flow of traffic and act as a firebreak. A second boulevard was planned to cross the southern section of the city. Trunk roads would run down the length of each island. Tange also called for the building of numerous parks, including a seaside park at Ujina, and the preservation of green areas along Hiroshima's riverbanks. Open squares and plazas would, Tange hoped, dot Hiroshima's landscape. His plan also called for an airport at Kanon. Few of these ideas were brand-new. The boulevard and street system had been proposed before the World War II and had been revisited at the various symposia and meetings in early 1946. One boulevard had already been partly constructed as a firebreak during the war. Many Hiroshima residents had begun thinking of the need for more parks and open spaces.[58] While unable for financial reasons to implement Tange's plan in 1946, Hiroshima's city and prefectural governments won approval for it from the national government as the guide for future development. They also agreed to the terms of the Special City Planning Act passed by the Diet in that year, which reinstituted zoning in the city. City officials later labeled the return to zoning "the start of reconstruction in Hiroshima."[59]

Rebuilding had in fact already begun, with, however, little adherence to Tange's plans or zoning of any sort. When some commentators suggested that Hiroshima be abandoned as an urban site, Mayor Hamai noted with pride that people were constructing shacks and shops amid the ashes.[60] "Without inquiring too closely into property rights or paying too much attention to the city administration's blueprints," noted one contemporary observer, "the homeless built house after house." This construction was done on an ad hoc basis: "First a post would be driven into the chosen plot, and to this would be nailed a board bearing the future householder's name, electrical cables would be connected, only the most conscientious citizens bothering first to obtain permission of the Electricity Workers, and in three or four weeks yet another family had a roof over its head." A reporter for the U.S. Army newspaper *Stars and Stripes* concluded that Hiroshima resembled a Wild West mining camp during a gold rush.[61] A shopkeeper later recalled how he had evaded restrictions: "There was a law at first, that no building covering an area more than fifteen tsubo [roughly 400 square feet] could be constructed. Well, I had enough property, so I built three buildings of fifteen tsubo each—and then later I knocked the walls down between them and had a store.... That's the way we had to do things in those days."[62]

Even as they started reconstruction, Hiroshima residents began to agree on an ideological mission for their city: that it be known as a "City of Peace." On August 6, 1946, sirens were sounded all over Hiroshima, and people stopped whatever they were doing to observe a minute of prayer for *hibaku-sha*. A simple ceremony was held in front of a tower built in remembrance of the souls of the dead. A year later, Mayor Hamai established the Hiroshima Peace Memorial Service held at what would become Hiroshima's Peace Park, a dignified convocation. Hamai read the first "Peace Declaration," in which he stated that nuclear weapons "must lead us to the realization of [the need for] unconditional peace and to the birth of a new way of life and a new world." General Douglas MacArthur, the Supreme Commander GHQ, sent a message saying, "The sufferings of the Day of Destiny will act as a warning to people of all races." A United Press reporter used the expression "No More Hiroshimas" in his writing. Published in *Stars and Stripes* and then reprinted in many American newspapers, those three words became the motto for Hiroshima. Even so, the Remembrance Day took on something of a carnival atmosphere in 1947, with jazz music being played over loudspeakers and the use of flashing neon signs to advertise goods in "atomic shops" of all kinds.[63]

Only in 1948 was August 6 fully institutionalized as a peace memorial day. "I pray at the bottom of my heart," intoned Mayor Hamai in his annual "Peace Declaration," that "No More Hiroshimas will be created on this earth." Hamai may not have initially supported the establishment of August 6 as a special day. According to some accounts, he did so only after the head of the newly formed Association for the Advancement of Tourism for Japan talked with him about the matter as a way of stimulating economic growth. At any rate, Hamai's words, translated into English, were displayed on a Peace Tower in large letters. From that time on, the phrase "No More Hiroshimas" has encapsulated what many of Hiroshima's leaders have thought their city should stand for.[64]

With residents in their city more ideologically unified than before and with Tange's plan available as a guide, Hiroshima leaders viewed 1948 as a propitious time to renew their quest for planned rebuilding. In August, members of the Hiroshima City Reconstruction Bureau invited the submission of designs for a Peace Memorial Park near the atomic bomb's hypocenter in the Nakajima District. Proposals for such a park had been made repeatedly at meetings of the city government and its advisory bodies. Some 145 plans were considered, but the joint plan of four faculty members at Tokyo University, one of whom was the same Kenzō Tange who had put forward a city plan two years before, was chosen. The plan called for a one-hundred-meter-wide boulevard running east–west through Hiroshima and skirting the south side of a Peace Park. The Peace Park would, according to the plan, have meeting halls, an arch-shaped peace memorial monument, and open spaces. To the north of the park there would be, the plan anticipated, a natural forest park and large plaza at which residents of the city could meet.[65]

Political lobbying helped make these plans reality. Mayor Hamai and others in the city government formed a "League" or "Peoples Lobby" containing "representatives of every section of society" to obtain help for Hiroshima. They traveled to Tokyo to meet with ministers and representatives of the Diet, asking for two closely related actions. First, they wanted the national government to return large tracts of land once held by Japan's military to the city. Special legislation was needed for this action. Simple land readjustment schemes, they realized, were not adequate for the tasks at hand. Second, they hoped for legislation greatly boosting financial aid from the national government for the actual reconstruction of Hiroshima. They wanted Hiroshima, as a casualty of atomic bombing, to be treated differently from other Japanese cities. Initially rebuffed, Hamai reentered the fray in 1949 with a lengthy petition in which he wrote of how declaring Hiroshima an official "Mecca of Peace" would help in the recovery of all of Japan. His timing was good.

Japan's leading political party was under particularly severe attack by other parties, and to regain lost ground its leaders were looking for dramatic ways to appeal to Japan's voters. Then, too, the American government, worried about the emergence of a communist government in China, was trying to make Japan a pro-western bastion in Asia. Without doubt, helping people in Hiroshima to rebuild their city fit in well with the needs of both American leaders and important Japanese politicians.[66]

Justin Williams, General MacArthur's representative to the Diet, actively supported the legislation with MacArthur's full backing, which practically ensured its passage. Mayor Hamai, whom Williams labeled "a man with bull-dog tenacity," had approached Americans for aid in rebuilding Hiroshima in late 1946, only to be turned away. At that time MacArthur did not want to set a precedent that might lead to many similar requests from other communities. American considerations had changed by 1949, and Williams recommended Hamai's plans favorably to MacArthur, who gave a "go-ahead signal."[67]

As a result of this convergence of interests, the Diet passed the Hiroshima Peace Memorial City Construction Law in May 1949. The legislation proclaimed Hiroshima to be a "City of Peace" and returned former military land in Hiroshima to the city, with the stipulation that it be used for parks, green areas, sports fields, railways, sewage and water plants, canals, cemeteries, and libraries. Moreover, the measure appropriated large sums for the rebuilding of the city along planned lines, with additional funding promised in the future. Similar legislation honored Nagasaki as a "City of International Culture" and set aside a smaller sum for that city's rebuilding, about one-third the amount given to Hiroshima. The smaller sum resulted from less effective lobbying by Nagasaki's leaders. The laws established a City of Peace and Culture Commission within the Ministry of Construction to oversee the rebuilding of the two cities, with the Ministry of Finance empowered to supervise the transfer of military lands to Hiroshima. A poll of Hiroshima's residents in July found a majority in favor of the legislation, and it went into effect on August 6, 1949. The first of seven articles of the measure proclaimed, "This law aims at the construction of Hiroshima as a Peace Memorial City, a symbol of the ideal of making lasting peace a reality."[68]

Hiroshima was fast becoming a worldwide symbol of peace. Nonetheless, in building their new city, Hiroshima residents used much from the past. Many of the features of Tange's plans had been talked about for years, even decades. As Hiroshima's residents planned the future of their city, they continued to respect top-down planning. They had little choice, of course, except to abide by the terms of national legislation. However, they were able to influence how that legislation was applied locally, as various groups and individuals at the local level took a stronger hand in matters than before.

Economic Growth, Urban Development, and City Planning

An astute visitor to Hiroshima in 1965 observed, "The shadows are fading in Hiroshima today, and the visible scars are few." He noted further that "Hiroshima is bigger and more prosperous than before, and within it is a new generation of young adults who do not remember or care."[69] While a symbol of peace for many, to others Hiroshima came to mean even more as a locus for economic development. Beginning with the Korean War in the early 1950s and continuing through the 1960s, Hiroshima participated in Japan's high-speed economic growth, and planners found themselves having to accommodate the 1949 legislation defining Hiroshima as a "City of Peace" to the realities of rapid economic development. National, prefectural, and city officials, with considerable local input, refined the 1949 law. As it was elaborated, the plan for Hiroshima consisted of new parks, boulevards and roads, and infrastructural improvements. Onto these elements were soon grafted additional planning measures designed to encourage economic expansion.

At the center of the rebuilding lay the Peace Park in the Nakajima District, close to the hypocenter of the atomic bomb. This region had been Hiroshima's main business center into the 1920s, boasting stores, theaters, restaurants, and inns. Nakajima possessed some 710 shops and 2,611 residents before its destruction by the atomic bomb. By the early 1950s, the city's major business district had shifted eastward into Hatchobori, but Nakajima remained a significant commercial district. The 1949 law called for the construction of the Peace Park in Nakajima and nearby Saiku-machi, covering an area of about thirty acres. By this time, the region was "full of shacks," perhaps as many as four hundred. The squatters were removed, according to a city government publication "with much difficulty," and given substitute lots in other parts of Hiroshima. Expansion of the Peace Park led to the relocation of more squatters in the late 1950s and early 1960s, which sometimes required bringing in police to force the clearances.[70] Thus, environmental justice issues were raised as a result of park construction, just as they had in the United States, where Native Americans and Alaskan Natives were removed from national parks. While the removals disturbed some Hiroshima residents, designs for buildings and monuments in the Peace Park upset still more.

Conflict over whether to preserve what became known as the A-Bomb Dome epitomized the many cross-currents of public opinion. Just across a branch of the Ota River from the Peace Park, the Dome had been a commercial exhibition hall constructed in 1915. Located almost directly under the hypocenter of the atomic bomb, the hall, made of reinforced concrete, was severely damaged by the blast and then gutted by fire, leaving only a skeleton, including the domed roof. As restoration work proceeded, many commercial and civic groups urged that the ruins of the building be torn down. Some business leaders saw the Dome as an unfortunate reminder of their city's past, a relic that might tarnish the image of economic growth they were eager to burnish. Many *hibakusha*—and, of course, this group included a number of business leaders—agreed. They resented how the Dome was becoming a tourist attraction and saw it as an inauthentic symbol of their experiences. However, most residents of Hiroshima, including a majority of *hibakusha,* called for the preservation of the Dome, and its preservation was

Preserving the A-Bomb Dome was controversial. (Author's collection)

The Peace Museum, here decorated for the 1985 remembrance, served as a focal point for Hiroshima's Peace Park. (Author's collection)

part of Tange's plans. Generally, peace advocates wanted the Dome saved as a reminder of the horror of the atomic bomb. "I would rather see it preserved," observed one survivor, "without it, we would tend to forget the event completely and be simply easygoing." In 1966, Hiroshima's city council voted to preserve the Dome's ruins, which were stabilized and remain to the present day.[71]

Other controversies swirled around buildings and monuments in the Peace Park itself. Begun in 1951 and finished four years later, the Peace Museum and Memorial Hall, designed by Tange and his associates as centerpieces for the park, faced some opposition from business groups eager to put the war behind them and from some *hibakusha,* who decried what they saw as contributing to the deleterious growth of tourism in Hiroshima. Thus, the buildings were viewed negatively by some Hiroshima residents for the same reasons that they disliked the preservation of the A-Bomb Dome. Even more controversy engulfed the construction of a large, high-rise ANA hotel just outside the park, for many of the same reasons. Constructed in 1951–1952, an A-Bomb Cenotaph attracted heated discussion on two counts. Originally intended to hold the remains of all of the victims of the atomic bombing, the cenotaph was reduced in size at the order of the Ministry of Construction, whose members decided that a large structure would cost too much. They concluded that only the names of the victims need be included. Taking the form of an ancient Japanese house, the cenotaph was intended to shield the souls of the victims from rain. Much more deeply resented was an inscription placed on the cenotaph, which reads (in translation): "Rest in Peace. The mistake shall not be repeated." Many *hibakusha* thought these sentences implied that they were responsible for the bombing.[72]

An eternal flame of peace, a pond and fountain, a memorial to children, and other buildings aroused little controversy. Over time, nearly everyone in Hiroshima came to accept, indeed cherish, the Peace Park and its buildings as central to their city's culture and economy. The cenotaph, eternal flame, and Dome formed a straight line in the eyes of viewers, making a north–south axis for the Peace Park, just as Tange had intended. With the passage of decades, concerns over appropriate forms of tourism, economic growth, and ideological values were successfully reconciled.

The 1949 law for the reconstruction of Hiroshima, as later elaborated, called for the use of land, much of it former military ground, as parks and green areas, well beyond the land set aside for the Peace Park. Planners decided to include seventy-nine parks and eight green areas spread over about 600 acres as part of Hiroshima's reconstruction. Most significant was the creation of a central park of 147 acres where the castle and military headquarters had once stood. Rebuilt of ferrous concrete, the castle now stands at an edge of this park. Then, too, green areas laced the banks of many of the branches of the Ota River, as many Hiroshima residents had urged during their discussions in 1946. These green banks are unique to Hiroshima among Japanese cities. However, not all early ideas came to fruition. Many had hoped that a forested area would blanket the region just to the north of the Peace Park, and a provision for the forest was included in the 1949 law. Instead, a major public housing development and sports-cultural complex went up in the Motomachi District. Nor did a seaside park at Ujina materialize.[73]

The 1949 law envisioned more than the creation of parks and green spaces, and numerous infrastructure improvements flowed from the measure. The oft-discussed east–west boulevard, running along the southern edge of the Peace Park, was built. About a hundred meters wide, this Peace Boulevard, as it was named, helped make Hiroshima's street system more efficient and provided a touch of nature in the heart of the city, for trees ran down its center. The boulevard became the focus for citywide celebrations, such as the parade for a Flower Festival held each spring from 1977. Even so, the highway attracted criticism in its early years. Its eastern end terminated at the foot of the hill Hijiyama, upon which the Atomic Bomb Casualty Commission, jointly sponsored by the American and Japanese governments, had in 1947 constructed facilities to study the results of the atomic bomb on its victims. The Peace Boulevard was called by its detractors a "Royal Road" built for the convenience of those in the commission. Other thoroughfares were less controversial. The 1949 law called for the construction of twenty-seven major new roads, and many were built in the 1950s and 1960s, though not a southern boulevard. As a group, these roads and streets composed a new grid system within the city, especially in the downtown Hatchobori District. The construction of the street system, combined with the use of the Nakajima area for the Peace Park, completed the migration of Hiroshima's downtown into this district. New comprehensive sewer and drainage systems were also constructed in the early 1950s and 1960s.[74]

Still other projects not originally part of the 1949 law won approval. A "Major Hiroshima Construction Plan of 1960" applied to 346 square kilometers (about 134 square miles) of the city and its nearby hinterland. Many improvements were additions to transportation. Hiroshima opened a commercial airport on land reclaimed from the Inland Sea in 1961 at about the same place Tange had designated, welcomed its first bullet trains three years later, and made numerous improvements to its port at Ujina throughout the 1950s and 1960s.[75] The provision of housing was also taken up by planners. Altogether, city authorities had 21,000 shanties removed by 1965, replacing those shacks with public housing.[76]

Nowhere was the effort to create public housing more apparent than in Hiroshima's Motomachi District just north of the Peace Park, an area that had been quarters for the Japanese Army's Fifth Division. Here city authorities put up 743 small, temporary prefabricated wooden houses in 1946–1947. Illegally constructed, nongovernment houses in the area came to about 1,400. The city built an additional 630 small apartments in 1956, moving in people from the deteriorating wooden houses. However, some three thousand families in the district still had inadequate housing. To meet their needs city officials decided in 1968 to build a group of high-rise public apartment buildings. To clear the land, squatters were removed and their homes demolished. The director of Hiroshima's City Planning Bureau explained at the time that the new apartments were necessary to improve the quality of life for Hiroshima residents. "The first element of the construction of a comfortable city," he observed, "is the development of a living infrastructure in relation to the construction of a community based on the principle of setting a value on civil life." Made of concrete and steel, the apartments replaced the older wooden apartments and houses. Situated in buildings eight to twenty stories tall, the 4,500 new apartments were constructed in a fashion that took the natural environment into account: the layout of the buildings was altered from the original design to preserve a camphor tree that had survived the atomic bomb; public spaces including flower gardens and parks were incorporated into the plans for the apartments; and the skyline of the buildings was designed so "as not to give a feeling of oppression." Completed in 1978, the Motomachi apartments provided middle-class living for their residents.[77]

It was Japan's high-speed economic growth that made the planned reconstruction of Hiroshima possible. By 1970, Japan's real national income was six times greater than it had been in the mid-1930s and industrial output was ten times larger.[78] With greater tax revenues resulting from the nation's economic growth, Japan's national government could help to fund Hiroshima's rebuilding. (United States aid was also of considerable importance in spurring Japan's economic growth, especially American spending in Japan for supplies for United Nations forces in the Korean conflict during the early and mid-1950s. Like so many of those Pacific regions affected by the United States, Japan benefited from American military spending.) The contribution of Japan's national government to local government finances tripled from 109 billion yen in 1950 to 333 billion yen in 1960, and to 1,777 billion yen in 1970.[79] Hiroshima reestablished itself as one of Japan's leading industrial centers after the Second World War, as part of the nation's "Pacific Belt" of heavy industry, a locus for shipbuilding and automaking in particular. By 1958, about one-third of the city's residents were employed directly in manufacturing establishments, a high proportion.[80] The economic boom attracted more people to Hiroshima, until by 1960 the city had 431,000 residents. Ten years later, the number had climbed to 542,000.[81] With more tax revenues, the city government, like the national government, could better afford reconstruction projects.

More than financing was involved, however. Equally important was the ability of government officials to assemble sites for the reconstruction projects—bodies of land for the Peace Park, other green areas, roads, and public housing. In addition to providing initial funding for reconstruction, the 1949 law and later legislation granted former military land to Hiroshima for many of these purposes. Land readjustment projects also helped. By the late 1970s, the city had acquired some 4,630 acres in these ways.[82] In contrast, it was difficulties in site assembly that often made city planning hard in San Francisco and Seattle.

Still more factors accounted for the relative success of planning in Hiroshima, chief among them being ideological unity. Over time, most Hiroshima residents came to see that through planning—ranging from the creation of the Peace Park to the construction of infrastructural improvements—their city could benefit from economic growth while also serving as a symbol of peace. An international incident in 1954 aroused renewed awareness on the dangers of nuclear weapons when a hydrogen bomb test by the United States at Bikini Atoll in Micronesia dusted the crew of a Japanese fishing boat, the *Lucky Dragon,* with radioactive fallout. All of the crew members soon complained of illnesses, and one died. It was this incident that led Eskimos in Alaska to oppose nuclear engineering through Project Chariot. Immediately after this atomic dusting, the Hiroshima Prefectural Diet called for the prohibition of nuclear weapons and international control of nuclear energy, requests endorsed by the national Diet.

Hiroshima then became a center for world peace movements. Foreign visitors, ranging from Jawaharlal Nehru of India in 1957 to Pope John Paul II in 1981, made a point of traveling to the Peace Park in the interest of furthering world peace. Regional and global peace organizations held meetings in Hiroshima, beginning with a World Conference against Atomic and Hydrogen Bombs in 1954. Hiroshima's mayor made a "Peace Declaration" every August 6 in a ceremony at the Peace Park, and those ceremonies became major international events. The one held in 1985 to commemorate the fortieth anniversary of the bomb attracted tens of thousands of people, including the famous author of the book *Hiroshima,* John Hersey.[83] The fiftieth anniversary attracted still more.[84]

This is not to say that all of the residents of Hiroshima approved of the directions their city was taking. Especially in the 1960s, some decried the increasingly fast pace of life. Others derided Hiroshima as a "Second Chicago" and denounced the continuing influx of outsiders.[85] Even so, more than people in most modern cities, Hiroshima residents, effectively led by Hamai as their mayor, generally agreed that urban planning was a valuable tool in Hiroshima's growth. The fact that planning came to encompass attractive public housing helped a great deal in this respect.

Toward Becoming a Technopolis?

Many of the same issues that concerned planners in the first two decades after World War II attracted attention during the 1970s and 1980s. More than in the past, however, planners took a regional approach to these matters, in line with shifts in emphasis in planning throughout much of the world. Then, too, as they moved into the 1990s, some planners sought to turn Hiroshima into a "technopolis," a high-technology city. As they continued their work in Hiroshima, they did so within a new legislative framework. The Diet passed laws in 1968 and 1970 that sought to alter urban planning in Japan fundamentally, the first major changes since 1919. Responding to grassroots citizens' protests and legal suits about air and water pollution, resulting diseases and deaths, and continuing rampant urban sprawl, the laws aimed to give much more authority to local municipalities to control growth, including the power to force developers to pay for infrastructural improvements. The laws also expanded the nation's zoning system to eight land-use types.[86]

In their attempts to make Hiroshima one of Japan's most livable cities, planners paid attention to the provision of parks and infrastructural improvements. In the late 1960s, the director of Hiroshima's City Planning Bureau observed that "the natural environment" was very important to urban life and noted that Hiroshima was fast becoming "a city with abundant water and greens."[87] By the early 1980s, Hiroshima possessed 213 parks and fourteen green areas covering 2,100 acres, far more than had been envisioned by the 1949 law, making the city a leader in Japan in the provision of open spaces for its citizens. The same was true of the city's infrastructure. By the early 1980s, 237 kilometers of major new roads had been built in Hiroshima. Whereas many of those constructed in the immediate postwar period aimed at creating a gridiron street pattern within the city, especially in its downtown area, many of the roads built in the 1970s and later sought to develop better connections with the surrounding regions and with a national highway system. An effective mass transit system of buses and streetcars operated on those roads and highways. Similarly, better sewers and drainage systems continued to be constructed. Particularly important in this respect was the movement toward a regional approach through the adoption in 1973 of a "Sewerage Improvement Total Plan" for the Ota and Seno river basins.[88]

New planning efforts lay behind Hiroshima's continuing development. In 1970, city officials, working with business leaders, drafted a "Comprehensive City Plan" including a new scheme for Hiroshima's traffic, which, while by no means as congested as traffic in larger cities such as Tokyo and Osaka, was more crowded than in the past. On their own initiative, business leaders donated a public hall and large baseball stadium to the city, along with statues for green areas along the banks of the Ota River. In 1971, Hiroshima's regional planning area was extended to cover two nearby cities, along with seventeen towns close to Hiroshima City. Two years later, extensive discussions among city officials, prefectural authorities, and local business leaders resulted in the formulation of a "Hiroshima Basic City New Plan." Amended slightly in 1978, this scheme merged thirteen towns and villages into Hiroshima City, bringing the city's population to 850,000 and its size to 673 square kilometers (almost 260 square miles). Within the new city boundaries, areas were designated for urbanization promotion, urbanization control, and zoning differentiating multiple types of residential, commercial, and industrial areas, elements required by the legislation that the Diet had passed in 1968.[89]

City officials listed six ambitious goals in their 1978 plan: "To achieve world peace; to conserve and carefully utilize nature; to create safety and a high standard of living; to assure a healthy and happy life; to cultivate human fulfillment; to create a stable living." Emphasizing social and cultural goals more than economic ones, this plan reached well beyond earlier bricks-and-concrete plans for Hiroshima's future. In 1980, Hiroshima won recognition from the national government as the tenth Government Ordinance Designated City of Japan, which bestowed the official designation of "metropolis" on Hiroshima, a source of tremendous local pride. City officials saw this designation as proof that Hiroshima had fully recovered from the destruction of the atomic bomb. By this time, Hiroshima's population had reached 900,000.[90]

As they were implemented, the plans for Hiroshima included ambitious area redevelopment and housing projects. The scope of the new projects went well beyond what had been achieved earlier in the Motomachi District. The Western Districts Development Project reclaimed 825 acres from the Inland Sea just west of the city for industrial, commercial, and residential uses. Designed to relieve traffic congestion and help make Hiroshima "a pivot of economic distribution," this development involved slicing away 135 acres of hillside for terraced housing. The Koyo New Housing Town Development put up housing on 688 acres upstream on the Ota River, about twelve kilometers north of the center of Hiroshima. Although the Koyo development included parks and playgrounds, it also obliterated a large natural area along the river. Similarly, the Suzugamine New Housing Town Development Project developed 136 acres of hillsides in western Hiroshima for additional housing.[91]

Perhaps most ambitious were plans to redevelop the Danbara District, just two kilometers from Hiroshima's center. Shielded by the hill Hijiyama, this was the only close-in area not destroyed or heavily damaged by the atomic bomb. Neglected by city authorities who faced more urgent rebuilding tasks in the destroyed parts of their city, Danbara deteriorated in the 1950s and 1960s, having no city sewerage facilities, public assembly halls, parks, or playgrounds. Many of the streets were dirt. Danbara also became congested, as twenty thousand people lived on its 185 acres. Under Hiroshima's 1971 city planning measure, it was decided to redevelop this district through the provision of 1,061 model houses and many new premises for local businesses. Parks, playgrounds, new streets, and sewer connections were also part of the plan. Begun in 1978, the redevelopment was completed in the 1990s.[92]

The processes involved in planning the new towns and the redevelopment of Danbara and the other districts reveal an underside to planning, demonstrating that planning had become more of a top-down affair by the 1970s and 1980s than it had been right after the destruction of Hiroshima, despite the passage of new national legislation in 1968 and 1970. There was still local input into planning, but not everyone was consulted. In the case of Danbara, many residents desired a redeveloped area with modern amenities. However, not all did. Some preferred what they described as an older, more relaxed, if also more crowded, way of life. They liked the flowers growing in their dirt streets and resented being told to change their ways. Then, too, the building of the Koyo and Suzugamine new towns and other projects suggests that, although city authorities had a genuine desire to integrate the natural environment into the new Hiroshima, when push came to shove, that desire took a back seat to economic development. Filling in more of the Inland Sea near Hiroshima cost fishermen more fishing grounds. The new towns, and the new suburbs, while having small parks and playgrounds in their plans, could be built only by degrading their regions' natural environments by slicing away hillsides and filling in the ocean.

Even so, Hiroshima was a more livable city than most other major metropolises in Japan. Its parks and green spaces, its public housing, and its infrastructure generally worked. These accomplishments came as a result of mediation in planning among municipal, prefectural, and national authorities. Locals, to be sure, had to follow national mandates. However, at least in the case of Hiroshima, local residents, despite some apparent return to centralized planning in the 1980s, had considerable say in the development. Not all had an equal voice, however, as bureaucrats in city and prefectural planning offices overrode the desires of local residents, especially those of poor people such as residents of Danbara.[93]

From the late 1980s on, heavy industry declined in significance in Hiroshima, as elsewhere in Japan, and some deindustrialization occurred.[94] Hiroshima prospered increasingly as a center for new high-technology firms. The city emerged as one of the few centers for computer software writing in Japan, possessing 35 software companies in 1982 and 120 four years later.

Rebuilt Hiroshima featured parks along the Ota River. (Author's collection)

Then, too, high-technology businesses grew up in plastics, printing, and some other fields. Hiroshima possessed an entrepreneurial energy not found in all Japanese cities—a result, perhaps, of the movement of new people into Hiroshima after the Second World War. Most of the firms they founded were small; some two-thirds of them started with less than $20,000 in capital. In this important respect, they resembled the small firms in Silicon Valley.[95]

Japan's Diet encouraged high-technology efforts through the passage of a Technopolis Law in 1983. The government hoped to create almost from scratch nineteen communities (the number was later raised to twenty-six) devoted to the development of new technologies needed for continuing economic growth in Japan. Located near larger "mother" cities, the new communities were to be home to relocated national universities, government research laboratories, and innovative businesses, all working together to develop new products for world markets. Beyond force-feeding the rapid growth of high-technology districts in the hope of creating new Silicon Valleys, an important objective was to move people out of overcrowded Tokyo and thus decentralize the population base of Japan.[96]

In 1984, the national government chose an area thirty kilometers to the east of Hiroshima City called Higashi-Hiroshima (*higashi* means "east" in Japanese) to become a technopolis. Encompassing 260 acres, this site was divided into an academic city including a fully relocated Hiroshima University by 1996, two industrial parks, and a residential town. Hiroshima, wrote scholars who studied the city in the early and mid-1990s, "represents a case of a large, aging industrial city where technopolis activity has acted as a sub-urbanizing magnet for relocation of activity from the city center, as well as a pole of attraction for branch plants." Higashi-Hiroshima attracted mainly large firms, as companies such as Chugoku Electric Company, Matsushita Home Electronics, and Panasonic built branch plants and some research facilities in the parks.[97]

The expected economic stimulus for Hiroshima did not fully material-ize. Researchers in the large relocated firms did not cooperate as well as had been hoped with scholars at Hiroshima University. This failure is not surpris-ing. Contrary to what some observers have written, the culture of academic–business collaboration that exists in the United States is more muted in Japan. Most scholars in Japan treasure their independence from business. As a result, few research breakthroughs occurred in Higashi-Hiroshima. What did happen was that the city of Hiroshima lost its university to the new area, along with a number of corporate research and production facilities. Be-tween 1982 and 1992, Higashi-Hiroshima gained sixty-eight new plants and increased its employment from 11,000 to more than 16,000 workers, mainly at the expense of Hiroshima. Hiroshima also lost its airport, which relocated from within the city to an area near Higashi-Hiroshima. In the end, the city proper gained little directly from the creation of a technopolis.[98]

Rebuilding on Okinawa

Rebuilding on Okinawa offers a valuable comparison to developments in Hiroshima. Between 1945 and 1972, when Okinawa and the other Ryūkyū Islands reverted to Japan, American authorities exercised extensive controls over that island. Reconstruction there "resulted from a synthesis of influ-ences," including "Japanese city planning practices and American efforts to shape planning, control the actual construction, and regulate the flow of building."[99] Between 1945 and 1950, the U.S. Navy and Army were in charge of Okinawa. Military jurisdiction was superseded by civilian control with the creation of the U.S. Civil Administration of the Ryukyus (USCAR) in 1950. In 1952, a full civil government composed of Okinawans was set up, but its ac-tions needed to comply with USCAR's guidelines and ordinances. American authorities had the right to intervene in Okinawan affairs until reversion.[100]

American occupation policies were most apparent in Naha, Okinawa's capital, located on the southern end of the island. Naha's prewar population of 68,000 shrank to just several hundred after American bombing leveled the city in October 1944. As in Hiroshima, recovery was fairly swift. By 1948, people returning from refugee camps had swelled the city's population to 26,000, and a year later the return of Okinawans who had been evacuated to mainland Japan boosted it to 109,000. As in Hiroshima, the most pressing need was housing. In late 1945, the American military set standards for the building of new homes. Between 1946 and 1949, 50,000 houses were constructed and given to refugees free of charge. Another 78,000 houses followed in the 1950s, financed mainly by American aid. In addition, roughly $50 million flowed from Congress to the Okinawan government for infrastructure improvements during the mid-1950s.[101]

This substantial American aid stood in marked contrast to the situation in the rest of Japan, where most cities were thrust back onto their own resources to rebuild. Even Hiroshima struggled until the 1949 law was passed. It was America's strategic plans for Okinawa that helps to explain the greater aid given that island. Especially with the "fall" of China to communism in 1949, the United States came to see its large and growing military bases on Okinawa as essential to its position in Asia during the Cold War. More than mainland Japan, Okinawa came to be viewed by some military planners as almost an extension of the United States. As we shall see in the next chapter, the onset of the Cold War also greatly increased American military activity on Guam.[102]

Even as American authorities addressed housing needs, they turned to more comprehensive reconstruction. In 1946, army officers devised a plan for Naha encompassing new highways that would divide the city into quadrants, with government offices and a shopping district at the center of the city, the creation of residential and industrial zones in outlying areas, and the establishment of parks. The plan called for the building of a water reservoir, a city hall, a theater, a hotel, a post office, and a fire station. However, this scheme was largely ignored in the haste to put up housing. Instead, comprehensive planning was soon turned over mainly to Okinawans.[103]

Planning devolved to local residents. In 1950, Naha officials organized a city planning committee and held a city planning conference, from which came comprehensive plans. Harkening back to Japan's 1919 zoning law, and informed by Japan's 1946 legislation, the plan divided about 1,215 acres of Naha and nearby villages into residential, commercial, and industrial areas, along with a governmental district, and provided for roads, green areas, and parks. The plan won approval from American authorities, who insisted, however, that military areas be excluded from the plan and that major highways be widened. Although not immediately enacted in full, this plan set the stage for later efforts. The Okinawan government adopted a road law and a building standards law in 1952 and a city planning law in 1953, all similar to legislation passed by the Japanese Diet in 1945–1946.[104]

Planned rebuilding of Naha occurred during the 1950s. Local authorities, with American approval, established a planning area encompassing Naha and several nearby villages. Planners thought big, projecting a population for the region of 234,000 by 1966 and 326,000 in 1976 (there were 156,000 people in the area in 1956). The new plans were based on a gridiron street system, slum clearances, zoning, and land readjustment schemes. While the USCAR took a hands-off approach, basically approving Okinawan plans and providing guidance by preparing transportation, population, and industrial planning studies, it underwrote much of the cost of rebuilding. USCAR provided 52 percent of the costs of capital improvements for Naha, with the city government paying most of the rest.[105]

As in Hiroshima, the plans for Naha, and more generally for the Ryūkyū Islands, aimed mainly at stimulating economic growth, with much less attention paid to environmental protection. This was not at all surprising, given that survival and reconstruction were the order of the day. American planning studies in the 1950s, for example, called for land reclamation from the ocean, including the reclamation of reefs near Naha. Japanese planners were far from alone in filling in coastlines. Only decades later did the preservation of reefs become important in some parts of America's Pacific possessions, most notably in Hawai'i and Guam.[106]

American influence in Okinawa extended well beyond reversion. Into the early 2000s, the United States maintained major military bases on the island, sometimes leading to conflicts with residents. About 50,000 American personnel were on Okinawa in the 1980s and 1990s. When I served as a Fulbright Lecturer to Japan in the 1980s, I gave several lectures at Ryūkyū University on Okinawa. An entry in a diary I kept then observed of the area around Moon Beach, "We saw Americans wherever we went—especially at a U.S.-style shopping center in Okinawa City where we stopped for ice cream at a Baskin and Robbins." Okinawans welcomed American and Japanese-government dollars spent to support the bases. As late as 2005, 8,800 Japanese worked at American military bases on Okinawa. In addition, the 29,000 Okinawans on whose land the bases were built received $670 million annually in rent. Even so, Okinawans increasingly objected to the American presence on their island as an infringement on their sovereignty.[107]

The situation on Okinawa was complex, the result of more than a simple contest between Japanese authorities and the American military. The Ryūkyūs had once been an independent kingdom, partly subservient to China, and became a Japanese prefecture only in the late nineteenth century. Many residents had long seen themselves as partially separate from Japan. The Okinawan government often found itself at odds with Japan's national government about land-use matters. Americans took over about 45,000 acres of land on Okinawa for military purposes at the close of the World War II and seized even more in the 1950s. Old villages were bulldozed to create military bases. Within the city limits of Kadena, 83 percent of the land was occupied by the largest U.S. airbase in the Pacific. Social issues, such as the occasional rape of Okinawan women by American servicemen, also arose. The prefectural government employed local animosity toward the American military as leverage to try to assert independence from national policies. In 2005, after years of controversy, the U.S. Marines agreed to relocate a major airbase on Okinawa in accord with the wishes of local residents. Thus, the peripheral Okinawa government was often in opposition to the metropoles in Tokyo and Washington, DC, or, if one thinks of CINCPAC, in Honolulu.[108]

Conclusions

Government officials were much more successful in rebuilding Hiroshima after World War II than they were in revitalizing the city through the creation of a nearby technopolis in the 1980s and 1990s. The national legislation passed in 1949 to rebuild Hiroshima and Nagasaki offered adequate funding to accomplish its goals, and those objectives were limited to only two cities. Japan's high-speed growth during the 1950s and 1960s, spurred in part by American military expenditures, provided tax revenues for the rebuilding. In contrast, the Japanese economy collapsed in the early 1990s, and Japan endured economic hard times for over a decade, so the plans for technopolises had to be scaled back. Then, too, the creation of a technopolis at Higashi-Hiroshima never had solid support from Hiroshima residents. It was a case of top-down planning imposed with little consideration for local sensibilities. Many of the faculty members at Hiroshima University with whom I talked in the mid-1980s opposed the relocation of their university to Higashi-Hiroshima, an action which they said would force them into an inconvenient commute to work. One of the few benefits they saw as resulting from the move was that at its new site the university would have additional tennis courts. Of course, there was no unanimity at first over all aspects of re-

building Hiroshima after the war. Nonetheless, considerable agreement soon
evolved around the motto of "No More Hiroshimas." Nothing comparable
occurred with regard to Higashi-Hiroshima.

To the extent that Hiroshima nurtured a high-technology district in Higashi-Hiroshima, that district differed markedly from what developed in Silicon Valley or in Seattle. As we saw in Chapter 3, Silicon Valley evolved over
many decades as a district composed mainly of hundreds, even thousands,
of small and medium-sized firms with permeable boundaries. In Seattle, a
hub-and-spoke system of high-technology companies developed around
three major centers—the Boeing Company, Microsoft, and the University
of Washington. In Hiroshima, government-directed, top-down planning decreed the development of a new technopolis composed of a relocated university and the research and production facilities of mainly large firms. Rarely
have such government-directed efforts to create high-technology districts
worked well. Success in South Korea was more the exception than the rule.
And, when they have succeeded, they have done so with ample government
funding, which the Japanese government did not provide in the 1990s. Hiroshima gained more from the development of software companies and other
high-technology businesses within the city than from the efforts to create a
technopolis at Higashi-Hiroshima.

If Hiroshima's postwar development is revealing about what govern-
ment-generated growth can and cannot accomplish, it also elucidates important aspects of environmentalism in Japan. In many ways, environmental developments in Hiroshima paralleled changes taking place elsewhere in
Japan. However, in some respects Hiroshima stood out as almost unique.[109]

In the 1950s and 1960s, high-speed economic development lay at the
center of the work of the Japanese government. With militarism and territorial expansion discredited, economic growth at almost any cost became the
number one goal. Water and air pollution, along with the continued filling
in of coastal areas for the sites of industrial plants, oil refineries, and power
plants, were seen acceptable trade-offs in the quest for economic development. "During the high economic-growth period, production efficiency was
the primary concern in the uncritical and rapid adaptation of new technologies," a leading Japanese environmental historian has written. "This stance,"
he has concluded, "resulted in unprecedented damage to natural ecosystems
and to human health and well-being."[110] Only in the late 1960s and early
1970s did local grassroots efforts to limit industrial pollution, stemming
mainly from health concerns, coalesce into a significant national movement
to place some environmental restrictions on economic growth. In 1970, the

Diet, influenced much more by local indigenous movements than by foreign developments, passed meaningful environmental protection legislation.

In Hiroshima, as in most of Japan, rapid economic growth took precedence over environmental protection for decades after the Second World War. Resuming a process begun in Tokugawa times, Hiroshima residents filled in parts of the Inland Sea to create ground upon which new factories, an airport, and port facilities could be constructed. At first, there was not much concern about the pollution caused by these developments. Factories were seen as emblematic of a prosperous future for Hiroshima, even though they harmed long-established fisheries, such as the growing of oysters, a regional specialty. As in American cities such as Pittsburgh and Saint Louis, factory smoke was seen as a symbol of industrial progress. Similarly, outlying green areas gave way to new housing developments, construction that often involved the cutting away of hills. Again, economic growth was seen as more important than environmental protection. Far from all the changes occurring in Hiroshima were environmentally insensitive, however. The provisions of parks, boulevards, and green areas within the rebuilt city made Hiroshima more livable than most major Japanese cities. So did the building of new roads and other infrastructural improvements, along with public housing.

Finally, it is worth stressing Hiroshima's unique status as a center for world peace movements. This development provided considerable ideological unity within the city as time progressed. Even more, with the Peace Park as its physical manifestation, Hiroshima attracted attention from peace advocates throughout the Pacific and beyond. Like native Hawaiians seeking a new future for Kahoʻolawe, Hiroshima residents came to see their city in similar terms—that is, as having a mission to bring the message of peace to the world. Native Hawaiians and other Pacific Islanders were among those attracted to Hiroshima as a peace center and, more generally, to Japan's antinuclear stance. They were, of course, responding to the dropping of the atomic bomb. Guam also became a site of immense military actions by American forces and a focus for protests in the postwar period, the subject of the next chapter.

CHAPTER 6

Guam, the Philippines, and American Samoa

W riting on behalf of the Guam Legislature in 1971, that body's secretary and speaker jointly observed, "The dominance of America's presence in the Pacific explains so much of Guam's economic
growth and current land problems." Continuing, they noted, "Although the
U.S. interest in the Pacific dates back to the mid-19th century, it was really
World War II that precipitated the major involvement by the Americans in
the Far East and Pacific realms." Finally, they observed that "for the central
Pacific much of the U.S. military administration and strike forces centered
in Guam."[1] They were correct. As in so many Pacific places, World War II
was a watershed in Guam's history. After the conflict, with the onset of the
Cold War, the military presence of the United States became even more pronounced in Guam than it was in the Hawaiian Islands or Alaska.

After looking at Guam's history as the framework within which later
developments played out, this chapter explores how the increased American
military presence on Guam affected the lives of Guamanians and how they
responded to the changes caused by it. The chapter focuses on controversies
on three interrelated issues: where to build a new ammunition wharf for
the U.S. Navy, how to establish a national park to commemorate America's
World War II campaigns in the Pacific, and where to place a national seashore in Guam's waters. Divisions on these topics well illustrate how inter-
twined economic, environmental, and cultural matters had become. So, too,
did efforts to understand and control the brown tree snake on Guam, the
fourth major topic of this chapter. An alien species inadvertently introduced
by the American military at the close of World War II, the brown tree snake
proliferated to such an extent that it disrupted the social and economic well-

being of Guamanians. The chapter also compares developments on Guam to those on the Philippine Islands and American Samoa.

As in the Hawaiian Islands, conflicts with the navy on Guam and in the Philippines, and to a lesser extent American Samoa, reached a series of climaxes in the 1970s and 1980s. Guamanians and Filipinos especially wanted to win economic independence from the American military. Guamanians, in particular, sought at the same time to protect the physical environment of their island and to preserve what remained of its native culture. In this complex situation, American military authorities were far from simply acting as "heavies." Navy officials, perhaps influenced by events in Hawai'i, learned to be sensitive to the wishes of others while also pursuing their own agendas, making compromises the order of the day.[2]

Development in Micronesia and Guam

Micronesia means "tiny islands" in Greek, an apt description. Some 2,373 islands in the Caroline, Marshall, Gilbert, Mariana, and Southwest island groups compose Micronesia. Scattered over an area in the western Pacific larger than the continental United States, Micronesia is mostly ocean. It encompasses 7 million square kilometers of ocean but only 2,700 square kilometers of land, an area smaller than the state of Rhode Island. More than any other segment of Oceania, Micronesia fits scholar and activist Epeli Hau'ofa's description of Oceania as a "sea of islands."

Guam is the largest and most populous island in Micronesia. It is one of the fifteen islands composing the Marianas, a north–south archipelago nearly 500 miles long located about 1,500 miles east of the Philippines. Other major islands in the Marianas include Rota, Tinian, and Saipan. Covering 214 square miles, about 137,000 acres, Guam is roughly thirty miles long and nine miles wide. By itself, Guam constitutes one-fifth of the dry land of Micronesia and over one-half of that of the Marianas. It narrows to about four miles in width at its center, giving it something of the shape of a bowtie. While northern Guam consists of a raised limestone plateau, parts of which have steep cliffs, southern Guam is a mixture of volcanic hills and valleys containing rivers and waterfalls. Swept by Southeast Asian monsoon rains, the island endures a typhoon once about every three years and a super typhoon roughly once a decade. Some 166,000 people were residing on Guam in 2004, and about 412,000 in all of Micronesia.[3]

Micronesia was probably colonized by people from southeastern China

and Taiwan. Migrating to the Philippines, Indonesia, and the Malay Peninsula, they populated the Marianas perhaps five to ten thousand years ago.
Archaeological sites discovered in the Marianas so far date firmly, however,
to only about thirty-five hundred years ago. Making pottery and using looms
to weave cloth, the inhabitants had a rich subsistence lifestyle based on culti-
vated agriculture—especially breadfruit, taro, sugarcane, yams, bananas, and
a limited amount of rice—and near-shore and pelagic fishing using outrigger
canoes called *proa*. As they moved into the Marianas, people altered their
physical environments, though less so than in some other Pacific regions
such as the Hawaiian Islands. They brought with them rats, but not the more
destructive dogs and pigs (or chickens) that commonly made up the portable
biota of later Pacific voyagers. Some Micronesians organized extensive trading and tribute empires that lasted for centuries. On Guam, they lived in
settlements, usually near freshwater sources and wetlands for growing taro
and other root crops. Known as the Chamorros, they used stone pillars called
latte as foundations for their most prominent buildings beginning around
1,000 A.D. Organized in matrilineal clans, they were not a unified people, a
fact that left them vulnerable to conquest by Europeans.[4]

That conquest came in the 1600s, ushering in three centuries of colonial rule. "Discovered" by Ferdinand Magellan in 1521, Guam was claimed by
Spain in 1565, but was not colonized until after the Chamorros were defeated
in a series of battles in the late 1600s. Organized resistance to the Spanish
ended in 1685, by which time the Chamorro population on Guam had been
reduced to about two thousand from roughly twelve thousand in 1668. Diseases unintentionally introduced by the Spanish, as well as warfare, caused
this precipitous decline, just as diseases introduced by westerners decimated
the ranks of native Hawaiians and Alaskan Natives at later dates. Tinian, Saipan, and Rota were also conquered by the Spanish. The Spanish transported
all of the Chamorros to Guam and organized them into villages laid out
in the Spanish fashion, with plazas, churches, government buildings, and
schools. Only about a century later were some Chamorros allowed to return to their home islands. Beginning in the late 1600s, Guam and the other
Marianas entered what has been described by Robert F. Rogers, the foremost
historian of Guam, as "a twilight period of 200 years of solitude until the
next invasion." The Spanish converted the Chamorros to Catholicism, but
did little to develop Guam or the other Marianas economically. The Spanish
empire was stretched thin, and Guam was useful to the Spanish mainly as a
way station to the Philippines.[5]

The United States purchased Guam, along with the Philippines and
Puerto Rico, from Spain after its victory in the Spanish-American War in

1898. Germany established a protectorate over the Marshalls in 1885 and bought the Carolines and Marianas (except Guam) in 1899. The United States put its navy in charge of governing Guam, a situation that endured for decades. "The island would be administered as if it were a ship," Rogers has written, "the 'USS *Guam*,' with the governor as captain, U.S. military personnel as crew, and the Chamorros as mess attendants."[6] Military not economic development considerations dominated American thinking about Guam. Nonetheless, some favorable changes occurred, especially as sanitation and medical services improved, leading to a resurgence in the Chamorro population from 9,630 in 1901 to 21,000 in 1940. Even so, as Rogers has observed, Guam "still had a subsistence 'bull cart' economy" with the navy's efforts to foster agricultural production "only marginally successful." Moreover, the navy treated the Chamorros as a distinctly inferior people. Denied citizenship in the United States, they were for a time forbidden to marry whites.[7]

Meanwhile, as a result of defeat in World War I, Germany lost its islands in Micronesia to Japan. Under the terms of the Treaty of Versailles, Japan was awarded all German lands in the Pacific north of the equator—including Tinian, Saipan, and Rota—as a Class C mandate of the League of Nations. Japan promptly integrated them into its growing Asian empire and developed them economically through commercial fishing, sugarcane plantations, and copra production.[8]

World War II brought major changes to Guam. Japanese forces bombed it on December 8, 1941, and landed troops on the island two days later. The capture of Guam took less than six hours. The Japanese then tried to incorporate Guam into their empire. Japanese replaced English in the schools, and Chamorro men were mobilized to build airstrips. In general, people on Guam, Rogers has concluded, assumed an "attitude of guarded, submissive neutrality toward the Japanese, while hoping for the return of the Americans." A few helped American servicemen try to avoid capture, at great personal cost, even death. As the war wound down, living conditions worsened. Forced labor became brutal, food supplies dwindled, and a breakdown of Japanese military discipline led to the massacre of a number of Chamorros. In July 1944, American forces invaded Guam, storming ashore at Asan just north of Apra harbor and at Agat a few miles south of the port. After fierce fighting, the island was secured in mid-August. The cost was high; 1,769 Americans and about 11,000 Japanese died. Some 578 Chamorros also lost their lives and another 258 were injured between 1941 and 1944, according to official claims later submitted to the United States Congress. In addition, many Chamorros lost their lands.[9]

The coming of peace led to major alterations to Micronesia. At the urging of the American delegation, the United Nations Security Council made most of Micronesia (but not Guam) a trust territory of the United States in 1947, with the new dependency assuming the title of the Trust Territory of the Pacific Islands (TTPI). President Harry S. Truman vested control over the TTPI in the navy and appointed the Commander in Chief, Pacific (CINC-PAC) as the first high commissioner for it. CINCPAC administered the vast reaches of the TTPI from headquarters in Honolulu. Guam was not part of the TTPI. Instead, as a United States flag territory, it continued to be administered separately by the navy.[10]

Micronesia and Guam did not return to their sleepy prewar existence, for the coming of the Cold War heightened their strategic significance. America hoped to build a network of bases in Micronesia to support a forward deployment of military forces around the western Pacific. Then, too, the United States sought nuclear test sites in Micronesia, conducting atomic tests at the Bikini Atoll in 1946 even before the TTPI was created. All-in-all, the United States had grand ambitions for Micronesia. As a leading historian of America in Micronesia, Hal H. Friedman, has observed, "Between 1945 and 1947, the United States sought to, and largely succeeded in, developing an exclusive, strategic sphere of influence in the Pacific Basin," which turned much of the Pacific into an "American lake."[11]

American actions, Friedman has noted, meant that the "military and economic development of Micronesia" during these years "demanded quite a bit of political and cultural change to be bequeathed or imposed on the inhabitants of the islands." Saipan, Tinian, and especially Guam were to support major American military bases, and some of the military plans envisioned removing indigenous peoples, or as the military described them, "natives," from their lands. This action was never taken in full. It was anticipated that 71,000 acres, half of the land on Guam, would be needed for bases. Ideas were floated to turn Kwajalein Atoll into a hub for air transportation and to use Enewetok as a fleet anchorage. Most of the proposed changes took decades to complete, with military installations concentrated on Guam and Kwajalein. The latter island group continued to be used as a nuclear test site by the United States into the late 1950s and as a missile range into the 1980s.[12]

World War II, then, was of great importance for Micronesia and Guam, as it was for most of the Pacific. Above all, the war greatly heightened America's long-standing involvement in the Pacific and, more specifically, in Guam. The development of the Cold War, along with trade possibilities, meant that that increased interest would not fade away. Rogers summarized the situation well. "The geopolitics of the Pacific," he observed, "were thus transformed from the prewar situation, in which Guam was a lonely American outpost surrounded by hostile Japanese islands, to one in which Guam was the center of an American-dominated lake that encompassed the entire western Pacific."[13] Not surprisingly, the American military, especially the navy, long remained the major force in Guam's political and economic development.

The wartime government of Guam was replaced in 1946 by a peacetime administration, with Rear Admiral Charles A. Pownall, formerly the commander of America's naval air forces in the Pacific, as the appointed governor. Shortly thereafter the Eighth Guam Congress, a locally elected body with limited powers, convened in a Quonset hut in Hagatna (Agana). Most Guamanians, as residents of Guam started calling themselves right after World War II, could not become American citizens at this time unless they entered America's armed services. Guamanians could not qualify for citizenship by being born in the United States, since Guam was an unincorporated territory; nor could they be naturalized as citizens of a foreign nation—a real Catch-22 situation. Disenfranchised except in local elections—and the appointed governor could veto any measures passed by the Guam Congress (later the Guam Legislature)—Guamanians had little say over their political lives.[14]

Political impotence carried over into economic matters, especially land-ownership. Despite the passage of legislation by the United States Congress in 1945 and 1946 designed to help them, Guamanians found it difficult to win reimbursement for losses incurred during World War II. The navy placed low ceilings on claims adjudicated by a Land and Claims Commission, and by the time the last claim was settled in 1957 the federal government had paid out only $8.3 million to 4,429 Guamanians. More galling was the loss of additional land. In 1946, the same Congress that authorized Guamanians to press claims for World War II losses approved legislation allowing the American military to acquire private land on Guam for the creation of bases.[15] The armed forces soon did so. When the United States had acquired Guam from Spain in 1898, it took over Spanish crown lands on the island, about 25 percent of the island's land area. As the federal government purchased more land, its holdings rose to 48,144 acres in 1937, roughly 35 percent of Guam's total land area. Further acquisitions brought federal government landholdings on Guam to about 56,500 acres, about 42 percent of Guam's land, by 1948. By 1950, the federal government owned or leased 58 percent of the land area of Guam. As two Guamanian historians accurately noted about a decade later, "this was a cause of bitter resentment among Guamanians."[16]

The loss of land troubled Guamanians for more than economic reasons. Family, not individual, landownership was central to Micronesian culture, and attacking that ownership was perceived as an assault on culture and family. As a leading scholar of Micronesian society has explained, "land was once . . . a cherished part of a group's and an individual's identity." In fact, "to have rights to land—understood as including the offshore flats and reef or fishing areas—was to be able to meet all one's basic needs: food, housing, transportation, and medicine. . . . People spoke of eating from their piece of land."[17] More was contested than simply the land itself, just as was the case with Kahoʻolawe in the Hawaiian Islands.

Moreover, in its desire to maintain tight security, the navy restricted commercial development on Guam. Guam's economy did well in the late 1940s, due mainly to war-surplus sales and military construction. However, restrictions soon limited growth and diversification. Local firms could not employ alien workers, such as Filipinos (unlike the military, which did), and local businesses had to be at least 51 percent owned by Guamanians. Moreover, only Guamanians could purchase land on Guam or lease it for more than five years. Well-meaning efforts to protect local residents from outside exploitation, these ordinances nonetheless limited development. Perhaps most harmful, the navy required security clearances—in effect, visas—for anyone traveling to Guam, a circumstance that made the development of tourism unlikely.[18]

Under mounting pressure from Guamanians, the federal government agreed to a major alteration in the island's political status in 1950. Through an Organic Act passed by Congress that year, a civilian government replaced the naval government and Guamanians were recognized as American citizens. The new governor, who was appointed by the president until 1969 and elected by Guamanians thereafter, still had veto power over measures passed by the Guam Legislature but usually tried to cooperate with members of that body. Because of security concerns, however, the navy controlled travel clearances until 1962, a circumstance that continued to retard tourism and also made it difficult for Guamanians to leave their island. It is worth remembering that tourism is partly structured by state actions. Once travel restrictions were lifted, tourism began expanding, and many Guamanians, often the best educated, left Guam for mainland America as part of the Pacific diaspora, the movement of Pacific Islanders to America, New Zealand, and Australia.[19]

Efforts to diversify Guam's economy accompanied political liberalization. One section of the Organic Act provided that products made on Guam could enter mainland America duty-free. Business leaders on Guam had visions of their island becoming a center of manufacturing, trade, and finance like Hong Kong. That never occurred. Guam lacked the resources and was too far from major consumption centers to develop much of an industrial base. Then, too, disputes with Congress over how much of a product needed to be made on Guam for that product to be classified as Guamanian and thus eligible for duty-free shipment limited exports.[20] Navy restrictions on the use of Guam's only commercial harbor at Apra, about two-thirds of the way down the island's west shore, also hurt. The placement of the navy's munitions wharf near the port's commercial facilities meant that trade was restricted, for a clear blast zone needed to be maintained in case an accidental explosion occurred. Relocating the ammunition wharf became a contentious issue in the 1970s and 1980s.

Nor did agriculture thrive. With much of the productive farmland in military hands, little was left for cultivation. "Lack of good farming land is the most serious problem Guam's farmers must contend with," observed a publication of the Guam government in 1953. "Condemnation of farm lands and the exodus of potential farm labor to occupations with the government or private firms have," it noted, "handicapped the re-building of the agricultural industry." In 1950, Guam had just 1,250 people employed in farming, and two years later only 3,759 acres were planted.[21] Nor did agriculture prosper much in later decades. Another report sponsored by the Guam government observed in 1971 that "agriculture has not been a growth industry during the sixties." In fact, the amount of land under cultivation fell, and fish production declined.[22]

Thwarted on most other fronts, Guamanians pinned their hopes on tourism, and in this endeavor they were partially successful. That Guam would emerge as a major tourist center in the Pacific was, however, not apparent in the 1950s. The Guam Legislature established the Guam Travel Bureau in 1952, but a year later even a booster publication admitted that "Guam today is definitely not the place for visitors." The pamphlet observed that there were "no hotel facilities and little likelihood for any in the near future." Guamanians liked to think of their island as "the Crossroads of the Pacific," but air transportation to Guam from mainland America was limited to two flights per week by Pan American Airlines and another two flights weekly by Philippine Airlines.[23] No flights yet connected Guam to Japan, which would later become the major source of tourists. Then, too, even Americans needed to have permission from the military in the form of security clearances to visit Guam.

When the requirement for permission to visit Guam was dropped in

1962, the number of tourists traveling to the island from mainland America rose. Federal government actions were important in another way as well. After doing little for about twenty years after World War II, the government spent considerable sums cleaning up war debris throughout American possessions in Micronesia. In 1963, about two thousand visitors called on Guam. Facilities were limited, mainly to seventy rooms in the Cliff Hotel above Hagatna. Only later in the decade, with Japan's economy doing well and Japanese tourists coming to make up the bulk of those visiting Guam, did tourism begin to take off. The number of people visiting Guam mushroomed to seventy-five thousand in 1970. About 83 percent of the tourists were Japanese, leading one writer to label the tourist boom "Japan's new invasion of Guam." Continental Airlines and TWA featured flights with jets between Honolulu, Guam, and Hong Kong, and Japan Airlines instituted service to Guam from Tokyo and Osaka. A growing number of hotels housed the tourists. Guam boasted eighteen, a number of them Japanese-owned, with a total of 1,034 rooms, by 1970. Many were along Tumon Beach, just north of Apra Harbor, an area destined to become overcrowded, much like Oʻahu's Waikiki.[24]

Guam's tourist boom continued into the 1990s. High-rise hotels lined Tumon Beach, stressing the island's electric-power, freshwater, and highway infrastructure. Increased air service, a runaway boom in Japan's economy, and legal changes (in 1988 a requirement that Japanese have visas to visit Guam for short trips was discontinued, once again underlining the importance of state actions to economic development) spurred development. In 1986, Guam possessed over three thousand hotel rooms and 585,000 visitors came to the island.[25] As restrictions on foreign investment were lifted, Japanese firms invested in the tourism of Guam and other parts of Micronesia, playing a leading role in the construction of new hotels in the 1980s, just as they did in the Hawaiian Islands. By 1994, Guam was hosting 1.1 million tourists annually, of whom 71 percent were Japanese, in four thousand hotel rooms. Some 275 commercial air flights entered or left Guam every week. A publication of the Guam government correctly observed in 2002 that "Guam's economy relies heavily on tourism revenue," although the number of tourists visiting the island remained about the same as it had been eight years earlier. The 1990s slump in the Japanese economy hurt tourism on Guam. However, in the early 2000s, as Japan's economy recovered, so did Guam's. In 2004, tourist arrivals topped one million for the first time in four years.[26]

The only partial success in economic diversification was not unique to Guam. The TTPI was dissolved in 1978, and American trusteeship of Micronesia began to end. In its place politically independent entities arose:

the Republic of the Marshall Islands, the Republic of Belau (Palau), and the Federated States of Micronesia (FSM). The northern Marianas became the Commonwealth of the Northern Mariana Islands, an American commonwealth. The Republic of Nauru and the Republic of Kiribati became members of the British Commonwealth. The Republic of the Marshall Islands and the FSM entered into a Compact of Free Association with the United States in 1985, and in 2002–2003 the United States Congress renewed that compact. By contrast, Guam remained an organized but unincorporated territory of the United States into 2005, despite a long-standing desire of many Guamanians that their island become a commonwealth. Even with their new political arrangements, the islands of Micronesia have encountered great difficulty in achieving balanced economic growth. As in so many of America's Pacific possessions, uneven growth has been the norm. A lack of varied resources, great distances to markets, and colonial legacies have dogged their efforts.[27]

Economic diversification and economic freedom from the United States have proven to be elusive. Throughout most of Micronesia, governments, subsidized by the United States government, were the largest employers, often providing work to as much as 60 percent of those employed in wage-earning jobs. Nor has full political freedom been achieved. In return for their political independence, the states formed from the TTPI have generally had to accede to American conditions: that no other country could use their islands for military purposes; that American military forces, including nuclear ones, would have free transit through the islands; and that the United States could establish military bases on the islands, including the continued use of the Kwajalein Atoll as a missile range. The United States paid for these rights, which made the new nations all that more dependent on America. Those payments, which were adjusted upward in the 1980s and 1990s, galled many Guamanians, who thought that they were not receiving their fair share of largesse from Uncle Sam.[28]

Continuing a long tradition, Guam's largest single employer in 1970 was government. The federal government employed 6,676 Guamanians, and the local government, known as GovGuam, gave work to an additional 5,486. This situation was not new. In 1948, nearly 40 percent of Guam's workers had found employment with the navy or other federal agencies on the island. Nor did this situation change much in later decades. Government—although now the local not the federal government—remained the largest employer in the late 1990s. Not until 2004, for example, was Guam's telephone exchange privatized. GovGuam provided jobs to about 14,000 people.[29] They were not low-paying ones, especially by Pacific Island standards. In fact, in 1990 Guam moved ahead of a state in per capita income for the first time, as the per capita income in Guam of $9,928 slightly exceeded that in Mississippi of $9,648. The per capita income for all of the United States was $14,420. This contrasted to a per capita income of $535 in the Republic of Kiribati, the lowest in Micronesia.[30]

These jobs supported a growing number of residents on Guam. About 22,000 people lived on the island in 1940, of whom 91 percent were Chamorros. By 1980, Guam's population had risen to roughly 105,000, of whom just 55 percent were Chamorros. Chamorros lived throughout Guam, but several old-time Chamorro settlements, Merizo and Umatac, were located in southwest Guam and became centers for debates about where to locate a national park and seashore on the island in the 1970s and 1980s. In 2000, the island's population stood at 155,000, including at least 50,000 residents who were foreign-born. Many of the immigrants had come from other parts of Micronesia, which under the terms of the Compact of Free Association had unrestricted immigration access to Guam. Yet, even as opportunities on Guam attracted other Micronesians, a perceived lack of opportunities propelled Guamanians from their territory. By 1990, 49,000 Guamanians were living in mainland America, over one-half of them in California.[31]

The unbalanced economy that Guam developed, one based mainly on the military, government, and tourism, influenced the interaction of environmental and developmental issues on the island. Guamanians, like others throughout the Pacific, sought to find a workable balance between economic development and environmental preservation. They did so, however, in the shadow of the United States military. The past history of the American military's actions on Guam, especially its taking of land, greatly affected Guamanians' perceptions of the issues.

Controversies about Military Facilities on Guam and the Philippines

Issues of military influence, economic development, environmental change, and indigenous people's rights merged in the question of where to build a new ammunition wharf on Guam. From the 1940s, the navy had maintained a pier known as Hotel Wharf well inside Apra harbor, at which ships unloaded ammunition for use by the navy and the air force. The ammunition was either trucked inland several miles to a storage magazine, which the navy called NAVMAG Guam and which supported the Seventh Fleet, or was taken directly to air-force bases on the island. The air-force bases included Strategic Air Command bases for B-52s armed with nuclear weapons. Surrounded by an extensive breakwater known as the Glass Breakwater, Apra harbor was protected from the open sea.

Problems arose in using Hotel Wharf as a munitions transfer point, especially as its usage intensified with the escalation of the Vietnam conflict in the 1960s. B-52 bombers flew from Guam airfields, armed with bombs brought in through Apra harbor. Simply put, Hotel Wharf was too close to commercial installations. To guard against damage should an accidental explosion of conventional weapons occur, the navy needed to locate its ammunition wharf about two miles from any such installations. Hotel Wharf's proximity to commercial facilities dampened development in Apra harbor just as tourism and other forms of economic activities were taking off, thus throttling efforts to make Guam's economy less reliant on the military. More than development issues were involved in building a new ammunition wharf. Wherever the wharf was placed, whether somewhere within Apra harbor far from commercial installations or at a location elsewhere on the island, it would likely hurt Guam's flora and fauna. It might also affect the activities of Guamanians, for any commercial building or home within a two-mile radius of the wharf would have to be relocated to clear the possible blast zone of people.

Still more was involved in relocating the ammunition wharf, for that issue was closely related to two others: where to establish a national park on Guam and where to locate a national seashore. The issues impinged upon one another, as decisions made about any one affected each of the others. As was so often the case in the Pacific, a seemingly simple matter quickly became complex. At first, navy officials viewed the relocation of their ammunition wharf mainly in technical terms. However, as Guamanians became involved in efforts both to develop their island economically and to preserve parts of its physical and cultural environments, navy officers had to broaden their outlooks, and over several decades viable compromises were worked out about where and how to construct a new ammunition wharf.[32]

The desires of military, especially navy, officials and the hopes of businesspeople on Guam coincided in pushing the federal government to end the use of Hotel Wharf as a munitions pier. The navy wanted the construction of a wharf capable of handling several ships simultaneously unloading up to 9 million pounds of ammunition, surrounded by a blast zone of 10,400 feet (this zone was called "an explosive safety quantity distance" or ESQD). Small, obsolete, and too close to commercial piers, Hotel Wharf no longer sufficed. A 10,400-foot blast zone around the wharf included virtually all of the outer Apra harbor and part of the inner Apra harbor, including many areas where new commercial development was desired. In fact, Hotel Wharf could operate as an ammunition wharf only with a special safety waiver granted by the federal government. With new, fast large ammunition ships coming into use, the need to relocate the wharf was seen as especially urgent by the navy.[33]

Business leaders feared that blast-zone restrictions were hampering economic development and strongly supported the navy's desire to construct a new wharf. The Guam Chamber of Commerce gave "its wholehearted support and approval" to the navy's proposal to move its wharf. Typical of the many Guamanian business leaders who testified favorably at public hearings was the general manager and vice president of Guam Oil & Refining. "The present location and the requisite restriction of operations in the harbor area," he complained, "severely restricts the necessary and orderly development and usage of the commercial port area" and thus acted as "a restrictive force on the economy of Guam."[34]

Navy officials agreed. They observed that "the potential for economic growth is excellent" on Guam. Containerized cargo handling began in 1969, strengthening Guam as a transportation hub, and "tourist steamers" were calling on the island in growing numbers. However, they also noted that "the lack of clear zones from explosives loading and unloading performed by the military is a considerable deterrent to commercial development of Apra Harbor." This unfortunate circumstance, they further recognized, "prevents the government of Guam from realizing the full tax base and revenue potential of the harbor." The relocation of the munitions wharf could open the way to economic growth.[35]

With business and military leaders in agreement, the only question remaining was where to construct a new wharf. Therein lay the rub. The selection of a new site proved difficult and time-consuming, and required compromises on the part of the many parties engaged in it. Specific site selection actions pitted the navy against Guamanians, but more was involved. As historian Michael Clement has written, the "controversy was just as much an internal conflict in the Government of Guam as it was a clash of military and Guamanian desires."[36] Technical considerations such as wind and wave directions, economic matters, especially the costs involved in building and maintaining a suitable wharf, and environmental and cultural issues all played important roles in the decisions of where to build the new wharf. Between 1964 and 1977, the navy investigated twenty-six potential sites, from

Ritidian Point in the north to Cetti Bay and Sella Bay in the southwest, in eight separate engineering and environmental studies.[37] Most possibilities were quickly discarded, but several received careful consideration.

Sella Bay attracted considerable favorable attention in the late 1960s and early 1970s. Without consulting Guamanians, navy officials announced in 1969 that they would build the pier at Sella Bay.[38] Compared to several other sites then also under review, it offered technical and cost advantages. Navy officials estimated that it would be less expensive to build a wharf, purchase land, and build roads at Sella Bay than at other places. Then, too, a wharf there could, they thought, be used 360 days per year, more days than at most other sites. Moreover, such a wharf would be close to the inland naval storage magazine, just seven miles away by truck. Finally, only twenty homes fell within the projected blast zone, compared to as many as a thousand at some possible locations.[39]

Initially there was a fair amount of local support for the Sella Bay option. The executive vice president of the Guam Chamber of Commerce argued forcefully for construction there. As Clement has observed, "A key concern of businessmen at the time was to establish a private sector not dependent on the U.S. military."[40] Above all, the chamber official stressed the need to move the munitions wharf out of Apra harbor to open that port to commercial development. The chamber's executive vice president thought that technical considerations made Sella Bay a logical choice. Few people, he observed, would have to be relocated. Moreover, building the wharf at Sella Bay would protect the area's physical and cultural environments. The blast zone surrounding the pier would preclude any hotel or resort developments nearby, thus enhancing "the area for such use as recreation, conservation, ecological and marine research." Sella Bay was at the time being considered for inclusion in a new national seashore, and building the ammunition wharf there would, he further asserted, save "the area for the eventual development of the proposed National Seashore Park." Moreover, he claimed that "artifacts in the area," including Chamorro *latte* stone sites, then subject to vandalism, would be better preserved.[41] Composed of Chamorros and non-Chamorros, the chamber backed the navy's plan, more generally, as helping Guamanians build a modern, capitalistic economy.[42]

Far from all Guamanians agreed with these arguments. A growing number argued that the navy had already claimed too much land on Guam and that the beauty of the island needed to be preserved to help tourism develop. One Guamanian explained, "Sella Bay is one of the most scenic spots on the island, and we greatly need it to promote tourism." He observed, moreover, that "Our economic situation on Guam is primarily derived from military expenditures," and concluded, "with the aid of tourism, our economic situation can be greatly enhanced."[43]

Responding to such complaints, the Guam legislature acted. The body held two public hearings on the matter in 1970 and passed a resolution "expressing deep concern over [the] ammo wharf" in July of that year. Additional protests led the legislature to pass a stronger resolution in early 1971 calling for the navy to abandon its plans for Sella Bay. Legislators pointed out that the American military already controlled much of Guam's land and that the navy was proposing to acquire at least an additional 4,400 acres to support the construction of the wharf. The military, they complained, had already placed many of the best fishing and swimming beaches off-limits to the Chamorros who had once lived on them. The members went on to protest against any additional land acquisitions by the military, stating, "One of the most prevalent threats to the cause of preservation and conservation of the lands of the territory is the proposed acquisition by the Federal Government of Sella Bay and the surrounding area, one of the most scenic on the island, being ideal for open beaches and the recreation for the people of Guam." Sovereignty was at issue. Far from protecting the ocean for inclusion in a national seashore or helping to preserve Chamorro culture, the wharf would cause serious environmental degradation. For several years the environmental organization Friends of the Earth had opposed the location of the munitions wharf at Sella Bay, and the Guam legislature closed its resolution by calling upon that group "to use its best efforts, including the taking of any legal action which it might feel appropriate to help the people of Guam in opposing the acquisition of Sella Bay by the Federal Government for the development of an ammunition wharf."[44]

That legal opposition was forthcoming. Members of the Guam legislature, together with representatives of several environmental bodies, sued the governor of Guam to prevent building the wharf at Sella Bay. In agreement with the navy and the Chamber of Commerce, the governor was trying to work out a land exchange—the navy would acquire extensive land holdings owned by the government of Guam around Sella Bay in return for ceding land elsewhere, especially in Apra harbor, to the government of Guam—which would allow construction at Sella Bay to begin. Backed by a petition signed by fifteen thousand Guamanians to "Save Sella Bay," those mounting the lawsuit were successful on appeal in 1973 to the Ninth Circuit Court in San Francisco—the same court that later ruled in favor of native Hawaiians occupying Kaho'olawe. Unable to acquire the shore land it needed, the navy reluctantly abandoned its efforts to establish a munitions pier at Sella Bay.[45]

Individuals as well as organizations played important roles in decisions involving developmental and environmental matters throughout America's Pacific possessions, a situation certainly true on Guam, as they acted through politics. Paul Bordallo emerged as the Chamorro champion for those opposing the navy's plans for Sella Bay. A senator in the Guam legislature, Bordallo had been educated at Stanford and Harvard Universities, from which institutions he had earned degrees in business administration. He was, in fact, a business leader on Guam. However, unlike most members of Guam's Chamber of Commerce, he opposed the navy out of a sense of outrage about how Guamanians, especially Chamorros, had been treated by it. At Stanford, he had earned a minor in anthropology and as part of his work on that degree had studied indigenous peoples of the Pacific. His father had been a member of the Guam Congress in the 1930s. Bordallo explained in a 2002 interview that "the central issue" in the Sella Bay controversy was "identity" and "sovereignty." "I conceived this Sella Bay," he said, "as a point that could lead to not just verbal confrontation between the Chamorro people of Guam and the United States military," but as one that contained "seeds to very serious consequences in Guam."[46]

The Guam legislature, supported by a public outcry, forced the navy to look elsewhere, in a major power reversal from earlier times. "Perhaps the most significant factor which weighs against the Sella Bay site," navy officers noted ruefully a few years later, "is the growing opposition of the local populace." More than technical and economic matters needed to be addressed. "A major issue," they continued, "is the proposal to use the Sella Bay area as an underwater conservation area." Environmental and cultural matters had trumped technical and economic considerations.[47]

With Sella Bay no longer a possibility, the navy turned its attention to Orote Island, a large rock formation that forms the western tip of the Orote Peninsula, which in turn comprised the southern shore of Apra harbor. Some Guamanians had suggested this location as early as 1972. Orote Peninsula terminated in high cliffs, which could, they thought, contain blasts from accidental explosions. Deep water for moorage was available, as was nearby land for the temporary storage of explosives. All of the peninsula and island was uninhabited federal land, making it unnecessary for the federal government to acquire more land or to relocate people.[48] A commission established by the Guam legislature and the governor of Guam favored the site in no uncertain terms. Members of the commission pointed out that Orote Island was far enough from the commercial sections of Apra harbor, well beyond the blast zone, to allow port development to proceed with few restrictions. They noted that some 40 million dollars'-worth of projects were ready for construction inside the Apra harbor on Cabras Island, owned by the Guam government, if that island could be shown to be outside of any blast zone.[49]

Navy officials agreed that Orote Island was a possible location. Two wharves capable of handling 9 million pounds of ammunition could be built for what they considered a low cost in a technically suitable area. Environmental disturbances could be kept to a minimum, navy officials believed, although twenty-one acres of a coral reef would have to be dredged to a depth of forty-five feet. Most important, navy officials observed, "Placing the pier at the isolated Orote Point site will insure that the expanding commercial port facilities in Apra harbor, coexisting with Navy requirements, can be accommodated without endangering the lives of employees in this 'industrial area.'"[50]

Even so, no munitions wharf was constructed at Orote Island. Plans for such a wharf were prepared in 1974, only to be deleted from the federal government's construction budget in 1978, a victim of the general post-Vietnam conflict scaling back of the American military. More was involved than economics. Some Guamanians and some federal government officials believed that the environmental impact statement about Orote Island grossly underestimated the damage to flora and fauna likely to occur and opposed building wharves there.[51]

Opposition on environmental grounds, combined with economic considerations, killed construction possibilities. As the navy later admitted, "When the Draft EIS was circulated in 1977, the proposal drew heavy criticism on the basis of its environmental impact," and that criticism "plus a high construction cost led to the project being dropped in 1978."[52] Historian Rogers later wrote of Orote Island, "It is a lovely place where I have hiked, fished and scuba dived many times. It would have been obliterated by the wharf complex, hence the objections to building the wharf there."[53] The navy learned once again that it could not ignore environmental issues.

Attention shifted to new areas in the 1980s, as the presidential administration of Ronald Reagan greatly increased federal government expenditures on the military. Two sites within Apra harbor, both having blast zones that would exclude most of the commercial sections of the port and both to be located on land already owned by the federal government, received careful scrutiny. One was a site on Adotgan Point on the Orote Peninsula just a short distance inside the harbor from Orote Island on the tip of the peninsula. The other possibility was a site on the Glass Breakwater, which formed the northern boundary of Apra harbor. Navy officials preferred the Adotgan site for economic and technical reasons. Learning from their past experiences, they were quick to admit that there were environmental drawbacks to building wharves at the Adotgan site. However, the navy believed that mitigation measures could limit most of the problems.[54]

Testimony about the navy's proposal to build its munitions wharf at Adotgan Point in the early 1980s revealed divisions of opinion among both Guamanians and federal government officials. The testimony also showed that the navy had become more responsive to the desires of others. Everyone agreed that it was necessary to relocate munitions handling from Hotel Wharf. The governor of Guam, the Guam legislature, and Guam's representative to the United States Congress endorsed relocation wholeheartedly. All were glad that no more land would need to be acquired by the federal government to construct a pier at either Adotgan Point or the Glass Breakwater.[55] While all could agree that relocating the munitions wharf was necessary, there was initially no consensus about which of the two sites was preferable. Not all favored the choice of Adotgan Point, as environmental and cultural issues again intruded.

Questions quickly arose about the impact a wharf at Adotgan Point would have on Guam's physical and cultural environments, despite the navy's assurances about mitigation measures. Leaders of federal and territorial agencies voiced objections. Officials of the Fish and Wildlife Service in the Department of the Interior had "serious concerns" about the effects of construction on coral reefs and saltwater fish, as did members of the National Marine Fisheries Service in the Department of Commerce. The head of the Environmental Protection Agency also wondered if Adotgan Point was the best location from an environmental point of view. Members of the Guam Planning Agency favored the Glass Breakwater, because placing a wharf there "would do far less environmental damage" and would help preserve "scenic vistas." The chairman of Guam's Division of Aquatic and Wildlife Resources agreed that the site at the Glass Breakwater was "the least environmentally damaging alternative" and concluded that there "was no justification in selecting the Adotgan Point alternative." Likewise, the head of the Guam Environmental Protection Agency stated that he "[could not] agree with the choice of Adotgan Point," for too much coral reef would be lost.[56] Guam's Department of Parks and Recreation officials observed that important historic and prehistoric sites might be damaged in the construction of roads and other shore-based facilities to serve a munition wharf there. Members of the Advisory Council on Historic Preservation in Washington, DC seconded those concerns and added that the pier would be "a visual intrusion" on historic sites.[57]

Demonstrating sensitivity that they had not previously displayed, navy officials responded carefully to all of the objections, leading to acceptance for their plans. They went further. In the fall of 1982, they agreed in a formal memorandum with the government of Guam to design any facilities on Adotgan Point in ways to minimize their impacts, including their visual impact, on historic sites. A year later, they entered into a still more far-reaching memorandum of understanding in which they agreed to establish two substantial ecological reserves on federal land as compensation for any harm the construction at Adotgan Point might do to flora and fauna. One would be a cliff area on the Orote Peninsula, a special habitat for birds; the other would encompass shore lands, the home of several endemic Guamanian birds and the rare fruit bat, and a substantial reef area.[58] Embracing these concessions, nearly all of those who had initially questioned the Adotgan site now supported it. The new ammunitions wharf was completed with federal funding in the late 1980s. Hotel Wharf was turned over to the government of Guam and in the 1990s was used by cruise ships.[59]

Controversies about the location of the munitions wharf on Guam, together with the general matter of land occupied by military bases on that island, resonated with disputes about American military bases in the nearby Philippine Islands. When the Philippines achieved independence from the United States in 1946, the American military retained military bases there. With the coming of the Cold War, and especially with America's involvement in the Vietnam conflict, political leaders in the United States viewed the bases, like those on Okinawa and Guam, as essential bastions against the spread of communism in the Far East. Filipinos were more circumspect about the presence of American bases on their soil. They saw it as a challenge to their national sovereignty. The issue of the bases was complicated, however; for it became tied up in two other disputed matters: American aid to the Philippines and trade tariffs. Filipinos generally pressed Americans for more economic aid and for trade legislation aimed at keeping the American market open to goods from the Philippines, while allowing Filipinos to levy tariffs on goods imported from the United States. In the minds of many Filipinos, economic aid and trade concessions were necessary to reduce their nation's dependence on the United States, a dependency, they argued, that had begun well before 1946.[60]

The story of disputes over the bases was one of declining American, and growing Filipino, power. In 1947, the newly independent Philippines granted the United States ninety-nine-year-long leases over a number of bases, most notably a large air base at Clark Field and a major naval installation at nearby

Subic Bay. In return, United States officials pulled American troops out of Manila, the capital of the Philippines, gave economic aid to the new nation, and met their Filipino counterparts partway on trade issues. During the 1940s and 1950s, the presidential administrations of Harry S. Truman and Dwight D. Eisenhower resisted Filipino efforts to assert any control over the bases, though Eisenhower acknowledged that ownership of the land the bases occupied resided with the Philippines. The U.S. Justice Department had claimed that the United States retained sovereignty to the bases' lands when it transferred title to the rest of the islands to the Philippine government in 1946. A bit later, the United States accepted new boundaries for the Subic Bay base to give jurisdiction over eighty thousand Filipinos in Olongapo to the Philippine government. As part of the base, those in Olongapo had had their lives governed by American law, for American, not Filipino, laws governed the bases—a major bone of contention. In the early 1960s, Filipino leaders successfully renegotiated the length of the bases' leases from ninety-nine to just twenty-five years. Further negotiations concluded in 1979 reduced the size of the bases at Clark Field and Subic Bay, labeled the bases "Philippine," and called for a review the bases' situation every five years.[61] By the late 1980s, the bases employed seventy thousand Filipinos and contributed $1 billion annually to the economy of the Philippines. Even so, mounting Filipino pressures and a reassessment by Americans of the value of the bases led to America's exit from the bases in the early 1990s, ending the United States' century-long direct presence on Filipino soil.[62]

While the controversies involving American bases in the Philippines rarely touched on environmental issues, those concerning where to locate the munitions wharf in Guam did. Moreover, the debates about the wharf had ramifications far beyond that single issue. The heated arguments spilled over into contemporary discussions about the creation of a national park and a national seashore on Guam.

The Creation of the Guam National Seashore

In 1971, Representative Harold Johnson of California, the acting chairman of the Subcommittee on National Parks and Recreation of the House Committee on Interior and Insular Affairs, introduced a joint resolution to the Senate and House to create a national seashore on Guam. Intended to "preserve for public use and enjoyment certain areas possessing outstanding natural, historic, and recreational values," the proposed seashore would encompass a region mapped out for inclusion in a park in 1967. That area was large, a total of 18,470 acres, of which 5,400 would be reef and water. The remaining nearly 13,000 acres would consist of land on Guam either already owned by the federal government or to be purchased by the federal government. Proposed for southwest Guam, the park would include the seashore from Nimitz Beach in the north down through Cetti Bay, Sella Bay, and Umatac Bay, all the way to Cocos Lagoon and Cocos Island in the south. The seashore would also include inland areas adjacent to the beaches, even embracing Mount Lamlam, the highest peak on Guam.[63]

Well aware of local antipathy toward the federal government, those preparing the resolution included safeguards for Guamanians. Property owned by the territory of Guam could be acquired only with the consent of the Guamanian government. There were also limitations on how the federal government could use its powers to purchase privately owned land for the seashore. For one year after the passage of an act establishing the seashore, the federal government was explicitly forbidden from using condemnation powers to buy lands in the villages of Umatac and Merizo, which were populated mainly by Chamorro people pursuing traditional lifestyles. Even after that time period had passed, condemnation would be difficult, hemmed in by many restrictions. It was assumed that considerable stretches of private land would always exist within the boundaries of the seashore, and that hunting and fishing would be allowed to continue within the seashore as long as the activities conformed to Guam's laws.[64]

In early 1972, Johnson and other members of his subcommittee traveled to Guam to hold a series of public hearings on the proposed seashore, and they revealed that, while support did exist for the seashore, Guamanians also harbored reservations about it. Paul Bordallo, chairman of the Committee on Agriculture, Resources, and Development for the Guam legislature and the same legislator who was most adamantly opposed to the relocation of the navy's ammunition wharf to Sella Bay, summed up the feelings of many residents. Bordallo praised the congressmen for holding hearings on Guam and listening to local opinions, something, he pointedly said, navy officials never did. He then opened his testimony by observing that the Guam legislature "sincerely and enthusiastically" supported the creation of the seashore.[65]

However, Bordallo spent most of his time expressing doubts. "First," he noted, "we think the proposed size of the park is too large." It would be a mistake, he continued, "to deduct a substantial part of our limited area from the tax rolls and from the jurisdiction of our government," for to do so would "seriously inhibit the development of Guam." After denouncing the navy's effort to appropriate land in Sella Bay, he stressed "how much the people of Guam resent involuntary condemnation and how important it is that the Park Service negotiate with private landowners within the taking and permit them to remain within the seashore so long as they conform to the master plan." He went further in his defense of the rights of Guamanians, saying that the National Park Service should share responsibility for the administration of the seashore with the government of Guam. Administrators should also, Bordallo asserted, give preference to Guamanians for jobs, especially in running concessions for the park. "We don't want to see a system develop," he concluded, "where the chiefs are all from the mainland United States and the Indians are all from the local reservation."[66]

In his recommendations for the treatment of the Chamorro villages of Merizo and Umatac, Bordallo demonstrated ambivalence, as did many Guamanians. On the one hand, he urged that the seashore be established in ways that would not disrupt the lives of people in those areas. On the other hand, Bordallo said that park planners needed "to recognize the needs of the villages of Merizo and Umatac for normal growth." It would not, he continued, be "appropriate to freeze these communities and preserve them like a fly in amber for all eternity." Perhaps, he thought, controlled tourism, "not a Coney Island type of development," in which the seashore could play a major part, offered a way out of this dilemma. The southern part of Guam, Bordallo finished his testimony, should remain "peaceful and serene."[67]

The Guam legislature had in 1971 passed a resolution introduced by Bordallo calling on all governmental bodies "to preserve and enhance the ancient features and traditions of the southern districts of Guam . . . most akin to the ancient Chamorro way of life." However, the resolution went on to incorporate some of the same contradictions as Bordallo's later testimony. It noted that "tourists find the atmosphere of the southern districts particularly appealing and picturesque, which gives another reason to take whatever steps necessary to preserve this atmosphere and thereby maintain a great natural tourist attraction." The resolution urged the construction "at an appropriate site within the locale of an old Chamorro village, complete with thatched roof buildings, latte stone sites, and all else required to recreate in the southern part of Guam an authentic habitat of the autochthonous inhabitants of the Marianas." It further called for the building of "a by-pass highway system so as to preserve the slow pace of the three southern villages and yet permit motor vehicles a rapid transit to the area."[68]

Most Guamanians who testified agreed with Bordallo. Nearly all said that the creation of seashore could help preserve Guam's environment. Many noted with satisfaction that it would preclude the navy's building an ammunition wharf in Sella Bay while encouraging desired forms of economic development. They believed, that, if done carefully, the creation of a national seashore could help free Guam's economy from dependence on the military. George Bamba, chairman of the Committee on Ecology and Environment for the Guam legislature, further explained that such a creation would keep the area out of the grips of outside entrepreneurs as well. He complained that "Japanese-run hotel" facilities were taking over his island, making Guam "an economic colony of Japan," and said that he favored the seashore, with locally owned and operated concessions, as a move in the direction of economic diversification and freedom. By this time, some were calling this part of Guam "the Japanese Riviera."[69]

More than economics was involved. The president of the Guam Environmental Council, who described his group as being composed of "local residents who are dedicated to the maintenance of quality environment for the people and community of Guam," asserted that his organization desired a national seashore because it would "enhance the social, economic, cultural, and natural environment of the island." He noted in particular that it could protect "the people's heritage" and Chamorro lifestyle. Much was seen as being involved in the creation of a national seashore. Indeed, a petition sponsored by the Guam Environmental Council, signed by sixty-five hundred Guamanians, captured well the sometimes conflicting thoughts. A National Seashore was needed, the petition to the secretary of the interior read, "for its potential contribution to knowledge of tropical Pacific ecology, and for its recreational benefits to local residents and to the large and growing number of tourists on the island."[70]

Like Bordallo, most of the same Guamanians testifying in favor of the creation of a national seashore had reservations. Above all, they feared that its establishment might become an excuse for the federal government to seize more land. The example of the navy's designs on Sella Bay was never far from their minds. A lawyer, who was at the time representing several Guamanians claiming that they had lost land unfairly to the navy, expressed such thoughts when he said that, if not done justly, setting aside land for the seashore would "force still more Guamanians off of their land and into the urban mold." He called upon members of the subcommittee to "at least require that the individual landowners of this island be given the opportunity of acquiring land of like character and dimension in exchange for that which they must surrender" and pleaded, "Don't give a man a handful of dollars." A resident of Umatac was even more blunt. In a letter published in Guam's leading newspaper in 1971 and then entered into the 1972 hearings, he addressed the "Uprooted People of Guam." He urged that they "let themselves be heard before they all wither and die from so many transplantings," a reference to land losses attributable to the federal government.[71]

The impassioned testimony of the Guamanians made its impression on the visiting congressmen. Representative Philip Ruppe of Michigan noted at the conclusion of the hearings that he was glad to learn that Guamanians supported the idea of a national seashore and believed that they were "correct in expressing your concern over the land use that would be part of such a development."[72] Over the next few years, the measure creating a national seashore on Guam was reworked to embody many of the desires of the Guamanians. In 1978, the U.S. Congress established a Territorial Seashore Park, encompassing 12,500 acres of Sella Bay and surrounding land from Agat in the north to Merizo in the south, thus setting up an area considerably smaller than the one that had been surveyed a decade earlier. Development was restricted and, according to the leading historian of Guam in 1995, "Sella Bay remains uninhabited and pristine."[73] A publication of the Guam Visitors Bureau noted in 2004 that Sella Bay, the center of the seashore, "is accessible only on foot, by way of a 1.5-mile hike beginning south of the town of Agat." The guide continued, "The bay has good corals and underwater caves, making it excellent for swimming and snorkeling." Culture, as well as flora and fauna, might be enjoyed: "Hikers will discover ancient latte stones and pottery shards, which are all that remain of Sidya, a Chamorro village that was deserted nearly 200 years ago."[74]

The Establishment of the War-in-the-Pacific National Historical Park on Guam

Even as the Congressional Subcommittee on National Parks and Recreation was conducting hearings on Guam about the creation of a national seashore there in 1972, its members listened to testimony about a proposed national park for the island. To be called the War-in-the-Pacific National Historical Park, it would commemorate American military campaigns during World War II, especially the one to retake Guam from the Japanese in 1944. Introduced into Congress by Representative Richard C. White of Texas, who as a marine had landed on Guam to recapture the island, the park bill raised many of the same issues that the act to create a national seashore had stirred up, but contained some interesting twists. White's measure envisioned the establishment of a park encompassing beaches on which the marines had landed and a substantial inland region composed of places at which battles had been fought, for a total of about 2,800 acres in areas including Asan, Agat, and Mount Tenjo. It was proposed that a museum and commemorative markers would grace these lands.[75]

Nearly all Guamanians who testified said they favored the park's creation. A member of the Guam legislature observed that the park "has met with favorable consideration from the people of Guam and the members of the Guam legislature." It would be, he thought, "a fine tribute to the battles on Guam" and "a living memorial to the entire Pacific campaign." He noted further that "Guam has developed into a key position of U.S. military activity in the Pacific" and that "the military personnel stationed on Guam would receive a sense of pride and historical perspective from a national park such as that proposed." More was involved than patriotism. After discussing the increase in tourism on Guam, he supported constructing the park, because doing so "would be of substantial assistance to Guam's developing tourism." The director of Guam's Department of Commerce made the same point, testifying that he thought a national park would aid "our budding tourist industry and our economy." Others favored the establishment of the park more as a way to preserve increasingly scarce open space. A representative of the Guam Environmental Council praised the proposal for saving "open space needed to maintain the charm and dignity of Guam." Quality-of-life matters concerned him the most. "For all of our construction, new highways and all of the growth that we see on your island of Guam," he explained, "I hope we and certainly you never lose sight of the fact that the environment of the island should be one where it is very fine and very good for the people of Guam to live and enjoy."[76]

Nonetheless, even proponents had questions. Many thought that the proposed park was too large and gave too much power to the federal government. The same Guam legislator who testified in favor of the park noted that "land on Guam is exceedingly dear" and called for a park of more limited size. He thought that the federal government should be allowed to acquire land only with the concurrence of the governor of Guam and the Guam legislature, and wanted provisions added to the legislation to provide the people of Guam with a say in the administration of the park. The director of Guam's Department of Commerce noted that "our recent past has demonstrated that we cannot allow a Federal agency to have carte blanche in Guam." He, too, said that the government of Guam must have veto power over any land acquisitions and that Guamanians needed to be involved in running the park. Even the member of the Guam Environmental Council who favored the park as a means of preserving open space cautioned, "We would like to see some publicity here on the island so that we will know that they are not going to include three-fourths of the area of Guam." All made reference in their park testimony to the controversy over the plan to build a munitions wharf in Sella Bay, which was made with almost no local consultation, as a poor way to conduct matters.[77]

Congress authorized the expenditure of $16.5 million to create the War-in-the-Pacific National Historical Park in 1978, with all except $500,000 to be spent on the acquisition of land. It included seven different units of land. A second park called the American Memorial Park was created on Saipan. However, for over a decade little was done. In the fifteen years after 1978, the U.S. Congress actually appropriated only $3 million to purchase land for the park on Guam. Of this amount just $2.5 million were spent, enough to acquire less than 40 percent of the private land within the park's boundaries. Congressman Morris Udall, chair of the House Committee on Natural Resources, visited Saipan and Guam in 1989 with other committee members to try to drum up support for the parks, to little avail. Acres of privately owned land remained inside the park on Guam. Meanwhile, it was only in 1983 that the National Park Service submitted a general management plan to congressional committees. Federal government budgetary restrictions retarded park development.[78] Even in beginning to construct the park, the National Park Service, despite all of the voices of Guamanians heard at public hearings, rode roughshod over some local desires. The government of Guam had planned to build a new small boat harbor at Agat. However, this location was one of the places where the marines had landed, and the federal government took it over, despite protests from outraged Guamanians, for the park. The Park Service seized the land by declaring a rusty World War II sewer pipe on the land to be a historic landmark.[79]

The park remained unfinished in the early 1990s, a situation that dismayed many as the fiftieth anniversary of World War II approached. To determine how best to proceed, Congress held a new round of hearings on a measure to fund the park adequately in 1993. The bill would appropriate $8 million for the park on Saipan and $11 million for the one on Guam. Held in Washington, DC, the hearings were a love feast, with no one dissenting from the park plans. The governor of Guam, representatives of the Guam legislature, members of Guam's American Legion post, and many marine veterans, including a former commandant of the Marine Corps, testified either in person or by correspondence in favor of the park. Gone were any doubts about the acquisition of land by the federal government or any misgivings about how the park might be administered. Instead, a new element not present in the hearings two decades before rose to prominence—Chamorro culture. Many Chamorros had lost their lives during the Japanese occupation of Guam and in the fighting by Americans to retake the island.[80]

In 1993, a proposal to include in the park on Guam a memorial to those Chamorros won overwhelming support. Typical was the handwritten letter of one Guamanian to the Congress, which argued that with a memorial "our unique Chamorro culture will be appreciated and will touch other people across the globe so this world can be peaceful that was meant to be [sic]." The chair of the Guam legislature's Committee on Youth, Senior Citizens and Cultural Affairs went further in linking Chamorro lifestyles, economic development, and the need for the park. She began her testimony by observing that "the comfortable lifestyle we maintain today is tied to that period of turbulence in Guam's history," a reference to World War II. She then stated that in recent years Guam had "undergone an unprecedented frenetic rate of development ... which has diluted the dynamics of our island culture." She concluded that "the same economics that has upgraded our lifestyle has strained the cultural fabric that provides strength and blurs the identity of our people" and supported the measure to build the park "as a means of providing a tangible approach in the preservation of our culture." Another Guamanian urged the construction of the park as a way of saving "our ancient artifacts like the latte stones," which "the native Chamorros once used."[81]

In the end, Congress appropriated the necessary funds, and the War-in-the-Pacific National Historical Park was completed, including a memorial to the Chamorros who had lost their lives during World War II. Covering 1,960 acres in seven units, the park has a visitor center at Asan, where there are interpretive exhibits and audiovisual programs. Designed to "honor all people from all nations who participated in the Pacific War," the park includes in its visitor center exhibits on Chamorro culture and history, as well as exhibits about the war. It also features environmental exhibits, including one on the brown tree snake.[82]

The Invasion of the Brown Tree Snake

A government publication noted with pride in 1953 that Guam was "completely free of poisonous snakes," making the island "a virtual utopia from poisonous bites of any kind."[83] A scant forty-three years later, a scientific report prepared for the U.S. Congress observed the very damaging impacts the brown tree snake was having on Guam. "The brown tree snake *(Boiga irregularis),*" the document noted, "has been a major factor in a modern extinction episode beyond its native range that is unprecedented in its scope: the extirpation of most of Guam's native terrestrial vertebrates, lizards, and virtually all of the island's forest birds." In addition, the report continued, brown tree snakes on Guam had caused "more than a thousand power outages, damaged agricultural interests by preying on poultry, killed many pets, and envenomated numerous children."[84] Journalists reporting on the damage done by the brown tree snake were blunt. One titled his account "The Snake That Ate Guam."[85]

Inadvertently introduced by the American military, the brown tree snake overran the island. Native to Indonesia, New Guinea, the Solomon Islands, and northern Australia, the snake probably entered Guam as a stowaway in a navy ship's cargo shortly after World War II.[86] Having no natural predators on the island and proving to be very adaptable in its exploitation of habitat and food sources, the reptile reached a population density of thirty-five to fifty per acre in the mid-1980s. This meant that there were perhaps 2 million brown tree snakes on Guam, about 20,000 per square mile. The snake was more than simply another pest; it was the cause of a major ecological disaster on Guam and a significant hindrance to the development of the island's economy. Moreover, the brown tree snake threatened to spread to other Pacific Islands, including the Hawaiian Islands, where it could be expected to wreak similar damage.[87]

Julie Savidge, a doctoral candidate in ecology at the University of Illinois, who worked in Guam's Division of Aquatic and Wildlife Resources (DAWR), was the first scientist to fully understand and publicize the harm the brown tree snake was causing. By the 1970s, Guamanians noticed that birdlife on many parts of their island was becoming increasingly rare. Guam's avifauna consisted of eighteen native birds, mainly forest dwellers such as the bridled white-eye, the Guam flycatcher, and the Rufous fantail. Many of these were unique to Guam, not even living on nearby islands like Rota. In 1978, those with the DAWR proposed that ten of Guam's native birds and two species of fruit bats be placed on the federal government's list of endangered species. Two of these birds, the Guam rail and the Micronesian broadbill, lived nowhere else in the world. The agency also advanced a plan to try to discover the causes for the decline in the populations of the birds. Savidge was tapped for that investigation.[88]

Her work showed conclusively that the brown tree snake was responsible for the plummeting numbers of birds. Scientists and nonscientists alike had suspected other causes, for up to that time no snake had been implicated in the wholesale destruction of birdlife anywhere in the world; thus the situation on Guam was a new one. Through extensive field work, Savidge and others at the DAWR had ruled out other possibilities: pesticide contamination, loss of habitat, competition from introduced birds, exotic diseases (avian malaria was at the time decimating bird species endemic to the Hawaiian Islands), and the depredations of rats. Then, through careful research in old newspapers and written reports and through the use of interviews and questionnaires with people throughout Guam, Savidge determined both when brown tree snakes were first noticed in different regions and when birdlife began disappearing from those areas. When it became clear that the arrival of snakes corresponded to the decline in birdlife, Savidge thought she had uncovered why the birds were disappearing. When additional fieldwork revealed that brown tree snakes ate all kinds of birds—and lizards and fruit bats, which were also becoming scarce—she was sure of it.[89]

Savidge was able to determine how the brown tree snake had spread on Guam. Introduced through Apra harbor sometime in the late 1940s or early 1950s, the snakes spread to southern Guam in the 1950s, to central Guam in the mid-1960s, and to Guam's northern extremities in the late 1970s and early 1980s. By early 1983, ten forest bird species managed to survive only in a small forest below the cliff line at the northern tip of Guam, a place the snakes could not reach. Birds also flourished on Cocos Island, a small islet just south of Guam—again, a place snakes had not reached. By this time, several of Guam's bird species were presumed to be extinct in the wild. Some survived in captivity through the heroic efforts of zoo curators, and some of these birds were later reintroduced to the wild. Others were completely lost.[90]

The impacts of the brown tree snake were multiple. By 1986, nine species of birds had been extirpated and others were endangered. At a time when the protection of their flora and fauna, including birdlife, featured prominently in debates about where to build the navy's ammunition wharf and where to locate parks, the depredations of the snakes alarmed Guamanians, especially as they came to see birds endemic to Guam as part of their natural and cultural heritage. There were also unexpected consequences. With most birds gone, growing swarms of mosquitoes might spread diseases such as the deadly dengue fever. Then, too, as they invaded buildings, the nocturnal snakes, which are mildly venomous, bit babies and children as they slept. By 1994, some 206 snakebites had been recorded, including eleven serious cases involving babies less than one year old. In addition, snakes climbed guy wires leading to poles supporting electrical power lines, often creating short circuits. Power outages became common just as uninterrupted electric flows were most needed for touristic developments. Between 1978 and 1994, there were twelve hundred such outages, and it was "conservatively estimated that power outages on Guam caused by brown tree snakes have cost millions of dollars a year." These power disruptions had many ramifications. As a government report observed, "Snakes startle people, and power outages frequently cut short their enjoyment of Guam's nightlife and shopping centers." Power outages also shut down refrigeration units and computers. Not only were the snakes dangerous and spreading diseases, they were also bad for business.[91]

Brown tree snakes threatened to become a problem throughout the Pacific. Very hardy, they could hitchhike to other islands in the wheel wells and cargo holds of airplanes and in cargo containers leaving Guam by ship. Biologists warned that "exotic snakes pose an enormous threat to other islands" and observed that it was "imperative that they be eliminated from interisland transport." Brown tree snakes were repeatedly found on Oʻahu in the 1980s and 1990s, brought in accidentally by military airplanes. Closer to Guam, numerous sightings of brown tree snakes occurred on Saipan, Tinian, and Rota. It was deemed likely that a colony of the snakes was established on Saipan by the 1990s. Kwajalein, Pohnpei, Wake Island, Okinawajima, and the Diego Garcia Atoll (in the Indian Ocean) reported less frequent sightings.[92]

Conceding that the snakes would never be completely eliminated from Guam, scientists and governmental officials hoped in the early 2000s to reduce their numbers through an integrated management plan that would alter their habitat and use both chemical and biological controls.[93] Recognizing the danger that the snakes might spread beyond Guam, in 1991 Congress added a section to the Nonindigenous Aquatic Nuisance Prevention and Control Act of 1990 to authorize a cooperative program to control the snake. Representatives of the Departments of Agriculture, Commerce, Defense, and the Interior, the Commonwealth of the Northern Mariana Islands (in which Tinian and Saipan lay), the territory of Guam, and the state of Hawaiʻi formed a Brown Tree Snake Control Committee in 1993 to develop an integrated pest control approach.[94]

By the close of the 1990s, the most stringent controls applied to the Hawaiian Islands. Working with the Brown Tree Snake Control Committee, the Hawaiian legislature established an Alien Species Action Plan in 1994. As it was applied to brown tree snakes over the next few years, this plan meant that all airplanes leaving Guam for Hawai'i were inspected for snakes on the ground in Guam and were checked again once they landed at a Hawaiian airport. Finally, the state established Snake Watch Alert Teams (SWAT) to seek out and destroy any snakes that might somehow have gotten loose in the Hawaiian Islands. Fears that brown tree snakes might run wild on Maui contributed substantially to a decision not to extend the length of the major runway of that island's main airport. A longer runway might allow airplanes to fly in directly from Guam, and those airplanes, many Mauians feared, might bring in brown tree snakes. Even so, in the summer of 2004 some residents suspected that brown tree snakes had gotten loose in the Hana region of Maui. In the winter of 2005, residents expressed similar fears about O'ahu.[95]

Developments in American Samoa

Developments in American Samoa, the only possession of the United States south of the equator, offer a valuable contrast to those on Guam.[96] Along with other European nations, the United States developed an interest in the Samoan Islands in the late nineteenth century for strategic purposes. The United States annexed the islands of Tutuila and Aunu'u in 1900 and the nearby island group of Manu'a four years later, despite the desire of chiefs in the last group to remain independent. These annexations were confirmed by Congress in 1929. The main goal was to create a naval coaling station and communications center at Pago Pago on Tutuila. To this end, American Samoa, like Guam, was placed under the administration of the navy, which gave tremendous leeway to local commanders. The naval administration lasted until 1951, when administration was shifted to the Department of the Interior, just as took place on Guam.[97]

The land area of American Samoa comes to about seventy-three square miles and is mainly mountainous. The climate is tropical. Comprising about three-quarters of American Samoa's land and 95 percent of its population, Tutuila is the most important island, home to the port of Pago Pago, which serves as the commercial center. Possessing several tuna-fish canneries, its harbor is, according to recent descriptions, "polluted and muddy." On "bad tuna days" the stench "will take your breath away." The three small islands of the Manu'a group, about sixty-two miles east of Tutuila, are much less developed, "100 years away" from the commercialization on Tutuila.[98]

As on Guam and Hawai'i, indigenous inhabitants in the Samoan Islands altered the landscape through their cultivation practices well before the coming of westerners, as a detailed study of Ofu Island in the Manuʻa group has shown. Bringing rats, pigs, dogs, and chickens with them, settlers reached Ofu about three thousand years ago. They exterminated five of ten native seabirds and one of three native land birds. Moreover, their cultivation largely modified Ofu's coastal terrace, with their slash-and-burn agriculture contributing to the loss of native birdlife through habitat destruction.[99]

By contrast, the naval administration, in the words of historian Steven Fischer, "transformed little in this part of Samoa."[100] For the most part, U.S. Navy administrators ruled in consultation with established local leaders and tried not to upset established ways of doing things. When a consultative legislature was established, members were chosen from established village districts, and, not surprisingly, well-known local leaders won election. Nor did many changes come to the economies of the islands. Subsistence agriculture and fishing continued as before, with copra about the only export. A 1952 naval report observed, "It is difficult to conceive of any nation gaining economic or financial benefit from American Samoa," for "the island resources have no potential." In a major difference from the situation on Guam, the navy appropriated little land for military usage, just 121 acres, and enforced ordinances preventing the loss of land by Samoans to outsiders. Nor were many nonresidents allowed to set up businesses in American Samoa, for fear that they might exploit residents. Some 99 percent of the land remained in Samoan hands in 1951. Even so, all was not harmony. In the 1920s, a strong movement for autonomy developed among Samoans, including those in American Samoa. Called "Mau," which means opinion, the movement called for the establishment of a civilian government. Those in the campaign accomplished little in the eyes of naval officers except to disrupt economic development by their interminable meetings. Naval officers improved health in American Samoa, leading to a doubling of the population every twenty-five years after 1900, until it reached about 24,000 in 1950. They also established an elementary and secondary public school system enrolling about 3,500 pupils. Another 1,175 students were in private missionary schools. Technological advancements made Pago Pago obsolete as a naval station, and the navy pulled out in 1951–1952. Here was a basic difference from Guam where, of course, the U.S. military increased its presence and its land acquisitions during the Cold War.[101]

Only in the 1960s did economic circumstances begin to change in American Samoa, but even then not nearly as much as on Guam. Under the administration of President John F. Kennedy, infrastructure improvements were made: new roads, an international airport, sewage-treatment facilities, and so on. The number of tuna canneries increased. The first tourist hotel was constructed. Even so, tourism failed to develop into a mainstay of the economy. In 2003, a leading guidebook still described accommodation options as "very limited" and labeled the largest hotel, which was government-run, as "infamous." There was one national park in American Samoa, with three units totaling nine thousand acres on the islands of Tutuila, Taʻu, and Ofu. One of the park's goals was to help preserve native society, and villagers were allowed to continue gathering plants from park areas for cultural and medicinal purposes. Nonetheless, traditional society eroded, and alcohol, juvenile delinquency, and crime problems surfaced. Moreover, civilian administrators created "a small welfare state." Appropriations to American Samoa from the U.S. government came to about $34 million annually in the early 2000s. Per capita income reached $8,000 annually.[102]

Even as Samoan society began to become commercialized, traditional titles and land tenures remained largely unchanged, and outside entrepreneurs were restricted in their access to American Samoa. The establishment of the tuna canneries was the exception, not the rule. Unlike native Hawaiians, American Samoans benefited handsomely from American subsidies and spoke little of seeking independence from the United States. In 2005, American Samoa remained an unincorporated, unorganized territory of the United States—by choice, not coercion. Unlike what occurred on Guam, American Samoan leaders opted not to try to win an organic act from Congress. To do so, they realized, would force them to give up racial preferences in landownership, which are unconstitutional under American law. An organic act might also force them to adhere to minimum-wage laws, thus undercutting advantages enjoyed by the tuna canneries.[103]

In fact, American Samoa became (and is) a prime example of a MIRAB economy, dependent on the migration of its people abroad and their remittances home, as well as on congressional appropriations. One-third of the workforce is employed by the territorial government. About sixty-two thousand American Samoans lived beyond their islands in the 1990s, mainly in California and Hawaiʻi, considerably more than the forty thousand residing in American Samoa.[104] Author Tom Conger captured well the "push" and "pull" forces that led many to leave American Samoa. Writing in 1996, he observed that the only major business in Pago Pago, the tuna-packing plant, imported its seasonal workers from Japan, and that most of the fishing boats were crewed by non-Samoans. "There's a bit of government work . . . and a few work in the hotel," he noted. However, in general, there was "Nothing for the Samoan kids to look forward to. That's why so many head to the U.S. as soon as their families can arrange."[105]

World traveler Paul Theroux, perhaps a bit jaded, has left an equally vivid and dispiriting picture of life in American Samoa. Commenting on the congressional subsidies, he concluded, "Life in American Samoa is one long Yankee boondoggle, and the people are so hoggishly contented that they cannot stand the idea of ever forming an independent political entity." He called residents "corrupted" and "fat jolly people, with free money, having a wonderful time." Samoa, Theroux believed, "had become part of the American family and was content." "Samoans," he thought, "were generally unenthusiastic, but similarly they were uncomplaining."[106] What Theroux missed, of course, was the lack of opportunities available in American Samoa, which led to the massive involvement of American Samoans in the Pacific diaspora.

Conclusions

Events on Guam in the years after World War II amply illustrate some of the difficulties involved in trying to reconcile economic development matters, environmental protection issues, the rights of indigenous peoples, and the desires of the American military in the Pacific. Developments on Guam also showed, however, that compromises could be reached. Navy officers initially approached matters such as the location of its new ammunition wharf from a technical and economic viewpoint but, pushed by other groups, widened their outlook to include environmental considerations. The growing sensitivity of navy officials coincided with the problems they faced in the Hawaiian Islands with regard to Kahoʻolawe, and to similar problems elsewhere in the Pacific. Because CINCPAC was ultimately responsible for the navy's stances on local issues in Guam and the Hawaiian Islands, it is likely that the thinking of navy officers about issues in both regions was related, although no "smoking gun" in the way of documentation exists.

As in most other areas dealt with in this study, compromises were arranged in the political arena, and the political process on Guam grew more pluralistic as time went on. More and more people and their organizations had effective access to political decision making. That process, as in other Pacific areas in which the United States had influence, was tinged with a dislike of federal government authority, leading to increased questioning about the roles of the American military on Guam.

Decisions to establish a national park and seashore on Guam were, like that involved in siting the ammunition pier, made through political debate. Guamanians, including those favoring the preservation of the Chamorro culture, were active in shaping the contours of the enabling legislation. The situation on Guam provides a contrast to the much more inhumane treatment meted out to Native Americans in the earlier creation of many national parks on the American mainland. Largely because of the input of Guamanians, Chamorro rights received attention in establishing the parks and in deciding on a location for the ammunition wharf on Guam. Circumstances on the island resembled the growing attention Alaskan Natives received in planning for the Beringian Heritage International Park. Times changed as new groups demanded and received places at the political table.

The park, seashore, and wharf issues contributed to the development of a Chamorro rights movement on Guam. Like indigenous peoples' movements throughout the Pacific, such as the native Hawaiian renaissance, that movement sought to restore native culture (including language), political influence, and economic power.[107] The Chamorro rights movement also aimed at the restoration of lost lands. Underlying specific concerns was again the issue of sovereignty. In the 1980s and 1990s, Guamanians, especially Chamorros, renewed their quest to regain lands lost to the navy right after World War II. In 1983, the United States Justice Department offered to settle the claims with a total payment of $39.5 million. Most claimants accepted the settlement, and the money was distributed to fifty-two hundred former landowners or their heirs. About two hundred disgruntled claimants held out for larger settlements, and the issue has not yet been resolved.[108] In a related move, in 2000 Congress agreed to take another look at claims for compensation for property, personal injury, and deaths. By 2003, a commission set up by the House of Representatives had collected more than five thousand questionnaires from Guamanians and was considering what actions to take.[109]

While the issues swirling around decisions about where to place the parks and the munitions wharf could be divisive, there was unanimity of opinion about the need to control the brown tree snake. The damages caused by the snake hurt Guam's environment and its business climate. The snake even threatened to bite into tourism, upon which many Guamanians banked to free themselves from the economic grip of the American military. In this case, the problem was not lack of consensus, but lack of knowledge. Until Julie Savidge conducted her research in the 1980s, no one really understood what the snakes were doing to their island, and even in the early 2000s no fully effective control mechanisms had been devised. Like other Pacific Islands, such as Kahoʻolawe, Guam possessed a fragile environment, in which one change could quickly "cascade" to create other alterations: it took less than a generation for most of Guam's birds to disappear. Invasive alien species, while certainly a global issue, had perhaps their greatest immediate impacts on small Pacific islands such as Guam.

Conclusions

I t is worth repeating in closing that the Pacific—one-third of the globe, encompassing millions of square miles and millions of people—has always been, and remains, a large, complex region composed of subregions. Even Oceania, one of the subregions, is itself conventionally divided into Melanesia, Micronesia, and Polynesia. The complexity of the Pacific makes generalizations difficult and fraught with possibility for error. Restricting the scope of investigations to some of the regions owned or controlled by the United States helps a bit, but even within these areas considerable diversity remains. Nonetheless, my work supports several important conclusions.

America's Pacific possessions, from the Aleutian Islands in the north to American Samoa in the south, and from Seattle and Silicon Valley in the east to Guam and the Philippines in the west, may be considered as one region, especially in modern times. Distinctly Pacific issues have been played out in these territories in decision making about economic development and environmental protection matters. World War II was certainly a watershed for all of these territories, but the issues that have arisen since then have also been closely related to the long history of the region. While current events have affected the choices people have made, the historical roots of those choices have been of equal import. History matters. Of course, each of the areas covered has had its own long history, and those local histories have shaped events in discrete ways. Still, several matters have transcended local developments as Pacific phenomena.

The political and economic colonialism of the region has been of particular significance in shaping the parameters within which decisions have been made. Control by westerners was preeminent in the recent history of much of the Pacific, and that history greatly affected developments. Among America's Pacific possessions the legacy of colonialism was perhaps most obvious in the cases of Hawai'i and Guam, but colonialism was also influential elsewhere. Residents in all of these regions harbored the feeling that they were being treated as second-class citizens—or worse—in America's Pacific empire. Their rebellions against that position fueled some of the environmental efforts to control economic growth on their own terms. Pacific peoples particularly had misgivings about America's military presence. From the opposition to the use of Kahoʻolawe as a bombing range, to disdain for federal regulation of fishing in Alaska, to efforts to revise plans for the ammunition dock in Guam, a desire to cast off perceived colonial standing motivated local residents. These feelings persisted as the twenty-first century opened.

World War II served as a catalyst for the development of many economic and environmental improvements in America's Pacific possessions. Pacific peoples were generally glad to have the American military rid their region, especially Micronesia, of Japanese influence and control. They also welcomed the economic growth that accompanied America's increased presence in the Pacific, as military spending for World War II and the Cold War boosted local economies. The conflict and its aftermath opened the Aleutian Islands to new types of fishing, brought economic growth to Hawaiʻi as servicemen later returned as tourists, helped spur the development of Guam, and brought major changes to America's Pacific Coast cities and to southern Japan's urban centers. However, people had short memories. Remembrances of World War II faded, and with that dimming went many favorable opinions of the U.S. military. Moreover, with economic growth came new environmental challenges. Pacific peoples soon found themselves at loggerheads with the American military, especially the U.S. Navy, and with some of the courses developments were taking. Even as some benefited from development, they questioned the various costs it entailed. Developments increased fishing pressures along the Aleutians, created the military ground that became pivotal to Hawaiian protests, altered Guam's ecosystem, and intensified urban growth in the Seattle and Silicon Valley regions.

However, conflict was not a simple matter of locals against outsiders. Divisions existed within the ranks of those living in the various regions. Nowhere were these divisions clearer than in the splits separating indigenous peoples from Euro-Americans moving into their areas. Environmental contests regularly came to involve the rights of indigenous peoples, most obviously in the efforts of native Hawaiians to halt the bombing of Kahoʻolawe, but also in the work of Chamorros to modify park plans on Guam and the desire of Alaskan Natives for input into schemes for an international park for Beringia. Similarly, efforts by Native Americans, especially the Duwamish

Indians, to affect land-use and waterway issues in Seattle became important in the 1990s and later. One exception to this generalization may be Japan, where the native Ainu of northern Japan had little say after the early 1800s. Even in Hiroshima, however, minorities mattered, at least for a short time, as Koreans and *burakumin* influenced the reconstruction of the city for a few years. Nor were outsiders united. In Guam, for example, navy officers sometimes found themselves at odds with other federal government officials on park and dock issues.

What comes through in these controversies is the importance of the state as the arena in which the disputes were resolved. More than that, the state itself was often one of the most important actors on the scene and helped to structure the developmental activities. The U.S. Navy greatly affected developments over much of America's Pacific, especially Guam and Hawai'i. As scholars studying modern American history for twenty years or so have been reemphasizing, state actions matter. My study reaffirms the need to bring the state back into the big picture of economic and cultural development. People as agents of change also deserve attention, however. Individuals were influential in shaping events across the Pacific: Noa Emmett Aluli in Hawai'i, Frederick Terman in Silicon Valley, Lowell Wakefield in Alaska, Shinzō Hamai in Hiroshima, and Paul Bordallo on Guam. People work in modern societies within the frameworks of state organizations, and they often do so through the formation of voluntary bodies, a mark of the development of civil societies. They frequently then use state agencies to achieve their goals. Aluli helped start the voluntary private organization of the PKO but later employed the state agency of the KIRC to restore Kaho'olawe. My study shows how the state interacted with the emergence of numerous cultural and social groups on a wide variety of developmental and environmental issues.

In looking at the Pacific, this study has revealed relationships between urban and rural issues, emphasizing similarities rather than differences between the two types. In all of the areas, with again perhaps the exception of Hiroshima, environmental justice issues were important. The rights of minority peoples often intersected with environmental and developmental issues. From Filipino women dealing with chemical solvents and polluted water supplies in Silicon Valley, to native Hawaiians grappling with land-use matters on Kaho'olawe, to Chamorros reasserting claims to their lands, environmental justice issues cut through the lives of city dwellers and rural peoples alike. Even in Hiroshima, the rights of minorities called for, but did not receive, justice in the reconstruction of the city. Throughout America's

Pacific possessions, economic growth was uneven. Parts of regions benefited more than others, and different groups had varying experiences.

What transpired in the Pacific, and especially on Pacific islands, resonates with developments in other regions. Large as it is, the Pacific is, of course, only part of the globe. In his *Something New under the Sun,* historian John McNeill has emphasized that the rapidity of global population and economic growth in the twentieth century created environmental challenges not known in earlier times, a discontinuity with the past. As he has explained, "There is something new under the sun ... the place of humankind within the natural world is not what it was." In terms of the scale and scope of environmental changes caused by people, he has written, "there has never been anything like the twentieth century."[1] That was certainly true of the Pacific, especially after the Second World War, when the pace of economic and environmental changes accelerated. Economic growth and the integration of the Pacific with other parts of the world altered lifestyles and forced Pacific peoples into making increasingly difficult environmental choices—choices similar to those people were having to make elsewhere in the world; and the types of decisions arrived at by Pacific peoples resembled those made by peoples in some specific parts of the globe.

Many of the same economic development and environmental protection matters Pacific peoples faced were played out in the American West. Here, too, perceived colonialism—often exemplified by the federal government and especially the U.S. military—irked, to put it mildly, Americans moving westward. Moreover, in the American West, as in the American Pacific, outside business enterprises, which provided much of the capital and expertise needed for development, were viewed by many residents as evil predatory interests. It was to counter such perceptions that Wakefield Seafood moved its headquarters from Seattle to an island near Kodiak after Alaska became a state.

The efforts of indigenous peoples in America's Pacific possessions have also resembled in important ways the work of some Native Americans to protect their environments, often by ending or limiting military use of their lands, especially in the West. In the American West, some tribes found themselves opposed to the military over land-use issues. The Western Shoshone, for example, successfully worked with non-Indian groups to derail plans to base a proposed mobile MX missile system in the Great Basin region in the 1980s.[2] Yet, one must be careful not to push this analogy too far. While well aware of these matters, and while sympathizing with the Native Americans, native Hawaiians took little part in these protests against the military, viewing themselves as a Pacific people and most concerned with developments in the Hawaiian and other Pacific islands. Protests on Kahoʻolawe connected more directly with changes taking place in other parts of the Pacific, especially with attempts to stop the use of Pacific islands as nuclear-testing sites and military bases.

Beyond the American West, other regions call for direct comparison to the Pacific. The circumpolar Arctic has in recent decades shared major similarities with parts of the Pacific in its development. Both regions have had very fragile environments; both have suffered from extractive industrial development at the hands of colonial powers, including the Soviet Union and Russia; and in both regions indigenous peoples have been harmed and are now reasserting their rights, especially to aboriginal lands.[3] Certainly, one important issue running through Pacific and Arctic environmentalism has been the fate of native flora and fauna under pressure from alien species. This problem is, of course, global in scope, but it is probably most pronounced in the Pacific, especially on Pacific islands, and in the Arctic.

Possessing especially fragile environments, these regions face situations in which one environmental change can very quickly "cascade" into many others. Thus, brown tree snakes devastated Guam. Nor was this circumstance unusual. In 2005, the Pacific harbored 24 percent of the world's threatened birds, many at risk because of the introduction of invasive species. A Regional Invasive Species Programme devised for the Pacific in 1998 belatedly recognized the problem.[4] Similarly, the introduction of fox farming to the Aleutian Islands in a misguided attempt to create a vehicle for economic development there led to the decimation of native bird populations when hungry foxes escaped into the countryside. Exactly how to revegetate Kahoʻolawe became an important issue in the 1990s and early 2000s. It was decided, at first, to remove all tamarisk trees, an alien species. However, when it was discovered that they provided shade in which many native species thrived, tamarisk trees were retained. Ideology played a role in this and similar decisions made throughout the Pacific, as culture and economics went hand in hand. Writing about native species in his poem "Native Plants" in 1985, activist botanist Rene Sylva observed:

> The Hawaiian plants are social plants.
> If you go look underneath the Hawaiian tree
> There's all kinds of plants that grow under them. . . .
> But the non-native plants are antisocial trees. . . .
> Nothing grows under there. . . .[5]

Notes

Introduction

1. Otis Hays, Jr., *Alaska's Hidden Wars: Secret Campaigns on the North Pacific Rim* (Fairbanks: University of Alaska Press, 2004), 135–141, esp. 141, reprints Tatsuguchi's diary.

2. Ibid., 32–39, 125.

3. Ibid.

4. Dennis O. Flynn and Arturo Giraldez offered a useful definition of the Pacific Rim. "In its current usage the concept 'Pacific Rim' geographically embraces mainland Asia, Japan, and the United States. Australia and New Zealand are afterthoughts, while archipelagos between the coasts and Latin American countries are ignored altogether," they noted. They continued, "It is imperative that the evolution of the Pacific Rim structures be studied beyond the narrow limitations imposed by popular misconceptions." See Dennis O. Flynn and Arturo Giraldez, "Introduction: The Pacific Rim's Past Deserves a Future," in Sally M. Miller, A. J. H. Latham, and Dennis O. Flynn, eds., *Studies in the Economic History of the Pacific Rim* (London: Routledge, 1998), 1–18, esp. 16.

5. Scholars debate the importance of the impact of World War II on developments in the American West and in the Pacific. For the argument that the conflict fundamentally transformed the trans-Mississippi West, see Gerald Nash, *The American West Transformed: The Impact of the Second World War* (Lincoln: University of Nebraska Press, 1985). To the contrary, Roger Lotchin, *The Bad City in the Good War: San Francisco, Los Angeles, and San Diego* (Bloomington: Indiana University Press, 2003), argues persuasively that most of the alterations associated with the war were more evolutionary than revolutionary in nature. My work on the United States' Pacific holdings strongly suggests that, while World War II was certainly important in bringing changes to those territories, they were based, as well, on a long history of change.

6. Until recently, most historians described works like mine as studies in political economy. Over the past decade, they have characterized such studies as works in state and society. Only rarely, however, have scholars of political economy or state-and-society studies included the environment as central to their stories. See Mark Rose, "Technology

and Politics: The Scholarship of Two Generations of Urban-Environmental Historians," *Journal of Urban History* 30 (July 2004): 769–785. One historian who has done so is J. R. McNeill. See especially J. R. McNeill, *Something New under the Sun: An Environmental History of the Twentieth-Century World* (New York: W. W. Norton, 2000); and J. R. McNeill, ed., *Environmental History in the Pacific World* (Aldershot, Hants: Ashgate, 2001).

7. Adam Rome, " 'Give Earth a Chance': The Environmental Movement and the Sixties," *Journal of American History* 90 (Sept. 2003): 525–554, esp. 527. See also Samuel P. Hays, *Beauty, Health and Permanence: Environmental Politics in the United States, 1955–1985* (Cambridge: Cambridge University Press, 1987); and Lizabeth Cohen, *A Consumers' Republic: The Politics of Mass Consumption in Postwar America* (New York: Vintage, 2003), 345–397.

8. Carolyn Merchant, "Shades of Darkness: Race and Environmental History," *Environmental History* 8 (July 2003): 380–394, esp. 380. See also Robert Bullard, *Dumping in Dixie: Race, Class and Environmental Justice* (Boulder, CO: Westview Press, 1990); Jennifer Clapp, *Toxic Exports: The Transfer of Hazardous Wastes from Rich to Poor Countries* (Ithaca, NY: Cornell University Press, 2001); Luke Cole and Sheila Foster, *From the Ground Up: Environmental Racism and the Rise of the Environmental Justice Movement* (New York: New York University Press, 2001); Richard Hofrichter, ed., *Toxic Struggles: The Theory and Practice of Environmental Justice* (Salt Lake City: University of Utah Press, 2002); Jonathan Keyes, "A Place of Its Own: Urban Environmental History," *Journal of Urban History* 26 (March 2000): 380–390; Alex Hurley, *Environmental Inequalities: Class, Race, and Industrial Pollution in Gary, Indiana, 1945–1980* (Chapel Hill: University of North Carolina Press, 1995); Martin Melosi, "Equity, Eco-Racism, and Environmental History," *Environmental History Review* 19 (Fall 1995): 1–16; David Pellow, *Garbage Wars: The Struggle for Environmental Justice in Chicago* (Cambridge, MA: MIT Press, 2002); Edwardo Lao Rhodes, *Environmental Justice in America: A New Paradigm* (Bloomington: Indiana University Press, 2003); Gerald R. Visgilio and Diana M. Whitelaw, eds., *In Our Backyard: A Quest for Environmental Justice* (Lanham, MD: Rowland & Littlefield, 2003); and Sylvia Hood Washington, *Packing Them In: An Archaeology of Environmental Racism in Chicago, 1865–1954* (Lanham, MD: Lexington Books, 2004).

9. Peder Anker, *Imperial Ecology: Environmental Order in the British Empire, 1895–1945* (Cambridge, MA: Harvard University Press, 2001), 2; Richard H. Grove, *Green Imperialism: Colonial Expansion, Tropical Island Edens and the Origins of Environmentalism, 1600–1860* (Cambridge: Cambridge University Press, 1995), 3, 12. See also Tom Griffiths and Libby Robin, eds., *Ecology and Empire: Environmental History of Settler Societies* (Seattle: University of Washington Press, 1997).

10. See Douglas R. Weiner, "A Death Defying Attempt to Articulate a Coherent Definition of Environmental History," *Environmental History* 10 (July 2005): 404–411.

11. Christine Meisner Rosen and Christopher C. Sellers, "The Nature of the Firm: Towards an Ecocultural History of Business," *Business History Review* 73 (Winter 1999): 577–600, esp. 577. The entire issue of the *Business History Review* 73 (Winter 1999) is devoted to relationships between business and the environment. See also Christine Meisner Rosen, "The Business–Environment Connection," *Environmental History* 10 (Jan. 2005):

77–79. For business history dealing with the Pacific, see Colin Newbury, "Mammon in Paradise: Economic Enterprise in Pacific Historiography," *Pacific Studies* 19 (June 1996): 37–58.

12. Robert Borofsky, ed., *Remembrance of Pacific Pasts: An Invitation to Remake History* (Honolulu: University of Hawai'i Press, 2000); Donald Denoon et al., eds., *The Cambridge History of the Pacific Islanders* (New York: Cambridge University Press, 1997); K. R. Howe, Robert C. Kiste, and Brij V. Lal, eds., *Tides of History: The Pacific Islands in the Twentieth Century* (Honolulu: University of Hawai'i Press, 1994); and Vijay Naidu, Eric Waddell, and Epeli Hau'ofa, eds., *A New Oceania: Rediscovering Our Sea of Islands* (Suva: University of South Pacific Press, 1993).

13. Jean Heffer, *The United States and the Pacific: History of a Frontier,* trans. W. Donald Wilson (Notre Dame, IN: University of Notre Dame Press, 2002); Roger Buckley, *The United States in the Asia-Pacific since 1945* (Cambridge: Cambridge University Press, 2002); and Hal M. Friedman, *Creating an American Lake: United States Imperialism and Strategic Security in the Pacific Basin, 1945–47* (Westport, CT: Greenwood Press, 2001). On recent migrations, see Paul Spickard, Joanne L. Rondilla, and Debbie Hippolite Wright, eds., *Pacific Diaspora: Island Peoples in the United States and across the Pacific* (Honolulu: University of Hawai'i Press, 2002). On tourism, see Michel Picard and Robert E. Wood, eds., *Tourism, Ethnicity, and the State in Asian and Pacific Societies* (Honolulu: University of Hawai'i Press, 1997).

14. John Whitehead, "Alaska and Hawai'i: The Cold War States," in *The Cold War American West, 1945–1989,* ed. Kevin Fernlund (Albuquerque: University of New Mexico Press, 1998), 189–210. See also Arthur Dudden, *The American Pacific: From the Old China Trade to the Present* (New York: Oxford University Press, 1992); Arrell Morgan Gibson, *Yankees in Paradise: The Pacific Basin Frontier* (Albuquerque: University of New Mexico Press, 1993); David Pletcher, *The Diplomacy of Involvement: American Economic Expansion across the Pacific, 1784–1900* (Columbia: University of Missouri Press, 2001); and Earl Pomeroy, *American Strategy in Guam and Micronesia* (Stanford, CA: Stanford University Press, 1951).

15. Bruce Hevly and John M. Findlay, eds., *The Atomic West* (Seattle: University of Washington Press, 1998); Nash, *The American West Transformed;* and William G. Robbins, *Colony and Empire: The Capitalist Transformation of the American West* (Lawrence: University Press of Kansas, 1994).

16. On the historic pros and cons of tourism for host communities, see Hal Rothman, *Devil's Bargains: Tourism in the Twentieth-Century American West* (Lawrence: University Press of Kansas, 1998). See also Mansel G. Blackford, "Historians Approach Tourism in the American West," *Business History Review* 75 (Autumn 2001): 579–585.

17. For an examination of Pacific developments with Hawai'i at their center, see Walter M. McDougall, *Let the Sea Make a Noise: Four Hundred Years of Cataclysm, Conquest, War and Folly in the Pacific* (New York: Avon Books, 1992).

18. McNeill, *Something New under the Sun.*

Chapter 1. Pacific Developments

1. Ben Finney, *Voyage of Rediscovery: A Cultural Odyssey through Polynesia* (Berkeley: University of California Press, 1994), esp. xiii, 74, 96, 308. A professor of anthropology at the University of Hawai'i, Mānoa, Finney was a sparkplug behind the building and voyaging of the *Hōkūle'a*.

2. Frank Graham, Jr., "U.S. and Soviet Environmentalists Join Forces across the Bering Strait," *Audubon* 93 (July–Aug. 1991): 42–61, esp. 53.

3. Paul Spikard, Joanne L. Rondilla, and Debbie Hippolite Wright, eds., *Pacific Diaspora: Island Peoples in the United States and Across the Pacific* (Honolulu: University of Hawai'i Press, 2002). See also James T. Fawcett and Benjamin V. Carino, eds., *Pacific Bridges: The New Immigration from Asia and the Pacific Islands* (New York: Center for Migration Studies, 1987).

4. Steven Roger Fischer, *A History of the Pacific Islands* (New York: Palgrave, 2002), xvi. Valuable histories also include Douglas Oliver, *The Pacific Islands* (Honolulu: University of Hawai'i Press, 1989); and Deryck Scarr, *The History of the Pacific Islands: Kingdom of the Reefs* (Sydney: Macmillan, 1990). See the works of Epeli Hau'ofa on the Pacific as a large, rich, and unified region before contact with the West, especially Epeli Hau'ofa, "Our Sea of Islands," *Contemporary Pacific* 6 (Spring 1994): 148–161. Paul D'Arcy has also stressed the size of the Pacific and the connections among peoples of the Pacific in pre-contact times. See Paul D'Arcy, "No Empty Ocean: Trade and interaction across the Pacific Ocean to the middle of the eighteenth century," in Sally Miller, A. J. H. Latham, and Dennis Owen Flynn, eds., *Studies in the Economic History of the Pacific Rim* (London: Routledge, 1998), 21–43.

5. R. Gerard Ward, "Earth's Empty Quarter? The Pacific Islands in a Pacific Century," *Geographical Journal* 155 (July 1989): 235–246, esp. 239.

6. Ben Finney, "The Other One-Third of the Globe," *Journal of World History* 5 (Fall 1994): 273–297.

7. Greg Dening, "History 'in' the Pacific," *Contemporary Pacific* 1 (Fall 1989): 134–139, esp. 134–135.

8. Arif Dirlik, "The Asia-Pacific Idea: Reality and Representation in the Invention of a Regional Structure," *Journal of World History* 3 (Spring 1992): 55–79, esp. 62. On the diversity of the Pacific, see also David A. Chappell, "Peripheralizing the Center: An Historical Overview of Pacific Island Micro-States," in Miller, Latham, and Flynn, eds., *Economic History of the Pacific Rim,* 63–71.

9. Jocelyn Linnekin, "Contending Approaches," in Donald Denoon et al., eds., *The Cambridge History of the Pacific Islanders* (Cambridge: Cambridge University Press, 1997), 3–36, esp. 3.

10. Kerry R. Howe, "Pacific Islands History in the 1980s: New Directions of Monograph Myopia?" *Pacific Studies* 61 (Fall 1979): 81–90, esp. 88. On the need for environmental historians to study ocean basins, especially the Pacific, see David Igler, "Longitudes and Latitudes," *Environmental History* 10 (Jan. 2005): 44–46.

11. J. R. McNeill, ed., *Environmental History in the Pacific World* (Aldershot: Ashgate, 2001), xi.

12. D'Arcy, "No Empty Ocean," 25. Published too late for discussion in this volume is Paul D'Arcy, *The People of the Sea: Environment, Identity, and History in Oceania* (Honolulu: University of Hawai'i Press, 2005). The literature on migrations into the Pacific, especially Oceania, is vast. For an overview, see Patrick Vinton Kirch, *On the Road of the Winds: An Archaeological History of the Pacific Islands before European Contact* (Berkeley: University of California Press, 2002), 63–246. Oceania is usually taken to consist of three areas—Melanesia, Micronesia, and Polynesia—labels first applied to the regions by a French explorer in 1831. Oceania, thus, does not encompass the North Pacific.

13. D'Arcy, "No Empty Ocean," 38; Paul D'Arcy, "The People of the Sea: Three Centuries of History and Culture in an Oceanic Environment," paper presented at the annual meeting of the American Society for Environmental History, Victoria, B.C., March 30–April 4, 2004, pp. 11, 15–16; and Hau'ofa, "Our Sea of Islands," 153. For examples of island empires, see Paul D'Arcy, "Connected by the Sea: Towards a Regional History of the Western Caroline Islands," *Journal of Pacific History* 36, no. 2 (2001): 163–182; and Glenn Petersen, "Indigenous Island Empires: Yap and Tonga Reconsidered," *Journal of Pacific History* 35 (Jan. 2000): 5–27.

14. D'Arcy, "People of the Sea," 17–18.

15. J. R. McNeill, "Of Rats and Men: A Synoptic Environmental History of the Island Pacific," *Journal of World History* 5 (Fall 1994): 299–349, esp. 299–300, 305, 309. See also Patrick Kirch and Terry Hunt, *Historical Ecology in the Pacific Islands: Prehistoric Environment and Landscape Change* (New Haven, CT: Yale University Press, 1997), esp. 1–21, which emphasizes environmental changes caused by the actions of indigenous peoples. For an additional examination of how indigenous peoples altered their environments in the Pacific, see Jared Diamond, *Collapse: How Societies Choose to Fail or Succeed* (New York: Viking, 2005), 79–135.

16. On the Spanish in the Pacific, see Oscar Spate, *Spanish Lake* (Minneapolis: University of Minnesota Press, 1979). On Captain Cook, see J. C. Beaglehole, *The Life of Captain James Cook* (Stanford, CA: Stanford University Press, 1974). For a very different view, see Gananath Obeyesekere, *The Apotheosis of Captain Cook: European Mythmaking in the Pacific* (Princeton, NJ: Princeton University Press, 1992). See also Robert Borofsky, ed., *Remembrance of Pacific Pasts: An Invitation to Remake History* (Honolulu: University of Hawai'i Press, 2000), 101–172.

17. McNeill, "Of Rats and Men," 312. Taking a very long-term approach to environmental change, some scholars have downplayed the impact of Captain Cook and other westerners on Pacific environments. See Eric Rolls, "The Nature of Australia," and John M. MacKenzie, "Empire and the Ecological Apocalypse: The Historiography of the Imperial Environment," in Tom Griffiths and Libby Robin, eds., *Ecology and Empire: Environmental History of Settler Societies* (Seattle: University of Washington Press, 1997), 35–45, 215–228.

18. Fischer, *History of the Pacific Islands*, 120–171, esp. 123, 167, 171. See also K. R. Howe, Robert C. Kiste, and Brij V. Lal, eds., *Tides of History: The Pacific Islands in the Twentieth Century* (Honolulu: University of Hawai'i Press, 1994), 29–146.

19. Hau'ofa, "Our Sea of Islands," 155. However, the historian David Igler has emphasized the reintegration of the eastern Pacific around the twin nodes of trade and disease

as early as 1770–1850. See David Igler, "Diseased Goods: Global Exchanges in the Eastern Pacific Basin, 1770–1850," *American Historical Review* 109 (June 2004): 692–719.

20. J. S. Holliday, *The World Rushed In: The California Gold Rush Experience* (New York: Simon & Schuster, 1981).

21. For an introduction to the westward movement of Americans, see Patricia Nelson Limerick, *The Legacy of Conquest: The Unbroken Past of the American West* (New York: W. W. Norton, 1987). For a comparative look at the history of America's Pacific-Coast cities, see Mansel G. Blackford, *The Lost Dream: Businessmen and City Planning on the Pacific Coast, 1890–1920* (Columbus: Ohio State University Press, 1993), 13–30.

22. Claus-M. Naske and Herman E. Slotnick, *Alaska: A History of the 49th State* (Norman: University of Oklahoma Press, 1987), 301. See also Lydia T. Black, *Russians in Alaska, 1732–1867* (Fairbanks: University of Alaska Press, 2004).

23. Mark R. Peattie, *Nan'yo: The Rise and Fall of the Japanese in Micronesia, 1885–1945* (Honolulu: University of Hawai'i Press, 1988).

24. Arrell Morgan Gibson, *Yankees in Paradise: The Pacific Basin Frontier* (Albuquerque: University of New Mexico Press, 1993); John H. Whitehead, "Noncontiguous Wests: Alaska and Hawai'i," in David M. Wrobel and Michael C. Steiner, eds., *Many Wests: Place, Culture and Regional Identity* (Lawrence: University Press of Kansas, 1997), 315–341. On Philadelphia's trade with China, see Jonathan Goldstein, *Philadelphia and the China Trade, 1682–1846* (University Park: Pennsylvania University Press, 1978).

25. Even so, far from all of the integration can be traced to American actions. The activities of other Pacific peoples, including Pacific Islanders, have been important. Pacific Islanders have not simply been passive victims of western aggression, but active shapers of their futures. See Fischer, *History of the Pacific Islands*, xviii–xix.

26. Stewart Firth, "The War in the Pacific," in Denoon, ed., *Cambridge History of Pacific Islanders*, 293–323, esp. 312–313; and Fischer, *History of the Pacific Islands*, 205.

27. Firth, "War in the Pacific," 319.

28. Roger Buckley, *The United States in the Asia-Pacific since 1945* (Cambridge: Cambridge University Press, 2002), 12, 94.

29. Stewart Firth, "A Nuclear Pacific," in Denoon, ed., *Cambridge History of Pacific Islanders*, 324–358; and Stewart Firth, *Nuclear Playground* (Honolulu: University of Hawai'i Press, 1987).

30. Jean Heffer, *The United States and the Pacific: History of a Frontier* (Notre Dame, IN: University of Notre Dame Press, 2002), trans. W. Donald Wilson, 310–335, esp. 311, 322; and Carl Abbott, *The Metropolitan Frontier: Cities in the Modern American West* (Tucson: University of Arizona Press, 1993), 80. On trade, see also J. T. Fawcett and B. V. Carino, "International Migration and Pacific Basin Development," in Fawcett and Carino, *Pacific Bridges*, 3–25, esp. 8–9. Strategic concerns and economic interests went hand in hand. American policy makers worked hard to keep Japan from trading with Communist China by sponsoring Japan's membership in the General Agreement on Tariffs and Trade in 1955, over the objections of Great Britain and some other western allies, and by opening American markets to Japanese goods. See William S. Borden, *The Pacific Alliance: United States Foreign Economic Policy and Japanese Trade Recovery, 1947–1955* (Madison: University of Wisconsin Press, 1984); and Sayuri Shimizu, *Creating People of Plenty: The*

United States and Japan's Economic Alternatives, 1950–1960 (Kent, OH: Kent State University Press, 2001).

31. Heffer, *United States and the Pacific*, 313, 398. In 1992, the Pacific as a whole accounted for about 20 percent of the cumulative stock of direct foreign investment by American companies.

32. Much has been written about MIRAB economies. Scholars like Hau'ofa have pointed out, for example, that remittances are an extension of older family exchange patterns and should not be seen negatively. On the other hand, scholars like D'Arcy have noted, "While many academics celebrate Hau'ofa's vision of Oceania to counter the prevailing image of Pacific states as too small to ever be viable without heavy dependence on external aid, few believe it offers any way of addressing contemporary problems." See D'Arcy "People of the Sea," 18; Finney, "Other One-Third of the Globe," 295–296; Hau'ofa, "Our Sea of Islands," 156; and Charles J. Stevens, "Introduction: Defining and Understanding Sustainability in Small Island States," *Pacific Studies* 22 (Sept./Dec. 1999): 2–12.

33. For some island groups, commercial fishing seemed to offer possibilities. Under Law of the Sea covenants sponsored by the United Nations, island governments established economic exclusion zones and leased fishing rights in those regions to foreign nations and companies. See Sandra Tarte, "Negotiating a Tuna Management Regime for the Western and Central Pacific: The MHLC Process, 1994–1999," *Journal of Pacific History* 34 (Fall 1999): 273–280. A 2005 report from the United Nations described possibilities for tuna-fishery development by Pacific Island nations. See United Nations Environment Programme, *Pacific Environment Outlook* (New York: United Nations, 2005), 34–35.

34. Martin Oppermann, ed., *Pacific Rim Tourism* (Wallingford, UK: CAB International, 1997), 12–13, 20, 31, 38. On Pacific tourism, see also C. M. Hall, *Tourism in the Pacific Rim: Development, Impacts, and Markets* (Melbourne: Halsted Press, 1994).

35. Michel Picard and Robert E. Wood, eds., *Tourism, Ethnicity, and the State in Asian and Pacific Societies* (Honolulu: University of Hawai'i Press, 1997). For a valuable case study, see Simon Milne, "The Economic Impact of Tourism in Kiribati," *Pacific Studies* 14 (March 1991): 53–70. For an examination of tourism in Pacific cities, see Patrick Mullins, "Tourism Urbanism," *International Journal of Urban and Regional Research* 15 (Sept. 1991): 326–342.

36. UN, *Pacific Environment Outlook*, 3, 76.

37. Buckley, *United States in the Asia-Pacific*, 157, 212–213; Firth, *Nuclear Playground*, 138; Fischer, *History of the Pacific Islands*, 214, 238–239; Michael Hamel-Green, "Regional Arms Control in the South Pacific: Island State Responses to Australia's Nuclear Free Zone Initiative," *Contemporary Pacific* 3 (Spring 1991): 59–84; Hau'ofa, "Our Sea of Islands," 158–159; and John Ravenhill, *APEC and the Construction of Pacific Rim Regionalism* (Cambridge: Cambridge University Press, 2001). On recent developments, see *Economist*, June 21, 2003, p. 34, Oct. 25, 2003, pp. 37, 38, July 10, 2004, pp. 36–37, July 23, 2005, pp. 23–25; and *Maui News*, Aug. 15, 2003, p. 10. For more complete descriptions of some of these groups, and of regional agreements among Pacific Island Countries and Territories (PICTs), see UN, *Pacific Environment Outlook*, 51–69.

38. Ibid.

39. Spikard, Rondilla, and Wright, eds., *Pacific Diaspora*, 1–2, 20. See also Dennis A. Ahlburg, "Do Pacific Islanders in the United States Hold 'Good' Jobs?" *Pacific Studies* 20 (June 1997): 87–103; and Geoffrey Hayes, "Migration, Metascience, and Development Policy in Island Polynesia," *Contemporary Pacific* 3 (Spring 1991): 1–58.

40. Mary M. Kritz, "The Global Picture of Contemporary Immigration," in Fawcett and Carino, eds., *Pacific Bridges*, 29–52, esp. 29.

41. Spikard, Rondilla, and Wright, eds., *Pacific Diaspora*, 1–2, 20. See also John Connell, "Paradise Left? Pacific Island Voyagers in the Modern World," in Fawcett and Carino, eds., *Pacific Bridges*, 375–404, esp. 383.

42. On the issue of Pacific identity, see Roger M. Keesing, "Creating the Past: Custom and Identity in the Contemporary Pacific," *Contemporary Pacific* 1 (Spring and Fall, 1989): 19–39; and Norman Meller, "Indigenous Self-Determination and Its Implementation," *Pacific Studies* 23 (March/June 2000): 1–19.

43. Spikard, Rondilla, and Wright, eds., *Pacific Diaspora*, 169–194.

44. On the legislation, see Greg Johnson, "Naturally There: Discourses of Permanence in the Repatriation Context," *History of Religion* 44 (Winter 2004): 36–55.

45. On alien species worldwide, see Yvonne Baskin, *A Plague of Rats and Rubber-vines: The Growing Threat of Species Invasions* (Washington, DC: Island Press, 2002); and Alfred D. Crosby, *Ecological Imperialism: The Biological Expansion of Europe, 900–1900* (Cambridge: Cambridge University Press, 1986).

46. Buckley, *United States in the Asia-Pacific*, 239. Even so, in 2000–2001 China joined Japan, Taiwan, and South Korea in measuring acid-rain depositions in the North Pacific, with much of the funding and expertise coming from Japan, which suffered from rain originating in China. See Kenneth E. Wilkening, *Acid Rain Science and Politics in Japan* (Cambridge, MA: MIT Press, 2004), 219–222.

47. McNeill, ed., *Environmental History in the Pacific World*, xiii, xxi.

48. Harold Brookfield, "Global Change and the Pacific: Problems for the Coming Half-Century," *Contemporary Pacific* 1 (Spring and Fall 1989): 1–18; Patrick D. Nunn, "Recent Environmental Changes on Pacific Islands," *Geographical Journal* 156 (July 1990): 125–140. Rising waters threatened the small Pacific-island nation of Tuvalu with extinction. In 2004, its political leaders prepared legal suits against the United States and Australia for the roles they had played in global warming and sought the status of "ecological refugee" for their citizens. See Leslie Allen, "Will Tuvalu Disappear beneath the Sea?" *Smithsonian* 35 (August 2004): 44–52.

49. UN, *Pacific Environment Outlook*. This 2005 report cites "small physical size and geographical remoteness, fragile biodiversity, exposure to natural hazards, high population growth, a limited natural resource base, remoteness from world markets, and small economies of scale" as being typical of PICTs (p. 1).

Chapter 2. The Hawaiian Islands

1. U.S. Navy, *Final Environmental Statement Concerning the Military Use of the Kahoolawe Target Complex in the Hawaiian Archipelago* [February 1972] (n.p., n.d.),

2–4. For a year-by-year chronicle, see Walter M. Barnard, *Kahoʻolawe* (Freedonia: self-published, 1996).

2. George Helm, "Notes," 1977, file 7, box 1, George Helm Collection (Hawaiiana Room, Hamilton Library, University of Hawaiʻi, Mānoa); and anon., "Kahoʻolawe Island Reserve: A Hawaiian Cultural Sanctuary," *Manoa* 7 (Summer 1995): 18. In a recent political history of the Hawaiian Islands, the journalist Tom Coffman has correctly assessed the importance of Kahoʻolawe to the native Hawaiian rights movement and to Hawaiian politics in general. "The political fallout of Kahoʻolawe remains incalculable," he observes, "Hawaiians were once again culture heroes in their homeland, not only to fellow Hawaiians but to a generally admiring and sympathetic public." See Tom Coffman, *The Island Edge of America: A Political History of Hawaiʻi* (Honolulu: University of Hawaiʻi Press, 2003), 299–304, esp. 304.

3. Kahoʻolawe Island Reserve Commission (KIRC), *Use Plan, December 1995*, www. hawaii.gov/kirc/main/home/html, pp. 17–30 (accessed June 17, 2002). Formed through volcanic action 1.5 million years ago, Kahoʻolawe was probably originally connected to the other three islands that now comprise Maui County: Maui, Molokaʻi, and Lānaʻi. Erosion and a rise in the ocean levels later separated the islands. See Peter MacDonald, "Fixed in Time: A Brief History of Kahoʻolawe," *Hawaiian Journal of History* 6 (1972): 69–90.

4. Investigations undertaken during the 1970s and 1980s showed that earlier archaeological work suggesting that Kahoʻolawe was unimportant to Hawaiians was misleading. The later work found thousands of sites and features that led to a basic reassessment of the island's significance. For a summary of the earlier work, see Elspeth P. Sterling, *Sites of Maui* (Honolulu: Bishop Museum Press, 1998), 80–81, esp. 81. On the population of Kahoʻolawe, see Robert C. Schmitt and Carole L. Silva, "Population Trends on Kahoolawe," *Hawaiian Journal of History* 18 (1984): 39–46. On the early history of Kahoʻolawe, see Pauline N. King, "A Local History of Kahoʻolawe Island: Tradition Development, and World War," a report prepared in typescript for the Kahoʻolawe Island Conveyance Commission (KICC) in 1993; population figures are on pp. 39 and 43. Archaeological discoveries in the summer of 2004 suggested that the number of Hawaiians living on Kahoʻolawe was probably greater than earlier estimates.

5. King, "Local History," 39–42.

6. Noa Emmett Aluli and Daviana Pōmaikaʻi McGregor, "*Mai Ke Mai Ke Ola*, From the Ocean Comes Life: Hawaiian Customs, Uses, and Practices on Kahoʻolawe Relating to the Surrounding Ocean," *Hawaiian Journal of History* 26 (1992): 231–254.

7. William F. Allen to Messrs. Wyllie & Allen, May 31, 1858, reprinted in *Paradise of the Pacific* 50 (May 1, 1938): 22, 27, 28.

8. Patrick Vinton Kirch, *Feathered Gods and Fishhooks: An Introduction to Hawaiian Archaeology and Prehistory* (Honolulu: University of Hawaiʻi Press, 1985), 153–154. The matter of population increases and declines in the Pacific is contentious. Many scholars now think that the population of the Hawaiian Islands as a whole, not just Kahoʻolawe, peaked before contact and was in decline, having encountered environmental limits. See O. A. Bushnell, *The Gifts of Civilization: Germs and Genocide in Hawaiʻi* (Honolulu: University of Hawaiʻi Press, 1993); O. A. Bushnell, " 'The Horror' Reconsidered: An Evaluation of the Historical Evidence for Population Decline in Hawaiʻi, 1778–1803," *Pacific Studies*

16 (Sept. 1993): 115–161; Tom Dye, "Population Trends in Hawai'i before 1778," *Hawaiian Journal of History* 28 (1994): 1–21; Thegn Ladefoged, "Hawaiian Dryland Agricultural Intensification and the Pacific Economy," *Pacific Studies* 16 (June 1993): 119–131; Robert Schmitt and Eleanor Nordyke, "Death in Hawai'i: The Epidemics of 1848–49," *Hawaiian Journal of History* 35 (2001): 1–14; and David Stannard, *Before the Horror: The Population of Hawai'i on the Eve of Western Contact* (Honolulu: University of Hawai'i Press, 1989).

9. Sherwin Carlquist, *Hawaii: A Natural History* (Lawa'i: Pacific Tropical Botanical Garden, 1980), unpaged preface; George Cox, *Alien Species in North America and Hawaii* (Washington, DC: Island Press, 1999); and Kenneth Nagata, "Early Plant Introductions in Hawai'i," *Hawaiian Journal of History* 19 (1985): 35–61. See also MacDonald, "Fixed in Time," 71; and King, "Local History," 57–108.

10. King, "Local History," 57–108; and State of Hawai'i, "Kaho'olawe: Aloha No: A Legislative History of the Island of Kaho'olawe," typescript, 1978, 40–41.

11. KICC, *Kaho'olawe Island: Restoring a Cultural Treasure: Final Report of the Kaho'olawe Island Conveyance Commission to the Congress of the United States, March 31, 1993* (Wailuku, 1993), 19, 24. For the most accurate estimate of ungulates on the island, see Hardy Spoehr, *Kaho'olawe's Forest Reserve Period, 1910–1918* (Wailuku, 1992), 3.

12. Spoehr, *Forest Reserve Period,* 1.

13. Robert Holt, "The Maui Forest Trouble: Reassessment of an Historic Forest Dieback," Ph.D. diss., University of Hawai'i, Mānoa, 1988.

14. Spoehr, *Forest Reserve Period,* 7. *Na'ulu* rains have also been called "showers" or "rains falling from a cloudless sky." See King, "Local History," 128–129.

15. Spoehr, *Forest Reserve Period,* 15.

16. King, "Local History," 131, and MacDonald, "Fixed in Time," 74.

17. Inez MacPhee Ashdown, *Kaho'olawe* (Honolulu: Topgallant Publishing, 1979), 4, 7. See also Inez Ashdown, "Kahoolawe," *Paradise of the Pacific* 59 (Dec. 1, 1947): 47–48; and *Los Angeles Times,* Sept. 22, 1968. Armine von Tempski, a friend of the MacPhee family, visited Kaho'olawe with Angus and remembered that he wanted to restore the land. See Armine von Tempski, *Born in Paradise* (New York: Hawthorn Books, 1940), 246–257.

18. Ashdown, *Kaho'olawe,* 8–9; KICC, *Restoring a Cultural Treasure,* 24–25; and MacDonald, "Fixed in Time," 75.

19. Ashdown, *Kaho'olawe,* 11; KICC, *Restoring a Cultural Treasure,* 24; and State of Hawai'i, "Kaho'olawe: Aloha No," 43–44.

20. Ashdown, *Kaho'olawe,* 15.

21. Ibid. See also KICC, *Cultural Treasure,* 24; King, "Local History," 153; and State of Hawai'i, "Kaho'olawe: Aloha No," 44.

22. KICC, *Restoring a Cultural Treasure,* 119. For negative western views of Kaho'olawe as a wasteland in the 1930s and 1940s, see Garland Greene, "Kahoolawe: Time and Tide," *Paradise of the Pacific* 53 (March 1, 1941): 28; and Jeanne Skinner, "A Week-End on Kahoolawe," *Paradise of the Pacific* 45 (June 1, 1933): 16.

23. Ashdown, "Kahoolawe," 48.

24. Ibid., 67–69; KICC, *Restoring a Cultural Treasure,* 25; King, "Local History," 160–172; and MacDonald, "Fixed in Time," 77.

25. Exec. Order no. 10,436, 18 Fed. Reg. 1051 (Feb. 20, 1953), reprinted in KICC, *Restoring a Cultural Treasure*, 110.

26. Thomas Hitch, *Islands in Transition: The Past, Present, and Future of Hawaii's Economy* (Honolulu: First Hawaiian Bank, 1992), 171–173, 198–201. On the military in the Hawaiian Islands, see Kathy Ferguson and Phyllis Turnbull, *Oh Say, Can You See? The Semiotics of the Military in Hawai'i* (Minneapolis: University of Minnesota Press, 1999).

27. "Navy Calls Operation Sailor Hat a Rocking Success," *Honolulu Star-Bulletin*, June 24, 1965; and U.S. Navy, *Final Environmental Statement Concerning the Military Use of the Kahoolawe Target Complex in the Hawaiian Archipelago*, 2–4.

28. Mansel G. Blackford, *Fragile Paradise: The Impact of Tourism on Maui, 1959–2000* (Lawrence: University Press of Kansas, 2001); and Bryan H. Farrell, *Hawaii: The Legend That Sells* (Honolulu: University of Hawai'i Press, 1982).

29. Blackford, *Fragile Paradise*, 20, 22, 37.

30. *Los Angeles Times*, Sept. 22, 1968.

31. Dorothy Pyle interview by Mansel G. Blackford, Sept. 17, 2003, audiotape (in Blackford's possession), side 1, tape 1; *Maui News*, Feb. 12, 1969, p. 8; and *Sunday Honolulu Star-Bulletin and Advertiser*, Feb. 9, 1969, p. A-1.

32. The situation was even more complicated. Some visitors to Maui viewed the bombing, especially night bombing well lit by flares, as a tourist attraction. On numerous visits to Maui in the 1970s and early 1980s, I saw visitors on lawn chairs at South Maui resorts watching the bombing as a spectator event like fireworks.

33. *Honolulu Star-Bulletin*, Sept. 15, 1969, p. B-1, March 2, 1970, p. A-13, June 8, 1970, p. D-20, and Oct. 30, 1971, p. A-3; *Maui News*, Nov. 23, 1971, p. 1; and Elmer Cravalho interview by Mansel G. Blackford, July 16, 2002, audiotape (in Blackford's possession), tape 1, side 1.

34. "Minutes of the Meetings of the Maui County Council," Oct. 3, 1969, Jan. 16, 1970, and March 19, 1971 (Office of the Clerk for Maui County in Wailuku, Hawai'i); *Honolulu Advertiser*, Oct. 4, 1969, p. D-8.

35. *Honolulu Star-Bulletin*, Oct. 30, 1971, p. A-3; and *Maui News*, July 31, 1971, p. 1.

36. U.S. Navy, *Final Environmental Statement Concerning the Use of Kahoolawe Target Complex in the Hawaiian Archipelago*, 1, 15, 30.

37. Ibid., 1, 14, 15, 23–30; *Maui News*, Dec. 11, 1971, p. C-8; and Pyle interview, tape 1, side 1.

38. Haunani-Kay Trask, "The Birth of the Modern Hawaiian Movement: Kalama Valley, O'ahu," *Hawaiian Journal of History* 21 (1987): 126–153, esp. 126–127. See also Lilikala Kame'eleihiwa, "The Hawaiian Sovereignty Movement: An Update from Honolulu," *Journal of Pacific History* 28 (Fall 1993): 214–218; Haunani-Kay Trask, *From a Native Daughter: Colonialism and Sovereignty in Hawai'i* (Honolulu: University of Hawai'i Press, 1993); and Robert and Anne Mast, *Autobiography of Protest in Hawai'i* (Honolulu: University of Hawai'i Press, 1996), 353–428.

39. Blackford, *Fragile Paradise*, 10–18; Theodore Morgan, *Hawaii: A Century of Economic Change, 1778–1876* (Cambridge, MA: Harvard University Press, 1948). See also

Noenoe K. Silva, *Aloha Betrayed: Native Hawaiian Resistance to American Colonialism* (Durham, NC: Duke University Press, 2004).

40. Blackford, *Fragile Paradise,* 104–105.

41. For a valuable comparative account, see Linda S. Parker, *Native American Estate: The Struggle over Indian and Hawaiian Lands* (Honolulu: University of Hawaiʻi Press, 1989). Working through an Indian Claims Commission and through the federal court system, Native Americans tried, with some success, to win back rights lost in earlier times. On Native American cultural renewal, see Joane Nagel, *American Indian Ethnic Renewal: Red Power and the Resurgence of Identity and Culture* (New York: Oxford University Press, 1996), 187–212. For a look at Native American activism, see Paul Chaat Smith and Robert Allen Warrior, *Like a Hurricane: The Indian Movement from Alcatraz to Wounded Knee* (New York: New Press, 1996). On Maori efforts to regain lands and treaty rights on New Zealand, see Jean Rosenfeld, *The Island Broken in Two Halves: Land and Renewal Movements among the Maori of New Zealand* (University Park: Pennsylvania University Press, 1999); Alan Ward, "Interpreting the Treaty of Waitangi: The Maori Resurgence and Race Relations in New Zealand," *Contemporary Pacific* 3 (Spring 1991): 85–115; and Alan Ward, "Treaty-Related Research and Versions of New Zealand History," in *Remembrance of Pacific Pasts,* ed. Robert Borofsky (Honolulu: University of Hawaiʻi Press, 2000), 401–419.

42. Ken S. Coates, *A Global History of Indigenous Peoples: From Prehistory to Age of Globalization* (New York: Palgrave, 2005).

43. "County Council Minutes," Sept. 7, 1973; Charles Maxwell, "Public Testimony on the Navy's Revised Environmental Impact Statement," April 10, 1978, file 9, box 1, Navy Kahoolawe Collection (Maui Historical Society, Wailuku, Hawaiʻi).

44. Walter Ritte, Jr., and Richard Sawyer, *Na Manaʻo O Kahoʻolawe* (Meaning of Kahoʻolawe) (Honolulu: Aloha ʻĀina O Kupuna, 1978), 106–107; and Walter Ritte, Jr., to Jimmy Carter, July 6, 1976, file 5, box 1, Helm Collection.

45. Ritte and Sawyer, *Na Manaʻo,* 3.

46. Maxwell, "Testimony," 1978; Francis Norris, "Kahoʻolawe: Island of Opportunity," M.A. thesis, University of Hawaiʻi, Mānoa, 1992, 92–97; and Myra Jean F. Tuggle, "The Protect Kahoʻolawe ʻOhana: Cultural Revitalization in a Contemporary Hawaiian Movement," M.A. thesis, University of Hawaiʻi, Mānoa, 1982, 44–45.

47. Norris, "Kahoʻolawe," 93; Tuggle, "Protect Kahoʻolawe ʻOhana," 45; and "Fund-Raising Luau Set for Anti-Bombing Group," *Maui News,* March 10, 1976, and "Mauians All Shook Up by Bombing of Island," ibid., March 12, 1976.

48. *Sunday Honolulu Advertiser,* Jan. 11, 1976, p. 2; and State of Hawaiʻi, "Kahoʻolawe: Aloha No," 50–51, 174. The report does not say how many people took part in these discussions or who they were. In early 1968, the Maui County Council praised members of the PKO for their landings and reiterated their stance that Kahoʻolawe should be retuned to the state. See "County Council Minutes," Jan. 17, 1968.

49. State of Hawaiʻi, "Kahoʻolawe: Aloha No," 74, 242.

50. Blackford, *Fragile Paradise,* 44–80, 139–169. On Aluli, see Brett Uprichard, "Interview with Dr. Emmett Aluli," *Honolulu* 22 (July 1988): 10.

51. *Honolulu Star-Bulletin and Advertiser,* Dec. 23, 1979, p. A-3; State of Hawai'i, "Kaho'olawe: Aloha No," 50.

52. Rodney Morales, "George Helm—The Voice and Soul," *Ho'i Ho'i Hou: A Tribute to George Helm and Kimo Mitchell* (Honolulu: Bamboo Ridge Press, 1984), 11–33, esp. 11. See also Aunty Mae Helm, "George Helm: A Profile of the Man and His Music," in Ritte and Sawyer, *Na Mana'o,* xvi; and Catherine Kekoa Enomoto, "Hawaiian Treasure," in the Native Hawaiian Chamber of Commerce, *'O'o Pulekina* 24 (April 1996), n.p. Helm's charisma may be sensed in two videotapes of him speaking and singing based on newsclips from 1975–1977: "Enduring Pride: E Mau Ana ka Ha'aheo" (videotape; Juniora Productions, 1987), vol. 7; and "Kaho'olawe: Aloha 'Āina—George Helm" (videotape; Nā Maka O Ka 'Āina, 1978). Helm performs 24 songs on George Helm, *The Music of George Helm: A True Hawaiian* (compact disk; Cord International HOCD 3000; 1996). For valuable contemporary accounts, see Pam Smith, "The Ohana: Birth of a Nation or Band-Aid Brigade?" *Hawaii Observer,* May 19, 1977, pp. 19–25; Pam Smith, "Kahoolawe: Hawaiians on Trial," ibid., July 28, 1977, pp. 14–15; and Jimmy Shimabukuro, "Kahoolawe: a Different Meaning," ibid., March 10, 1977, p. 9.

53. Morales, "Helm," 22, 25; and State of Hawai'i, "Kaho'olawe: Aloha No," 15–26.

54. Norris, "Kaho'olawe," 103–104; Tuggle, "Protect Kaho'olawe 'Ohana," 46–47; Protect Kaho'olawe 'Ohana, "Official Statement," Feb. 1, 1977, file 7, box 1, Helm Collection; State of Hawai'i, "Kaho'olawe: Aloha No," 51. On developments on March 5–7, 1977, see Morales, "Helm," 29–32; and *Maui News,* March 9, 1977, p. 1.

55. On reactions to the deaths, see *Maui News,* March 14, 1977, p. 1; and Smith, "Ohana," 22–25.

56. State of Hawai'i, "Kaho'olawe: Aloha No," 65; and Tuggle, "Protect Kaho'olawe 'Ohana," 74–80.

57. Smith, "Ohana," 19, 25. Women were important to the PKO. A few took part in the landings, with many more active in networking, organizing rallies and protests, fundraising, and the like. Older women, like older men, were respected as *kūpuna.* On the importance of elders in native Hawaiian society, see M. J. Harden, *Voices of Wisdom: Hawaiian Elders Speak* (Kula: Aka Press, 1999); and Jay Hartwell, *Na Mamo: Hawaiian People Today* (Honolulu: 'Ai Pohaku Press, 1996). Aunty Clara Ku has been described as "A kupuna, cultural and spiritual counselor to movement leaders, especially on Molokai"; see "Fallen Warriors," *Honolulu Star-Bulletin,* Aug. 11, 1998.

58. Aluli also had an important career in medicine, dedicating himself to improving the health of native Hawaiians. He became president of Na Pu'uwai, Inc., a native Hawaiian health organization that sponsored studies of native Hawaiian health on Moloka'i. He went on to set up a community health system on Moloka'i and Lāna'i and to serve as the coexecutive medical director of the Moloka'i General Hospital. See "To Live and Die on Moloka'i," *Honolulu Star-Bulletin,* Sept. 1, 1998; "A Man for Kahoolawe: 'Dr. Noa Emmett Aluli,' "*Maui News,* June 17, 2001; *Native Hawaiian Center of Excellence Newsletter,* April 2002, unpaged, http:www.hawaii.edu/nhcoe/newsletter/html (accessed June 19, 2002); and Uprichard, "Interview," 47.

59. Aluli and McGregor, *"Mai Ke Kai,"* 231–234; "Uncle Harry Kūhini Mitchell,"

(videotape, two cassettes, Nā Makaoka ʻĀina, 1996), cassette 2; and Ron Youngblood, *On the Hana Coast* (Honolulu: Emphasis International, 1983), 94.

60. "Harry Mitchell," first cassette.

61. Norris, "Kahoʻolawe," 108–120. The main suit was Aluli v. Brown. 602 F.2d 876 (1979); Harold Brown was the secretary of the navy.

62. U.S. Navy, *Draft Supplement 10-31-77 to Final Environmental Statement Concerning Military Use of the Kahoolawe Island Target Complex in the Hawaiian Archipelago, February 1972,* n.p. , n.d., pp. 9g–9i, 14a, 29m, 29v, and A6. The archaeological work was carried on by the Hawaiian Historic Places Review Board, a state body, which found numerous archaeological sites and features and urged that the entire island of Kahoʻolawe be listed in the National Register. See Pyle interview, tape 1, side 1 (Pyle was a member of the Review Board).

63. Walter Ritte and Emmett Aluli, "Public Testimony on the Navy's Revised Environmental Impact Statement," April 25, 1978, file 5, box 2, Navy Kahoolawe Collection. Isaac Hall, "Testimony," April 10, 1978, file 9, box 1, Navy Kahoolawe Collection. In September 2003, the Sierra Club honored Hall with its prestigious William O. Douglas Award.

64. Karl Mowat, Jon Van Dyke, and Leilanai Hiaaa Mitchell, "Testimony," April 25, 1978, file 5, box 2, Navy Kahoolawe Collection; Ry Barbin, John Bose, and Ricky Tugenkamp, "Testimony," April 10, 1978, file 9, box 1, Navy Kahoolawe Collection.

65. For reporting on the archaeological discoveries, see "Kahoolawe Uncovered," *Sunday Honolulu Star-Bulletin and Advertiser,* July 24, 1977; and *Honolulu Advertiser,* Aug. 19, 1980, p. A-3. For reporting on the signing of the consent decrees, see "Kahoolawe Cleanup Agreement Signed," *Honolulu Advertiser,* Dec. 2, 1980.

66. See articles in the newsletter of the Office of Hawaiian Affairs, an agency of the state of Hawaiʻi: Jeff Clark, "KICC Reschedules Draft Report Release, Hearings," *Ka Wai Ola O Oha* 9 (Sept. 1992): 1, 8; and Jeff Clark, "Cleaning Rites of Healing and Rejuvenation," ibid. 9 (Oct. 1992): 12, 13.

67. "Ohana Criticizes Navy for Kahoolawe Policies," *Honolulu Star-Bulletin,* May 5, 1984; *Maui News,* May 17, 1882, p. 1; and *New York Times,* April 25, 1982, p. 15.

68. *Honolulu Advertiser,* March 7, 1988, p. A-3, and May 24, 1988, p. A-3; *Honolulu Star-Bulletin & Advertiser,* March 27, 1988, p. A-9, and May 24, 1988, p. 1.

69. *Honolulu Advertiser,* March 7, 1988, p. A-3.

70. For reprints of the acts and the memorandum, see KICC, *Restoring a Cultural Treasure,* 111–115. See also KICC, *Interim Report to the United States Congress, July 31, 1993* (Honolulu, 1993). For Hannibal Tavares' remarks, see Hannibal Tavares, "Opening Comments, May 14, 1991," KICC, *Preliminary Public Hearing* (Wailuku, 1991), 4–5; this report is a verbatim transcript of the hearings.

71. Rendell (Kaʻimipono) Tong, Dana Hall, Charles Maxwell, and Inez McPhee Ashdown, "Testimony," May 14, 1991, KICC, *Preliminary Public Hearing,* 25, 47–52, 66–67, 135–136.

72. KICC, *Restoring a Cultural Treasure,* 36–37.

73. For a valuable comparison, see John Whitehead, "Alaska and Hawaiʻi: The Cold War States," in *The Cold War American West, 1945–1989,* ed. Kevin Fernlund (Albuquerque: University of New Mexico Press, 1998), 189–210.

74. KICC, *Restoring a Cultural Treasure*, 36–37.

75. *Maui News*, May 9, 1994, p. 1.

76. U.S. Navy and the State of Hawai'i, "Memorandum of Understanding Concerning the Island of Kaho'olawe, Hawai'i, May 6, 1994" (n.p., 1994); State of Hawai'i, "Quitclaim Deed from the United States of America to the State of Hawaii for the Island of Kaho'olawe, Hawai'i, May 7, 1994" (Honolulu, 1994); U.S. Department of Defense, "Appropriations Act, Fiscal Year 1994, Title X," Public Law 103–139, 107 Stat. 1418 (Washington, DC, 1994); State of Hawai'i, *Session Laws of Hawai'i Passed by the Seventeenth State Legislature, Special Session 1993 and Regular Session 1994, Act 161, Chapter 6-K* (Honolulu, 1995), 355–358; KIRC and the Protect Kaho'olawe 'Ohana, "Letter of Understanding Pertaining to the Island of Kaho'olawe, February 16, 1995," http://wwww.brouhaha.net/ohana/lou.pdf (accessed June 19, 2002); and State of Hawai'i, *Hawai'i Revised Statutes, 1997, Cumulative Supplement, Chapter 6-K* (Honolulu, 1998), 52–55.

77. KIRC, *Use Plan, December 1995*.

78. *Honolulu Advertiser*, March 20, 2000, p. 1; and *Maui News*, August 5, 2000, p. 1, Jan. 31, 2003, p. 3, Feb. 9, 2003, p. 1, and Feb. 26, 2004, p. 4.

79. *Maui News*, May 3, 24, and June 7, 2002.

80. *Columbus Dispatch*, June 18, 25, 26, Oct. 18, 2000, April 27, June 16, Aug. 5, 2001, June 8, 2002; and *Economist*, Aug. 4, 2001, pp. 30–31.

81. Samuel P. Hays, *Beauty, Health and Permanence: Environmental Politics in the United States, 1955–1985* (Cambridge: Cambridge University Press, 1987), 13.

82. Jeff Clark, "Kaho'olawe Draft Use Plan Presented," *Ka Wai Ola O Oha* 12 (Sept. 1995): 6.

83. Robert Gottlieb, "Reconsidering Environmentalism: Complex Movements, Diverse Roots," *Environmental History Review* 17 (Winter 1993): 2–3; and David Pellow, *Garbage Wars: the Struggle for Environmental Justice in Chicago* (Cambridge, MA: MIT Press, 2002), vii.

84. George Helm, "Notes," n.d., files 9 and 10, box 1, Helm Collection. On how Pacific peoples have reconstructed their pasts to deal with the present, see Roger Keesing, "Creating the Past: Custom and Identity in the Contemporary Pacific," *Contemporary Pacific* 1 (Spring and Fall 1989): 19–39.

Chapter 3. The Pacific Coast

1. Philip Herrara, "Megalopoplis Comes to the Northwest," *Fortune Magazine* 76 (Dec. 1967), 118–123, 194, esp. 118, 194.

2. Ronald R. Boyce, "Paths to Pugetopolis," *Journal of the West* 41 (Spring 2002): 59–67, esp. 65.

3. Carl Abbott, *The Metropolitan Frontier: Cities in the Modern American West* (Tucson: University of Arizona Press, 1993). See also Gerald D. Nash, *The American West in the Twentieth Century: A Short History of an Urban Oasis* (Englewood Cliffs, NJ: Prentice-Hall, 1973), 193–296. *Journal of the West* 41 (Spring 2002), is devoted to the history of western cities, especially their development after World War II.

4. Glenna Matthews, *Silicon Valley, Women, and the California Dream: Gender, Class, and Opportunity in the Twentieth Century* (Stanford, CA: Stanford University Press, 2003), 13.

5. Cathy Newman, "Inside the Dream Incubator: Silicon Valley," *National Geographic* 200 (Dec. 2001): 52–75, esp. 57.

6. Martin Kenney, "Introduction," in *Understanding Silicon Valley: The Anatomy of an Entrepreneurial Region,* ed. Martin Kenney (Stanford, CA: Stanford University Press, 2000), 1–12, esp. 3.

7. Newman, "Inside the Dream Incubator," 57.

8. Matthews, *Silicon Valley,* 133–136.

9. Annalee Saxenian, *Regional Advantage: Culture and Competition in Silicon Valley and Route 128* (Cambridge, MA: Harvard University Press, 1994), 2.

10. Matthews, *Silicon Valley,* 13–112. See also David Naguib Pellow and Lisa Sun-Hee Park, *The Silicon Valley of Dreams: Environmental Justice, Immigrant Workers, and the High-Tech Global Economy* (New York: New York University Press, 2002), 23–59; and Stephen J. Pitti, *The Devil in Silicon Valley: Northern California, Race, and Mexican Americans* (Princeton, NJ: Princeton University Press, 2003), 8–78.

11. Timothy J. Sturgeon, "How Silicon Valley Came to Be," in *Understanding Silicon Valley,* ed. Kenney, 15–47.

12. Stuart W. Leslie and Robert H. Kargon, "Selling Silicon Valley: Frederick Terman's Model for Regional Advantage," *Business History Review* 70 (Winter 1996): 435–472, esp. 435. Scholars differ in their assessment of Terman's importance. See Christopher Lecuyer, "Making Silicon Valley: Engineering Culture, Innovation, and Industrial Growth, 1930–1970," *Enterprise and Society* 2 (Dec. 2002): 666–672. For a biography, see Steven Erie, *Fred Terman at Stanford: Building a Discipline, a University, and Silicon Valley* (Stanford, CA: Stanford University Press, 2005).

13. Margaret Pugh O'Mara, *Cities of Knowledge: Cold War Science and the Search for the Next Silicon Valley* (Princeton, NJ: Princeton University Press, 2005), 98–141. See also John M. Findlay, *Magic Lands: Western Cityscapes and American Culture after 1940* (Berkeley: University of California Press, 1992), 117–159.

14. O'Mara, *Cities,* 127.

15. Leslie R. Berlin, "Robert Noyce and Fairchild Semiconductor, 1957–68," *Business History Review* 75 (Spring 2001): 63–101.

16. Stuart W. Leslie, "The Biggest 'Angel' of Them All: The Military and the Making of Silicon Valley," in *Understanding Silicon Valley,* ed. Kenney, 48–67, esp. 50, 52. For a detailed examination of the impact of World War II on California's major cities, see Roger W. Lotchin, *The Bad City in the Good War: San Francisco, Los Angeles, Oakland, and San Diego* (Bloomington: Indiana University Press, 2003).

17. Leslie, "Biggest 'Angel,'" 49, 53–62.

18. Mia Gray, Elyse Golob, Ann R. Markusen, and Sam Ock Park, "The Four Faces of Silicon Valley," in *Second Tier Cities: Rapid Growth Beyond the Metropolis* (Minneapolis: University of Minnesota Press, 1999), ed. Ann R. Markusen, Yong-Sook Lee, and Sean DiGiovanna, 291–310. On the importance of entrepreneurs, see Leslie Berlin, "Entrepreneurship and the Rise of Silicon Valley," Ph.D. diss., Stanford University, 2001.

19. Saxenian, *Regional Advantage,* 43–44. See also David P. Angel, "High-Technology Agglomeration and the Labor Market: The Case of Silicon Valley," in *Understanding Silicon Valley,* ed. Kenney, 124–140. On the importance of a regional identity in the development of Silicon Valley, see Stephen B. Adams, "Regionalism in Stanford's Contribution to the Rise of Silicon Valley," *Enterprise and Society* 4 (Sept. 2003): 521–543.

20. Saxenian, *Regional Advantage,* 50; Gray, "Four Faces," 299–306; and Matthews, *Silicon Valley,* 122. See also Christopher Lecuyer, "High-Technology Corporatism: Management–Employee Relations in U.S. Electronics Firms, 1920–1960s," *Enterprise and Society* 4 (Sept. 2003): 502–520.

21. Gray, "Four Faces," 295.

22. On the long-term importance of military spending to Silicon Valley, see Thomas Heinrich, "Cold War Armory: Military Contracting in Silicon Valley," *Enterprise and Society* 3 (June 2002): 247–284.

23. Matthews, *Silicon Valley,* 240.

24. Mark C. Suchman, "Dealmakers and Counselors: Law Firms as Intermediaries in the Development of Silicon Valley," in *Understanding Silicon Valley,* ed. Kenney, 71–97.

25. Martin Kenney and Richard Florida, "Venture Capital in Silicon Valley: Fueling New Firm Formation," in *Understanding Silicon Valley,* ed. Kenney, 98–123.

26. Matthews, *Silicon Valley,* 143.

27. Saxenian, *Regional Advantage,* 3.

28. Matthews, *Silicon Valley,* 227–230; and Saxenian, *Regional Advantage,* 83–104.

29. *Wall Street Journal,* Dec. 10, 1999, p. C-1.

30. *Economist,* Jan. 8, 2000, p. 69. See also *Wall Street Journal,* Jan. 10, 2000, p. 1, April 17, 2000, p. 1, and April 19, 2000, p. 1.

31. *Wall Street Journal,* May 25, 2000, p. 1; *Economist,* July 1, 2000, p. 24.

32. *Wall Street Journal,* August 16, 2001, p. C-1. See also John Cassidy, *Dot.Con: The Greatest Story Ever Sold* (New York: Harper Collins, 2002); and Roger Lowenstein, *Origins of the Crash: The Great Bubble and Its Undoing* (New York: Penguin, 2004).

33. Matthews, *Silicon Valley,* 230–233.

34. Leslie and Kargon, "Selling Silicon Valley."

35. Stuart W. Leslie, "Regional Disadvantage: Replicating Silicon Valley in New York's Capital Region," *Technology and Culture* 42 (April 2001): 236–264.

36. O'Mara, *Cities,* 142–222.

37. Ibid., 216, 220.

38. Robert W. Preer, *The Emergence of Technopolis: Knowledge-Intensive Technologies and Regional Development* (New York: Praeger, 1992); and Susan Rosengrant and David R. Lampe, *Route 128: Lessons from Boston's High-Tech Community* (New York: Basic Books, 1992).

39. See MEDB, "Mission Statement," a self-published, unpaged, and undated pamphlet available at MEDB headquarters, Kīhei, Hawai'i. For more detail on high-technology efforts on Maui, see Mansel G. Blackford, *Fragile Paradise: The Impact of Tourism on Maui, 1959–2000* (Lawrence: University Press of Kansas, 2001), 26–33.

40. MEDB, *Maui's Economic Future: Activities in Site Selection, October, 1983,* self-published, unpaged pamphlet, available at MEDB headquarters, Kīhei.

41. MEDB, "Timeline," typescript available at MEDB headquarters in Kīhei.

42. Maui Research and Technology Park, "MRTP Tenants, 1998," www.mrtp.com/tenants.html (accessed March 3, 1998).

43. *Forbes Magazine,* May 31, 1999, pp. 220–233.

44. Leslie and Kargon, "Selling Silicon Valley," 457–461.

45. Ibid., 461–467.

46. For an assessment of the many factors needed for success in the creation of high-technology districts, see O'Mara, *Cities,* 225–231.

47. Pellow and Park, *Silicon Valley of Dreams,* 19.

48. Matthews, *Silicon Valley,* 146.

49. Pitti, *Devil in Silicon Valley,* 173.

50. Pellow and Park, *Silicon Valley of Dreams,* 77.

51. Ibid., 100.

52. Robin Baker and Sharon Woodrow, "The Clean Light Image of the Electronics Industry: Miracle or Mirage?" in *Double Exposure: Women's Health Hazards on the Job and at Home,* ed. Wendy Cavkin (New York: Monthly Review Press, 1984), 21–36, esp. 24–25.

53. Fred Arnold, Urmil Minocha, and James T. Fawcett, "The Changing Face of Asian Immigration to the United States," and B. V. Carino, "The Philippines and Southeast Asia: Historical Roots and Contemporary Linkages," in James T. Fawcett and Benjamin V. Carino, eds., *Pacific Bridges: The New Immigration from Asia and the Pacific Islands* (New York: Center for Migration Studies, 1987), 105–152, 305–327, esp. 307.

54. Pellow and Park, *Silicon Valley of Dreams,* 67.

55. Baker and Woodrow, "Clean, Light Image," 22; and Matthews, *Silicon Valley,* 163.

56. Matthews, *Silicon Valley,* 172–173; and Pellow and Park, *Silicon Valley of Dreams,* 75–77. For more detail, see Baker and Woodrow, "Clean, Light Image," 28–35. Pressure from the federal government was more important than pressure from the state government in bringing about changes. Since the 1970s, the state of California possessed a California Environmental Quality Act, modeled on federal legislation, but in the water-pollution cases of Silicon Valley it was the Superfund designations that made the most difference. See Stephanie S. Pincetl, *Transforming California: A Political History of Land Use and Development* (Baltimore: Johns Hopkins University Press, 1999), 184.

57. Pitti, *Devil in Silicon Valley,* 151, 163, 169, esp. 163.

58. Matthews, *Silicon Valley,* 173. For more detail, see Baker and Woodrow, "Clean, Light Image," 28–35, esp. 30.

59. Matthews, *Silicon Valley,* 248.

60. Ibid.

61. Pellow and Park, *Silicon Valley of Dreams,* 214.

62. On the development of San Francisco, see especially William Issel and Robert W. Cherney, *San Francisco, 1865–1932: Politics, Power, and Urban Development* (Berkeley: University of California Press, 1986). On urban planning in Pacific Coast Cities, see Mansel G. Blackford, *The Lost Dream: Businessmen and City Planning on the Pacific Coast, 1890–1920* (Columbus: Ohio State University Press, 1993). On the failure of American cities to rebuild in new ways after major fires, see Christine Meisner Rosen, *The Limits*

of Power: Great Fires and the Process of City Growth in America (Cambridge: Cambridge University Press, 1986).

63. O'Mara, *Cities,* 105–106.

64. Ibid., 132–139.

65. Paul Chaat Smith and Robert Allen Warrior, *Like a Hurricane: The Indian Movement from Alcatraz to Wounded Knee* (New York: New Press, 1996), 1–87, esp. 81.

66. Gary L. Peters, "Urban Change in California: A Perspective," *Journal of the West* 41 (Spring 2002): 50–58, esp. 55.

67. Pellow and Park, *Silicon Valley of Dreams,* 69–71.

68. Matthews, *Silicon Valley,* 191–198, esp. 195.

69. Ibid., 193; and Pellow and Park, *Silicon Valley of Dreams,* 71.

70. Newman, "Inside the Dream Incubator," 62–63, 67, 72–73.

71. *Wall Street Journal,* June 20, 2000, p. 1.

72. Newman, "Inside the Dream Incubator," 75.

73. *Wall Street Journal,* Nov. 15, 2000, p. B-1.

74. Ronald R. Boyce, "Paths to Pugetopolis," *Journal of the West* 41 (Spring 2002): 59–67, esp. 65; *Economist,* July 10, 2004, p. 27.

75. Investigations in the early and mid-1960s found that some insecticides and toxic chemicals were being carried into the groundwater in the Seattle area but concluded that pollution by sewage was a much more serious problem. See Leon Robinette, "Caution: Living May be Dangerous to Your Health," *Seattle Magazine* 6 (June 1969): 24–31, esp. 24.

76. On Seattle's early development, see Blackford, *Lost Dream,* 13–30, esp. 14. For more detail, see Alexander Norbert MacDonald, "Seattle's Economic Development, 1880–1910," Ph.D diss., University of Washington, 1959.

77. Matthew W. Klingle, "Urban by Nature: An Environmental History of Seattle, 1880–1970," Ph.D diss., University of Washington, 2001, pp. 1–163. See also Grant Redford, ed., *That Man Thomson* (Seattle: University of Washington Press, 1950).

78. Ibid. See also Coll Thrush, "It's Along the Rivers and Lakes: Watershed Transformations and Indigenous Persistence in Seattle," paper presented at the annual meeting of the American Society for Environmental History, March 31–April 4, 2004, Victoria, B.C. For more detail, see Coll Thrush, "City of Changers," *Pacific Historical Review* 75 (Feb. 2006): 89–117. See also Sarah S. Elkind, "Environmental Inequality and the Urbanization of West Coast Watersheds," *Pacific Historical Review* 75 (Feb. 2006): 53–61, which looks at developments in Los Angeles, the San Francisco Bay area, and Seattle.

79. Blackford, *Lost Dream,* 98–127. See also William H. Wilson, *The City Beautiful Movement* (Baltimore: Johns Hopkins University Press, 1989), 213–233.

80. Norbert MacDonald, *Distant Neighbors: A Comparative History of Seattle and Vancouver* (Lincoln: University of Nebraska Press, 1987), 155. For more detail on Seattle's development during the interwar years, see Richard Berner, *Seattle, 1921–1940: From Boom to Bust* (Seattle: Charles Press, 1992).

81. On Seattle's growth after World War II, see Abbott, *Metropolitan Frontier,* 53–98; Richard C. Berner, *Seattle Transformed: World War II to the Cold War* (Seattle: Charles Press, 1999); Roger Sale, *Seattle Past to Present* (Seattle: University of Washington Press,

1976), 173–252; and T. M. Sell, *Wings of Power: Boeing and the Politics of Growth in the Northwest* (Seattle: University of Washington Press, 2001).

82. Abbott, *Metropolitan Frontier*, 54.

83. Richard S. Kirkendall, "The Boeing Company and the Military-Metropolitan-Industrial Complex, 1945–1953," *Pacific Northwest Quarterly* 85 (Oct. 1994): 137–149.

84. Sell, *Wings of Power*, esp. 33–51.

85. Ibid., 29. See also Carl Abbott, "Regional City and Network City: Portland and Seattle in the Twentieth Century," *Western Historical Quarterly* 23 (Aug. 1992): 293–321, esp. 320; and MacDonald, *Distant Neighbors*, 155.

86. John M. Findlay, "The Off-center Seattle Center: Downtown Seattle and the 1962 World's Fair," *Pacific Northwest Quarterly* 80 (Jan. 1989): 2–11, esp. 4; and MacDonald, *Distant Neighbors*, 156.

87. Sale, *Seattle*, 190.

88. Findlay, "Off-center Seattle Center." See also Findlay, *Magic Lands*, 214–264. The fair was also intended to be an urban renewal effort to rid Seattle of a run-down area, at the expense of residents there, raising yet another environmental justice issue. For a more positive appraisal of the world fair's impact on Seattle, see Abbott, "Regional City and Network City," 306–308.

89. Abbott, "Regional City and Network City."

90. Klingle, "Urban by Nature," 380.

91. Rillmond Schear, "The Great Big Boom over in Bellevue," *Seattle Magazine* 2 (June 1965): 28–37, 45–47, esp. 29–31. For details on Bellevue's development, see Alan J. Stein and the HistoryLink staff, *Bellevue Timeline: The Story of Washington's Leading Edge City from Homesteads to High Rises, 1863–2003* (Bellevue, WA: City of Bellevue, 2004), 46, 63.

92. Matthew Klingle to the author, Oct. 26, 2004.

93. Klingle, "Urban by Nature," 379–412. For a contemporary account, see Sale, *Seattle*, 196–200.

94. Ibid. Seattleites had turned down a regional sewage initiative in 1954, a vote which had spurred Ellis to action.

95. Klingle, "Urban by Nature," 410. The success story was complex. It was not simply that Seattleites convinced others to accept their Metro Plan. In fact, John Henry, the head of the Bellevue Sewer District, was the first person to propose a regional system of interceptor sewers and helped spearhead early attempts to have them approved. During the 1958 campaigns, he worked hard to get residents in Bellevue, Kirkland, and other eastside suburbs to support regional government. Klingle to the author, Oct. 26, 2004.

96. Klingle, "Urban by Nature," 410–435, esp. 434.

97. Sale, *Seattle*, 227–232.

98. Ruth Wolf, "Block that Freeway," *Seattle Magazine* 6 (Feb. 1969): 30–36; and Ruth Wolf, "Getting There Could Be Half the Battle," *Seattle Magazine* 6 (June 1969): 32–41.

99. See Raymond Mohl, "Stop the Road: Freeway Revolts in American Cities," *Journal of Urban History* 30 (July 2004): 674–706, esp. 676; and Zachary M. Schrag, "The Freeway Fight in Washington, D.C.: The Three Sister Bridge in Three Administrations," *Journal of Urban History* 30 (July 2004): 648–673.

100. Editor, "Rapid Transit: An Agonizing Reappraisal," *Seattle Magazine* 7 (May 1970): 70. See also Richard L. Morrill, "Opinion," *Seattle Magazine* 7 (May 1970): 13.

101. To deal with the growing congestion, in 2002 Seattleites approved building a 14-mile-long monorail from North Seattle to the city's southwestern area, at a cost estimated to amount to $9.3 billion. See *Economist,* July 2, 2005, p. 33.

102. Brian Casserly to the author, e-mail, June 8, 2005. A doctoral candidate in history at the University of Washington, Casserly is writing his dissertation on "Landscapes of Security: The Evolution of Civilian–Military Relations in the Puget Sound Region, 1890–1990."

103. Brian Casserly, "Confronting the U.S. Navy at Bangor, 1973–1982," *Pacific Northwest Quarterly* 95 (Summer 2004): 130–139, esp. 135, 138.

104. Casserly to the author; Brian Casserly, "Abstract: Missiles or Picnics in Pugetopolis? Conflicting Visions of Seattle's Fort Lawton," www.pnwhistorians.org/Research/abstractDetail.sap?id=149 (accessed June 7, 2005).

105. Smith and Warrior, *Like a Hurricane,* 89–90.

106. MacDonald, *Distant Neighbors,* 155; and Sell, *Wings of Power,* 29. There were 1.6 million residents in Seattle's SMSA (1960 boundaries) or 2.1 million residents in Seattle's Consolidated Metropolitan Area. See Abbott, "Regional City and Network City," 320.

107. Mia Gray, Else Golob, and Ann R. Markusen, "Seattle: A Classic Hub-and-Spoke," in *Second-Tier Cities,* ed. Markusen, 267–289.

108. Ibid., 268–269. See also Julie Creswell, "Boeing Plays Defense," *Fortune Magazine,* April 19, 2004, pp. 90–98; *Economist,* April 27, 2002, pp. 67–69, and April 19, 2003, pp. 26–27; and *Seattle Post-Intelligencer,* March 31, 2004, p. D-1. Boeing's future looked better by 2005. See *Economist,* June 4, 2005, pp. 59–60; and *Fortune Magazine,* June 13, 2005, pp. 27–28.

109. Rosabeth Moss Kanter, *World-Class: Thriving Locally in the Global Economy* (New York: Simon & Schuster, 1995), 361.

110. Gray, "Hub-and-Spoke."

111. Abbott, "Regional City and Network City," 320; and Stein, *Bellevue Timeline,* 93.

112. Sell, *Wings of Power,* 45–49.

113. Boyce, "Paths to Pugetopolis," 66.

114. Jerry Adler, "Seattle Reigns," *Newsweek,* May 20, 1996, pp. 46–59, esp. 46, 50.

115. *Seattle Post-Intelligencer,* March 31, 2004, p. B-3.

116. In 1990, the per capita income of residents of King County (home to Seattle) was $18,587; that of all Washingtonians came to just $14,293. The per capita income of residents of Santa Clara County was $20,423; that of all Californians was the lower $16,409. See Gray, "Hub-and-Spoke," 284.

117. Adam Rome, *The Bulldozer in the Countryside: Suburban Sprawl and the Rise of American Environmentalism* (Cambridge: Cambridge University Press, 2001).

118. Traffic congestion was a problem throughout the United States, but was especially pronounced in the United States' Pacific Coast and western cities. See *Economist,* June 4, 2005, pp. 28–29, and Nov. 5, 2005, pp. 33–34.

Chapter 4. Alaska

1. Spike Walker, *Working on the Edge: Surviving in the World's Most Dangerous Profession, King Crab Fishing on Alaska's High Seas* (New York: St. Martin's Press, 1991), xvii–xxiii.

2. Mansel G. Blackford, *Pioneering a Modern Small Business: Wakefield Seafood and the Alaskan Frontier* (Greenwich, CT: JAI Press, 1979), 2. See also Patrick Dillon, *Lost at Sea: An American Tragedy* (New York: Dial Press, 1998); Todd Lewan, *The Last Run: A True Story of Rescue and Redemption on the Alaska Seas* (New York: Harper Collins, 2004); and Brad Matsen, *Fishing up North: Stories of Luck and Loss in Alaskan Waters* (Anchorage: Alaskan Northwest Books, 1998). Fishing became safer with the passage by Congress of the Commercial Fishing Industry Vessel Safety Act in 1988. The number of vessels lost each year in Alaska remained about the same, but fatalities among crew members were halved. See Terry Johnson, *Ocean Treasure: Commercial Fishing in Alaska* (Fairbanks: University of Alaska Sea Grant Program, 2003), 45–46.

3. Stephen Haycox, *Frigid Embrace: Politics, Economics and Environment in Alaska* (Corvallis: Oregon State University Press, 2002); and Daniel Nelson, *Northern Landscapes: The Struggle for Wilderness Alaska* (Washington, DC: Resources for the Future, 2004). On attitudes in Alaska, see also Claus-M. Naske and Herman E. Slotnick, *Alaska: A History of the 49th State* (Norman: University of Oklahoma Press, 1987), 3. For a description of life in modern-day Alaska, see Peter Jenkins, *Looking for Alaska* (New York: St. Martin's Press, 2001).

4. See Roderick Nash, *Wilderness and the American Mind* (New Haven, CT: Yale University Press, 1967). Nash argues that most people on frontiers sought to put nature to immediate use for personal gain. For a nuanced examination of attitudes and actions, see Richard W. Judd, *Common Lands, Common People: The Origins of Conservation in New England* (Cambridge, MA: Harvard University Press, 1997). Judd sees a complex set of relationships governing people, their communities, and nature. Community norms and traditional ways of dealing with new lands (and bodies of water) were, he shows, important in the development of twentieth-century conservation movements.

5. John McPhee, *Coming into the Country* (New York: Farrar, Straus and Giroux, 1976), 87. See also John S. Dryzek, *Conflict and Change in Resource Management: The Case of Alaska* (Boulder, CO: Westview Press, 1983), 35. For a cautionary tale of difficulties in getting ahead in modern Alaska, see Norma Cobb and Charles W. Sasser, *Arctic Homestead* (New York: St. Martin's Press, 2000), a firsthand account.

6. Ken Ross, *Environmental Conflict in Alaska* (Boulder: University Press of Colorado, 2000), 3.

7. Naske and Slotnick, *Alaska*, 5–6.

8. Ibid., 45–62. For more detail, see Lydia Black, *Russians in Alaska, 1732–1867* (Fairbanks: University of Alaska Press, 2004). Black argues that most Russians treated Aleuts reasonably, at least by the 1800s, and that the Russians followed meaningful conservation measures in their hunting of fur-bearing animals, including sea otters. See also Mark Bassin, *Imperial Visions: Nationalist Imagination and Geographical Expansion in the Russian Far East, 1840–1965* (Cambridge: Cambridge University Press, 1999).

9. Haycox, *Frigid Embrace,* ix; Naske and Slotnick, *Alaska,* 16. As early as 1967, historian William H. Wilson urged scholars of Alaska's economic history "to join the Russian and American periods more closely together." See William H. Wilson, "Landmarks and Open Questions in Alaskan Economic History," *Proceedings of the Conference on Alaskan History* (Anchorage: Alaska Methodist University Press, 1967), 129.

10. Haycox, *Frigid Embrace,* x.

11. Victoria Wyatt, "Alaska and Hawaiʻi," in Clyde A. Milner II, Carol A. O'Connor, and Martha A. Sandweiss, eds., *The Oxford History of the American West* (New York: Oxford University Press, 1994), 565–600.

12. Arrell Morgan Gibson, *Yankees in Paradise: The Pacific Basin Frontier* (Albuquerque: University of New Mexico Press, 1993); John H. Whitehead, "Noncontiguous Wests: Alaska and Hawaiʻi," in David M. Wrobel and Michael C. Steiner, eds., *Many Wests: Place, Culture and Regional Identity* (Lawrence: University Press of Kansas, 1997), 315–341. Some commercial whaling lasted into the twentieth century. For a firsthand account, see Arthur James Allen, *A Whaler and Trader in the Arctic, 1895 to 1944* (Anchorage: Alaska Northwest Publishing Company, 1978).

13. Naske and Slotkin, *Alaska,* 70–71, 77–87, 301. On the environmental consequences of gold mining, see Kathryn Morse, *The Nature of Gold: An Environmental History of the Klondike Gold Rush* (Seattle: University of Washington Press, 2003). On copper mining, see Melody Grauman, "Kennecott: Alaskan Origins of a Copper Empire, 1900–1938," *Western Historical Quarterly* 9 (April 1978): 197–212.

14. Haycox, *Frigid Embrace,* 36; Naske and Slotnick, *Alaska,* 87, 301.

15. Richard Cooley, *Politics and Conservation: The Decline of the Alaskan Salmon* (New York: Harper-Row, 1963); Haycox, *Frigid Embrace,* 27–28, 33; Anthony Netboy, *The Salmon: Their Fight for Survival* (Boston: Houghton Mifflin, 1974), 410–433, esp. 409. For a valuable contemporary work, see C. L. Andrews, "The Salmon of Alaska," *Washington Historical Quarterly* 9 (Oct. 1918): 243–254.

16. Haycox, *Frigid Embrace,* 33, 46–47; Naske and Slotkin, *Alaska,* 103–105.

17. There were the bare beginnings of farming and lumbering in Alaska. In the 1930s and 1940s, the federal government sponsored the resettlement of several hundred farmers from northern Great Plains states to the Matanuska Valley just north of Anchorage as a New Deal project. Never very successful, this experiment did little to boost Alaska's economy. Lumbering, which developed into a major industry after World War II, was just beginning in the prewar years. Alaskans produced most of the lumber they used by the 1920s and 1930s but had not yet developed an export business in timber. See Haycox, *Frigid Embrace,* 61; Naske and Slotnick, *Alaska,* 73–74, 85–86, 94–98, 106, 112–117; and Whitehead, "Noncontiguous Wests," 328–329. For attitudes toward farming in the north, see James Shortridge, "The Alaskan Agricultural Empire: An American Agrarian Vision, 1898–1929," *Pacific Northwest Quarterly* 69 (Oct. 1978): 145–158.

18. Robert A. Frederick, "On Imagination and New Paths: Our Multi-Frontier in the Far North," *Proceedings of the Conference on Alaskan History,* 158.

19. Brian Garfield, *The Thousand-Mile War: World War II in Alaska and the Aleutians* (Fairbanks: University of Alaska Press, 1969); and Otis Hayes, Jr., *Alaska's Hidden Wars: Secret Campaigns on the North Pacific Rim* (Fairbanks: University of Alaska Press, 2004).

20. Hayes, *Hidden Wars,* 11, 127. For the details of Aleut relocation, see Dean Kohl-hoff, *When the Wind Was a River: Aleut Evacuation in World War II* (Seattle: University of Washington Press, 1995). See also Ethel Ross Oliver, *Journal of an Aleutian Year* (Seattle: University of Washington Press, 1988). Ross taught on Atka Island in 1956. In addition to describing how Aleut life was changing in the 1950s, this diary is valuable because it reprints firsthand accounts of the experiences of Aleuts during and after World War II.

21. Whitehead, "Alaska and Hawai'i," 197. See also Naske and Slotkin, *Alaska,* 14, 136–139, 301.

22. Dan O'Neill, "Alaska and the Firecracker Boys: The Story of Project Chariot," in Bruce Hevly and John M. Findlay, eds., *The Atomic West* (Seattle: University of Washington Press), 179–199. See also Ross, *Environmental Conflict,* 96–109; and Peter A. Coates, *The Trans-Alaska Pipeline Controversy: Technology, Conservation, and the Frontier* (Fairbanks: University of Alaska Press, 1993), 111–133. Soviet scientists and political leaders had similar plans for their arctic regions. As historian John McNeill has written, "They used nuclear explosions to create reservoirs and canals and to open mine shafts. In 1972 and 1984 they detonated three nuclear bombs to try to loosen ores from which phosphate (for fertilizer) was derived." See J. R. McNeill, *Something New under the Sun: An Environmental History of the Twentieth-Century World* (New York: W. W. Norton, 2000), 343.

23. O'Neill, "Alaska and the Firecracker Boys."

24. Ross, *Environmental Conflict,* 110–120. For more detail, see Dean W. Kohlhoff, *Amchitka and the Bomb: Nuclear Testing in Alaska* (Seattle: University of Washington Press, 2002). Amchitka was eventually restored at a cost of $6.7 million. Amchitka had been part of the 3-million-acre Aleutian Islands Reservation formed in 1913, and by the time of World War II the island was part of the Refuge of the National Wildlife Reservation. Amchitka became part of the 1-million-acre Alaska Maritime National Wildlife Refuge in 1976. Even so, the island continued to be used for military purposes through the 1980s.

25. Naske and Slotkin, *Alaska,* 140–185, esp. 169. For more detail, see George W. Rogers, *The Future of Alaska: the Economic Consequences of Statehood* (Baltimore: Johns Hopkins University Press, 1962).

26. Naske and Slotkin, *Alaska,* 158–159, 171, 174–175, 247; Netboy, *Salmon,* 409.

27. Ibid. See also Kathy Durbin, *Tongass: Pulp Politics and the Fight for the Alaska Rain Forest* (Corvallis: Oregon State University Press, 1999); David Smith, "Pulp, Paper, and Alaska," *Pacific Northwest Quarterly* 66 (April 1975), 61–70; and Mike Dunning, "Tourism in Ketchikan and Southeast Alaska," *Alaska History* 15 (Fall 2000): 31–43.

28. George W. Rogers, "Alaskan Economic History," *Proceedings of the Conference on Alaskan History,* 123.

29. Johnson, *Ocean Treasures,* 1, 98.

30. Terry Johnson, *The Bering Sea and the Aleutian Islands: Region of Wonders* (Fairbanks: University of Alaska Press, for the Alaska Sea Grant Program, 2003), 19–44. For still valuable observations, see the report of expeditions sponsored by the Smithsonian Institute to the Aleutians in 1936–1938: Ales Hrdlicka, *The Aleutian and Commander Islands and Their Inhabitants* (Philadelphia: Wistar Institute of Anatomy and Biology,

1945), esp. 5–18. For a popular history, see William R. Hunt, *Arctic Passage: The Turbulent History of the Land and People of the Bering Sea, 1697–1975* (New York: Charles Scribner's Sons, 1975).

31. For a survey of fisheries in the North Pacific, including Alaskan waters, see Robert J. Browning, *Fisheries of the North Pacific: History, Species, Gear and Processes* (Anchorage: Alaska Northwest Publishing Company, 1974). King crabs are found in Japanese and Russian waters, and before World War II Japanese vessels fished for king crabs off the Alaskan coast.

32. Blackford, *Pioneering,* 4–7. On the king crab industry, see also Sybil Beale, "The King Crab Industry of Alaska, 1953–1969: An Economic Analysis," M.A. thesis, University of Washington, 1971; and Graham Miller, "The Development of the King Crab Industry in Alaska up to 1964," M.S. thesis, University of Alaska, 1965.

33. Blackford, *Pioneering,* 4–10. On the development of America's frozen-food industry, see Charles H. Harrison, *Growing a Global Village: Making History at Seabrook Farms* (New York: Holmes & Meier, 2003); and Shane Hamilton, "The Economies and Conveniences of Modern-Day Living: Frozen Foods and Mass Marketing, 1945–1965," *Business History Review* 77 (Spring 2003): 33–60.

34. Blackford, *Pioneering,* 8–11.

35. Ibid., 12–17.

36. Ibid., 39–40.

37. Ibid., 9, 26, 30–31.

38. Ibid., 168. These are live-weight pounds, the weight of the entire crabs, not just the meat eaten by consumers.

39. Blackford, *Pioneering,* 139–140.

40. Ibid., 141–144. To deflect criticism that it was an outside interest, Wakefield Seafood moved its headquarters to Alaska in 1960.

41. Blackford, *Pioneering,* 145–146; Johnson, *Ocean Treasure,* 10. In 1974, the state legislature limited the number of fishing permits in the salmon, herring, and some other fisheries.

42. Blackford, *Pioneering,* 146–150.

43. By this time, some nations had unilaterally taken this step: for instance, the United States (concerned mainly about undersea oil resources, not fish or crab) and Iceland. Thus, the United States insisted that other nations respect its rights over its continental shelves but was at first unwilling to respect the rights of other nations over their continental shelves. In addition, Argentina, Panama, Mexico, Peru, and Chile claimed exclusive rights to their continental shelves to a distance of 200 miles from shore. See Rognvaldur Hannesson, *The Privatization of the Oceans* (Cambridge, MA: MIT Press, 2004), 31–38.

44. Francis T. Christy, Jr., and Anthony Scott, *The Commonwealth in Ocean Fisheries: Some Problems of Growth and Economic Allocation* (Baltimore: Johns Hopkins University Press, 1965), 153–174; and J. V. R. Prescott, *The Political Geography of the Oceans* (New York: John Wiley & Sons, 1975), 116–141.

45. Blackford, *Pioneering,* 150–153.

46. Johnson, *Bering Sea,* 141, 158–159; Richard Adams Carey, *Against the Tide: The Fate of the New England Fisherman* (New York: Houghton Mifflin, 1999), 51–56. The Japanese protested the proclamation of the American EEZ, estimating that 1.6 million tons of their nation's 10 million-ton annual fish catch came from within that zone. See *Wall Street Journal,* Nov. 11, 1976, p. 38. On the talks more generally, see *Time,* March 14, 1977, p. 1; and *Wall Street Journal,* June 18, 1974, p. 1, and March 1, 1976, p. 1. For a close look at how the council governing Alaskan waters operated, see Matsen, *Fishing up North,* 63–79.

47. Elizabeth Mann Borghese, *The Oceanic Circle: Governing the Seas as a Global Resource* (New York: United Nations University Press, 1998), 109–131.

48. Sandra Tarte, "Negotiating a Tuna Management Regime for the Western and Central Pacific: The MHLC Process 1994–1999," *Journal of Pacific History* 34 (Fall 1999): 273–280.

49. Hannesson, *Privatization,* 41–42.

50. Carey, *Against the Tide,* 302–304. See also Daniel Pauly Jay MacLean, *In a Perfect Ocean: The State of Fisheries and Ecosystems in the North Atlantic Ocean* (Washington, DC: Island Press, 2003). Nations varied tremendously in how successful they were in managing fish stocks within the 200-mile limit. See Hannesson, *Privatization,* 85–162, for a close look at regulatory developments in the waters of New Zealand, Chile, Norway, Canada, Iceland, and the United States.

51. Matsen, *Fishing up North,* 7.

52. For an overview of global fishery problems, see McNeill, *Something New,* 243–253. See also *Attaché,* May 2002, p. 8; *Economist,* March 18, 1995, p. 46, Dec. 1, 2001, p. 78, and May 17, 2003, p. 70; and *U.S. News & World Report,* June 22, 1992, pp. 64–75. On recent efforts to study overfishing, see Lance Van Sittert, "The Other Seven Tenths," *Environmental History* 10 (Jan. 2005): 106–109. There were hopeful signs. Some consumers began calling for the certification that the fish they purchased came from healthy, not overused, fish stocks. See *Economist,* Oct. 8, 2005, p. 66.

53. *Fortune,* Jan. 29, 1979, p. 53.

54. *Wall Street Journal,* June 26, 1995, p. 1. For a close look at the 1981 crash in king crabs catch, see Matsen, *Fishing up North,* 15–23.

55. *Wall Street Journal,* Sept. 4, 1996, p. 1, and Jan. 15, 2002, p. 1; *Columbus Dispatch,* Nov. 12, 2000, p. B-6. See also Johnson, *Bering Sea,* 169–178; Johnson, *Ocean Treasure,* 143–144; and Nature Conservancy, *Newsletter,* Summer 2004, http://nature.org/magazine/summer2004/pribilof/features/art12831.html (accessed June 11, 2004).

56. Hannesson, *Privatization,* 158–159. Many questions surrounded the granting of ITQs, however, making their implementation difficult. Most controversial were the decisions about which fishermen would be granted ITQs and which would not, thus excluding them from the fishery. Usually only those fishermen who had provable long-term histories of taking part in a given fishery were granted ITQs.

57. Johnson, *Ocean Treasure,* 136.

58. Ibid., 77–78, 159; and Naske and Slotkin, *Alaska,* 284. For firsthand accounts, see Bob Durr, *Down in Bristol Bay: High Tides, Hangovers, and Harrowing Experiences on Alaska's Last Frontier* (New York: St. Martin's Press, 1999); and Joe Upton, *Alaska Blues: A Fisherman's Journal* (Anchorage: Alaska Northwest Publishing Company, 1977).

59. Naske and Slotkin, *Alaska*, 241–269.

60. Ibid., 186–208. For more detail, see Donald Craig Mitchell, *Take My Land, Take My Life: The Story of Congress's Historic Settlement of Alaska Native Land Claims, 1960–1971* (Fairbanks: University of Alaska Press, 2001).

61. Coates, *Trans-Alaska Pipeline*, 19.

62. Naske and Slotkin, *Alaska*, 206–207. On the political battles, see Nelson, *Northern Landscapes*.

63. Ross, *Environmental Conflict*, 197–202.

64. Coates, *Trans-Alaska Pipeline*, 251–302; and Robert Douglas Meade, *Journeys Down the Line: Building the Trans-Alaska Pipeline* (New York: Doubleday & Co., 1978). On the impacts of oil income on Alaska, see Mim Dixon, *What Happened to Fairbanks: The Effects of the Trans-Alaska Oil Pipeline on the Community of Fairbanks, Alaska* (Boulder, CO: Westview Press, 1978); Lawrence A. Palinkas, Bruce Murray Harris, and John S. Petterson, *A Systems Approach to Social Impact Assessment: Two Alaskan Case Studies* (Boulder, CO: Westview Press, 1985); and George W. Rogers, *Change in Alaska: People, Petroleum, and Politics* (Fairbanks: University of Alaska Press, 1970).

65. U.S. Department of the Interior, Bureau of Land Management, Geological Survey, *Leasing and Management of Energy Resources on the Outer Continental Shelf* (Washington, DC: Government Printing Office, 1976), 10–11, 21–25. For background information, see Sarah S. Elkind, "Black Gold and the Beach: Offshore Oil, Beaches, and Federal Power in Southern California, *Journal of the West* 44 (Winter 2005): 8–17.

66. Dryzek, *Conflict and Choice*, 19–24. For analyses of the details of the legislation, see Russell O. Jones, Walter M. Mead, and Philip E. Sorenson, "The Outer Continental Shelf Lands Amendments of 1978," *Natural Resources Journal* 19 (Oct. 1979): 885–908; and Robert B. Krueger and Louis H. Singer, "An Analysis of the Outer Continental Shelf Lands Act Amendments of 1978," *Natural Resources Journal* 19 (Oct. 1979): 909–927.

67. Department of Interior, *Leasing and Management of Energy Resources*, 6–9.

68. On arctic offshore oil developments, see Dorene A. Bolze, "Outer Continental Shelf Oil and Gas Development in the Alaskan Arctic," *Natural Resources Journal* 30 (Winter 1990): 17–64; and W. F. Weeks and G. Weller, "Offshore Oil in the Alaska Arctic," *Science* 225 (July 27, 1984): 371–378.

69. U.S. Department of the Interior, Bureau of Land Management, *Draft Environmental Statement: Proposed Five-Year OCS Oil and Gas Lease Schedule March 1980–February 1985* (Washington, DC: Government Printing Office, 1979), 36. See also Dryzek, *Conflict and Choice*, 16–17.

70. Dryzek, *Conflict and Choice*, 16–17; and Department of Interior, *Draft Environmental Statement: Proposed Five-Year OCS . . . Schedule*, 36.

71. Nelson, *Northern Landscapes*, 72; U.S. Department of Commerce, National Oceanic and Atmospheric Administration (NOAA), *Cook Inlet Interim Synthesis Report* (Boulder, CO: Science Applications, 1979), 29, 45.

72. NOAA, *Cook Inlet*, 150, 159, 161.

73. Eugene H. Buck et al., *Kadyak: A Background for Living* (Fairbanks: University of Alaska Arctic Information and Data Center, 1975), 304.

74. Nelson, *Northern Landscapes*, 159.

75. Robert Panitch, "Offshore Drilling: Fishermen and Oilmen Clash in the Gulf of Alaska," *Science* 189 (July 18, 1975): 204–206, esp. 205.

76. Nelson, *Northern Landscapes*, 161–163.

77. George Rogers, "Off-Shore Oil and Gas Developments in Alaska: Impacts and Conflicts," *Polar Record* 17 (Sept. 1974): 255–275, esp. 265.

78. Nelson, *Northern Landscapes*, 162–163.

79. Department of the Interior, *Draft Environmental Statement: Proposed Five-Year . . . Schedule*, 48, 187, 195; NOAA, *Cook Inlet*, 31; and Nelson, *Northern Landscapes*, 166.

80. Jones, Mead, and Sorenson, "Outer Continental Shelf Lands Act," 925; NOAA, *Cook Inlet*, 111–112.

81. Department of Interior, *Draft Environmental Statement: Proposed Five-year Lease OCS . . . Schedule*, 182–184. See also Johnson, *Bering Sea*, 114–115; and Matsen, *Fishing up North*, 18.

82. Tom Kizzia, "Feuding Groups Make an Oil Deal," *Sierra* 71 (Sept.–Oct. 1986): 76–77; and Matsen, *Fishing up North*, 31.

83. Colleen S. Brenner and Robert W. Middleton, *Fisheries and Oil Development on the Continental Shelf* (Bethesda, MD: American Fisheries Society, 1991), vii, 1; Johnson, *Bering Sea*, 116.

84. Ibid. In 2005, the moratorium on offshore drilling for natural gas came under attack. It seemed likely that Congress might allow some drilling in previously prohibited areas. See *Wall Street Journal*, August 22, 2005, p. A-4.

85. William Brown, "A Common Border: Soviets and Americans Work to Create a Joint Park in the Bering Strait," *National Parks* 62 (Nov.–Dec. 1988): 18–23, esp. 21.

86. NPS, "What Is Beringia?" www.nps.gov/akso/beringia/whatisberingia2.htm (accessed May 20, 2004). For a description of Beringia's flora and fauna, see Frank Graham, Jr., "U.S. and Soviet Environmentalists Join Forces across the Bering Strait," *Audubon* 93 (July–Aug. 1991): 42–61. For more detail, see Frederick Hadleigh West, *The Archaeology of Beringia* (New York: Columbia University Press, 1981). Exactly when people traversed the land bridge(s), and how many times they did so, remains a matter of debate.

87. Brown, "Common Border," 18–20; Graham, "U.S. and Soviet Environmentalists," 53; and NPS, "Shared Beringian Heritage Program," www.nps.gov/akso/beringia/ beringiaprogram.htm (accessed May 20, 2004). The 1990 study may be read at www.nps. gov/akso/beringia/recon2.htm (accessed May 20, 2004).

88. NPS, *Bridge of Friendship: A Progress Report on the Establishment of Beringia International Park* (Washington, DC: Government Printing Office, 1992), 1, 6. For a look at native life on the Russian side, see *Economist*, Sept. 24, 2005, p. 63.

89. Graham, "U.S. and Soviet Environmentalists," 58. For an Alaskan Native's view of life there, see Susan B. Andrews and John Creed, eds., *Authentic Alaska: Voices of Its Native Writers* (Lincoln: University of Nebraska Press, 1998), 130–131.

90. NPS, "Shared Beringian Heritage Program," 1.

91. Mark David Spence, *Dispossessing the Wilderness: Indian Removal and the Making of the National Parks* (New York: Oxford University Press, 1999). See also Karl Jacoby,

Crimes against Nature: Squatters, Poachers, Thieves and the Hidden History of American Conservation (Berkeley: University of California Press, 2001), 149–192.

92. Theodore Catton, *Inhabited Wilderness: Indians, Eskimos, and National Parks in Alaska* (Albuquerque: University of New Mexico Press, 1997).

93. NPS, "Shared Beringian Heritage Program," 1.

94. NPS, "Projects Funded under Shared Beringian Heritage Program," www.nps. gov/akso/beringia/projects.htm (accessed May 20, 2004).

95. NPS, "Shared Beringian Heritage Program," 2. Some tourism was beginning in the Bering Sea in the early 2000s, and the park was expected to play a role in this development. The 114-passenger ship *Spirit of the Oceans* offered two-week cruises in the Bering Sea in the summer of 2004 for $7,200 per person. See www.cruisewest.com (accessed June 20, 2004).

96. Samuel P. Hays, *Conservation and the Gospel of Efficiency: The Progressive Conservation Movement, 1890–1920* (New York: Athenaeum, 1969).

97. *Economist,* May 26, 2005, p. 36.

98. Blackford, *Pioneering,* 145. For a particularly valuable discussion of the concept of the "tragedy of the commons" in fisheries, see Arthur F. McEvoy, *The Fisherman's Problem: Ecology and Law in the California Fisheries, 1850–1980* (Cambridge: Cambridge University Press, 1986), 10–12.

99. Johnson, *Bering Sea,* 129.

Chapter 5. Southern Japan during American Occupation

1. Michihiko Hachiya, *Hiroshima Diary: The Journal of a Japanese Physician, August 6–September 30, 1945* (Chapel Hill: University of North Carolina Press, 1955), 1–2. For a discussion of atomic bomb literature and art, see Robert Jay Lifton, *Death in Life: Survivors of Hiroshima* (New York: Basic Books, 1967), 397–479. On the atomic bombing of Nagasaki, see F. W. Chinnock, *Nagasaki—The Forgotten Bomb* (London: George Allen & Unwin, 1970).

2. The Committee for the Compilation of Materials on Damage Caused by the Atomic Bombs in Hiroshima and Nagasaki, *Hiroshima and Nagasaki: The Physical, Medical, and Social Effects of the Atomic Bombings* (New York: Basic Books, 1981), 37–66, 335–392. This lengthy volume summarizes and reprints many Japanese reports. Most of the important reports and documents on the bombing of Hiroshima are available in the English language, as in this compilation.

3. Andre Sorensen, *The Making of Urban Japan: Cities and Planning from Edo to the Twenty-first Century* (London: Routledge, 2002).

4. Yorifusa Ishida, "Japanese Cities and Planning in the Reconstruction Period, 1945–55," *Rebuilding Urban Japan after 1945,* ed. Carola Hein, Jeffrey M. Diefendorf, and Yorifusa Ishida (Houndmills, Hants: Palgrave Macmillan, 2003), 17–49, esp. 26.

5. Cherie Wendelken, "Aesthetics and Reconstruction: Japanese Architectural Culture in the 1950s," in Hein et al., *Rebuilding Urban Japan,* 188–209, esp. 192. See also T. Su-

gimoto, "Atomic Bombing and Restoration in Japan," *Destruction and Rebirth of Urban Environment* (Tokyo: Sagami Shobo Publishing, 2000), ed. N. Fukui and H. Jinnai, 17–37 (this work is published in Japanese and English on each page); and Carola Hein, "Hiroshima, the Atomic Bomb and Kenzō Tange's Hiroshima Peace Center," in Joan Ockman, ed., *Out of Ground Zero: Case Studies in Urban Reinvention* (Munich: Pestel, 2002).

6. Norioki Ishimaru, "Reconstructing Hiroshima and Preserving the Reconstructed City," in Hein et al., *Rebuilding Urban Japan*, 87–107, esp. 87.

7. Yoshiteru Kosakai, *Hiroshima Peace Reader* (Hiroshima: Keisuisha, 1980), 5–22. Kosakai was chief editor of the Hiroshima City Historical Collective and the director of the Hiroshima City Archives. See also "There Have Been Two Versions of the Name Hiroshima and Kure," one-page manuscript in the Hiroshima City Archives.

8. Kosakai, *Hiroshima Peace Reader*, 6. See also City of Hiroshima, *Hiroshima* (Hiroshima: Nakamoto Sogo Publishing, 1983), 91.

9. Ishimaru, "Reconstructing Hiroshima," 87; Kosakai, *Hiroshima Peace Reader*, 8–9; Yoshida Mitsukuni, *Hiroshima and Beyond: A Heritage of Technology* (Tokyo: Mazda Corporation, 1985), 15–19, 26–27, 49–55. This conflict between miners and farmers resembles a contest between gold miners and early-day farmers in northern California, with the farmers complaining that mining caused the silting up of rivers. Going to their state capital in Sacramento, the farmers succeeded in having the state's first environmental legislation passed in an attempt to prevent that silting.

10. For a pioneering work on castle towns, see John Hall, "The Castle Town and Japan's Modern Urbanization," in John Hall and Marius Jansen, eds., *Studies in the Institutional History of Early Modern Japan* (Princeton, NJ: Princeton University Press, 1968), 169–188. For more recent interpretations, see Tsuneo Sato, "Tokugawa Villages and Agriculture," and Katsuhisa Moriya, "Urban Networks and Information Systems," in Chie Nakane and Shinzaburo Oishi, eds., *Tokugawa Japan* (Tokyo: University of Tokyo Press, 1990), 37–80, 97–123. On the changing relative importance of castle towns and smaller villages in the economic growth of Tokugawa Japan, see Thomas Smith, *Native Sources of Japanese Industrialization, 1750–1920* (Berkeley: University of California Press, 1988), 15–49. For an overview, see Sorensen, *Urban Japan*, 11–44. Sorensen stresses that, unlike the case in western Europe, there were no self-governing cities in feudal Japan. To the contrary, Japanese castle towns initially served military purposes. Their rulers decreed that for defensive reasons streets be narrow and winding and bridges restricted, thus making an attack on the inner part of the town, where the castle keep was located, difficult. Open spaces and parks were almost nonexistent.

11. For a classic work on Japanese urbanization, see R. P. Dore, *City Life in Japan* (Berkeley: University of California Press, 1963). Sorensen sees developments in Nara and Kyoto as exceptional and as having little long-lasting impact on urbanization in Japan. See Sorensen, *Urban Japan*, 13. However, Sugimoto considers Hiroshima to have been partially modeled on Kyoto in Tokugawa times, especially in efforts to construct something of a grid of streets, albeit one distorted by the irregularities of city's river system. See Sugimoto, "Atomic Bombing and Restoration of Hiroshima," 23.

12. Takafusa Nakamura, *Economic Growth in Prewar Japan* (New Haven, CT: Yale University Press, 1983).

13. City of Hiroshima, *Hiroshima*, 92–93; Committee, *Hiroshima and Nagasaki*, 387, 410; Ishimaru, "Reconstructing Hiroshima," 87; Kosakai, *Hiroshima Peace Reader*, 9, 12–14; Averill Liebow, *Encounter with Disaster: A Medical Diary of Hiroshima, 1945* (New York: W. W. Norton, 1970), 22. Liebow headed an American military medical team to assess the effects of the bomb on Hiroshima residents in the fall of 1945.

14. City of Hiroshima, "City Planning in Hiroshima," pamphlet, March 31, 1981, pp. 6–9, available at the City Planning Division, Hiroshima. See also Kosakai, *Hiroshima Peace Reader*, 11.

15. Sorenson, *Urban Japan*, 53–57, 61. From 1889, mayors were appointed from one of three elected candidates, and there were elected city councils. However, the electorate was very limited until 1925, and the powers of the mayor and councilmen were severely restricted.

16. Sorensen, *Urban Japan*, 85–150, esp. 85.

17. Ibid.

18. Ibid.

19. City of Hiroshima, "City Planning in Hiroshima," 6–9; Ishimaru, "Reconstructing Hiroshima," 87–88.

20. Ibid. For a detailed look at prewar neighborhoods, see Sugimoto, "Atomic Bombing and the Restoration of Hiroshima."

21. Committee, *Hiroshima and Nagasaki*, 344–353.

22. Ibid., 21–83. See also Walter Enloe, *Oasis of Peace: A Hiroshima Story* (St. Paul, MN: Hamline University Press, 1998), 132; John Hershey, *Hiroshima* (New York: Bantam, 1981); Liebow, *Encounter with Disaster*, 24–27.

23. Robert Jungk, *Children of the Ashes: The Story of Rebirth* (New York: Harcourt, Brace & World, 1959), 23. "We called it 'the atomic desert.' I never thought people would be able to live there again," recalled Ichiro Moritaki, a survivor of the bomb and later an advocate for survivors' rights, in 1985. See *Asahi Evening News* (English-language edition), July 12, 1985, p. 3.

24. Committee, *Hiroshima and Nagasaki*, 335–392. The committee estimated that the total property loss in Hiroshima came to about 884 million yen, about three times the aggregate earning power of Hiroshima's resident population in 1944. For graphic photographs of the destruction, see Yuchiro Sasaki, "Witness of A-Bomb: Diary of Hiroshima," pamphlet, undated, n.p. See also Ishimaru, "Reconstructing Hiroshima," 89.

25. Committee, *Hiroshima and Nagasaki*, 105–482. On the effects of radiation sicknesses, see also Liebow, *Encounter with Disaster*, 96–180.

26. Committee, *Hiroshima and Nagasaki*, 347, 410, 421, 455. For more detail, see Kenneth Werrell, *Blankets of Fire: U.S. Bombers over Japan during World War II* (Washington, DC: Smithsonian Institute Press, 1996); and William M. Tsutsui, "Landscapes in the Dark Valley: Toward an Environmental History of Wartime Japan," *Environmental History* 8 (April 2003): 294–311. On Japan's home front during World War II, see Thomas Havens, *Valley of Darkness: The Japanese People and World War II* (New York: W. W. Norton, 1978); and John Dower, *Japan in War and Peace* (New York: New Press, 1993).

27. Committee, *Hiroshima and Nagasaki*, 80–86; and Tsutsui, "Landscapes," 295–297. The radiation effects of the atomic bomb did not last long, for the half-life of the bomb's

radioactive material was short. Within a few weeks it was safe to move back into Hiroshima. Interestingly, Tsutsui finds that the impact of the Second World War on Japan's flora and fauna was far from one-sided. There were negative consequences flowing from wartime exigencies—increased clear-cut logging, industrial pollution of the air and water, and the decimation of wildlife (especially through the use of birds as a food source). On the other hand, relieved of diminution by the removal of Japanese fishing vessels, fish and crab stocks in nearby and offshore waters recovered. So did fur seals in the Pacific Islands once Japanese hunting ended with the war. Tsutsui concludes that "while the Second World War clearly had a deleterious impact on many aspects of Japan's natural environment, there were also significant ways in which the war brought unexpectedly beneficial environmental consequences" (p. 295).

28. Committee, *Hiroshima and Nagasaki,* 339.

29. Ishida, "Japanese Cities," 17–18; and Sorensen, *Urban Japan,* 158–159.

30. Lifton, *Death in Life,* 145; Sorensen, *Urban Japan,* 162.

31. Hershey, *Hiroshima,* 34.

32. Ibid., 73; and Liebow, *Encounter with Disaster,* 116.

33. Committee, *Hiroshima and Nagasaki,* 356–357, 380, 518–519.

34. Hershey, *Hiroshima,* 89; Jungk, *Children of the Ashes,* 91–92, 109; Kosakai, *Hiroshima Peace Reader,* 16–17; Lifton, *Death in Life,* 85.

35. Liebow, *Encounter with Disaster,* 120.

36. City of Hiroshima, *Hiroshima,* 102.

37. Kosakai, *Hiroshima Peace Reader,* 16.

38. Committee, *Hiroshima and Nagasaki,* 380, 516–517.

39. Jungk, *Children of the Ashes,* 63–64. Following their general procedure of allowing the Japanese to rule themselves, especially at the local level, American authorities acquiesced in this choice, even though the mayor had been a right-wing politician in the past. On the American occupation of Japan, see Theodore Cohen, *Remaking Japan: The American Occupation as New Deal* (New York: Free Press, 1987).

40. Jungk, *Children of the Ashes,* 47–48, 135. On Hamai's leadership, see also City of Hiroshima, *Hiroshima,* 100; and Lifton, *Death in Life,* 210–215.

41. Sorensen, *Urban Japan,* 156–158.

42. Committee, *Hiroshima and Nagasaki,* 455.

43. Otis Carey, *From a Ruined Empire: Letters—Japan, China, Korea, 1945–46* (Tokyo: Kodansha International, 1984), 249; Committee, *Hiroshima and Nagasaki,* 468; Jungk, *Children of the Ashes,* 46–47, 76, 78–79; Liebow, *Encounter with Disaster,* 118; Lifton, *Life in Death,* 268; Rafael Steinberg, *Postscript from Hiroshima* (New York: Random House, 1965), 110. Only much later was discrimination against minority groups seen as bad by most Japanese. In 1980, while I was serving as a Fulbright Lecturer in Fukuoka, I was asked by two of my students, who wanted to marry, to serve as a go-between for their families, one of which was *eta*. With considerable reluctance, I agreed to do so. At what quickly became a very uncomfortable dinner, family members sat on opposite sides of a table in a Chinese restaurant (they probably felt that they could not refuse my invitation). They talked only to me, not to each other. The students did not marry.

44. On the meaning of the term *hibakusha,* see especially Lifton, *Death in Life,* 6–7. Survivors were also called *higaisha* and *seizonsha.*

45. Lifton, *Death in Life,* 100–101, 262–264; Steinberg, *Postscript from Hiroshima,* 36–37.

46. Sorensen, *Urban Japan,* 158–162, esp. 159. See also Ishida, "Japanese Cities and Planning," 28–30.

47. Ishida, "Japanese Cities and Planning," 27–34.

48. Sorensen, *Urban Japan.* Sorensen concludes that postwar planning in Japan was at best "a qualified success" (p. 167). See also City Bureau, Ministry of Construction, *City Planning in Japan* (Tokyo: n.p., 1974), 26–27.

49. City of Hiroshima, *Hiroshima,* 109.

50. Ibid., 110; and Jungk, *Children of the Ashes,* 92–93. See also Ishida, "Reconstructing Hiroshima," 92–93.

51. For reprints of the testimony, see City of Hiroshima, *Hiroshima,* 110; and Kosakai, *Hiroshima Peace Reader,* 18–19. See also *Asahi Evening News,* July 12, 1985, p. 3.

52. Ibid. On the planning ferment in 1946, see also Mark Gayn, *Japan Diary* (Rutland, VT: Charles E. Tuttle, 1981), 267; and Hershey, *Hiroshima,* 102–103.

53. Jungk, *Children of the Ashes,* 94–95, 104. Advice came from all over Japan. The former head of city planning in Tokyo urged that Hiroshima residents pay special attention to devising new layouts for shopping streets and that they create landscaped parks along the banks of the Ota River. See Ishida, "Reconstructing Hiroshima," 91–92.

54. Jungk, *Children of the Ashes,* 94–95, 104. See also Ishimaru, "Reconstructing Hiroshima," 96.

55. City of Hiroshima, *Hiroshima,* 108.

56. Jungk, *Children of the Ashes,* 104.

57. *New York Times,* March 23, 2005, p. A-20. See also *Time,* March 30, 1987, p. 81; and Wendelken, "Aesthetics and Reconstruction," 190–194.

58. City of Hiroshima, *Hiroshima,* 111; Ishida, "Reconstructing Hiroshima," 92; Kosakai, *Hiroshima Peace Reader,* 20.

59. City of Hiroshima, "City Planning of Hiroshima," 10–11; Ishida, "Reconstructing Hiroshima," 94.

60. Lifton, *Death in Life,* 213.

61. Jungk, *Children of the Ashes,* 106.

62. Steinberg, *Postscript from Hiroshima,* 25–26.

63. City of Hiroshima, *Hiroshima,* 120; Kosakai, *Hiroshima Peace Reader,* 20–21; and Lifton, *Death in Life,* 280–281.

64. Kosakai, *Hiroshima Peace Reader,* 21. On Hamai's initial doubts, see Jungk, *Children of the Ashes,* 61–62, 135. This account also argues that an Australian journalist, among the first to view Hiroshima after its bombing, coined the phrase "No More Hiroshimas."

65. Kosakai, *Hiroshima Peace Reader,* 44.

66. City of Hiroshima, *Hiroshima,* 111; Ishida, "Reconstructing Hiroshima," 95; Jungk, *Children of the Ashes,* 168–169.

67. Justin Williams, Sr., *Japan's Political Revolution under MacArthur: A Participant's Account* (Athens: University of Georgia Press, 1979), 254–257, esp. 254.

68. City of Hiroshima, *Hiroshima*, 111; Jungk, *Children of the Ashes*, 171; Kosakai, *Hiroshima Peace Reader*, 22.

69. Steinberg, *Postscript from Hiroshima*, 4–5.

70. Kosakai, *Hiroshima Peace Reader*, 42–44. See also Betty Jean Lifton, *A Place Called Hiroshima* (Tokyo: Kodansha International, 1985), 108; Jungk, *Children of the Ashes*, 183; and Sugimoto, "Atomic Bombing and Restoration of Hiroshima," 25–29.

71. Lifton, *Death in Life*, 275–280. Mayor Hamai and the president of Hiroshima University opposed preservation, because they thought the Dome was ugly. See Ishimaru, "Reconstructing Hiroshima," 104. A second preservation of the Dome was carried out in 1989, and in 1996 the Dome was added to UNESCO's world heritage list. See Sugimoto, "Atomic Bombing and Restoration of Hiroshima," 30–31.

72. Lifton, *Life in Death*, 271–274; Kosakai, *Hiroshima Peace Reader*, 45–51.

73. City of Hiroshima, "City Planning in Hiroshima," 12, 20–21.

74. Ibid., 18, 22; Steinberg, *Postscript from Hiroshima*, 63–64.

75. City of Hiroshima, "City Planning in Hiroshima," 36; City of Hiroshima, *Hiroshima*, 113, 128.

76. Steinberg, *Postscript from Hiroshima*, 30.

77. "Motomachi District Redevelopment Project, Hiroshima City," typescript in the City Planning Office, Hiroshima. See also City of Hiroshima, "City Planning of Hiroshima," 32; and Ishida, "Reconstructing Hiroshima," 99–100. I had numerous opportunities to visit the apartments in the 1980s. The grounds were always meticulously clean and free of the graffiti.

78. On Japan's economic ascent, see Mansel G. Blackford, *The Rise of Modern Business in Great Britain, the United States, and Japan* (Chapel Hill: University of North Carolina Press, 1998), 176–210.

79. Takafusa Nakamura, *The Postwar Japanese Economy: Its Development and Structure* (Tokyo: University of Tokyo Press, 1981), 135.

80. Committee, *Hiroshima and Nagasaki*, 410.

81. City of Hiroshima, "City Planning of Hiroshima," 6. See also City of Hiroshima, "Hiroshima of Today," a 1985 pamphlet in the Hiroshima City Clerk's office, p. 17.

82. City of Hiroshima, "City Planning of Hiroshima," 26.

83. City of Hiroshima, *Hiroshima*, 120–123, 131–133. On the Bikini tests, see Stewart Firth, *Nuclear Playground* (Honolulu: University of Hawai'i Press, 1987), 16, 20, 26.

84. Ironically, the fact that *hibakusha* were a shrinking proportion of Hiroshima's population contributed to the city's growing ideological unity. *Hibakusha* had composed about one-third of the city's population in 1950, but a scant one-fifth fourteen years later. Affected by feelings of guilt and shame, and often physically debilitated, *hibakusha* found it difficult to cooperate in trying to win aid from their national government. The medical needs of the *hibakusha* were long ignored by governmental authorities. In 1954, prodded by the *Lucky Dragon* incident, the Japanese Diet made its first appropriation, one of less than $10,000, to aid hospitals in Hiroshima and Nagasaki dealing with nuclear-bomb

victims. By 1956, national government aid had risen to almost $100,000. Finally, in 1957 the Diet passed legislation recognizing the special medical needs of *hibakusha* and appropriated a significant sum to aid them. Even so, it was not until extensions of that legislation were made in the 1970s that the needs of *hibakusha* were adequately met. See Lifton, *Death in Life,* 267. See also Committee, *Hiroshima and Nagasaki,* 503–603; and Walter Enloe and Randy Morris, *Encounters with Hiroshima* (St. Paul, MN: Hamline University Press, 1998).

85. Lifton, *Death in Life,* 262–263; Jungk, *Children of the Ashes,* 228–229; and Steinberg, *Postscript from Hiroshima,* 42–43.

86. Sorensen, *Urban Japan,* 200–255, esp. 213.

87. "Motomachi District Improvement Project."

88. City of Hiroshima, "City Planning of Hiroshima," 20–22.

89. Ibid., 6, 12, 14, 16, 38; City of Hiroshima, *Hiroshima,* 128–129.

90. City of Hiroshima, *Hiroshima,* 129.

91. City of Hiroshima, "City Planning of Hiroshima," 28–31.

92. Ibid., 34; "Overview of Danbara Living Environment Development Model Project," typescript in City Planning Office, Hiroshima.

93. Hiroshima thus seems to have fared better than most Japanese cities. Sorensen judges the 1968 and 1970 laws to have largely failed in empowering local authorities, curbing urban sprawl, and, more generally, remaking cities. There were many loopholes in the laws, which developers in most localities exploited to carry on much as before. Not until the late 1990s and early 2000s did new legislation passed by the Diet in response to continuing citizen protests change the situation. See Sorensen, *Urban Japan,* 288–332.

94. In 1983, Hiroshima possessed 874 companies in heavy industry and chemicals and 1,494 enterprises in light industries. Some 126,000 of its 425,000 workers labored directly in industry, about the same proportion as had in 1958. In 1985, Hiroshima ranked fourteenth among Japanese cities by value of manufacturing shipments; City of Hiroshima, "Hiroshima Today," 22–23. See also Kuniko Fujita and Richard Hill, "Global Production and Regional 'Hollowing Out' in Japan," in Michael Peter Smith, ed., *Pacific Rim Cities in the World Economy* (New Brunswick, NJ: Transaction Publishers, 1989), 202.

95. Sheridan Tatsuno, *The Technopolis Strategy: Japan, High Technology, and the Control of the 21st Century* (New York: Prentice-Hall, 1986), 163–165; and Michael Cusumano, *Japan's Software Factories: A Challenge to U.S. Management* (New York: Oxford University Press, 1991).

96. Cusumano, *Software Factories,* 130, 165; and Sorensen, *Urban Japan,* 261–264.

97. Funaba, Sasaki, Lee, and Markusen, "View," 263.

98. Ibid. Sorensen has tentatively concluded that "it does not seem likely a majority of the technopolises will be successful in the long run" and that "the concept of creating many small Silicon Valleys is flawed." See Sorensen, *Urban Japan,* 263.

99. Takayuki Ikeda, "War Damage Reconstruction, City Planning and US Civil Administration in Okinawa," in *Rebuilding Urban Japan,* 127–155, esp. 127.

100. Ibid., 131–132.

101. Ibid., 134–139.

102. Robert D. Eldredge, *The Origins of the Bilateral Okinawa Problem: Okinawa in Postwar U.S.–Japan Relations, 1945–1952* (New York: Garland Publishing, 2001); and Nicholas Evan Sarantakes, *Keystone, the American Occupation of Okinawa and U.S. Japanese Relations* (College Station: Texas A&M University Press, 2000).

103. Ikeda, "War Damage Reconstruction," 136–139, esp. 139.

104. Ibid., 138–141.

105. Ibid., 140–152.

106. Ibid., 154–155.

107. Mansel G. Blackford, "Diary" (unpublished), Nov. 30, 1980. See also *Economist,* Oct. 29, 2005, p. 44.

108. See *Columbus Dispatch,* Oct. 26, 2005, p. A-10, Oct. 30, 2005, p. A-7; and *Economist,* Oct. 29, 2005, p. 44. I experienced a taste of Okinawan independence in 1980. My diary recorded: "Okinawa is very different from Fukuoka in culture and people. The people do not consider themselves to be part of Japan. An old woman at a Bingata factory told us that she had never been to Japan." At the end of my visit, my hosts took me to the airport outside of Naha for my return flight to Fukuoka and bid me farewell, saying, "Bye, bye; have a good trip back to Japan." See Blackford, "Diary," Nov. 29, 30, 1980.

109. For an overview, see A. Radha Krishnan and Malcolm Tull, "Resource Use and Environmental Management in Japan," in *Environmental History in the Pacific,* ed. J. R. McNeill (Aldershot, Hants: Ashgate, 2001), 337–358. See also J. R. McNeill, *Something New under the Sun* (New York: W. W. Norton, 2000), 292–294.

110. Yoshiro Hoshino, "Japan's Post–Second World War Environmental Problems," in Jun Ui, *Industrial Pollution in Japan* (Tokyo: United Nations University Press, 1992), 71. For a case study of Oita Prefecture, see Jeffrey Broadbent, *Environmental Politics in Japan: Networks of Power and Protest* (Cambridge: Cambridge University Press, 1998). See also Timothy S. George, *Minamata: Pollution and the Struggle for Democracy in Postwar Japan* (Cambridge, MA: Harvard University Press, 2001); and Kenneth E. Wilkening, *Acid Rain Science and Politics in Japan* (Cambridge, MA: MIT Press, 2004).

Chapter 6. Guam, the Philippines, and American Samoa

1. U.S. Congress, House, Subcommittee on National Parks and Recreation (of the Committee on Interior and Insular Affairs), *Hearings on the Proposed War-in-the-Pacific National Historic Park—Proposed Guam National Seashore, Held on Guam, Jan. 15, 1972* (Washington, DC: Government Printing Office, 1972), 52–53. Hereafter cited as *Hearings, 1972.*

2. See Robert F. Rogers, *Destiny's Landfall: A History of Guam* (Honolulu: University of Hawai'i Press, 1995). See also Paul Carano and Pedro C. Sanchez, *A Complete History of Guam* (Rutland, VT: Charles E. Tuttle Company, 1964). Scholars disagree on what islands compose Micronesia. Francis X. Hezel has recently observed that Micronesia "is an equivocable term and one that some feel is meaningless." See Francis X. Hezel, *The New Shape of Old Island Cultures: A Half Century of Social Change in Micronesia* (Honolulu: University of Hawai'i Press, 2001), viii. There has, in fact, been a heated debate among

scholars about Micronesia as a viable construct for a generation or more. See Paul Rainbird, *The Archaeology of Micronesia* (Cambridge: Cambridge University Press, 2004), 43–69.

3. Hal M. Friedman, "Facelift: American Plans for Changes to the Physical Landscape of Postwar Micronesia, 1945–1947," paper presented at the annual meeting of the American Society for Environmental History, Providence, Rhode Island, March 26–30, 2003, pp. 1–2; Hal M. Friedman to the author, October 27, 2004, letter in author's possession; "Guam," *Pacific Magazine* 30 (Jan. 2005): 30; and Rogers, *Destiny's Landfall*, 1.

4. Paul D'Arcy, "Connected by the Sea: Towards a Regional History of the Western Caroline Islands," *Journal of Pacific History* 36 (April 2001): 163–182; Steven Roger Fischer, *A History of the Pacific Islands* (New York: Palgrave, 2002), 27–30; Rogers, *Destiny's Landfall*, 6, 21–40; Rainbird, *Archaeology*, 101–133. The indigenous people of Guam were known variously as Marianos, Chamorris, and by 1668 as Chamorros. In the present day, some want to be called Chamoru. Scholars disagree on how many migrations populated Micronesia and where they came from.

5. Rogers, *Destiny's Landfall*, 41–107, esp. 73.

6. Ibid., 126.

7. Ibid., 145, 158. For more detail, see Timothy Maga, *Defending Paradise: The United States and Guam* (New York: Garland Publishing, 1950); Dirk Ballendorf, "An Historical Perspective on Economic Development in Micronesia, 1783 to 1945," *Asian Culture Quarterly* 19 (Summer 1991): 56; Hezel, *New Shape*, 1–3.

8. Mark R. Peattie, *Nan'yo: The Rise and Fall of the Japanese in Micronesia, 1885–1945* (Honolulu: University of Hawai'i Press, 1988).

9. Rogers, *Destiny's Landfall*, 163–203, esp. 173, 194. See also Ronald H. Spector, *Eagle against the Sun: The American War with Japan* (New York: Random House, 1985), 298–323.

10. After World War II, the U.S. military wanted to annex all of Micronesia and make Guam its capital. However, when the Soviet Union invaded Japan in 1945, it took several small Japanese islands north of Hokkaido and held them for strategic purposes. The United States wanted the Soviet Union to return those islands to Japan. The U.S. secretary of state advised President Truman that if the U.S.A. unilaterally annexed Micronesia, the Soviet Union would use that action as a precedent to keep the northern islands. From Undersecretary of the Interior Abe Fortas came the idea of making much of Micronesia a strategic trusteeship of the United States. The Soviet Union agreed to this compromise in return for American assurances that it would not press too hard for the return of the northern islands to Japan.

11. Friedman, "Facelift: American Plans." See also Hal M. Friedman, *Creating an American Lake: United States Imperialism and Strategic Security in the Pacific Basin, 1945–1947* (Westport, CT: Greenwood Press, 2001); Hal M. Friedman, "The Limitations of Collective Security: The United States and the Micronesian Trusteeship, 1945–1947," *ISLA: A Journal of Micronesian Studies* 3 (Dry Season 1995), 339–370; and Hal M. Friedman, "The Open Door in Paradise: United States Strategic Security and Economic Policy in the Pacific Islands, 1945–1947," *Pacific Studies* 20 (March 1997): 63–87.

12. Friedman, "Open Door in Paradise."

13. Rogers, *Destiny's Landfall*, 207.

14. Ibid., 208–211.

15. Ibid., 214. It was the same 1946 Congress that passed legislation allowing Native Americans to take legal actions against the United States government for compensation due to broken treaties.

16. Carano and Sanchez, *Complete History of Guam*, 335–336; Rogers, *Destiny's Landfall*, 216.

17. Hezel, *New Shape*, 34.

18. Rogers, *Destiny's Landfall*, 210.

19. Ibid., 224–225. In 1962, a CIA training base on Saipan was relocated to Okinawa, thus enabling the security restrictions to be lifted.

20. Carano and Sanchez, *Complete History of Guam*, 367; and Joseph R. Holmes, *This Is Guam* (Agano: Pacific Press, 1953), 53–54.

21. Holmes, *This Is Guam*, 57.

22. Richard Barrett Lowe, *Problems in Paradise: The View from Government House* (New York: Pageant Press, 1967), 392.

23. Holmes, *This Is Guam*, 17.

24. Department of Commerce, Government of Guam, *Guam 1970: An Economy in Transition* (Agana, 1971), 6, 8, 13–14; Peattie, *Nan'yo*, 314; Albert Ravenholt, "Guam U.S.A.: America's Western Pacific Destiny?" *Southeast Asia Series* 18 (1970): 1, 11; and Rogers, *Destiny's Landfall*, 240.

25. Rogers, *Destiny's Landfall*, 247, 277.

26. The Annie E. Casey Foundation and the Population Reference Bureau, *Children in Guam* (n.p., 2002), 2; "Guam," *Pacific Magazine* 30 (Jan. 2005): 30; Thomas J. Iverson, "Japanese Visitors to Guam: Lessons from Experience," in John C. Crotts and Chris Ryan, eds., *Marketing Issues in Pacific Area Tourism* (New York: Haworth Press, 1997), 39–54, esp. 45; Peattie, *Nan'yo*, 317. The number of tourists visiting the Northern Marianas rose fourfold annually between 1984 and 1994, reaching 500,000. See Rainbird, *Archaeology*, 62.

27. Stewart Firth, *Nuclear Playground* (Honolulu: University of Hawai'i Press, 1987), 52–69; David Hanlon, *Remaking Micronesia: Discourses over Development in a Pacific Territory, 1944–1982* (Honolulu: University of Hawai'i Press, 1998), 21–50; and Rainbird, *Archaeology*, 58–60. It took into the 1990s for other nations to fully recognize some of these political changes, which were complicated by global geopolitical concerns.

28. The United States could play hard ball. When the Republic of Belau unexpectedly adopted a nuclear-free constitution in 1979, the United States sought repeatedly to have it altered. In 1994, the Republic of Belau agreed to American terms and was then allowed into a Compact of Free Association with the United States. See Firth, *Nuclear Playground*, 53–64; and Rainbird, *Archaeology*, 59. On Micronesian economies, see Hanlon, *Remaking Micronesia*, 87–185; and Hezel, *New Shape*, 4–5, 13, 55. For a more optimistic account, see John Cameron, "Economic Options for the Federated States of Micronesia at Independence," *Pacific Studies* 14 (Dec. 1991): 35–70. P. F. Kluge, *The Edge of Paradise: America in Micronesia* (New York: Random House, 1991), is critical of the United States.

29. Carano and Sanchez, *Complete History of Guam*, 328; and Galbraith, *Micronesia*, 84. See also *Economist*, April 20, 2004, unpaginated announcement.

30. Rogers, *Destiny's Landfall*, 288. Per capita income varied tremendously throughout Micronesia in the early 2000s: $21,000 in Guam; $8,000 in the Commonwealth of the Northern Mariana Islands; $2,000 in the Federated States of Micronesia; $1,900 in the Marshall Islands; and $800 in Kiribati. See *Pacific Magazine* 30 (Jan. 2005): 24, 26, 30, 32, 33.

31. Casey Foundation, *Children in Guam*, 1–2; Hezel, *New Shape*, 143–147; and Paul Spikard, Joanne L. Rondilla, and Debbie Hippolite Wright, eds., *Pacific Diaspora: Island Peoples in the United States and across the Pacific* (Honolulu: University of Hawai'i Press, 2002), 20. For a history of the out-migration of Chamorros, see Robert A. Underwood, "Excursions into Inauthenticity: The Chamorros of Guam," *Pacific Viewpoint* 26 (April 1985): 160–184. So many Micronesians migrated to Guam, Hawai'i, the Northern Mariana Islands, and American Samoa that the U.S. Congress agreed in the fall of 2003 to give those areas $30 million to help cover health, education, and social service costs resulting from the migrations. Some $14.2 million went to Guam. In 2004, the population of Guam was 37 percent Chamorro, 26 percent Filipino, 10 percent Caucasian, 10 percent Korean, Japanese, and Chinese, and 27 percent other. See "Guam," *Pacific Magazine* 30 (Jan. 2005): 30.

32. Rogers, *Destiny's Landfall*, 248–249, offers a brief examination of some of these issues. For a detailed look at one of them, see Michael R. Clement, Jr., "The Sella Bay Ammunition Wharf Controversy, 1969–1975: Economic Development, Indigenous Rights and Colonialism in Guam," M.A. thesis, University of Guam, 2002.

33. Department of the Navy, *Draft Environmental Impact Statement: U.S. Naval Magazine Guam, Mariana Island Ammunition Port Facility, P-620 & P-621* (n.p., 1977), esp. A-1, D-1. (Hereafter cited as *DEIS, 1977*.) All environmental impact statements cited in this chapter may be found at the Hamilton Library, University of Hawai'i, Mānoa. See also Clement, "Sella Bay," 21.

34. *Hearings, 1972*, 52.

35. *DEIS, 1977*, A-13, A-20, A-21.

36. Clement, "Sella Bay," 1.

37. VTN Pacific, *Draft Environmental Impact Statement for an Ammunition Wharf in Outer Apra Harbor, Guam* (n.p., 1981), 11-2–11-7, reviews the studies. Hereafter cited as *DEIS, 1981*.

38. Rogers, *Destiny's Landfall*, 248.

39. *DEIS, 1977*, appendix A, 14, and III-6.

40. Clement, "Sella Bay," 15.

41. *Hearings, 1972*, 53–58.

42. Clement, "Sella Bay," 31–32, 83.

43. Ibid., 28.

44. *Hearings, 1972*, 84–85; Clement, "Sella Bay," 41–45, 95.

45. Rogers, *Destiny's Landfall*, 248; Clement, "Sella Bay," 53–57.

46. Clement, "Sella Bay," 104, 112.

47. *DEIS, 1977,* III-6.

48. *Hearings, 1972,* 86. Rogers has written that "Orote Island is not really an island, but a large rock formation at the tip of Orote Peninsula, and is separated from the peninsula by a ravine that is partly submerged only at high tides." Robert Rogers to the author, November 11, 2004, letter in the author's possession.

49. *DEIS, 1977,* A-iii.

50. Ibid., C-1.

51. *DEIS, 1981,* vi and II-6.

52. VTN Pacific, *Final Environmental Impact Statement for an Ammunition Wharf in the Outer Apra Harbor Guam, Mariana Islands* (n.p., 1984), I-13 (hereafter cited as *EIS, 1984*).

53. Rogers to the author, November 11, 2004.

54. *EIS, 1984,* ii.

55. Ibid., F-1, F-20, F-33.

56. Ibid., D-18–D-21, D-28, D-29, F-21, F-22, F-29.

57. Ibid., D-12.

58. Ibid., D-13, D-14, D-30, D-32.

59. Rogers, *Destiny's Landfall,* 249.

60. H. W. Brands, *Bound to Empire: The United States and the Philippines* (New York: Oxford University Press), 220–223. See also George E. Taylor, *The Philippines and the United States: Problems of Partnership* (New York: Praeger, 1964). On issues of dependency, see Sharon Delmendo, *The Star-Entangled Banner: One Hundred Years of America in the Philippines* (New Brunswick, NJ: Rutgers University Press, 2004).

61. Brands, *Bound to Empire,* 233–234, 250–251, 270–271, 274, 304–311.

62. Ibid., 340–344; Stanley Karnow, *In Our Image: America's Empire in the Philippines* (New York: Random House, 1989), 23.

63. *Hearings, 1972,* 19–21.

64. Ibid.

65. Ibid., 22–25.

66. Ibid.

67. Ibid., 24–25.

68. Ibid., 27–28.

69. Ibid., 37–38.

70. Ibid., 44–48.

71. Ibid., 64–67, 75.

72. Ibid., 81.

73. Rogers, *Destiny's Landfall,* 249.

74. Guam Visitors Bureau, "Guide to Hiking on Guam," p.1, www.avisonic.com/client (accessed Jan. 2, 2004).

75. *Hearings, 1972,* 1–6.

76. Ibid., 3, 4, 11, 16.

77. Ibid., 5, 11, 17.

78. U.S. Congress, House, Subcommittee on the National Parks, Forests, and Public Lands (of the Committee on Natural Resources), *Hearing to Provide for Additional De-*

velopment at War in the Pacific National Historical Park (Washington, DC: Government Printing Office, 1993), 1, 26, 28, 80. (Hereafter cited as *Hearing, 1993*.)

79. Rogers, *Destiny's Landfall*, 260.

80. *Hearing, 1993*, 30–43

81. Ibid., 104, 107.

82. U.S. National Park Service, "War in the Pacific National Historical Park," p. 1, http://www.nationalparks.com/war_in_the_pacific_national_historical_park.htm (accessed Dec. 5, 2004). See also Russell D. Butcher, *Guide to National Parks, Pacific Region* (Old Saybrook, CT: Globe Pequot Press, 1999), 92.

83. Holmes, *This Is Guam*, 11.

84. Brown Tree Snake Control Committee (of the Aquatic Nuisance Species Task Force), *Brown Tree Snake Control Plan* (n.p., 1996), 1.

85. For a valuable journalistic account, see Mark Jaffe, *And No Birds Sing: The Story of an Ecological Disaster in a Tropical Paradise* (New York: Simon & Schuster, 1994). See also David Quammen, *The Song of the Dodo: Island Biogeography in an Age of Extinction* (New York: Scribner's, 1996), 321–344; and Oliver Sacks, *Island of the Colorblind* (New York: Alfred Knopf, 1997), 153–154. For a collection of essays by leading scientists, see Gordon H. Rodda et al., eds., *Problem Snake Management: The Habu and Brown Treesnake* (Ithaca, NY: Cornell University Press, 1999).

86. The brown tree snake was only the most notorious of alien species to invade the Mariana Islands in the wake of World War II. On Saipan, the navy planted *tangan-tangan* grasses to hold earth in place. The soil was eroding due to destruction by bombing and shelling during the conflict. *Tangan-tangan* quickly spread over Saipan, creating what one scholar has called "an impenetrable barrier." See Peattie, *Nan'yo*, 313.

87. Brown Tree Snake Control Committee, *Brown Tree Snake Control Plan*, 5–8.

88. Jaffe, *No Birds Sing*, 11–28.

89. Julie A. Savidge, "Extinction of an Island Forest Avifauna by an Introduced Snake," *Ecology* 68 (June 1987): 660–668.

90. Ibid., 661.

91. Brown Tree Snake Control Committee, *Brown Tree Snake Control Plan*, 12–13. See also Thomas H. Fritts and David Chiszar, "Snakes on Electrical Transmission Lines: Patterns, Causes, and Strategies for Reducing Electrical Outages Due to Snakes," in *Problem Snake Management*, Rodda et al., eds., 89–103.

92. Brown Tree Snake Control Committee, *Brown Tree Snake Control Plan*, 8; and Thomas H. Fritts, Michael J. McCoid, and Douglas M. Gomez, "Dispersal of Snakes to Extralimital Islands: Incidents of the Brown Treesnake *(Boiga irregularis)* Dispersing to Islands in Ships and Aircraft," in *Problem Snake Management*, Rodda et al., eds., 209–223.

93. Earl W. Campbell III, Gordon H. Rodda, Thomas H. Fritts, and Richard L. Bruggers, "An Integrated Management Plan for the Brown Treesnake *(Boiga irregularis)* on Pacific Islands," in *Problem Snake Management*, Rodda et al., eds., 422–435. See also U.S. Department of Agriculture, "No Escape from Guam: Stopping the Spread of the Brown Tree Snake" (n.p., 1998), 1–5.

94. Brown Tree Snake Control Committee, *Brown Tree Snake Control Plan*, 1.

95. Mansel G. Blackford, *Fragile Paradise: The Impact of Tourism on Maui, 1959–2000* (Lawrence: University Press of Kansas, 2001), 170–190.

96. For a bibliography of popular and scholarly studies, see H. G. A. Hughes, *Samoa (American Samoa, Western Samoa, Samoans Abroad)* (Oxford: Clio Press, 1997).

97. Capt. T. F. Darden, *Historical Sketch of the Naval Administration of the Government of American Samoa, April 17, 1900–July 1, 1951* (Washington, DC: Government Printing Office, 1952), ix–xiii, 1–6. See also John Gray, *Amerika Samoa: A History of American Samoa and its United States Naval Administration* (Annapolis: Naval Institute Press, 1960). For a coffee-table history, see Robert J. Shaffer, *American Sāmoa: 100 Years under the United States Flag* (Honolulu: Island Heritage Publishing, 2000).

98. Michelle Bennett, Dorinda Talbot, and Deanna Swaney, *Samoan Islands* (Melbourne: Lonely Planet Publications, 2003), 129, 132, 151.

99. Terry L. Hunt and Patrick V. Kirch, "The Historical Ecology of Ofu Island, American Samoa, 3000 B.P. to the Present," in Patrick V. Kirch and Terry L. Hunt, eds., *Historical Ecology in Pacific Islands: Prehistoric Environmental and Landscape Change* (New Haven, CT: Yale University Press, 1997), 105–123.

100. Steven Roger Fischer, *A History of the Pacific Islands* (Hounsmills, Hants: Palgrave, 2002), 182.

101. Darden, *American Samoa*, esp. 5, 17. Some commercial development occurred, but not much. In the mid-1950s, only 9 percent of the adult population held full-time jobs in one of the most commercially developed towns on Tutuila; of those who lived in a less-developed village on Ofu, the proportion came to only 1 percent. See Melvin Ember, "Commercialization and Political Change in American Samoa," *Explorations in Cultural Anthropology: Essays in Honor of George Peter Murdock* (New York: McGraw-Hill, 1964), 95–110, esp. 104.

102. "American Samoa," *Pacific Magazine* 30 (Jan. 2005): 23; Bennett, *Samoan Islands,* 120–122, 136–137; Butcher, *Guide,* 82; and Fischer, *Pacific Islands,* 222.

103. Ibid.

104. Bennett, *Samoan Islands,* 122; and Paul Spikard, Joanne L. Rondill, and Debbie Hippolite Wright, *Pacific Diaspora: Island Peoples in the United States and across the Pacific* (Honolulu: University of Hawai'i Press, 2002), 19–20. American Samoa's resident population was 57,291 in 2000.

105. Tom Conger, *Banana Moon* (Makawao, HI: Jungle Press, 1996), 108–109.

106. Paul Theroux, *The Happy Isles of Oceania: Paddling the Pacific* (New York: Ballantine Books, 1992), 346–359, esp. 346–347, 359.

107. Vincente Diaz, "Fight Boys, 'til the Last . . .': Islandstyle Football and the Remasculization of Indigeneity in the Militarized American Pacific Islands," in *Pacific Diaspora,* Spikard, Rondilla, and Wright, eds., 169–194; and Vincente Diaz, "Simply Chamorro: Telling Tales of Demise and Survival in Guam," in *Remembrance of Pacific Pasts,* Borofsky, ed., 362–382. In mid-2004, Dirk Ballendorf, a faculty member at the University of Guam, wrote, "On Guam today there is a small, but loud minority of 'Chamorro activists' who might be something less than ten per cent of the total population" (Dirk Ballendorf to the author, May 7, 2004; letter in the author's possession). Women were important leaders, just as in the Hawaiian Islands. See Rainbird, *Archaeology,* 35; and Laura Maria Torres

Souder, *Daughters of the Island: Contemporary Chamorro Women Organizers on Guam* (Lanham, MD: University Press of America, 1992).

108. Rogers, *Destiny's Landfall*, 265.

109. *Maui News*, Dec. 12, 2003, p. A-6, and Feb. 17, 2004, p. A-4.

Conclusions

1. J. R. McNeill, *Something New under the Sun: An Environmental History of the Twentieth-Century World* (New York: W. W. Norton, 2000), xxi, 3. In the 1990s and early 2000s, the World Bank (WB) and the International Monetary Fund (IMF) became deeply involved in pushing a "green" agenda coupled with neoliberal ideas touting the values of markets for borrowers worldwide. For generally favorable accounts of globalization and the actions of the WB and the IMF, see Jagdish Bhagwati, *In Defense of Globalization* (New York: Oxford University Press, 2004), and Martin Wolf, *Why Globalization Works* (New Haven, CT: Yale University Press, 2004). For criticisms, see Michael Goldman, *Imperial Nature: The World Bank and Struggles for Social Justice in the Age of Globalization* (New Haven, CT: Yale University Press, 2005), and Joseph E. Stiglitz, *Globalization and Its Discontents* (New York: W. W. Norton, 2003).

2. The relationships between Native Americans and environmentalism in modern America are complex. On the one hand, some tribes, like the Western Shoshone, have sought to protect their lands from environmental degradation. See Matthew Glass, "Air Force, Western Shoshone, and Mormon Rhetoric of Place and the MX Conflict," in Bruce Hevly and John M. Findlay, eds., *The Atomic West* (Seattle: University of Washington Press, 1998), 255–275. On the other hand, some tribes have sought waste sites for their reservations as a way of boosting tribal income. See Shepard Krech III, *The Ecological Indian: Myth and History* (New York: W. W. Norton, 1999), epilogue. The literature on these topics is growing. See Brett Clark, "The Indigenous Environmental Movement in the United States: Transcending Borders in Struggles against Mining, Manufacturing, and the Capitalist State," *Organization & Environment* 15 (Dec. 2002): 410–442; and Patrick Impero Wilson, "Native Peoples and the Management of Natural Resources in the Pacific Northwest: A Comparative Assessment," *American Review of Canadian Studies* 32 (Autumn 2002): 397–414. For a look at how four tribes in Canada and the United States negotiated mining agreements for their lands, see Saleem H. Ali, *Mining, the Environment, and Indigenous Development Conflicts* (Tucson: University of Arizona Press, 2003).

3. Eric Alden Smith and Joan McCarter, eds., *Contested Arctic: Indigenous Peoples, Industrial States, and the Circumpolar Environment* (Seattle: University of Washington Press, 1997).

4. United Nations, *Pacific Environment Outlook* (New York: United Nations, 2005), 47.

5. Rene Sylva, "Native Plants," in Dana Naome Hall, ed., *Mālama: Hawaiian Land and Water*, special issue of *Bamboo Ridge: The Hawaiian Writers' Quarterly* 29 (Winter 1985): 77.

Bibliographic Essay

I have indicated the major primary and secondary sources consulted in my research in the copious endnotes to this volume. In this bibliographic essay, I want simply to highlight those sources that have been most important for me and that might best lead readers into additional avenues of thought.

I have utilized many types of primary sources. Among the most important for anyone interested in recent debates on public issues having to do with business development and environmental protection issues are environmental impact statements. These statements are required by law to reprint verbatim all of the testimony at public hearings (called "scoping" hearings) and all of the written correspondence on such matters. Often running to hundreds, even thousands, of pages, these documents are invaluable in laying out the positions taken by various people, groups, and organizations. Many other types of government reports, along with newspapers and periodical articles, have also been useful sources. Talking with people—sometimes in formal oral-history interviews but often in more informal ways—proved essential in many cases. Less useful in the modern period for this project were manuscript collections, although the George Helm Collection at the University of Hawai'i, Mānoa, was helpful in understanding developments at Kaho'olawe.

The works of other scholars in environmental history, Pacific history, and business history have provided essential backdrops for my work, as laid out in the introduction and first chapter of my study. In the notes to each chapter, I have listed the most important local or regional studies upon which I have relied. Here, let me list some of the studies I have found most important.

Scholars have created the field of environmental history over the past generation. For guides to the literature, see Shepard Krech III, J. R. McNeill, and Carolyn Merchant, eds., *Encyclopedia of World Environmental History*, 3 vols. (New York: Routledge, 2004); and Carolyn Merchant, ed., *The Columbia Guide to American Environmental History* (New York: Columbia University Press, 2002). See especially J. R. McNeill, *Something New under the Sun: An Environmental History of the Twentieth-Century World* (New York: W. W. Norton, 2000), for global changes over the past century, and J. R. McNeill, ed., *Environmental History in the Pacific World* (Aldershot, Hants: Ashgate, 2001), for developments in the Pacific. For a basic collection of leading essays in global environmental history, see Char Miller and Hal Rothman, eds., *Out of the Woods: Essays in Environmental History* (Pittsburgh: University of Pittsburgh Press, 1997). On how an understanding of power over making choices is an important key to environmental history, see Douglas R. Weiner, "A Death Defying Attempt to Articulate a Coherent Definition of Environmental History," *Environmental History* 10 (July 2005): 404–411.

Much of my work connects with the findings of histories of environmental justice movements. On the need for scholars to examine such movements, see especially Carolyn Merchant, "Shades of Darkness: Race and Environmental History," *Environmental History* 8 (July 2003): 380–394. See also Robert Bullard, *Dumping in Dixie: Race, Class and Environmental Justice* (Boulder, CO: Westview Press, 1990); Jennifer Clapp, *Toxic Exports: The Transfer of Hazardous Wastes from Rich to Poor Countries* (Ithaca, NY: Cornell University Press, 2001); Luke Cole and Sheila Foster, *From the Ground Up: Environmental Racism and the Rise of the Environmental Justice Movement* (New York: New York University Press, 2001); Richard Hofrichter, ed., *Toxic Struggles: The Theory and Practice of Environmental Justice* (Salt Lake City: University of Utah Press, 2002); Jonathan Keyes, "A Place of Its Own: Urban Environmental History," *Journal of Urban History* 26 (March 2000): 380–390; Alex Hurley, *Environmental Inequalities: Class, Race, and Industrial Pollution in Gary, Indiana, 1945–1980* (Chapel Hill: University of North Carolina Press, 1995); Martin Melosi, "Equity, Eco-Racism, and Environmental History," *Environmental History Review* 19 (Fall 1995): 1–16; David Pellow, *Garbage Wars: The Struggle for Environmental Justice in Chicago* (Cambridge, MA: MIT Press, 2002); Edwardo Lao Rhodes, *Environmental Justice in America: A New Paradigm* (Bloomington: Indiana University Press, 2003); Gerald R. Visgilio and Diana M. Whitelaw, eds., *In Our Backyard: A Quest for Environmental Justice* (Lanham, MD: Rowland & Littlefield, 2003); and Sylvia Hood Washington, *Packing Them In: An Archaeology of Environmental Racism in Chicago, 1865–1954* (Lanham, MD: Lexington Books, 2004).

Business historians are beginning to address the environmental consequences of economic development. See especially Christine Meisner Rosen and Christopher C. Sellers, "The Nature of the Firm: Towards an Ecocultural History of Business," *Business History Review* 73 (Winter 1999): 577–600;

Business History Review 73 is devoted to relationships between business and the environment. See also Christine Meisner Rosen, "The Business–Environment Connection," *Environmental History* 10 (Jan. 2005): 77–79.

My study depends upon the work of numerous scholars in the field of Pacific history. For valuable overviews, see Robert Borofsky, ed., *Remembrance of Pacific Pasts: An Invitation to Remake History* (Honolulu: University of Hawai'i Press, 2000); Donald Denoon et al., eds., *The Cambridge History of the Pacific Islanders* (New York: Cambridge University Press, 1997); K. R. Howe, Robert C. Kiste, and Brij V. Lal, eds., *Tides of History: The Pacific Islands in the Twentieth Century* (Honolulu: University of Hawai'i Press, 1994); and Vijay Naidu, Eric Waddell, and Epeli Hau'ofa, eds., *A New Oceania: Rediscovering Our Sea of Islands* (Suva: University of South Pacific Press, 1993).

Much has been written about the United States in the Pacific. A useful place to start is Jean Heffer, *The United States and the Pacific: History of a Frontier,* trans. W. Donald Wilson (Notre Dame, IN: University of Notre Dame Press, 2002). For introductions to post-1945 developments, see also Roger Buckley, *The United States in the Asia-Pacific since 1945* (Cambridge: Cambridge University Press, 2002); and Hal M. Friedman, *Creating an American Lake: United States Imperialism and Strategic Security in the Pacific Basin, 1945–47* (Westport, CT: Greenwood Press, 2001). For earlier developments, see Arthur Dudden, *The American Pacific: From the Old China Trade to the Present* (New York: Oxford University Press, 1992); Arrell Morgan Gibson, *Yankees in Paradise: The Pacific Basin Frontier* (Albuquerque: University of New Mexico Press, 1993); David Pletcher, *The Diplomacy of Involvement: American Economic Expansion across the Pacific, 1784–1900* (Columbia: University of Missouri Press, 2001); and Earl Pomeroy, *American Strategy in Guam and Micronesia* (Stanford, CA: Stanford University Press, 1951).

INDEX

Abbott, Carl, 83, 85
Aboriginal Lands of Hawaiian Ancestry (ALOHA), 43, 44
Adotgan Point (Guam), 182–184
AEC. *See* Atomic Energy Commission
agriculture: in Alaska, 231n. 17; conflicts with mining, 238n. 9; in Guam, 173; in Hawaiʻi, 31, 42; in Kahoʻolawe, 30, 31; in Marianas, 168; in Samoan Islands, 197; in Silicon Valley, 63, 78, 79
Aina, Jack, 34
aircraft. *See* Boeing Company
Air Force, U.S., 160, 177. *See also* military, U.S.
Akaka, Daniel, 54
Alaska: acquisition by United States, 17, 98; agriculture, 231n. 17; Beringia Heritage International Park, 121–124; climate, 113–114; conservation concerns, 96, 125; development, 97–105; economy, 95–96, 98–99, 100–101, 104–105; environmentalism, 103, 124–125; federal government role, 104, 108–109; gold mining, 17, 81, 99; lumber industry, 98, 104, 125, 231n. 17; military presence, 20, 101, 102, 104; national parks, 116, 122, 123; natural resources, 95–96, 98, 101, 103–105, 125; oil industry, 98, 104–105, 114–115, 116, 117, 122; population, 17, 99, 102; relations with federal government, 98–99; Russians in, 17, 97–98, 99, 126, 230n. 8;

Shared Beringia Heritage Program, 121, 123–124; statehood, 19, 103–104; tourism, 104, 237n. 95; whalers, 18. *See also* Aleutian Islands; Bering Sea
Alaska Conservation Society, 103
Alaska Miners Association, 122
Alaska National Interest Lands Conservation Act (ANILCA), 116
Alaska Natives Claims Settlement Act (ANCSA), 115–116, 123
Alaskan Federation of Natives, 103
Alaskan Natives: activism, 103; land claims, 115–116; opposition to Beringia Heritage International Park, 122–123; opposition to use of nuclear explosives, 102–103, 155; population, 17, 99; visits to Chukotka region, 11, 122. *See also* Aleut Indians; Eskimos
Alcatraz Island, occupation by Native Americans, 44, 78, 90
Aleutian Islands: birds, 207; climate, 105–106; fox farming, 207; fur trading, 97–98, 230n. 8; Japanese attack and occupation, 1, 101–102; military use, 101, 232n. 24; nuclear testing, 20, 103; vegetation, 105. *See also* Bering Sea
Aleut Indians: employment in king crab industry, 109; hunters, 97–98, 230n. 8; population, 98; relocation during World War II, 101–102
Aleut League, 103

About the Author

Mansel Blackford is a professor of history at The Ohio State University, where he works primarily in the fields of business history and western American history. He has published ten previous books, many of which deal with the history of the Pacific, most recently *Fragile Paradise: The Impact of Tourism on Maui, 1959–2000* (2001). Professor Blackford has served as the president of the Business History Conference and as a Senior Fulbright Lecturer to Japan on two occasions. He was named the Distinguished Historian in the State of Ohio in 2005.